Analytical Methods and Convergence in Probability with Applications, 2nd Edition

Analytical Methods and Convergence in Probability with Applications, 2nd Edition

Guest Editors

Irina Shevtsova
Victor Korolev

MDPI

Basel • Beijing • Wuhan • Barcelona • Belgrade • Novi Sad • Cluj • Manchester

Guest Editors
Irina Shevtsova
Moscow State University
Moscow
Russia

Victor Korolev
Moscow State University
Moscow
Russia

Editorial Office
MDPI AG
Grosspeteranlage 5
4052 Basel, Switzerland

This is a reprint of the Special Issue, published open access by the journal *Mathematics* (ISSN 2227-7390), freely accessible at: https://mdpi.com/si/143635.

For citation purposes, cite each article independently as indicated on the article page online and as indicated below:

Lastname, A.A.; Lastname, B.B. Article Title. *Journal Name* **Year**, *Volume Number*, Page Range.

ISBN 978-3-7258-2695-7 (Hbk)
ISBN 978-3-7258-2696-4 (PDF)
https://doi.org/10.3390/books978-3-7258-2696-4

Contents

mathematics

Article

Comparing Compound Poisson Distributions by Deficiency: Continuous-Time Case

Vladimir Bening [1,2] **and Victor Korolev** [1,2,3,4,*]

[1] Faculty of Computational Mathematics and Cybernetics, Lomonosov Moscow State University, 119991 Moscow, Russia
[2] Moscow Center for Fundamental and Applied Mathematics, 119991 Moscow, Russia
[3] Federal Research Center "Computer Science and Control", Russian Academy of Sciences, 119333 Moscow, Russia
[4] Department of Mathematics, School of Science, Hangzhou Dianzi University, Hangzhou 310018, China
* Correspondence: vkorolev@cs.msu.ru

Abstract: In the paper, we apply a new approach to the comparison of the distributions of sums of random variables to the case of Poisson random sums. This approach was proposed in our previous work (Bening, Korolev, 2022) and is based on the concept of statistical deficiency. Here, we introduce a continuous analog of deficiency. In the case under consideration, by continuous deficiency, we will mean the difference between the parameter of the Poisson distribution of the number of summands in a Poisson random sum and that of the compound Poisson distribution providing the desired accuracy of the normal approximation. This approach is used for the solution of the problem of determination of the distribution of a separate term in the Poisson sum that provides the least possible value of the parameter of the Poisson distribution of the number of summands guaranteeing the prescribed value of the $(1-\alpha)$-quantile of the normalized Poisson sum for a given $\alpha \in (0,1)$. This problem is solved under the condition that possible distributions of random summands possess coinciding first three moments. The approach under consideration is applied to the collective risk model in order to determine the distribution of insurance payments providing the least possible time that provides the prescribed Value-at-Risk. This approach is also used for the problem of comparison of the accuracy of approximation of the asymptotic $(1-\alpha)$-quantile of the sum of independent, identically distributed random variables with that of the accompanying infinitely divisible distribution.

Keywords: limit theorem; compound Poisson distribution; Poisson random sum; asymptotic expansion; asymptotic deficiency; kurtosis; accompanying infinitely divisible distribution

MSC: 60E15; 60F05; 60G50; 60G55; 91B05

Citation: Bening, V.; Korolev, V. Comparing Compound Poisson Distributions by Deficiency: Continuous-Time Case. *Mathematics* **2022**, *10*, 4712. https://doi.org/10.3390/math10244712

Academic Editor: Iosif Pinelis

Received: 17 November 2022
Accepted: 8 December 2022
Published: 12 December 2022

1. Introduction

This paper is a complement to our previous work [1], where we considered a version of the problem of stochastic ordering and proposed an approach based on the concept of deficiency that is well-known in asymptotic statistics; see, e.g., [2] and later publications [3–6]. In the paper [1], we used the approach mentioned above in order to establish a kind of stochastic order for the distributions of sums of independent random variables (r.v.s) based on the comparison of the number of summands required for the distribution of the sum to have the desired asymptotic properties (for the problems and methods related to stochastic ordering, see, e.g., [7]). Here, we apply this approach to the comparison of the distributions of sums of random variables to the case of Poisson random sums.

In statistics, as well as in [1], the deficiency is measured in integer units and correspondingly has the meaning of either the number of additional observations required for a statistical procedure to attain the same quality as the 'optimal' procedure in statistics or the number of additional summands in the sum required to attain the desired accuracy of the normal approximation in [1]. Unlike these cases, in the present paper, we deal with the compound Poisson distributions and introduce a continuous analog of deficiency. The extension of the approach proposed in [1] for non-random sums of independent r.v.s to Poisson random sums is possible due to the asymptotic normality of the latter as the parameter of the Poisson distribution of the number of summands infinitely grows. In the case under consideration, by continuous deficiency, we mean the difference between the parameter of the Poisson distribution of the number of summands in a Poisson random sum and that of the compound Poisson distribution providing the desired accuracy of the normal approximation. This approach is used for the solution of the problem of determination of the distribution of a separate term in the Poisson sum that provides the least possible value of the parameter of the Poisson distribution of the number of summands guaranteeing the prescribed value of the $(1-\alpha)$-quantile of the normalized Poisson sum for a given $\alpha \in (0,1)$.

This problem is solved under the condition that possible distributions of random summands possess coinciding first three moments. Therefore, we can say that, in this problem, we deal with 'fine tuning' of the distribution of a separate summand since we assume that different possible distributions of random summands may differ only by their kurtosis. In the setting under consideration, the best distribution delivers the smallest value of the parameter of the compounding Poisson distribution. This problem is actually a particular case of the problem of quantification of the accuracy of approximations of the compound Poisson distributions provided by limit theorems of probability theory. The main mathematical tools used in the paper are asymptotic expansions for the compound Poisson distributions and their quantiles.

The formal setting mentioned above can be applied to solving some practical problems dealing with the collective risk insurance models where it is traditional to describe the cumulative insurance payments by the compound Poisson process. The approach under consideration makes it possible to determine the distribution of insurance payments providing the least possible time that provides the prescribed Value-at-Risk.

To make the above-mentioned more clear, consider an insurance company that starts its activity at time $t_0 = 0$. Within the classical collective risk model [8], the total insurance payments at some time t have the form of a sum of a random number (number of payments by the time t) of independent identically distributed r.v.s (insurance payments), that is, of a Poisson random sum. In this model, the number of insurance payments by time t follows the Poisson process $N_\lambda(t)$ with some intensity $\lambda > 0$. We assume that the parameter λ is uncontrollable and fixed. Since $N_\lambda(t)$ has the same distribution as $N_1(\lambda t)$ and the parameter λ is assumed fixed, the setting under consideration concerns the problem of determination of the distribution of an individual insurance payment providing the least possible t guaranteeing the prescribed Value-at-Risk for the average losses of the insurance company within the time interval $[0,t]$.

The approach considered in the paper can be used when the distributions of the summands (possible losses) are known only up to their first three moments, and the exact Value-at-Risk is not known for sure.

Within the framework of the collective risk model in the setting under consideration, the problem consists in the description of the best strategy of the insurance company. Here, the choice of the terms of a contract (e.g., the amount of insurance payment related to each possible insurance event) is meant as a strategy. That is, a strategy consists in the determination of the distribution of an insurance payment. Briefly, the problem is to choose an optimal distribution of a separate insurance payment among the distributions that have the same first three moments so that the desired goal is achieved within the least possible time interval.

We also consider the application of the proposed approach to the study of the asymptotic properties of non-random sums of independent identically distributed r.v.s as compared to those of the compound Poisson distributions with the same expectation. It is well-known that, in many respects, these properties coincide. This phenomenon manifests itself, for example, in the form of the method of accompanying infinitely divisible distributions (see, e.g., [9], Chapter 4, Section 24). Therefore, it is of certain interest to investigate the accuracy of the approximation of the characteristics of sums of independent r.v.s as compared to that of the accompanying infinitely divisible (that is, corresponding compound Poisson) laws. This problem was studied by many specialists; see, e.g., [10–13] and the references therein. Unlike most preceding works where the approximation of distribution functions was discussed, here we consider the application of accompanying laws to a somewhat inverse problem of approximation of quantiles.

The paper is organized as follows. Section 2 contains a short overview of the results concerning the asymptotic expansions for compound Poisson distributions. Here we also formulate basic lemmas to be used in the next sections. The main results are presented in Section 3. In Section 3.1, we introduce the notion of the α-reserve in the collective risk model and present some asymptotic expansions for this quantity. In Section 3.2, a continuous-time analog of the notion of deficiency is introduced. Here we also prove some general results concerning the continuous-time deficiency. In Section 3.3, we consider the problem of comparison of compound Poisson distributions by deficiency and present the asymptotic formula for the deficiency of one compound Poisson distribution with respect to the other. In Section 3.4, we deal with the problem of comparison of the distributions of Poisson random sums with those of non-random sums. Actually, this problem consists in the comparison of the accuracy of approximation of the asymptotic $(1-\alpha)$-quantile of the sum of independent identically distributed random variables with that of the accompanying infinitely divisible distribution.

2. Notation and Auxiliary Results

Throughout what follows, we will assume that all the random variables and processes are defined on the same probability space $(\Omega, \mathfrak{F}, \mathsf{P})$. The expectation and variance with respect to the measure P will be, respectively, denoted E and D. The set of real numbers and natural numbers will be, respectively, denoted $\mathbb{R}$ and $\mathbb{N}$. The distribution function of the standard normal law will be denoted $\Phi(x)$,

$$\Phi(x) = \frac{1}{\sqrt{2\pi}} \int_{-\infty}^{x} \varphi(y)dy, \quad \varphi(x) = \frac{1}{\sqrt{2\pi}} \exp\Big\{-\frac{x^2}{2}\Big\}, \quad x \in \mathbb{R}.$$

The distribution of a random variable X will be denoted $\mathcal{L}(X)$.

Let $X_1, X_2, \ldots$ be independent identically distributed random variables. Let N_λ be the random variable with the Poisson distribution with parameter λ. Assume that for each $\lambda > 0$, the random variables $N_\lambda, X_1, X_2, \ldots$ are independent. Let S_λ be the Poisson random sum, $S_\lambda = X_1 + \ldots + X_{N_\lambda}$. If $N_\lambda = 0$, then S_λ is assumed to equal to zero. Assume that $\mathsf{E}X_1 = a$ and $\mathsf{D}X_1 = \sigma^2 > 0$ exist. For integer $k \geq 0$, denote $\mathsf{E}X_1^k = \alpha_k$. Of course, $\alpha_0 = 1$, $\alpha_1 = a$ and $\alpha_2 = \sigma^2 + a^2$.

Recall some facts concerning the asymptotic expansions for the compound Poisson distributions (sf. [8,14,15]).

Denote the characteristic functions of the random variables X_1 and S_λ as $f(t)$ and $h_\lambda(t)$, respectively. It is well-known that if $f(t)$ has r continuous derivatives, then, as $t \to 0$, we have

$$f(t) = 1 + iat - \frac{\alpha_2 t^2}{2} + (it)^2 \sum\nolimits_{k=1}^{r-2} \frac{(it)^k \alpha_{k+2}}{(k+2)!} + o(t^r). \quad (1)$$

A random variable X_1 is said to satisfy the Cramér condition (C), if

$$\limsup_{|t|\to\infty} |f(t)| < 1. \quad (2)$$

For $k = 0, 1, 2, \dots$ define the function $H_k(x) : \mathbb{R} \to \mathbb{R}$ as

$$H_k(x) \equiv (-1)^k \frac{\phi^{(k)}(x)}{\phi(x)}.$$

The function $H_k(x)$, $x \in \mathbb{R}$, so defined, is a polynomial of degree k and is called the *Hermite polynomial* of degree k.

It is easy to calculate that

$$H_0(x) = 1, \quad H_1(x) = x, \quad H_2(x) = x^2 - 1, \quad H_3(x) = x^3 - 3x, \quad H_4(x) = x^4 - 6x^2 + 3,$$

$$H_5(x) = x^5 - 10x^3 + 15x, \quad H_6(x) = x^6 - 15x^4 + 45x^2 - 15.$$

Let m be a nonnegative integer and $q_k \in \mathbb{R}$, $k = 0, \dots, m$. Consider the polynomial

$$q(x) = \sum_{k=0}^{m} q_k x^k.$$

Let $H_0(x), \dots, H_m(x)$ be Hermite polynomials. Let

$$Q(x) = \sum_{k=0}^{m} q_k H_k(x).$$

Then it is easy to make sure that the function $v(t) = q(it)\exp\{-t^2/2\}$ is the Fourier transform of the function $V(x) = Q(x)\phi(x)$. Throughout what follows, we will assume that $r \geq 3$ is a fixed integer number.

For a complex z, let

$$\widetilde{f}(z) = \sum_{k=1}^{r-2} \frac{\alpha_{k+2} z^k}{(k+2)!}.$$

Obviously, $\widetilde{f}(z)$ is a polynomial of degree $\leq r - 2$ with real coefficients; moreover, $\widetilde{f}(0) = 0$. From (1), it follows that

$$f(t) - 1 - iat + \frac{\alpha_2 t^2}{2} = (it)^2 \widetilde{f}(it) + o(t^r)$$

as $t \to 0$. For $\lambda > 0$ and a complex z let

$$p_\lambda(z) = \sum_{k=1}^{r-2} \frac{1}{k!} \left[\frac{z^2}{\alpha_2} \widetilde{f}\left(\frac{z}{\sqrt{\lambda \alpha_2}} \right) \right]^k. \tag{3}$$

It can be easily made sure that there exist integer $m \geq 3$ and polynomials $q_k(z)$ with real coefficients, $k = 3, \dots, m$, not depending on λ such that

$$p_\lambda(z) = \sum_{k=3}^{m} \lambda^{-k/2+1} q_k(z) \tag{4}$$

for all $\lambda > 0$ and complex z. Moreover, these polynomials $q_k(z)$ are uniquely determined by (3) and (4). Let

$$q_k(z) = \sum_{j=3}^{L_k} q_{k,j} z^j \tag{5}$$

be the corresponding representation of $q_k(z)$ with $q_{k,j} \in \mathbb{R}$ $(j = 3, \dots, L_k)$, $L_k \geq 3$ $(k = 3, \dots, m)$. Let $H_j(x)$ be the Hermite polynomials. For $x \in \mathbb{R}$ and $k = 3, \dots, m$ let

$$R_k(x) = -\sum_{j=3}^{L_k} q_{k,j} H_{j-1}(x). \tag{6}$$

The function $R_k(x)$ is called the *Edgeworth polynomial* of degree k.

For $\lambda > 0$ and complex z from (3) and (4), we easily obtain

$$p_\lambda(z) = \sum_{k=3}^{(r-2)^2+2} \lambda^{-k/2+1} \sum_{\frac{k-2}{r-2} \leq j \leq k-2} \alpha_{k,j} z^{k+2(j-1)},$$

where

$$j!\alpha_{k,j} = \sum_{\substack{3\le n_1\le\ldots\le n_j\le r\\ n_1+\ldots+n_j=k+2(j-1)}} \frac{\alpha_{n_1}\cdot\ldots\cdot\alpha_{n_j}}{n_1!\cdot\ldots\cdot n_j!}\alpha_2^{-k/2-j+1}.$$

Therefore, in (4) and (5), we should set $m = (r-2)^2+2$ and $L_k = 3(k-2)$ $(k = 3,\ldots,m)$.

For $x \in \mathbb{R}$, $\lambda > 0$ and $r \in \mathbb{N}$ define the functions $G_{\lambda,r}(x)$ as

$$G_{\lambda,r}(x) = \Phi(x) + \phi(x)\sum_{k=3}^{r}\lambda^{-k/2+1}R_k(x).$$

In particular, for $r = 3$, we have

$$R_3(x) = -\frac{\alpha_3}{6\alpha_2^{3/2}}H_2(x)$$

and

$$G_{\lambda,3}(x) = \Phi(x) - \frac{\alpha_3}{6\alpha_2^{3/2}\sqrt{\lambda}}(x^2-1)\phi(x). \tag{7}$$

For $r = 4$, we have

$$R_4(x) = -\frac{\alpha_4}{24\alpha_2^2}H_3(x) - \frac{\alpha_3^2}{72\alpha_2^3}H_5(x)$$

and

$$G_{\lambda,4}(x) = \Phi(x) - \frac{\alpha_3}{6\alpha_2^{3/2}\sqrt{\lambda}}(x^2-1)\phi(x) - \frac{\phi(x)}{\lambda}\left[\frac{\alpha_4}{24\alpha_2^2}(x^3-3x) - \frac{\alpha_3^2}{72\alpha_2^3}(x^5-10x^3+15x)\right]. \tag{8}$$

Moreover, if $\varkappa_3(S_\lambda)$ and $\varkappa_4(S_\lambda)$ are the skewness and kurtosis of the random variable S_λ,

$$\varkappa_3(S_\lambda) \equiv \mathsf{E}\left(\frac{S_\lambda - \mathsf{E}S_\lambda}{\sqrt{\mathsf{D}S_\lambda}}\right)^3 = \mathsf{E}\left(\frac{S_\lambda - \alpha_1\lambda}{\sqrt{\lambda\alpha_2}}\right)^3 = \frac{\alpha_3}{\sqrt{\lambda}\alpha_2^{3/2}},$$

$$\varkappa_4(S_\lambda) \equiv \mathsf{E}\left(\frac{S_\lambda - \mathsf{E}S_\lambda}{\sqrt{\mathsf{D}S_\lambda}}\right)^4 - 3 = \mathsf{E}\left(\frac{S_\lambda - \alpha_1\lambda}{\sqrt{\lambda\alpha_2}}\right)^4 - 3 = \frac{\alpha_4}{\lambda\alpha_2^2},$$

then (7) and (8) can be rewritten as

$$G_{\lambda,3}(x) = \Phi(x) - \frac{\varkappa_3(S_\lambda)}{6}\Phi^{(3)}(x)$$

and

$$G_{\lambda,4}(x) = \Phi(x) - \frac{\varkappa_3(S_\lambda)}{6}\Phi^{(3)}(x) + \frac{\varkappa_4(S_\lambda)}{24}\Phi^{(4)}(x) + \frac{\varkappa_3^2(S_\lambda)}{72}\Phi^{(6)}(x).$$

Lemma 1. *Let $r > 3$. Assume that the distribution of the random variable X_1 satisfies the Cramér condition* (C) *(see* (2)*). Then*

$$\sup_x\left|\mathsf{P}\left(\frac{S_\lambda - a\lambda}{\sqrt{\lambda(a^2+\sigma^2)}} < x\right) - G_{\lambda,r}(x)\right| = o(\lambda^{-r/2+2}),$$

that is,

$$\lim_{\lambda\to\infty}\lambda^{r/2-1}\sup_x\left|\mathsf{P}\left(\frac{S_\lambda - a\lambda}{\sqrt{\lambda(a^2+\sigma^2)}} < x\right) - G_{\lambda,r}(x)\right| = 0.$$

This statement is a particular case of Theorem 4.4.1 in [15].

Our further reasoning is based on the following general statement dealing with the asymptotic behavior of the quantiles of univariate distributions of a random process.

Let $Z(t)$, $t \geq 0$, be a random process. Assume that for each $t \geq 0$ the distribution of the random variable $Z(t)$ is continuous. For $\beta \in (0,1)$ and $t \geq 0$, the left β-quantile of the random variable $Z(t)$ will be denoted $u_\beta(t)$:

$$u_\beta(t) = \inf\{u : \mathsf{P}(Z(t) < u) \geq \beta\}.$$

Lemma 2. *Assume that, as $t \to \infty$, the distribution function of the random process $Z(t)$ admits the asymptotic expansion of the form*

$$\mathsf{P}(Z(t) < x) = \Psi_0(x) + t^{-1/2}\Psi_1(x) + t^{-1}\Psi_2(x) + o(t^{-1}).$$

Moreover, let the functions $\Psi_0''(x)$, $\Psi_1'(x)$ and $\Psi_2(x)$ be continuous and $\Psi_0'(x) > 0$. Then for any $\beta \in (0,1)$, we have

$$u_\beta(t) = u_\beta - \frac{\Psi_1(u_\beta)}{\Psi_0'(u_\beta)\sqrt{t}} + \frac{\Psi_0'(u_\beta)\Psi_1(u_\beta)\Psi_1'(u_\beta) - \left(\Psi_0'(u_\beta)\right)^2\Psi_2(u_\beta) - \frac{1}{2}\Psi_1^2(u_\beta)\Psi_0''(u_\beta)}{\left(\Psi_0'(u_\beta)\right)^3 t} + o(t^{-1}),$$

where u_β is the left β-quantile of the distribution function $\Psi_0(x)$: $\Psi_0(u_\beta) = \beta$.

For the proof of this statement, see [15], Section 4.5.

Remark 1. *If we set*

$$\overline{u}_\beta(t) = u_\beta - \frac{\Psi_1(u_\beta)}{\Psi_0'(u_\beta)\sqrt{t}} + \frac{\Psi_0'(u_\beta)\Psi_1(u_\beta)\Psi_1'(u_\beta) - \left(\Psi_0'(u_\beta)\right)^2\Psi_2(u_\beta) - \frac{1}{2}\Psi_1^2(u_\beta)\Psi_0''(u_\beta)}{\left(\Psi_0'(u_\beta)\right)^3 t},$$

then it is not difficult to make sure that under the conditions of Lemma 2, we have

$$\mathsf{P}(Z(t) < \overline{u}_\beta(t)) = \beta + o(t^{-1}).$$

From Lemmas 1 and 2, it follows that if $\alpha_4 = \mathsf{E}X_1^4 < \infty$ and the random variable X_1 satisfies the Cramér (C) condition (2), then

$$\mathsf{P}\left(\frac{S_\lambda - a\lambda}{\sqrt{\lambda(a^2+\sigma^2)}} < x\right) = \Phi(x) + \frac{\Psi_1(x)}{\sqrt{\lambda}} + \frac{\Psi_2(x)}{\lambda} + o(\lambda^{-1}) \qquad (9)$$

where

$$\Psi_1(x) = -\frac{\alpha_3}{6\alpha_2^{3/2}}\phi(x)H_2(x), \quad \Psi_2(x) = -\phi(x)\left[\frac{\alpha_4}{24\alpha_2^2}H_3(x) + \frac{\alpha_3^2}{72\alpha_2^3}H_5(x)\right].$$

Therefore, setting $t = \lambda$, $Z(t) = S_\lambda$, $\Psi_0(x) = \Phi(x)$, from Lemma 2, we obtain the following result. For $\beta \in (0,1)$, let $w_\beta(\lambda)$ and u_β be the β-quantiles of the random variable S_λ and of the standard normal distribution, respectively.

Lemma 3. *Let $\mathsf{E}X_1^4 < \infty$, and let the random variable X_1 satisfy the Cramér (C) condition (2). Then, as $\lambda \to \infty$, we have*

$$w_\beta(\lambda) = a\lambda + u_\beta\sqrt{\lambda\alpha_2} + \frac{\alpha_3 H_2(u_\beta)}{6\alpha_2} +$$

$$+ \frac{1}{\sqrt{\lambda\alpha_2^{5/2}}}\left[\frac{\alpha_3^2}{72}\left(H_5(u_\beta) - 2H_2(u_\beta)H_3(u_\beta) + 4u_\beta H_2^2(u_\beta)\right) + \frac{\alpha_4\alpha_2}{24}H_3(u_\beta)\right] + o(\lambda^{-1/2})$$

where $H_k(x)$ are the Hermite polynomials.

3. Main Results

3.1. The Asymptotic Expansions for the α-Reserve in the Collective Risk Model

Let $X_1, X_2, \ldots$ be independent identically distributed r.v.s such that

$$\mathsf{E}X_1^2 > 0, \quad \mathsf{E}|X_1|^{4+\delta} < \infty, \quad \delta > 0. \tag{10}$$

Assume that the r.v. X_1 satisfies the Cramér (C) condition (2). For $t > 0$, let the r.v. N_t have the Poisson distribution with parameter λt, where $\lambda > 0$ is a fixed parameter. Assume that for each $t > 0$ the r.v.s $N_t, X_1, X_2, \ldots$ are independent. Consider the *Poisson random sum*

$$S_t = X_1 \ldots + X_{N_t}.$$

In terms of the collective risk model, the r.v.s X_j can be interpreted as individual insurance claims, and the r.v. S_t can be interpreted as the total insurance payment of an insurance company by the time t.

Let $\alpha \in (0,1)$. Define the *standardized α-reserve* $C^*_\alpha(t)$ by the formula

$$\mathsf{P}\left(\frac{S_t - \lambda t \mathsf{E}X_1}{\sqrt{\lambda t \mathsf{E}X_1^2}} \geq C^*_\alpha(t)\right) = \alpha + o(t^{-1}), \quad t \to \infty. \tag{11}$$

Along with the set $X_1, X_2, \ldots$ consider another set $Y_1, Y_2, \ldots$ of independent identically distributed r.v.s such that

$$\mathsf{E}Y_1^2 > 0, \quad \mathsf{E}|Y_1|^{4+\delta} < \infty, \quad \delta > 0. \tag{12}$$

Assume that the r.v. Y_1 satisfies the Cramér (C) condition (2). Also assume that for each $t > 0$, the r.v. N_t having the Poisson distribution with parameter λt is independent of the set $Y_1, Y_2, \ldots$ Denote

$$T_t = Y_1 + \ldots + Y_{N_t}.$$

In the same way as (11), define the *standardized α-reserve* $C^{**}_\alpha(t)$ for the sequence $Y_1, Y_2, \ldots$ as

$$\mathsf{P}\left(\frac{T_t - \lambda t \mathsf{E}Y_1}{\sqrt{\lambda t \mathsf{E}Y_1^2}} \geq C^{**}_\alpha(t)\right) = \alpha + o(t^{-1}), \quad t \to \infty.$$

Lemmas 2 and 3 directly imply the following statement. For $\alpha \in (0,1)$ let u_α be the $1-\alpha$-quantile of the standard normal distribution, that is, $\Phi(u_\alpha) = 1 - \alpha$.

Theorem 1. *Let $\alpha \in (0,1)$ and the r.v.s $X_1, X_2, \ldots$ and $Y_1, Y_2, \ldots$ satisfy conditions* (10), (12) *and* (2). *Then, as $t \to \infty$,*

$$C^*_\alpha(t) = u_\alpha + \frac{\mathsf{E}X_1^3(u_\alpha^2 - 1)}{6\sqrt{\lambda t}(\mathsf{E}X_1^2)^{3/2}} + \frac{1}{12\lambda t \mathsf{E}X_1^2}\left[\frac{(\mathsf{E}X_1^3)^2}{\mathsf{E}X_1^2}(5u_\alpha - 2u_\alpha^3) + \frac{\mathsf{E}X_1^4}{2(\mathsf{E}X_1^2)^2}(u_\alpha^3 - 3u_\alpha)\right] + o(t^{-1}),$$

$$C^{**}_\alpha(t) = u_\alpha + \frac{\mathsf{E}Y_1^3(u_\alpha^2 - 1)}{6\sqrt{\lambda t}(\mathsf{E}Y_1^2)^{3/2}} + \frac{1}{12\lambda t \mathsf{E}Y_1^2}\left[\frac{(\mathsf{E}Y_1^3)^2}{\mathsf{E}Y_1^2}(5u_\alpha - 2u_\alpha^3) + \frac{\mathsf{E}Y_1^4}{2(\mathsf{E}Y_1^2)^2}(u_\alpha^3 - 3u_\alpha)\right] + o(t^{-1}).$$

We see that if the first three moments of X_1 and Y_1 coincide, then $C^*_\alpha(t)$ and $C^{**}_\alpha(t)$ differ only by the terms of order $O(t^{-1})$.

Now if we define the *α-reserves* $\widetilde{C}^*_\alpha(t)$ and $\widetilde{C}^{**}_\alpha(t)$ as

$$\mathsf{P}\big(S_t \geq \widetilde{C}^*_\alpha(t)\big) = \alpha + o(t^{-1}), \text{ and } \mathsf{P}\big(T_t \geq \widetilde{C}^{**}_\alpha(t)\big) = \alpha + o(t^{-1}), \quad t \to \infty,$$

then

$$\widetilde{C}^*_\alpha(t) = \sqrt{\lambda t \mathsf{E}X_1^2} \cdot C^*_\alpha(t) + \lambda t \mathsf{E}X_1 \text{ and } \widetilde{C}^{**}_\alpha(t) = \sqrt{\lambda t \mathsf{E}Y_1^2} \cdot C^*_\alpha(t) + \lambda t \mathsf{E}Y_1.$$

3.2. A Continuous-Time Analog of Deficiency

In this section, we will propose an approach to the comparison of the two compound Poisson distributions in terms of the 'continuous' analog of deficiency. For the traditional definition of deficiency as the number of additional observations required for a statistical procedure to attain the desired quality, we refer the reader to the papers [1–3,5,6]. Here, we will introduce its continuous-time analog.

Consider two stochastic processes $X(t)$ and $Y(t)$, $t \geq 0$. We will be interested in the asymptotic behavior of the probabilities of $X(t)$ and $Y(t)$ to exceed a given threshold.

For $\alpha \in (0,1)$ let $c_\alpha(t)$ be the asymptotic $(1-\alpha)$-quantile of $X(t)$:

$$\mathsf{P}\big(X(t) \geq c_\alpha(t)\big) = \alpha + o(t^{-1}), \quad t \to \infty.$$

Lemma 2 directly implies the following statement.

Proposition 1. *Assume that there exist distribution function $G(x)$ and the functions $g_1(x)$ and $g_2(x)$ such that*

$$\sup_{x\in\mathbb{R}} \Big|\mathsf{P}\big(X(t) < x\big) - G(x) - \frac{1}{\sqrt{t}}g_1(x) - \frac{1}{t}g_2(x)\Big| = o(t^{-1}), \tag{13}$$

where the functions $G(x)$, $g_1(x)$ and $g_2(x)$ are smooth enough. Then the the asymptotic $(1-\alpha)$-quantile of $X(t)$ admits the asymptotic expansion

$$c_\alpha(t) = c_\alpha - \frac{g_1(c_\alpha)}{G'(c_\alpha)\sqrt{t}} - \frac{1}{t}\left[\frac{G''(c_\alpha)g_1^2(c_\alpha)}{2(G'(c_\alpha))^3} + \frac{G'(c_\alpha)g_2(c_\alpha) - g_1(c_\alpha)g_1{}'(c_\alpha)}{(G'(c_\alpha))^2}\right] + o(t^{-1}),$$

where c_α is the $(1-\alpha)$-quantile of the distribution function $G(x)$, that is, $G(c_\alpha) = 1-\alpha$.

Assume that the asymptotic expansion for the distribution function of $Y(t)$ has the form

$$\mathsf{P}\big(Y(t) < x\big) = G(x) + \frac{1}{\sqrt{t}}g_1(x) + \frac{1}{t}\overline{g}_2(x) + o(t^{-1}), \tag{14}$$

where the functions $G(x)$, $g_1(x)$ and $\overline{g}_2(x)$ are smooth enough. The asymptotic expansion (14) differs from that for the distribution function of $X(t)$ in Proposition 1 only by the term of order t^{-1}, that is, the two distributions are close enough.

Define the positive function $m(t)$, $t > 0$, by the equality

$$\mathsf{P}\big(\sqrt{t}\,Y(m(t)) \geq c_\alpha(m(t))\big) = \alpha + o(t^{-1}), \quad t \to \infty. \tag{15}$$

If $m(t) - t = d + o(1)$, $d \in \mathbb{R}$, $t \to \infty$, then the number d is called *the asymptotic deficiency* of the distribution $\mathcal{L}(Y(t))$ with respect to the distribution $\mathcal{L}(X(t))$. In other words, d is the asymptotic 'additional' time required for the process $Y(t)$ to attain the quantile of the same order as that of $X(t)$.

Theorem 2. *Assume that conditions* (13) *and* (14) *hold. Then the asymptotic deficiency d of the distribution $\mathcal{L}(Y(t))$ with respect to the distribution $\mathcal{L}(X(t))$ has the form*

$$d = \frac{2\big[g_2(c_\alpha) - \overline{g}_2(c_\alpha)\big]}{G'(c_\alpha)c_\alpha} + o(1).$$

The proof of this statement repeats that of Theorem 3.1 in [1] up to notation (furthermore, unfortunately, in formula (16) of [1], the coefficient $\sqrt{n}$ analogous to $\sqrt{t}$ in (15) of the present paper was erroneously omitted).

3.3. The Comparison of Compound Poisson Distributions by Deficiency

In this section, we will discuss the asymptotic deficiency of the compound Poisson distributions providing a given $(1-\alpha)$-quantile of the normalized Poisson random sums. For this purpose, we will use Theorem 2.

Define the *average Poisson random sums* $\overline{S}_t$ and $\overline{T}_t$ by the formulas

$$\overline{S}_t = \frac{S_t - \lambda t\, \mathsf{E}X_1}{t\sqrt{\lambda \mathsf{E}X_1^2}}, \quad \overline{T}_t = \frac{T_t - \lambda t\, \mathsf{E}Y_1}{t\sqrt{\lambda \mathsf{E}Y_1^2}}.$$

Define the *asymptotic deficiency* $d \in \mathbb{R}$ of $\overline{T}_t$ with respect to $\overline{S}_t$ by the formula

$$\mathsf{P}\big(\sqrt{t}\cdot \overline{T}_{\bar{t}} \geq C_\alpha^*(\bar{t})\big) = \alpha + o(t), \quad t \to \infty,$$

where $\bar{t} = t + d + o(1)$, that is, d is the 'additional time' required for the normalized average Poisson random sum $\sqrt{t}\cdot\overline{T}_t$ to exceed the asymptotic α-reserve $C_\alpha^*(t)$ of the normalized average Poisson random sum $\sqrt{t}\cdot\overline{S}_t$.

To apply Theorem 2, assume that

$$\frac{\mathsf{E}X_1^3}{(\mathsf{E}X_1^2)^{3/2}} = \frac{\mathsf{E}Y_1^3}{(\mathsf{E}Y_1^2)^{3/2}}. \tag{16}$$

Condition (16) holds, e.g., if the first three moments of X_1 and Y_1 coincide.

Theorem 2 directly implies the following statement.

Theorem 3. *Assume that the r.v.s $N_t, X_1, X_2, \dots; Y_1, Y_2, \dots$ satisfy conditions* (2), (10) *and* (16). *Then, as $t \to \infty$, the 'additional time' d has the form*

$$d = \frac{(3-u_\alpha^2)}{12}\left[\frac{\mathsf{E}X_1^4}{(\mathsf{E}X_1^2)^2} - \frac{\mathsf{E}Y_1^4}{(\mathsf{E}Y_1^2)^2}\right] + o(1). \tag{17}$$

Remark 2. *If $\mathsf{E}X_1 = \mathsf{E}Y_1 = 0$, then* (17) *can be rewritten as*

$$d = \tfrac{1}{12}(3-u_\alpha^2)\big(\varkappa_4(X_1) - \varkappa_4(Y_1)\big) + o(1),$$

That is, in this case, the continuous-time analog of asymptotic deficiency is determined by the difference of kurtoses.

3.4. Comparing the Distributions of Poisson Random Sums with Those of Non-Random Sums

It is well-known that the asymptotic properties of non-random sums of independent identically distributed r.v.s coincide with those of the compound Poisson distributions with the same expectation. This phenomenon manifests itself, for example, in the form of the method of accompanying infinitely divisible distributions (see, e.g., [9], Chapter 4, Section 24). Therefore, it is of certain interest to investigate the accuracy of the approximation of the characteristics of sums of independent r.v.s as compared to that of the accompanying infinitely divisible (that is, corresponding compound Poisson) laws. This problem was studied by many specialists, see, e.g., [10–13]. Unlike most preceding works where the approximation of distribution functions was discussed, here we consider the application of accompanying laws to a somewhat inverse problem of approximation of quantiles.

Here, we will not assume the possibility of the interpretation of the presented results in terms of a collective risk model where at least the expectations of X_j should be positive. Assume that the independent identically distributed r.v.s $X_1, X_2, \dots$ are standardized:

$$\mathsf{E}X_1 = 0, \quad \mathsf{E}X_1^2 = 1. \tag{18}$$

Again, let N_t be an r.v. with the Poisson distribution with parameter λt, where $\lambda > 0$ is fixed. Assume that for each $t > 0$ the random variables $N_t, X_1, X_2, \ldots$ are independent. Consider the problem of comparison of the distribution of a normalized Poisson random sum

$$S_t^* = \frac{X_1 + \ldots + X_{N_t}}{\sqrt{\lambda t}}$$

with the distribution of the corresponding non-random sum

$$U_t^* = \frac{X_1 + \ldots + X_{[\lambda t]}}{\sqrt{[\lambda t]}}$$

as $t \to \infty$, where the symbol $[a]$ denotes the integer part of a real number a. For definiteness, if $N_t = 0$, then S_t^* is assumed to be equal to zero.

If conditions (18), (10) and (2), then Lemmas 1 and 2 imply (see (9)) that, as $t \to \infty$,

$$\mathsf{P}(S_t^* < x) = \Phi(x) - \frac{\mathsf{E}X_1^3}{6\sqrt{\lambda t}}\varphi(x)(x^2 - 1) -$$

$$- \frac{\varphi(x)}{24\lambda t}\left[\mathsf{E}X_1^4(x^3 - 3x) + \frac{(\mathsf{E}X_1^3)^2}{3}(x^5 - 10x + 15x)\right] + o(t^{-1}), \tag{19}$$

whereas the classical theory of asymptotic expansions in the central limit theorem (e.g., see [16]) yields that

$$\mathsf{P}(U_t^* < x) = \Phi(x) - \frac{\mathsf{E}X_1^3}{6\sqrt{[\lambda t]}}\varphi(x)(x^2 - 1) -$$

$$- \frac{\varphi(x)}{24[\lambda t]}\left[(\mathsf{E}X_1^4 - 3)(x^3 - 3x) + \frac{(\mathsf{E}X_1^3)^2}{3}(x^5 - 10x + 15x)\right] + o(t^{-1}). \tag{20}$$

Note that (19) and (20) differ in that, in (19), the kurtosis of X_1 is present in the non-normalized form $\varkappa_4^*(X_1) = \mathsf{E}X_1^4$, whereas in (20), there stands the normalized kurtosis $\varkappa_4(X_1) = \mathsf{E}X_1^4 - 3$.

From the obvious inequalities

$$\lambda t - 1 \le [\lambda t] \le \lambda t$$

it follows that, as $t \to \infty$,

$$\frac{1}{\lambda t} \le \frac{1}{[\lambda t]} \le \frac{1}{\lambda t - 1} = \frac{1}{\lambda t}\Big(1 + \frac{1}{\lambda t} + O(t^{-2})\Big)$$

and

$$\frac{1}{\sqrt{[\lambda t]}} = \frac{1}{\sqrt{\lambda t}} + O(t^{-3/2}).$$

Therefore, relation (20) can be rewritten as

$$\mathsf{P}(U_t^* < x) = \Phi(x) - \frac{\mathsf{E}X_1^3}{6\sqrt{\lambda t}}\varphi(x)(x^2 - 1) -$$

$$- \frac{\varphi(x)}{24\lambda t}\left[\mathsf{E}(X_1^4 - 3)(x^3 - 3x) + \frac{(\mathsf{E}X_1^3)^2}{3}(x^5 - 10x + 15x)\right] + o(t^{-1}). \tag{21}$$

Denote $\overline{U}_t^* = U_t^* / \sqrt{t}$. Let $\alpha \in (0,1)$. Define the asymptotic $(1-\alpha)$-quantile $C_\alpha(t)$ of S_t^* by the relation

$$\mathsf{P}\big(S_t^* \ge C_\alpha(t)\big) = \alpha + o(t^{-1}), \quad t \to \infty.$$

Define the number $d \in \mathbb{R}$ by the formula

$$\mathsf{P}\big(\sqrt{t}\,\overline{U}_{\bar{t}}^{*} \geq C_{\alpha}(\bar{t})\big) = \alpha + o(t^{-1}), \quad t \to \infty,$$

where $\bar{t} = t + d + o(1)$. Now relations (19), (21) and Theorem 2 directly imply the following statement.

Theorem 4. *Let $\alpha \in (0,1)$. Assume that the r.v.s $N_t, X_1, X_2, \ldots$ satisfy conditions* (18), (10) *and* (2). *Then*

$$d = \frac{3 - u_{\alpha}^{2}}{4} + o(1)$$

as $t \to \infty$, where $\Phi(u_{\alpha}) = 1 - \alpha$.

Remark 3. *The quantity d can be interpreted as the asymptotic deficiency of the distribution of a non-random sum with respect to the corresponding accompanying compound Poisson distribution. Note that under the conditions of Theorem 4, d does not depend on the distribution of X_1. If $\alpha > 0.0417...$, then d is asymptotically positive, that is, the (accompanying) compound Poisson distribution of the r.v. S_t^* provides better accuracy for the approximation of the asymptotic $(1-\alpha)$-quantile of U_t^*.*

4. Conclusions

This paper is a continuation of our previous work [1] and deals with a version of the problem of stochastic ordering. We follow an approach based on the concept of deficiency, which is well-known in asymptotic statistics. In the present paper, we considered compound Poisson distributions and introduced a continuous analog of deficiency. It was suggested to understand the continuous deficiency as the difference between the parameter of the compounding distribution of a Poisson random sum and that of the compound Poisson distribution providing the desired accuracy of the normal approximation. The asymptotic representations for the continuous deficiency were obtained under the condition that possible distributions of random summands possess coinciding first three moments. Therefore, we can say that, in this problem, we deal with 'fine tuning' of the distribution of a separate summand since we assume that different possible distributions of random summands can differ only by their kurtosis. In the setting under consideration, the best distribution delivers the smallest value of the parameter of the compounding Poisson distribution. The main mathematical tools used in the paper are asymptotic expansions for the compound Poisson distributions and their quantiles. The formal setting mentioned above was applied to solving some practical problems dealing with the collective risk insurance models where it is traditional to describe the cumulative insurance payments by the compound Poisson process. The approach under consideration makes it possible to determine the distribution of insurance payments providing the least possible time that provides the prescribed Value-at-Risk. We also considered the application of the proposed approach to the study of the asymptotic properties of non-random sums of independent identically distributed r.v.s as compared to those of the compound Poisson distributions with the same expectation. We investigate the accuracy of the approximation of the characteristics of sums of independent r.v.s as compared to that of the accompanying infinitely divisible (that is, corresponding compound Poisson) laws. Unlike most preceding works where the approximation of distribution functions was discussed, here we considered the application of accompanying laws to a somewhat inverse problem of approximation of quantiles.

Author Contributions: Conceptualization, V.B. and V.K.; methodology, V.B. and V.K.; validation, V.B. and V.K.; formal analysis, V.B. and V.K.; investigation, V.B. and V.K.; writing—original draft preparation, V.K.; writing—review and editing, V.K.; supervision, V.K.; project administration, V.K.; funding acquisition, V.K. All authors have read and agreed to the published version of the manuscript.

Funding: This research was funded by the Russian Science Foundation, grant 22-11-00212.

Acknowledgments: The authors thank Alexander Zeifman for his help in the final preparation of the manuscript.

Conflicts of Interest: The authors declare no conflict of interest.

References

1. Bening, V.E.; Korolev, V.Y. Comparing distributions of sums of random variables by deficiency: Discrete case. *Mathematics* **2022**, *10*, 454. [CrossRef]
2. Hodges, J.L.; Lehmann, E.L. Deficiency. *Ann. Math. Stat.* **1970**, *41*, 783–801. [CrossRef]
3. Xiang, X. Deficiency of the sample quantile estimator with respect to kernel quantile estimators for censored data. *Ann. Stat.* **1995**, *23*, 836–854. [CrossRef]
4. Bening, V.E. *Asymptotic Theory of Testing Statistical Hypotheses: Efficient Statistics, Optimality, Power Loss, and Deficiency*; Walter de Gruyter: Berlin, Germany, 2011.
5. Torgersen, E. *Comparison of Statistical Experiments*; Cambridge University Press: Cambridge, UK, 1991.
6. Bening, V.E.; Korolev, V.Y.; Zeifman, A.I. Calculation of the deficiency of some statistical estimators constructed from samples with random sizes. *Colloq. Math.* **2019**, *157*, 157–171. [CrossRef]
7. Müller, A.; Stoyan, D. *Comparison Methods for Stochastic Models and Risks*; John Wiley & Sons: Chichester, UK, 2002.
8. Cramér, H. *Collective Risk Theory*; Skandia Jubilee Volume: Stockholm, Sweden, 1955.
9. Gnedenko, B.V.; Kolmogorov, A.N. *Limit Distributions for Sums of Independent Random Variables*; Addison-Wesley: Reading, MA, USA, 1954.
10. Prokhorov, Y.V. Strong stability of sums and infinitely divisible distributions. *Theory Probab. Its Appl.* **1958**, *4*, 141–153. [CrossRef]
11. Arak, T.V. On the approximation of n-fold convolutions of distributions having non-negative characteristic functions with accompanying laws. *Theory Probab. Its Appl.* **1981**, *25*, 221–245. [CrossRef]
12. Čekanavičius, V. Approximation by accompanying distributions and asymptotic expansions. I; II. *Lith. Math. J. (Liet. Mat. Rink.)* **1989**, *29*, 171–178. 402–415.
13. Zaitsev, A.Y. Approximation of convolutions of multi-dimensional symmetric distributions by accompanying laws. *J. Sov. Math.* **1992**, *61*, 1859–1872. [CrossRef]
14. Von Chossy, R.; Rappl, G. Some approximation methods for the distribution of random sums. *Insur. Math. Econ.* **1983**, *2*, 251–270. [CrossRef]
15. Bening, V.; Korolev, V. *Generalized Poisson Models and Their Applications in Insurance and Finance*; Walter de Gruyter: Berlin, Germany, 2012.
16. Bhattacharya, R.N.; Ranga Rao, R. *Normal Approximation and Asymptotic Expansions*; John Wiley & Sons: New York, NY, USA; London, UK; Sydney, Australia, 1976.

mathematics

MDPI

Article

Delicate Comparison of the Central and Non-Central Lyapunov Ratios with Applications to the Berry–Esseen Inequality for Compound Poisson Distributions

Vladimir Makarenko [1,2,*] and Irina Shevtsova [1,2,3,4,*]

1 Faculty of Computational Mathematics and Cybernetics, Lomonosov Moscow State University, Leninskie Gory, 1/52, 119991 Moscow, Russia
2 Moscow Center for Fundamental and Applied Mathematics, 119991 Moscow, Russia
3 Federal Research Center "Informatics and Control", Russian Academy of Sciences, Vavilov Str., 44/2, 119333 Moscow, Russia
4 Department of Mathematics, School of Science, Hangzhou Dianzi University, Hangzhou 310005, China
* Correspondence: vlamakarenko@gmail.com (V.M.); ishevtsova@cs.msu.ru (I.S.)

Abstract: For each $t \in (-1,1)$, the exact value of the least upper bound $H(t) = \sup\{\mathbb{E}|X|^3/\mathbb{E}|X-t|^3\}$ over all the non-degenerate distributions of the random variable X with a fixed normalized first-order moment $\mathbb{E}X_1/\sqrt{\mathbb{E}X_1^2} = t$, and a finite third-order moment is obtained, yielding the exact value of the unconditional supremum $M := \sup L_1(X)/L_1(X-\mathbb{E}X) = (\sqrt{17+7\sqrt{7}})/4$, where $L_1(X) = \mathbb{E}|X|^3/(\mathbb{E}X^2)^{3/2}$ is the non-central Lyapunov ratio, and hence proving S. Shorgin's (2001) conjecture on the exact value of M. As a corollary, an analog of the Berry–Esseen inequality for the Poisson random sums of independent identically distributed random variables $X_1, X_2, \ldots$ is proven in terms of the central Lyapunov ratio $L_1(X_1 - \mathbb{E}X_1)$ with the constant $0.3031 \cdot H(t)(1-t^2)^{3/2} \in [0.3031, 0.4517)$, $t \in [0,1)$, which depends on the normalized first-moment $t := \mathbb{E}X_1/\sqrt{\mathbb{E}X_1^2}$ of random summands and being arbitrarily close to 0.3031 for small values of t, an almost 1.5 size improvement from the previously known one.

Keywords: Lyapunov fraction; extreme problem; moment inequality; central limit theorem; Berry–Esseen inequality; compound Poisson distribution; normal approximation

MSC: 60F05; 60E15; 26D05

Citation: Makarenko, V.; Shevtsova, I. Delicate Comparison of the Central and Non-Central Lyapunov Ratios with Applications to the Berry–Esseen Inequality for Compound Poisson Distributions. *Mathematics* **2023**, *11*, 625. https://doi.org/10.3390/math11030625

Academic Editor: Francisco Chiclana

Received: 10 December 2022
Revised: 16 January 2023
Accepted: 23 January 2023
Published: 26 January 2023

1. Introduction

Let $X, X_1, X_2, \ldots$ be independent and identically distributed random variables (i.i.d. r.v.'s), N_λ be a Poisson r.v. with expectation $\lambda > 0$ and independent of the sequence $\{X_n\}_{n\geqslant 1}$ for each $\lambda > 0$. The r.v. is

$$S_\lambda = X_1 + X_2 + \ldots + X_{N_\lambda}$$

and is called a Poisson random sum, and its distribution is called a compound Poisson. Here, for definiteness, we assume that $\sum_{k=1}^{0}(\,\cdot\,) = 0$. Poisson random sums S_λ are popular mathematic models in many fields. In particular, in the classical collective risk model [1], the r.v. S_λ describes the total insurance claim amount per time unit with the intensity of the claim arrivals equaling λ. Many examples of applied problems that make use of Poisson random sums can be found, e.g., in the books [2–4]. As a rule, these problems can be successfully solved only if the distribution of the r.v. S_λ is either known or approximated accurately enough.

Assume that $\mathbb{E}X^2 \in (0, \infty)$. We denote

$$\widetilde{S}_\lambda = \frac{S_\lambda - \mathbb{E}S_\lambda}{\sqrt{\mathbb{D}S_\lambda}} = \frac{S_\lambda - \lambda\mathbb{E}X}{\sqrt{\lambda\mathbb{E}X^2}},$$

$$F_\lambda(x) := \mathbb{P}(\widetilde{S}_\lambda < x), \quad \Phi(x) = \frac{1}{\sqrt{2\pi}}\int_{-\infty}^{x} e^{-t^2/2}\,dt, \quad x \in \mathbb{R}.$$

As is well known, under the above assumptions, the compound Poisson distributions are asymptotically normal:

$$\Delta_\lambda(X) := \sup_x |F_\lambda(x) - \Phi(x)| \to 0, \quad \lambda \to \infty.$$

Therefore, irrespective of the common distribution $\mathscr{L}(X)$ of the summands $X_1, X_2, \ldots$, the distribution function (d.f.) of the Poisson random sum S_λ can be approximated by the normal law with the corresponding location and scale parameters under reasonable ("convenient," computable) estimates $\Delta_\lambda \leqslant \overline{\Delta}_\lambda$ for the uniform distance Δ_λ:

$$\Phi(x) - \overline{\Delta}_\lambda \leqslant F_\lambda(x) \leqslant \Phi(x) + \overline{\Delta}_\lambda, \quad x \in \mathbb{R}.$$

Under the above assumptions, Δ_λ may converge to zero arbitrarily and slowly ([5], Theorems 5 and 8). Some possible upper bounds for Δ_λ in this situation were presented in [6]. However, under some additional moment-type conditions, the rate of convergence of Δ_λ to zero can be rather universally estimated by a "convenient" power-type function. For example, if $\mathbb{E}|X|^{2+\delta} < \infty$ for some $\delta \in (0, 1]$, then $\Delta_\lambda = O(\lambda^{-\delta/2})$, as $\lambda \to \infty$. A particular form of $O(\ldots)$ is determined by the available moment characteristics of $\mathscr{L}(X)$.

The main attention was traditionally given to the case $\delta = 1$ since, generally, for $\delta > 1$, the convergence rate remains the same as for $\delta = 1$. Moreover, by analogy with convergence rate bounds for the sums of a non-random number of independent r.v.s', central moments were initially used in the moment-type bounds for Δ_λ since these bounds themselves were obtained by a more or less ingenious application of the formula of total probability in order to extend to random sums the bounds initially constructed for non-random sums. These bounds had a rather cumbersome form, as shown in [7,8].

However, in the construction of the estimates of the accuracy of the normal approximation to compound Poisson distributions, it turned out to be convenient and reasonable to use non-central moments. In these terms, the bounds take a pretty simple form [9,10]

$$\Delta_\lambda(X) \leqslant \frac{C_1}{\sqrt{\lambda}} \cdot L_1(X), \quad \lambda > 0, \tag{1}$$

where

$$L_1(X) = \frac{\mathbb{E}|X|^3}{(\mathbb{E}X^2)^{3/2}} \tag{2}$$

is the *non-central Lyapunov ratio* or *non-central Lyapunov fraction*. Estimate (1) is an analog of the Berry–Esseen inequality for Poisson random sums (or for compound Poisson distributions).

The first upper bounds for the constant C_1 [9–11] were greater than the then best-known upper bounds for the absolute constant C in the *classical* Berry–Esseen inequality [12,13]

$$\sup_{x\in\mathbb{R}}\left|\mathbb{P}\left(\frac{X_1 + \ldots + X_n - n\mathbb{E}X}{\sqrt{n\mathbb{D}X}} < x\right) - \Phi(x)\right| \leqslant \frac{C}{\sqrt{n}} \cdot L_0(X), \quad n \in \mathbb{N},$$

where

$$L_0(X) = \frac{\mathbb{E}|X - \mathbb{E}X|^3}{(\mathbb{D}X)^{3/2}} = L_1(X - \mathbb{E}X) \tag{3}$$

is known as the central Lyapunov ratio or the central Lyapunov fraction. Michel [14] was the first to prove that $C_1 \leqslant C$ (four years later, this result was independently re-proved in [15]). Finally, the authors of [16] succeeded in proving that $C_1 < C$. Namely, in that paper, the upper bound of $C_1 \leqslant 0.345$ was obtained, which was strictly less than the lower bound $C_E := (\sqrt{10}+3)/(6\sqrt{2\pi}) = 0.4097\ldots$ [17] for the absolute constant C. Later the upper bound of 0.345 for C_1 was lowered to 0.3041 [18] (see also [19], Theorem 2.4.3) and 0.3031 ([20], Theorem 4). The first lower bound, $C_1 \geqslant 0.2344$, for C_1, was obtained in the paper [21]. In ([5], Theorem 5) and ([22], Chapter 3, p. 50), this estimate was improved to

$$C_1 \geqslant \sup_{\gamma>0, m\in\mathbb{N}_0} \sqrt{\gamma}\left(e^{-\gamma}\sum_{k=0}^{m}\frac{\gamma^k}{k!} - \Phi\left(\frac{m-\gamma}{\sqrt{\gamma}}\right)\right) \geqslant 0.266012\ldots = \frac{2}{3\sqrt{2\pi}} + 0.0000505\ldots$$

In [5], an intermediate estimate was obtained in terms of the least upper bound with respect to γ and m, whereas in [22], exact values $\gamma = 6.4206$, $m = 6$, were found to provide the lower bound for this supremum. However, if we let $\gamma = m \to \infty$, then the limit value is $2/(3\sqrt{2\pi})$ only. The lower bound for the constant C_1 is presented here with the separation of the term $2/(3\sqrt{2\pi})$, and due to that, this number plays the same asymptotic role in inequality (1), as the Esseen lower bound C_E in the classical Berry–Esseen inequality. For more details concerning the asymptotically exact constants, see [5,23]. A detailed survey of the moment-type bounds for the accuracy of the normal approximation to the compound Poisson distribution, including both the case $0 \leqslant \delta < 1$ and asymptotic settings, can be found in [5] (for the case $\delta = 1$ and non-asymptotic setting see also [18], Section 3).

It should be noted that the estimate (1) in terms of the non-central Lyapunov ratio $L_1(X)$ implies a similar estimate in terms of the central Lyapunov ratio

$$\Delta_\lambda(X) \leqslant \frac{C_0}{\sqrt{\lambda}} \cdot L_0(X), \quad \lambda > 0, \tag{4}$$

where C_0 is an absolute constant, but not vice versa. Namely, let

$$J(X) = J(\mathscr{L}(X)) := \frac{L_1(X)}{L_0(X)} = \frac{\mathbb{E}|X|^3}{\mathbb{E}|X-\mathbb{E}X|^3}\left(\frac{\mathbb{D}X}{\mathbb{E}X^2}\right)^{3/2},$$

and let $\mathscr{P}$ be the class of all distributions on $\mathbb{R}$ with finite third moments. In 1996 S. Shorgin [24] proved that for any $\mathscr{L}(X) \in \mathscr{P}$

$$J(X) \leqslant 2\sqrt{2} < 2.8285 \quad \text{and} \quad \inf_{\mathscr{L}(X)\in\mathscr{P}} J(X) = 0,$$

hence, with the account of the upper bound $C_1 \leqslant 0.3031$ [20], it follows that $C_0 \leqslant 2\sqrt{2}C_1 < 0.8573$, and also that inequality (4) does not imply (1); that is, bounding (1) in terms of the non-central Lyapunov ratio not only obtains in a more natural way than (4) but is also more accurate. However, inequality (4) is more natural and extremely convenient in estimating the rate of convergence of distributions of randomly stopped random walks with equivalent elementary trends and variances to variance-mean mixtures of normal laws [25–29], in particular, to skew the exponential power law, skew the Student's law, and more generally, the variance-generalized gamma and generalized hyperbolic distributions. Note that such asymptotic behavior of the elementary trends and variances is typical for the increments of a Wiener process with drift, and due to the considerable trends, the central moments of elementary increments are computed in a much simpler way than the non-central ones, which gives an advantage to inequality (4) over inequality (1).

In 2001, S. Shorgin [30] suggested that

$$\sup_{\mathscr{L}(X)\in\mathscr{P}} J(X) = \sup_{\mathscr{L}(X)\in\mathscr{P}} \frac{L_1(X)}{L_0(X)} = \frac{\sqrt{17+7\sqrt{7}}}{4} = 1.48997\ldots =: C_{\mathrm{SH}} \tag{5}$$

and described the hypothetical extreme of the two-point distribution of the r.v. X.

In 2011, Korolev, Shevtsova, and Shorgin [31] demonstrated that the least upper bound $\sup_{\mathscr{L}(X)\in\mathscr{P}} J(X)$ can be found in the class of distributions concentrated in at most three points, and that the estimate $\sup_{\mathscr{L}(X)\in\mathscr{P}} J(X) \leqslant 1.49$ was computed numerically, which implies that $C_0 < 1.49C_1 \leqslant 1.49 \cdot 0.3031 < 0.4517$, see also ([19], Section 2.4). Note that, as of 2011, the best-known upper bound for C_1 was 0.3041 [18], yielding a worse upper bound $C_0 < 1.49 \cdot 0.3041 < 0.4532$, published in the cited works.

In the present paper, a complete proof of hypothesis (5) is given, but the main result consists of the solution to this problem in a more delicate setting. Namely, we suggest the fixing of the value of the normalized mathematical expectation $\mathbb{E}X/\sqrt{\mathbb{E}X^2} = t \in (-1,1)$ and instead of the unconditional optimization problem (5), we solve the problem of conditional optimization

$$\sup_{\substack{\mathscr{L}(X)\in\mathscr{P}:\\ \mathbb{E}X=t\sqrt{\mathbb{E}X^2}}} J(X) = \sup_{\substack{\mathscr{L}(X)\in\mathscr{P}:\\ \mathbb{E}X=t,\,\mathbb{E}X^2=1}} \frac{L_1(X)}{L_1(X-t)} = \left(1-t^2\right)^{3/2} \sup_{\substack{\mathscr{L}(X)\in\mathscr{P}:\\ \mathbb{E}X=t,\,\mathbb{E}X^2=1}} \frac{\mathbb{E}|X|^3}{\mathbb{E}|X-t|^3}, \tag{6}$$

which allows us to take the possible smallness of the centering parameter $\mathbb{E}X/\sqrt{\mathbb{E}X^2}$ into account and majorize the ratio $J(X) = L_1(X)/L_0(X)$ by a quantity close to unity, which is almost one and a half times more accurate, than is allowed by (5). The values $t = \pm 1$ are not considered here because the only distribution satisfying the conditions $\mathbb{E}X = t = \pm 1$ and $\mathbb{E}X^2 = 1$ is the degenerate in the point t one. The solution to the conditional optimization problem (6) reduces the calculation of the least upper bound to

$$H(t) := \sup\left\{\frac{\mathbb{E}|X|^3}{\mathbb{E}|X-t|^3} : \mathscr{L}(X) \in \mathscr{P},\ \mathbb{E}X = t,\ \mathbb{E}X^2 = 1\right\}, \quad -1 < t < 1. \tag{7}$$

In the present paper, $H(t)$ is calculated for each value of the centering parameter $t \in (-1,1)$ (Theorem 1 and Table 1), and hypothesis (5) is proved by writing the $\sup J(X)$ in the form

$$\sup_{\mathscr{L}(X)\in\mathscr{P}} J(X) = \sup_{t\in(-1,1)} H(t)\left(1-t^2\right)^{3/2}$$

and calculating the latest upper bound with respect to $t \in (-1,1)$ (Theorem 2 and Table 1). In particular, from (7), it follows that for any $\mathscr{L}(X) \in \mathscr{P}$, we have

$$J(X) = \frac{L_1(X)}{L_0(X)} \leqslant H\left(\frac{\mathbb{E}X}{\sqrt{\mathbb{E}X^2}}\right)\left(1 - \frac{(\mathbb{E}X)^2}{\mathbb{E}X^2}\right)^{3/2},$$

and hence, for any distribution $\mathscr{L}(X) \in \mathscr{P}$ with the known value of the normalized first-order moment $\mathbb{E}X/\sqrt{\mathbb{E}X^2} = t \in (-1,1)$, inequality (4) holds with a sharper value of the constant

$$C_0 = C_0(t) := C_1 \cdot H(t)\left(1-t^2\right)^{3/2} \leqslant 0.3031 \cdot \frac{\sqrt{17+7\sqrt{7}}}{4} < 0.4517.$$

The values of $C_0(t)$ rounded up to the fourth digit are presented for some $t \in [0,1)$ in the fourth column of Table 1. In addition, in Theorem 3, the form of the constant $C_0(t)$, $t \in (-1,1)$, is presented for the case where only an upper bound $|\mathbb{E}X|/\sqrt{\mathbb{E}X^2} \leqslant t$ is known for the normalized expectation.

Table 1. The values of the functions $H(t)$, $H(t)(1-t^2)^{3/2}$, $C_0(t) = 0.3031 \cdot H(t)(1-t^2)^{3/2}$, and the mass $p(t)$ of one of the atoms of the extreme distribution rounded up, for some $t \in [0,1)$.

t	$H(t)$	$H(t)(1-t^2)^{3/2}$	$C_0(t)$	$p(t)$
0	1	1	0.3031	$\frac{3-\sqrt{3}}{6}$
0.001	1.00111	1.00111	0.3035	0.2116
0.01	1.0108	1.0107	0.3064	0.21405
0.05	1.057	1.053	0.3192	0.22494
0.1	1.1225	1.1057	0.3352	0.23856
0.2	1.285	1.20871	0.3664	0.26593
0.3	1.5034	1.3051	0.3956	0.29365
0.4	1.805	1.3896	0.4212	0.32205
0.5	2.2392	1.4544	0.4409	0.35168
0.6	2.9067	1.4882	0.4511	0.38345
$\sqrt{\frac{5-\sqrt{7}}{6}}$	$\frac{1+2\sqrt{7}}{2}$	$\frac{\sqrt{17+7\sqrt{7}}}{4}$	0.4517	$\frac{5-\sqrt{7}}{6}$
0.7	4.04901	1.4747	0.447	0.41691
0.8	6.4739	1.3984	0.4239	0.44833
0.9	15.041	1.2457	0.3776	0.47783
1−	$+\infty$	1	0.3031	0.5

Regarding the methods, computation of the least upper bound in (7) is implemented in two steps: a reduction to the distributions concentrated in two points at most (see Section 3, "Reduction to the case of two-point distributions"), and the analysis of the two-point distributions (see Section 4, "Analysis of the two-point distributions"), the last step is, in fact, the most difficult one from a technical point of view. It also should be noted here that the standard technique based on the works [32–34] (see also [35]) allows the reduction of only up to the three-point distributions, since there are three linear conditions in total for $\mathscr{L}(X)$ in (6) and (7): the two moment conditions $\mathbb{E}X = t$ *and* $\mathbb{E}X^2 = 1$, plus one probability normalization condition $\mathbb{E}X^0 \equiv \mathbb{E}1 = 1$. In fact, the same moments should be fixed in (5) to make the objective function

$$L_1(X) - C_{SH} \cdot L_0(X) = \frac{\mathbb{E}|X|^3}{(\mathbb{E}X^2)^{3/2}} - C_{SH} \cdot \frac{\mathbb{E}|X-\mathbb{E}X|^3}{(\mathbb{D}X)^{3/2}},$$

linear with respect to $\mathscr{L}(X)$, and hence, no further reduction in (5) can be allowed by just the standard techniques. Therefore, we used an alternative approach based on the construction of a special lower bound to $|x-t|^3$ with two tangency points in the form of a linear combination of the functions $1, x, x^2, and |x|^3$, generating the required moment conditions $\mathbb{E}1 = 1$, $\mathbb{E}X = t$, $\mathbb{E}X^2 = 1$, $\mathbb{E}|X|^3 < \infty$ (Lemma 1 in Section 3), and then integrating the obtained inequality with respect to x (Lemma 2 in Section 3). This trick allows us to immediately reduce the calculation of the least upper bound in (7) to the analysis of the two-point distributions, which is implemented in Lemma 4 of Section 4.

Section 2, "Formulations of main results," contains accurate formulations of the main results, and Section 5, "Proofs of main results," contains their proofs.

To conclude this introductory overview, note as well that an "opposite" problem of comparing the central and non-central absolute moments

$$\frac{\mathbb{E}|X-\mathbb{E}X|^p}{\mathbb{E}|X|^p} \longrightarrow \sup$$

was considered in the papers [36], with $p=3$ and [37], with an arbitrary $p>1$; for a wider class of functions of X and $X-\mathbb{E}X$, including $|\cdot|^p$; and also in [38] with $p=3$ under an additional restriction $\mathbb{E}X/\sqrt{\mathbb{E}X^2}=t$ for each $t\in(-1,1)$.

2. Formulations of Main Results

Theorem 1. *For every* $t\in(-1,1)$

$$H(t) := \sup_{\substack{\mathscr{L}(X)\in\mathscr{P}:\\ \mathbb{E}X=t\sqrt{\mathbb{E}X^2}}} \frac{\mathbb{E}|X|^3}{\mathbb{E}|X-t|^3} = \begin{cases} 1, & t=0,\\ 1+\dfrac{3t^2}{1-t^2}\cdot\dfrac{1-z^2(t)}{1-3z^2(t)}, & 0<|t|<t_0,\\ \dfrac{2}{z(t)(3-z^2(t))}, & t_0\leqslant|t|<1, \end{cases} \tag{8}$$

where $t_0=\sqrt{\frac{5-\sqrt{7}}{6}}=0.6263\ldots,$

$$z(t) = \begin{cases} u(t), & 0<t<t_0,\\ v(t), & t_0\leqslant t<1, \end{cases} \tag{9}$$

$u(t),\, 0<t<\sqrt{3}/2=0.8660\ldots,$ *is the unique root of the equation*

$$\frac{4u\sqrt{1-u^2}}{3u^2-1} = \frac{4t^2-3}{3t\sqrt{1-t^2}} \tag{10}$$

on the interval $0<u<\frac{\sqrt{3}}{3}$; *and* $v(t),\, t\in(0,1)$, *is the unique root of the equation*

$$\frac{2(1-v^2)^{3/2}}{v(3-v^2)} = \frac{t(3-2t^2)}{(1-t^2)^{3/2}} \tag{11}$$

on the interval $0<v<1$. *The function* $H(t)$ *is continuous and monotonically increasing on* $[0,1)$ *with* $\lim\limits_{t\to1-}H(t)=+\infty$. *The supremum in* (7) *is attained for* $0<t<1$ *only on the two-point distribution of the form*

$$\mathbb{P}(X=x)=p=1-\mathbb{P}(X=y)=:1-q, \tag{12}$$

where $x=x(t)=t+\sqrt{(1-t^2)q/p},\, y=y(t)=t-\sqrt{(1-t^2)p/q}$, *and*

$$p=p(t)=\tfrac{1}{2}(1-z(t)), \quad t\in(0,1). \tag{13}$$

The values of the functions $H(t)$ and $p(t)$ for some $t\in[0,1)$ rounded up to the fourth digit are given in the second and fifth columns of Table 1. Since the function $p(t)$ is close to linear (see the left graph in Figure 1), for more clarity, the right graph in Figure 1 also represents the normalized function

$$\tilde{p}(t) := \frac{p(t)}{p(0+)+t(p(1-)-p(0+))} = \frac{p(t)}{\frac{3-\sqrt{3}}{6}+t\left(\frac{1}{2}-\frac{3-\sqrt{3}}{6}\right)}, \quad 0<t<1. \tag{14}$$

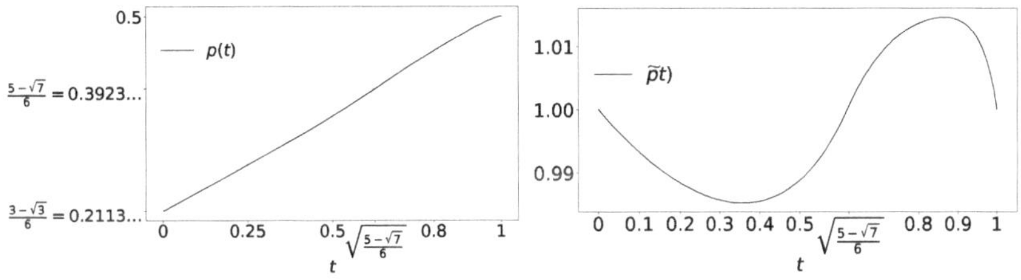

Figure 1. Plots of the functions $p(t)$ and $\widetilde{p}(t)$ defined in (13) and (14), respectively.

The next statement provides a simple upper bound for $H(t)$ for small $|t|$ in the form of a fractional-rational expression.

Proposition 1. *The function H defined in* (8) *admits the upper bound*

$$H(t) \leqslant \hat{H}(t) := \frac{5t + 6\sqrt{2}}{2(1-t^2)(3\sqrt{2}-2t)} \quad \textit{for every } 0 \leqslant t \leqslant t_0, \tag{15}$$

where $\hat{H}$ is continuous and monotonically increasing on $[0, t_0]$ with

$$\lim_{t\to 0+} \frac{\hat{H}(t)-1}{H(t)-1} = 1.$$

Theorem 2. *For every $t \in (-1, 1)$, we have*

$$\sup_{\substack{\mathscr{L}(X)\in\mathscr{P}:\\ \mathbb{E}X = t\sqrt{\mathbb{E}X^2}}} J(X) = \sup_{\substack{\mathscr{L}(X)\in\mathscr{P}:\\ \mathbb{E}X = t\sqrt{\mathbb{E}X^2}}} \frac{\mathbb{E}|X|^3}{\mathbb{E}|X-t|^3}(1-t^2)^{3/2} = H(t)(1-t^2)^{3/2},$$

where the function $H(t)(1-t^2)^{3/2}$ is even and continuous on the interval $(-1, 1)$, increases on the interval $0 < t < t_0 = \sqrt{\frac{5-\sqrt{7}}{6}} = 0.6263\ldots$, decreases on the interval $t_0 < t < 1$, and

$$\lim_{t\to\pm 1} H(t)(1-t^2)^{3/2} = 1, \tag{16}$$

$$\sup_{-1<t<1} H(t)(1-t^2)^{3/2} = \sup_{\mathscr{L}(X)\in\mathscr{P}} J(X) = \frac{\sqrt{1-t_0^2}}{1-2t_0^2+2t_0^4} = \frac{\sqrt{17+7\sqrt{7}}}{4} = 1.489971\ldots, \tag{17}$$

with the supremums attained only at the points $t = \pm t_0$ and only on the two-point distribution of the form

$$\mathbb{P}(X = t_0^{-1}) = t_0^2, \quad \mathbb{P}(X = 0) = 1 - t_0^2.$$

The existence of the upper bound (15) for H allows us to immediately construct a simple and rather tight majorant for the function $H(t)(1-t^2)^{3/2}$ for a small t.

Proposition 2. *For $0 \leqslant t \leqslant t_0$, we have*

$$H(t)(1-t^2)^{3/2} < \hat{H}(t)(1-t^2)^{3/2} = \frac{\sqrt{1-t^2}(5t+6\sqrt{2})}{2(3\sqrt{2}-2t)}, \tag{18}$$

where $\hat{H}(t)(1-t^2)^{3/2}$ is continuous and monotonically increasing on $[0, t_0]$ and satisfies

$$\lim_{t\to 0+} \frac{\hat{H}(t)(1-t^2)^{3/2}-1}{H(t)(1-t^2)^{3/2}-1} = 1,$$

$$\hat{H}(t_0)(1-t_0^2)^{3/2} = 1.5144\ldots = H(t_0)(1-t_0^2)^{3/2} + 0.0244\ldots$$

The values of the function $H(t)(1-t^2)^{3/2}$ for some $t \in [0,1)$, rounded up to the fourth digit, are presented in the third column of Table 1. The plots of the functions $H(t)(1-t^2)^{3/2}$ and $\hat{H}(t)(1-t^2)^{3/2}$ are given in Figure 2.

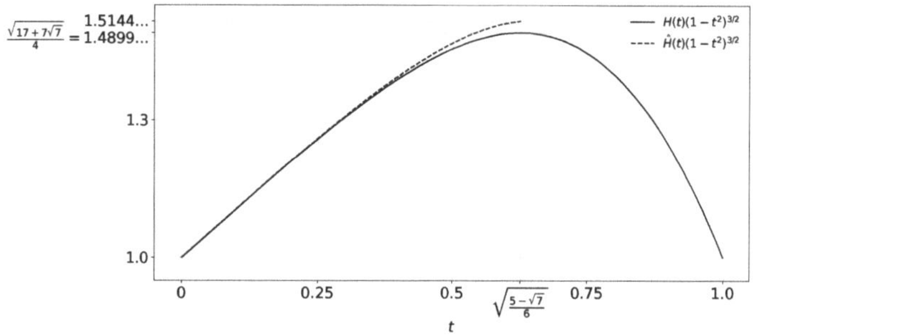

Figure 2. Plots of the functions $H(t)(1-t^2)^{3/2}$ and $\hat{H}(t)(1-t^2)^{3/2}$.

Theorem 2 and inequality (1) directly imply the following estimate of the accuracy of the normal approximation to the distribution of a Poisson random sum in terms of the central moments of the summands.

Theorem 3. *Using the notation from Section 1, for every $t \in (-1,1)$ and for any common distribution of random summands $\mathscr{L}(X) \in \mathscr{P}$ with $\mathbb{E}X = t\sqrt{\mathbb{E}X^2}$, we have*

$$\Delta_\lambda(X) \leqslant \frac{C_0(t)}{\sqrt{\lambda}} \cdot L_0(X), \quad \lambda > 0, \tag{19}$$

where

$$C_0(t) = C_1 \cdot H(t)(1-t^2)^{3/2} \leqslant 0.3031 \cdot \frac{\sqrt{17+7\sqrt{7}}}{4} < 0.4517, \quad t \in (-1,1).$$

If $|\mathbb{E}X| \leqslant t\sqrt{\mathbb{E}X^2}$, then inequality (19) holds for each $t \in [0,1)$ with $C_0(t)$ replaced by $C_0(t \wedge t_0)$, where $t_0 = \sqrt{\frac{5-\sqrt{7}}{6}} = 0.6263\ldots$ is defined in Theorem 1. Moreover, $C_0(t)$ admits the estimate

$$C_0(t) \leqslant 0.3031 \cdot \frac{\sqrt{1-t^2}(5t+6\sqrt{2})}{2(3\sqrt{2}-2t)}, \quad 0 \leqslant t \leqslant t_0,$$

whose right-hand side is monotonically increasing on $(0, t_0)$.

The values of $C_0(t)$, rounded up to the fourth digit, are presented for some $t \in [0,1)$ in the fourth column of Table 1.

Before turning to the proofs of these theorems, note that we obviously have $H(0) = 1$,

$$H(t) = \sup_{\substack{\mathscr{L}(X)\in\mathscr{P}:\\ \mathbb{E}X=t,\\ \mathbb{E}X^2=1}} \frac{\mathbb{E}|X|^3}{\mathbb{E}|X-t|^3} = \sup_{\substack{\mathscr{L}(X)\in\mathscr{P}:\\ \mathbb{E}X=t,\\ \mathbb{E}X^2=1}} \frac{\mathbb{E}|(-X)|^3}{\mathbb{E}|(-X)-(-t)|^3} = \sup_{\substack{Y\in\mathscr{P}:\\ \mathbb{E}Y=-t,\\ \mathbb{E}Y^2=1}} \frac{\mathbb{E}|Y|^3}{\mathbb{E}|Y-(-t)|^3} = H(-t),$$

and hence, it suffices to consider $t \in (0,1)$ only.

3. Reduction to the Case of Two-Point Distributions

The aim of the present section is to prove that for every r.v. X with $\mathbb{E}X = t$ *and* $\mathbb{E}X^2 = 1$, there exists an r.v. Y with the same expectation and variance, and with the third absolute moment matching X (and whose distribution is then uniquely defined), such that $\mathbb{E}|X-t|^3 \geqslant \mathbb{E}|Y-t|^3$. Since $\mathbb{E}|X|^3 = \mathbb{E}|Y|^3$, this would immediately imply that $\mathbb{E}|X-t|^3/\mathbb{E}|X|^3 \geqslant \mathbb{E}|Y-t|^3/\mathbb{E}|Y|^3$, and, hence, the investigation of the least upper bound in

$$H(t) = \sup_{\substack{\mathscr{L}(X)\in\mathscr{P}:\\ \mathbb{E}X=t,\,\mathbb{E}X^2=1}} \frac{\mathbb{E}|X|^3}{\mathbb{E}|X-t|^3} = \sup_{\rho\geqslant 1} \sup_{\substack{\mathscr{L}(X)\in\mathscr{P}:\\ \mathbb{E}X=t,\,\mathbb{E}X^2=1,\,\mathbb{E}|X|^3=\rho}} \frac{\rho}{\mathbb{E}|X-t|^3}$$

can be restricted to the analysis of the two-point distributions only.

Following Richter [39], we start with the construction (Lemma 1) of a special lower bound for the function $|x-t|^3$, $x\in\mathbb{R}$, which satisfies the following two important properties:

- it is a linear combination $a+bx+cx^2+d|x|^3$, $a,b,c,d\in\mathbb{R}$, of the functions $1, x, x^2, |x|^3$ generating the given moment conditions $\mathbb{E}1 = 1$, $\mathbb{E}X = t$, $\mathbb{E}X^2 = 1$, $\mathbb{E}|X|^3 = \rho \in [1,\infty)$; and
- it has exactly two tangent points with $|x-1|^3$.

Afterward, we integrate (Lemma 2) the obtained inequality with respect to x to construct a lower bound to $\mathbb{E}|X-t|^3$ as a linear combination of 1, $\mathbb{E}X$, $\mathbb{E}X^2$, and $\mathbb{E}|X|^3$ and note that equality in the obtained inequality is attained iff X is a two-point r.v. with possible special values. Finally, we prove in Lemma 3 that for every $\rho\geqslant 1$ and any r.v. X satisfying the above three moment conditions $\mathbb{E}X=t$, $\mathbb{E}X^2=1, and\ \mathbb{E}|X|^3=\rho$, there exists a two-point distribution (of the r.v. Y), whose support satisfies all the conditions in the coefficients $a, b, c, and\ d$ of $1, x, x^2, and |x|^3$ imposed by Lemma 2 and which then satisfies the required inequality

$$\mathbb{E}|X-t|^3 \geqslant a + b\mathbb{E}X + c\mathbb{E}X^2 + d\mathbb{E}|X|^3 = a + b\cdot t + c + d\cdot\rho = \mathbb{E}|Y-t|^3.$$

The last statement allows us to immediately conclude that only the two-point distributions may be extremal.

Lemma 1. *Let $t\in\mathbb{R}\setminus\{0\}$. Then for all $u,v\in\mathbb{R}$ such that*

$$\begin{cases} u+v>0,\\ u<1<v,\end{cases}$$

the inequality

$$|x-t|^3 \geqslant a+bx+cx^2+d|x|^3, \quad x\in\mathbb{R}, \tag{20}$$

holds, where

$$a = a_t(u,v) = |t|^3 a_1(u,v), \tag{21}$$
$$b = b_t(u,v) = t|t|b_1(u,v), \tag{22}$$
$$c = c_t(u,v) = |t|c_1(u,v), \tag{23}$$
$$d = d(u,v), \tag{24}$$

$$a_1(u,v) = \begin{cases} -\dfrac{(2uv-u-v)(2u^2v^2-2u^2v-u^2-2uv^2+4uv-v^2)}{(u-v)^3}, & u \geqslant 0, \\ \dfrac{6u^4v^2-u^4-12u^3v^2+4u^3v+6u^2v^4-12u^2v^3+6u^2v^2+4uv^3-v^4}{(u-v)(u+v)(u^2-4uv+v^2)}, & u < 0, \end{cases}$$

$$b_1(u,v) = \begin{cases} 3(2u^3v^2-4u^3v+u^3+2u^2v^3-4u^2v^2+ \\ \quad +5u^2v-4uv^3+5uv^2-4uv+v^3)/(u-v)^3, & u \geqslant 0, \\ -\dfrac{3(4u^3v-u^3-4u^2v^2-3u^2v+4uv^3-3uv^2+4uv-v^3)}{(u-v)(u^2-4uv+v^2)}, & u < 0, \end{cases}$$

$$c_1(u,v) = \begin{cases} \dfrac{3(u^3-4u^2v^2+5u^2v-4u^2+5uv^2-4uv+2u+v^3-4v^2+2v)}{(u-v)^3}, & u \geqslant 0, \\ \dfrac{3(u^4+4u^3v-4u^3-6u^2v^2+2u^2+4uv^3+v^4-4v^3+2v^2)}{(u-v)(u+v)(u^2-4uv+v^2)}, & u < 0, \end{cases}$$

$$d(u,v) = \begin{cases} -\dfrac{(u+v-2)(u^2-4uv+2u+v^2+2v-2)}{(u-v)^3}, & u \geqslant 0, \\ \dfrac{(u+v-2)(u^2-4uv+2u+v^2+2v-2)}{(u+v)(u^2-4uv+v^2)}, & u < 0, \end{cases}$$

with equality attained exactly in the two points: ut and vt.

Remark 1. *In [38], Lemma 1, it was demonstrated that for any $t \in \mathbb{R} \setminus \{0\}$ and real u, v such that*

$$\begin{cases} u+v<0, \\ v>1, \end{cases}$$

the inequality

$$|x-t|^3 \leqslant a_t(u,v) + b_t(u,v)x + c_t(u,v)x^2 + d_t(u,v)|x|^3, \quad x \in \mathbb{R},$$

holds with the same functions $a_t, b_t, c_t,$ and d_t, as in Lemma 1 for the case where $u < 0$ with equality attained exactly the two points ut and vt.

Let
$$f(x) = |x-1|^3 \quad \text{and} \quad g(x) = a + bx + cx^2 + d|x|^3, \quad x \in \mathbb{R},$$
be the left-hand and right-hand sides of (20) with $t = 1$, respectively. Figures 3–5 illustrate that several variants of the location of tangency points of the functions f and g with respect to the stationary points of g are possible. On the left side of these figures are the plots of $f(x)$ (solid line) and $g(x)$ (dotted line), whereas on the right side, for clarity, is the plot of the difference $f(x) - g(x)$.

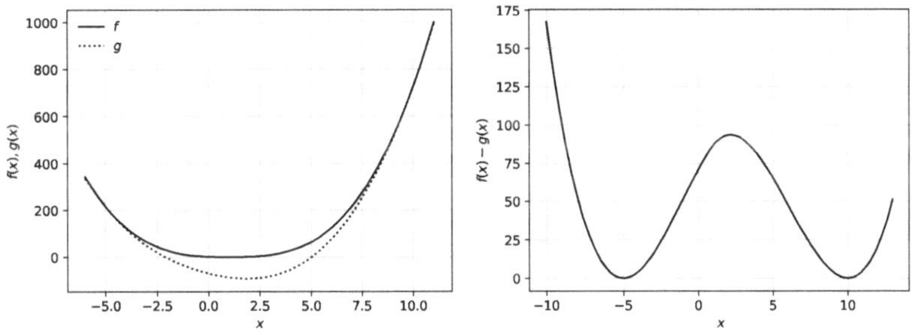

Figure 3. The graphs of the functions $f(x) = |x-1|^3$ and $g(x) = a + bx + cx^2 + d|x|^3$ from Lemma 1 (**left**) and the graph of the difference $f - g$ (**right**) for $u = -5$, $v = 10$ ($d > 0$). The unique minimum point of g lies between the tangency points u and v.

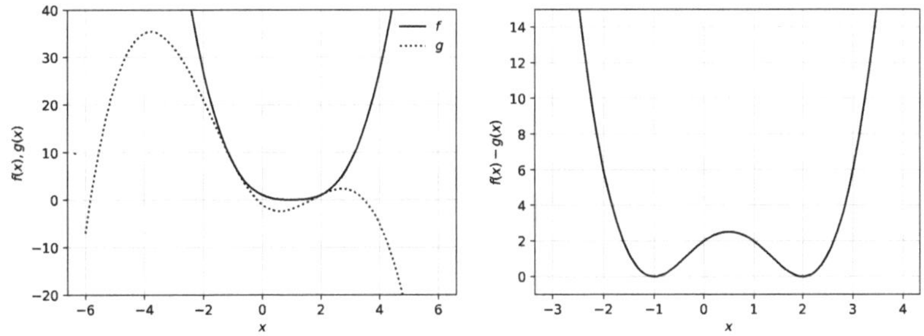

Figure 4. Plots of the functions $f(x) = |x-1|^3$ and $g(x) = a + bx + cx^2 + d|x|^3$ from Lemma 1 (**left**), and the plot of the difference $f - g$ (**right**) for $u = -1$, $v = 2$ ($d < 0$). The unique minimum point of g lies between the tangency points u and v. The maximum points lie to the left from u and to the right from v.

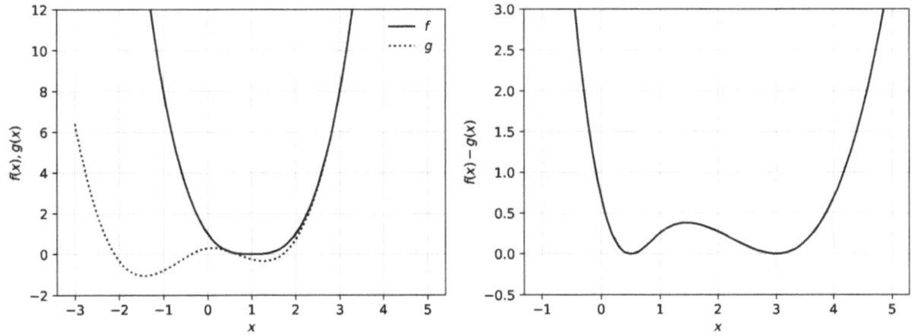

Figure 5. Plots of the functions $f(x) = |x-1|^3$ and $g(x) = a + bx + cx^2 + d|x|^3$ from Lemma 1 (**left**), and the plot of the difference $f - g$ (**right**) for $u = 0.5$, $v = 3$ ($d > 0$). The unique minimum point of g lies between the tangency points u and v. Two more stationary points, the minimum and the maximum points, lie to the left of u.

Proof. By virtue of the relations (21)–(24), the problem is reduced to the case of $t = 1$ by the scale transformation. We let

$$f(x) = |x-1|^3, \quad g(x) = a + bx + cx^2 + d|x|^3, \quad h(x) = f(x) - g(x), \quad x \in \mathbb{R}.$$

The coefficients a, b, c, and d given in the formulation of the lemma, were constructed so that points u and v were the tangency points of the functions $g(x)$ and $f(x)$; that is, these coefficients are defined as the solution to the system of the following four linear equations:

$$\left\{\begin{array}{lcl} g(u) & = & f(u), \\ g'(u) & = & f'(u), \\ g(v) & = & f(v), \\ g'(v) & = & f'(v), \end{array}\right. \iff \left\{\begin{array}{lcl} a+bu+cu^2+d|u|^3 & = & (1-u)^3, \\ b+2cu+3du|u| & = & -3(1-u)^2, \\ a+bv+cv^2+dv^3 & = & (v-1)^3, \\ b+2cv+3dv^2 & = & 3(v-1)^2. \end{array}\right.$$

Next, we proved that $h(x) \geqslant 0$ for any $x \in \mathbb{R}$.

1. Let $0 \leqslant u < 1$. Then

$$\begin{aligned} a_1(u,v) &= -\frac{(2uv-u-v)(2u^2v^2-2u^2v-u^2-2uv^2+4uv-v^2)}{(u-v)^3}, \\ b_1(u,v) &= \frac{3(2u^3v^2-4u^3v+u^3+2u^2v^3-4u^2v^2+5u^2v-4uv^3+5uv^2-4uv+v^3)}{(u-v)^3}, \\ c_1(u,v) &= \frac{3(u^3-4u^2v^2+5u^2v-4u^2+5uv^2-4uv+2u+v^3-4v^2+2v)}{(u-v)^3}, \text{ and} \\ d(u,v) &= -\frac{(u+v-2)(u^2-4uv+2u+v^2+2v-2)}{(u-v)^3}. \end{aligned}$$

(1a) Let $x \geqslant 1$. We have

$$h(x) = \frac{2(u-1)^2(x-v)^2(2uv+ux-3u-3vx+v+2x)}{(u-v)^3}.$$

Since

$$2(u-1)^2(x-v)^2 \geqslant 0, \quad (u-v)^3 < 0,$$

it suffices to show that

$$s_1(x) := 2uv+ux-3u-3vx+v+2x \leqslant 0.$$

We have

$$s_1(1) = 2(u-1)(v-1) < 0 \text{ and}$$

$$s_1'(x) = u-3v+2 < 0, \quad \text{since } v > 1 \geqslant \frac{u+2}{3},$$

therefore, $s_1(x) < 0$ and $h(x) \geqslant 0$. Moreover, $h(x) = 0$ if and only if $x = v$.

(1b) Let $0 \leqslant x < 1$. Then

$$h(x) = \frac{2(x-u)^2(v-1)^2(2uv-3ux+u+vx-3v+2x)}{(u-v)^3}.$$

Since

$$2(x-u)^2(v-1)^2 \geqslant 0, \quad (u-v)^3 < 0,$$

it suffices to show that

$$s_2(x) := (v-3u+2)x+2uv+u-3v \leqslant 0.$$

We have

$$s_2(0) = 2uv+u-3v < 0, \quad \text{since } v > 1 > \frac{u}{3-2u}; \text{ and}$$

$$s_2(1) = 2(u-1)(v-1) < 0,$$

$$\min\{s_2(0), s_2(1)\} \leqslant s_2(x) \leqslant \max\{s_2(0), s_2(1)\},$$

therefore, $s_2(x) < 0$ and $h(x) \geqslant 0$. Moreover, $h(x) = 0$ if and only if $x = u$.

(1c) Let $x < 0$. Then

$$h'(x) = -3(1-x)^2 - b - 2cx + 3dx^2,$$
$$h''(x) = 6(d-1)x + 2(3-c),$$
$$h(0) \geqslant 0,$$

moreover, $h(0) = 0$ if and only if $u = 0$ (as it was proved above),

$$h'(0) = -b - 3 = \frac{6u(v-1)^2(u^2+uv-2v)}{(v-u)^3},$$

$$d - 1 = \frac{2(u-1)^2(u-3v+2)}{(v-u)^3},$$

$$3 - c = \frac{6(v-1)^2(2u^2-u-v)}{(u-v)^3}.$$

Taking into account the relations

$$\frac{6u(v-1)^2}{(v-u)^3} \geqslant 0,$$

$$u^2 + uv - 2v < 0, \quad \text{since } v > 1 > \frac{u^2}{2-u},$$

we have $h'(0) \leqslant 0$. Moreover, $h'(0) = 0$ if and only if $u = 0$. Note that

$$\frac{2(u-1)^2}{(v-u)^3} > 0,$$

$$u - 3v + 2 < 0, \quad \text{since } v > 1 > \frac{u+2}{3},$$

$$\frac{6(v-1)^2}{(u-v)^3} < 0,$$

$$2u^2 - u - v < 0, \quad \text{since } v > 1 > 2u^2 - u,$$

therefore, $d - 1 < 0$, $3 - c > 0$, and $h''(x) > 0$. Hence, $h'(x)$ increases, and with the account of $h'(0) \leqslant 0$, we find that $h'(x) < 0$ for $x < 0$; that is, $h(x)$ decreases for $x < 0$. Since $h(0) \geqslant 0$, we have $h(x) > 0$ for $x < 0$.

2. Now let $u < 0$. We have

$$a_1(u,v) = \frac{6u^4v^2 - u^4 - 12u^3v^2 + 4u^3v + 6u^2v^4 - 12u^2v^3 + 6u^2v^2 + 4uv^3 - v^4}{(u-v)(u+v)(u^2-4uv+v^2)},$$

$$b_1(u,v) = -\frac{3(4u^3v - u^3 - 4u^2v^2 - 3u^2v + 4uv^3 - 3uv^2 + 4uv - v^3)}{(u-v)(u^2-4uv+v^2)},$$

$$c_1(u,v) = \frac{3(u^4 + 4u^3v - 4u^3 - 6u^2v^2 + 2u^2 + 4uv^3 + v^4 - 4v^3 + 2v^2)}{(u-v)(u+v)(u^2-4uv+v^2)},$$

$$d(u,v) = \frac{(u+v-2)(u^2-4uv+2u+v^2+2v-2)}{(u+v)(u^2-4uv+v^2)}.$$

(2a) Let $x \geqslant 1$. Then

$$h(x) = \frac{2(x-v)^2 s_3(x)}{(v-u)(u+v)(u^2-4uv+v^2)},$$

where

$$s_3(x) = 3u^4 - 6u^3 + 3u^2v^2 + 6u^2vx - 6u^2v - 3u^2x + 3u^2 - 6uv^2x + 4uv + 2ux + 3v^2x - v^2 - 2vx.$$

Note that

$$\frac{2(x-v)^2}{(v-u)(u+v)(u^2-4uv+v^2)} \geqslant 0$$

with the equality attained iff $x = v$. Therefore, it suffices to show that $s_3(x) > 0$. However, this follows from the relations

$$s_3(1) = 3u^4 - 6u^3 + 3u^2v^2 - 2u(v-1)(3v+1) + 2v(v-1) > 0,$$
$$s_3'(x) = 3u^2(2v-1) - 2u(3v^2-1) + v(3v-2) > 0.$$

(2b) Let $x \leqslant 0$. Then

$$h(x) = \frac{2(x-u)^2 s_4(x)}{(v-u)(u+v)(u^2-4uv+v^2)},$$

where

$$s_4(x) = 3u^2v^2 - 6u^2vx + 3u^2x - u^2 + 6uv^2x - 6uv^2 + 4uv - 2ux + 3v^4 - 6v^3 - 3v^2x + 3v^2 + 2vx.$$

Note that

$$\frac{2(x-u)^2}{(v-u)(u+v)(u^2-4uv+v^2)} \geqslant 0,$$

with the equality attained iff $x = u$. Therefore, it suffices to show that $s_4(x) > 0$. However, this follows from the relations

$$s_4(0) = u^2(3v^2-1) - 2uv(3v-2) + 3v^2(v-1)^2 > 0,$$
$$s_4'(x) = (v-u)(3u(2v-1) - (3v-2)) < 0.$$

(2c) Let $0 < x < 1$. For all $u < 0,\ v > 1,\ u+v > 0$, we have

$$h(0) = \frac{2u^2\left(u^2(3v^2-1) - 2uv(3v-2) + 3v^2(v-1)^2\right)}{(v-u)(u+v)(u^2-4uv+v^2)} > 0,$$

$$h(1) = \frac{2(v-1)^2\left(3u^4 - 6u^3 + 3u^2v^2 - 2u\left(3v^2-2v-1\right) + 2v(v-1)\right)}{(v-u)(u+v)(u^2-4uv+v^2)} > 0,$$

$$h'(0) = -\frac{6u\left(u^2(2v-1) - uv(2v-1) + 2v(v-1)^2\right)}{(v-u)(u^2-4uv+v^2)} > 0.$$

Moreover,

$$h'''(x) = \frac{12(1-u-v)(u^2+u(1-4v)+v^2+v-2)}{(u+v)(u^2-4uv+v^2)} \geqslant 0 \quad \Longleftrightarrow \quad u+v \leqslant 1.$$

Consider the case $u + v \geqslant 1$. Since $h'''(x) \leqslant 0$, the function h' is concave. Since $h'(0) > 0$, the function h' has at most one root x_0 on the interval $0 \leqslant x \leqslant 1$. Moreover, $h'(x) \geqslant 0$ for $0 \leqslant x \leqslant x_0$ and $h'(x) \leqslant 0$ for $x_0 \leqslant x \leqslant 1$. Therefore, $h(x)$ either increases on the whole interval $0 \leqslant x \leqslant 1$ (if h' is nonnegative), or increases on $0 \leqslant x \leqslant x_0$ and decreases on $x_0 \leqslant x \leqslant 1$, so that

$$\min_{0 \leqslant x \leqslant 1} h(x) = \min\{h(0), h(1)\}.$$

Since $h(0) > 0$ and $h(1) > 0$, we have $h(x) > 0$.

Now consider the case $0 < u + v < 1$. In this case, h' is convex. Note that

$$h'(1) = \frac{6(v-1)(2-u-v)\Big(2u^3 - 2u^2 v + u(2v^2 - v - 1) - v(v-1)\Big)}{(v-u)(u+v)(u^2 - 4uv + v^2)} < 0.$$

Since $h'(0) > 0,\ h'(1) < 0$, and h' is convex, the function h' has exactly one root x_1 on the interval $0 \leqslant x \leqslant 1$. Moreover, $h'(x) \geqslant 0$ for $0 \leqslant x \leqslant x_1$ and $h'(x) \leqslant 0$ for $x_1 \leqslant x \leqslant 1$. So, the function h increases on the interval $[0, x_1]$ and decreases on $[x_1, 1]$. Therefore,

$$\min_{0 \leqslant x \leqslant 1} h(x) = \min\{h(0), h(1)\}.$$

With the account of $h(0) > 0$ and $h(1) > 0$, we have $h(x) > 0$ for all $0 \leqslant x \leqslant 1$. □

Lemma 1 trivially yields the following statement.

Lemma 2. *For any $\mathscr{L}(X) \in \mathscr{P}, t \in \mathbb{R} \setminus \{0\}$ and every $u, v \in \mathbb{R}$ such that*

$$\begin{cases} u + v > 0, \\ u < 1 < v, \end{cases}$$

the inequality

$$\mathbb{E}|X - t|^3 \geqslant a_t(u,v) + b_t(u,v)\mathbb{E}X + c_t(u,v)\mathbb{E}X^2 + d(u,v)\mathbb{E}|X|^3,$$

holds with equality attained iff the distribution of the r.v. X is concentrated in the two points: ut and vt.

By $\mathscr{P}_2$, let us denote the class of all the non-degenerate two-point distributions. Obviously, $\mathscr{P}_2 \subset \mathscr{P}$.

Lemma 3. *For any $t \in (0,1)$*

$$H(t) := \sup_{\substack{\mathscr{L}(X) \in \mathscr{P}: \\ \mathbb{E}X = t, \\ \mathbb{E}X^2 = 1}} \frac{\mathbb{E}|X|^3}{\mathbb{E}|X - t|^3} = \sup_{\substack{\mathscr{L}(X) \in \mathscr{P}_2: \\ \mathbb{E}X = t, \\ \mathbb{E}X^2 = 1}} \frac{\mathbb{E}|X|^3}{\mathbb{E}|X - t|^3},$$

moreover, the least upper bound on the right-hand side can be attained only on the two-point distributions.

Proof. It suffices to prove that for any $\varrho \geqslant 1$ and r.v. X with

$$\mathbb{E}X = t, \quad \mathbb{E}X^2 = 1, \textit{ and } \quad \mathbb{E}|X|^3 = \varrho$$

there exists a two-point r.v. Y with

$$\mathbb{E}Y = t, \quad \mathbb{E}Y^2 = 1, \textit{ and } \quad \mathbb{E}|Y|^3 = \varrho,$$

satisfying the inequality

$$\mathbb{E}|X - t|^3 \geqslant \mathbb{E}|Y - t|^3.$$

Indeed, the above moment conditions imply that

$$H(t) = \sup_{\varrho \geqslant 1} \sup_{\substack{\mathscr{L}(X) \in \mathscr{P}:\, \mathbb{E}X = t,\\ \mathbb{E}X^2 = 1,\, \mathbb{E}|X|^3 = \varrho}} \frac{\varrho}{\mathbb{E}|X - t|^3} \leqslant \sup_{\varrho \geqslant 1} \sup_{\substack{Y \in \mathscr{P}_2:\, \mathbb{E}Y = t,\\ \mathbb{E}Y^2 = 1,\, \mathbb{E}|Y|^3 = \varrho}} \frac{\varrho}{\mathbb{E}|Y - t|^3}, \quad 0 < t < 1,$$

where only equality is possible since $\mathscr{P}_2 \subset \mathscr{P}$.

(1) Let $\varrho > 1$. Consider a two-point r.v. Y_p that takes values $x > y$ with probabilities p and $q = 1 - p$, respectively, and satisfies $\mathbb{E}Y_p = t, \mathbb{E}Y_p^2 = 1$. Then we necessarily have

$$x = x(p) = t + \sqrt{(1 - t^2)q/p}, \quad y = y(p) = t - \sqrt{(1 - t^2)p/q}.$$

We show that $x + y > 0$ iff $p < \frac{1+t}{2}$. We have

$$x + y > 0 \iff \frac{2t\sqrt{pq} + \sqrt{1 - t^2}(q - p)}{\sqrt{pq}} > 0 \iff 2t\sqrt{p(1 - p)} > \sqrt{1 - t^2}(2p - 1).$$

The last inequality trivially holds for $0 < p \leqslant \frac{1}{2}$ since the left-hand side is positive, whereas the right-hand side is non-positive. If $\frac{1}{2} < p < 1$, then both sides of this inequality are positive. Therefore, they can be squared:

$$4t^2 p(1 - p) > (1 - t^2)(4p^2 - 4p + 1) \iff t^2 > (2p - 1)^2 \iff p < \frac{1 + t}{2}.$$

Unifying the intervals under consideration, we obtain the desired statement. Note that on $\left(0, \frac{1+t}{2}\right)$ the function

$$\widetilde{\varrho}(p) \equiv \mathbb{E}|Y_p|^3 = p\left(t + \sqrt{\tfrac{q}{p}(1 - t^2)}\right)^3 + q\left|t - \sqrt{\tfrac{p}{q}(1 - t^2)}\right|^3$$

of the argument, p takes all the values from the interval $(1, +\infty)$ because, for any $0 < t < 1$, we have

$$\widetilde{\varrho}\left(\frac{1 + t}{2}\right) = 1, \quad \lim_{p \to 0+} \widetilde{\varrho}(p) = +\infty$$

and $\widetilde{\varrho}(p)$ is continuous. Hence, for every $\varrho > 1$ there exists $p_0 = p_0(\varrho) \in \left(0, \frac{1+t}{2}\right)$ such that $\mathbb{E}|Y_{p_0}|^3 = \varrho$. Furthermore, note that,

$$\begin{cases} y(p_0) < t < x(p_0), \\ x(p_0) + y(p_0) > 0, \end{cases}$$

and, hence, the couple $u = y(p_0)/t$ *and* $v = x(p_0)/t$ satisfy all the conditions of Lemma 2, according to which, with the account of the definition of the r.v. Y_{p_0}, we have

$$\mathbb{E}|X - t|^3 \geqslant a_t(u, v) + b_t(u, v)t + c_t(u, v) + d(u, v)\varrho = \mathbb{E}|Y_{p_0} - t|^3,$$

where the equality is attained iff the distribution of the r.v. X is concentrated in exactly two points $ut = y(p_0)$ and $vt = x(p_0)$; that is, iff $X \stackrel{d}{=} Y_{p_0}$. Therefore, the desired statement holds with the r.v. $Y \stackrel{d}{=} Y_{p_0}$.

(2) Now let $\varrho = 1$. By virtue of Jensen's inequality, for the strictly convex function $f(x) = x^{3/2}$, $x \geqslant 0$, we have

$$1 = \mathbb{E}|X|^3 = \mathbb{E}f(X^2) \geqslant f(\mathbb{E}X^2) = f(1) = 1,$$

where the equality holds iff

$$\mathbb{P}(X^2 = \mathbb{E}X^2) = 1, \quad \text{i.e., } \mathbb{P}(|X| = 1) = 1.$$

The condition $\mathbb{E}X = t$ immediately implies that, in this case, the r.v. X must have the two-point distribution of the form $\mathbb{P}(X = \pm 1) = (1 \pm t)/2$. So, the desired statement holds with $Y \stackrel{d}{=} X$. □

4. Analysis of Two-Point Distributions

Recall that by $\mathscr{P}_2$, we denoted the class of all the non-degenerate two-point distributions.

Lemma 4. **(a)** *For any $t \in (0,1)$*

$$\sup_{\substack{\mathscr{L}(X)\in\mathscr{P}_2:\\ \mathbb{E}X=t,\ \mathbb{E}X^2=1}} \frac{\mathbb{E}|X|^3}{\mathbb{E}|X-t|^3} = \max_{-1<z<1} M(z,t) = M(z(t),t), \tag{25}$$

where the function $z(t)$, $t \in (0,1)$, is defined in Theorem 1 (see (9))

$$M(z,t) = \begin{cases} M_1(z,t), & -1 < z < 1-2t^2, \\ M_2(z,t), & 1-2t^2 \leqslant z < 1, \end{cases}$$

$$M_1(u,t) = 1 + \frac{3t^2}{1-t^2} \cdot \frac{1-u^2-a(t)u\sqrt{1-u^2}}{1+u^2}, \quad u \in (-1,1),$$

$$M_2(v,t) = \frac{b(t)\sqrt{1-v^2}+2v}{v^2+1}, \quad v \in (-1,1),$$

$$a(t) = \frac{4t^2-3}{3t\sqrt{1-t^2}}, \quad b(t) = \frac{t(3-2t^2)}{(1-t^2)^{3/2}}, \quad t \in (0,1).$$

Moreover, the supremum in (25) is attained only on the two-point distribution defined in Theorem 1 (see (12)).

(b) *The functions M, M_1, and M_2 are differentiable in the domain $(z,t) \in (-1,1) \times (0,1)$ and have continuous derivatives there.*

(c) *There hold the equalities*

$$\lim_{z\to-1+} M_1(z,t) = \lim_{z\to1-} M_1(z,t) = 1, \quad t \in (0,1),$$

$$\lim_{z\to-1+} M_2(z,t) = -1, \quad \lim_{z\to1-} M_2(z,t) = 1, \quad t \in (0,1),$$

$$\lim_{t\to0} M_1(z,t) = 1, \quad \lim_{t\to0} M_2(z,t) = \frac{2z}{z^2+1}, \quad z \in (-1,1),$$

$$\lim_{t\to1} M_2(z,t) = +\infty, \quad z \in (-1,1).$$

(d) *The function $z(t)$ is continuously differentiable and monotonically decreasing on the interval $t \in (0,1)$ with*

$$z(0+) = \frac{\sqrt{3}}{3}, \quad z(t_0) = \frac{\sqrt{7}-2}{3}, \quad z(1-) = 0.$$

Moreover, the inequalities

$$z(t) \leqslant 1-2t^2, \quad t \in (0,t_0],$$
$$z(t) \geqslant 1-2t^2, \quad t \in [t_0,1),$$

hold, and the equality in each of them is attained only at the endpoint $t = t_0 := \sqrt{\frac{5-\sqrt{7}}{6}} = 0.6263\ldots$, *defined in Theorem* 1.

Proof. **(a)** Consider a two-point distribution

$$\mathbb{P}(X = x) = p = 1 - \mathbb{P}(X = y) = 1 - q, \tag{26}$$

with some $x > t > y,\ p \in (0,1)$. From the conditions

$$\mathbb{E}X = t \textit{ and } \mathbb{E}X^2 = 1,$$

it follows that

$$x = t + \sqrt{\tfrac{q}{p}(1-t^2)} \textit{ and } y = t - \sqrt{\tfrac{p}{q}(1-t^2)}. \tag{27}$$

Denote

$$\widetilde{H}(p,t) = \frac{\mathbb{E}|X|^3}{\mathbb{E}|X-t|^3} = \frac{p|x|^3 + q|y|^3}{p(x-t)^3 + q(t-y)^3}, \quad p \in (0,1),\ t \in (0,1). \tag{28}$$

Then

$$\widetilde{H}(t) := \sup_{\substack{\mathscr{L}(X)\in\mathscr{P}_2:\\ \mathbb{E}X=t,\ \mathbb{E}X^2=1}} \frac{\mathbb{E}|X|^3}{\mathbb{E}|X-t|^3} = \sup_{0<p<1} \widetilde{H}(p,t). \tag{29}$$

Let us show that the last supremum has the form (25) with $z(t)$ defined in (9).

For $0 < p \leqslant t^2$, we have $y \geqslant 0$ and

$$\widetilde{H}(p,t) = \frac{px^3 + qy^3}{p(x-t)^3 + q(t-y)^3} = \frac{t(3-2t^2) + \frac{q-p}{\sqrt{pq}}(1-t^2)^{3/2}}{\frac{p^2+q^2}{\sqrt{pq}}(1-t^2)^{3/2}} = \frac{b(t)\sqrt{pq} + (q-p)}{p^2+q^2}.$$

For $t^2 < p < 1$, we have $y < 0$ and

$$\widetilde{H}(p,t) = 1 + \frac{t(4t^2-3)(p-q) + 6t^2\sqrt{1-t^2}\sqrt{pq}}{\frac{p^2+q^2}{\sqrt{pq}}(1-t^2)^{3/2}} = 1 + \frac{3t^2}{1-t^2}\cdot\frac{a(t)\sqrt{pq}(p-q) + 2pq}{p^2+q^2}.$$

In terms of a new variable

$$z = q - p = 1 - 2p, \tag{30}$$

we have

$$pq = \frac{1-z^2}{4}, \quad p^2 + q^2 = \frac{1+z^2}{2}, \quad \text{and} \quad \sup_{p\in(0,1)} \widetilde{H}(p,t) = \sup_{z\in(-1,1)} \widetilde{H}\left(\frac{1-z}{2}, t\right)$$

Observing that

$$\widetilde{H}\left(\frac{1-z}{2}, t\right) = M(z,t), \tag{31}$$

we may finally write

$$\widetilde{H}(t) := \sup_{p\in(0,1)} \widetilde{H}(p,t) = \sup_{-1<z<1} M(z,t), \quad t \in (0,1).$$

We show that $z(t)$ is the unique global maximum point of the function $M(\,\cdot\,,t)$ for each $t \in (0,1)$, whence, with the account of relations (26), (27), (30), the item (a) would follow.

For M_1, we have

$$\frac{\partial M_1(u,t)}{\partial u} = \frac{3t^2}{1-t^2} \cdot \frac{a(t)(3u^2-1) - 4u\sqrt{1-u^2}}{\sqrt{1-u^2} \cdot (1+u^2)^2},$$

and hence, the stationary points of $M_1(\,\cdot\,,t)$ can be determined from the equation

$$g(u) := \frac{4u\sqrt{1-u^2}}{3u^2-1} = a(t),$$

which coincides with (10).

Note that the function $g(u)$ is even, continuously differentiable and monotonically decreasing on the intervals $(-1, -\sqrt{3}/3)$, $(-\sqrt{3}/3, \sqrt{3}/3)$, and $(\sqrt{3}/3, 1)$ and has discontinuity points of the second kind in the points $u = \pm\sqrt{3}/3$ (see the plot of $g(u)$ in Figure 6). Therefore, there exist the inverse functions

$$g_1^{-1} : (-\infty, 0) \to (-1, -\sqrt{3}/3),$$

$$g_2^{-1} : \mathbb{R} \to (-\sqrt{3}/3, \sqrt{3}/3),$$

$$g_3^{-1} : (0, +\infty) \to (\sqrt{3}/3, 1),$$

each of which is differentiable and monotonically decreasing in its domain.

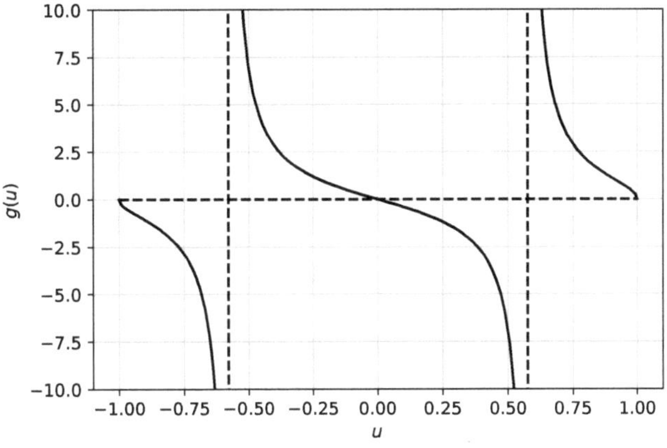

Figure 6. The plot of the function $g(u) = \frac{4u\sqrt{1-u^2}}{3u^2-1}$.

If $a(t) = 0$ (that is, $t = \sqrt{3}/2$), then it is easy to make sure that $u = 0$ is the unique maximum point and unique stationary point of the function $M_1(\,\cdot\,,t)$ on $(-1,1)$.

Now let $a(t) \neq 0$. By $u_1(t) < u_2(t)$ denote the roots of the equation $g(u) = a(t)$ on the interval $u \in (-1,1)$. If $a(t) > 0$ (that is, $t > \sqrt{3}/2$), then $u_1(t) = g_2^{-1}(a(t))$, $u_2(t) = g_3^{-1}(a(t))$ are respectively the points of local maximum and minimum of the function $M_1(\,\cdot\,,t)$ (see the plots of the function $M_1(\,\cdot\,,t)$ for some t in Figure 7). Moreover, $a(t)u_1(t) < 0$ and $M_1(u_1(t),t) > 1$. Since $a(t)$ is continuously differentiable and monotonically increasing, both $u_1(\cdot)$ and $u_2(\cdot)$ are continuously differentiable and monotonically decreasing with

$$u_1(\sqrt{3}/2+) = 0, \quad u_1(1-) = -\sqrt{3}/3,$$

$$u_2(\sqrt{3}/2+) = 1, \quad u_2(1-) = \sqrt{3}/3.$$

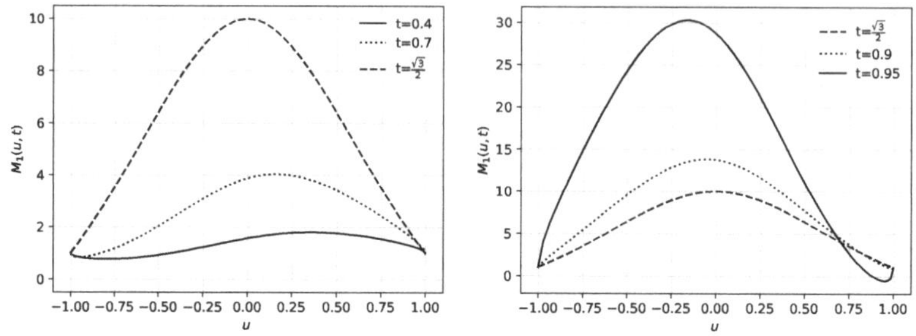

Figure 7. Plots of the functions $M_1(\,\cdot\,,t)$ for some t.

And if $a(t) < 0$ (that is, $t < \sqrt{3}/2$), then $u_1(t) = g_1^{-1}(a(t))$, $u_2(t) = g_2^{-1}(a(t))$ are the points of local minimum and maximum, respectively. Moreover, $a(t)u_2(t) < 0$ and $M_1(u_2(t),t) > 1$. Since $a(t)$ is continuously differentiable and monotonically increasing, both $u_1(t)$ and $u_2(t)$ are continuously differentiable and monotonically decreasing on the interval $t \in (0, \sqrt{3}/2)$ with

$$u_1(0+) = -\sqrt{3}/3, \quad u_1(\sqrt{3}/2-) = -1,$$

$$u_2(0+) = \sqrt{3}/3, \quad u_2(\sqrt{3}/2-) = 0.$$

Since $M_1(\pm 1, t) = 1$, the local maximum point of the function $M_1(\,\cdot\,,t)$ is the point of its global maximum on the whole interval $u \in (-1,1)$.

So, for an arbitrary $s \in (-1,1)$, we have

$$\sup_{-1<u<s} M_1(u,t) = \begin{cases} M_1(0 \wedge s, t), & a(t) = 0, \\ M_1(u_1(t) \wedge s, t), & a(t) > 0, \\ M_1(u_2(t) \wedge s, t) \vee 1, & a(t) < 0 \end{cases}$$

(here, the symbols $\vee$ and $\wedge$ denote the maximum and minimum, respectively). For $s = 1 - 2t^2$, we have

$$\sup_{-1<u<1-2t^2} M_1(u,t) = \begin{cases} M_1\left(-\frac{1}{2}, \frac{\sqrt{3}}{2}\right) = \frac{32}{5}, & t = \sqrt{3}/2, \\ M_1(u_1(t) \wedge (1-2t^2), t), & \sqrt{3}/2 < t < 1, \\ M_1(u_2(t) \wedge (1-2t^2), t) \vee 1, & 0 < t < \sqrt{3}/2. \end{cases}$$

Compare $1 - 2t^2$ with $u_2(t)$ for $0 < t < \frac{\sqrt{3}}{2}$ and with $u_1(t)$ for $\frac{\sqrt{3}}{2} < t < 1$. If $\frac{\sqrt{3}}{2} < t < 1$, then, as it has already been noted, $-\sqrt{3}/3 < u_1(t) < 0$, and hence, $u_1(t) > -\sqrt{3}/3 \geqslant 1 - 2t^2$ trivially for $\sqrt{\frac{1}{2} + \frac{\sqrt{3}}{6}} \leqslant t < 1$. And if $t \in \left(\frac{\sqrt{3}}{2}, \sqrt{\frac{1}{2} + \frac{\sqrt{3}}{6}}\right) = (0.866\ldots, 0.888\ldots)$, then $1 - 2t^2 \in \left(-\frac{\sqrt{3}}{3}, -\frac{1}{2}\right) \subset \left(-\frac{\sqrt{3}}{3}, \frac{\sqrt{3}}{3}\right)$, that is, point $1 - 2t^2$ belongs to the same interval $\left(-\frac{\sqrt{3}}{3}, \frac{\sqrt{3}}{3}\right)$ of the monotonic decrease of the function $g(u)$, as $u_1(t)$, and hence, on the interval of the values of t under consideration, we have

$$1 - 2t^2 \leqslant u_1(t) \quad \Leftrightarrow \quad g(1-2t^2) \geqslant g(u_1(t)) \equiv a(t) \quad \Leftrightarrow$$

$$\Leftrightarrow \quad \frac{4t(2t^2-1)\sqrt{1-t^2}}{-6t^4+6t^2-1} \geqslant \frac{4t^2-3}{3t\sqrt{1-t^2}} \quad \Leftrightarrow$$

$$\Leftrightarrow \quad 12t^2(2t^2-1)(1-t^2) \geqslant (4t^2-3)(-6t^4+6t^2-1) \quad \Leftrightarrow \quad 6t^4 - 10t^2 + 3 \leqslant 0 \quad \Leftrightarrow$$

$$\Leftrightarrow \quad t \in \left[\sqrt{\tfrac{5-\sqrt{7}}{6}}, \sqrt{\tfrac{5+\sqrt{7}}{6}}\right] \cap \left(\tfrac{\sqrt{3}}{2}, \sqrt{\tfrac{1}{2}+\tfrac{\sqrt{3}}{6}}\right) = \left(\tfrac{\sqrt{3}}{2}, \sqrt{\tfrac{1}{2}+\tfrac{\sqrt{3}}{6}}\right).$$

$\Big($In the third step here, we also took into account that $-6t^4+6t^2-1>0$ for $t \in \left(\sqrt{\tfrac{1}{2}-\tfrac{\sqrt{3}}{6}}, \sqrt{\tfrac{1}{2}+\tfrac{\sqrt{3}}{6}}\right) \supset \left(\tfrac{\sqrt{3}}{2}, \sqrt{\tfrac{1}{2}+\tfrac{\sqrt{3}}{6}}\right)\Big)$. So, unifying the obtained interval with the domain $t \geqslant \sqrt{\tfrac{1}{2}+\tfrac{\sqrt{3}}{6}}$, we finally conclude that

$$u_1(t) > 1-2t^2 \text{ for all } t \in \left(\tfrac{\sqrt{3}}{2}, 1\right).$$

It remains to compare $1-2t^2$ with $u_2(t)$ on the interval $0<t<\frac{\sqrt{3}}{2}$. As it has already been noted, on this interval, we have $0<u_2(t)<\frac{\sqrt{3}}{3}$, and hence, $u_2(t)>0 \geqslant 1-2t^2$ a fortiori for $0.707\ldots = \frac{\sqrt{2}}{2} \leqslant t < \frac{\sqrt{3}}{2}$ and $u_2(t) < \sqrt{3}/3 \leqslant 1-2t^2$ for $0<t\leqslant \sqrt{\tfrac{1}{2}-\tfrac{\sqrt{3}}{6}} = 0.459\ldots$ If $t \in \left(\sqrt{\tfrac{1}{2}-\tfrac{\sqrt{3}}{6}}, \tfrac{\sqrt{2}}{2}\right)$, then $1-2t^2 \in \left(0, \tfrac{\sqrt{3}}{3}\right) \subset \left(-\tfrac{\sqrt{3}}{3}, \tfrac{\sqrt{3}}{3}\right)$; that is, the point $1-2t^2$ belongs to the same interval $\left(-\tfrac{\sqrt{3}}{3}, \tfrac{\sqrt{3}}{3}\right)$ of the monotonic decrease of the function $g(u)$, as $u_2(t)$, and hence,

$$1-2t^2 \leqslant u_2(t) \quad \Leftrightarrow \quad g(1-2t^2) \geqslant g(u_2(t)) \equiv a(t).$$

Further calculations completely coincide with what has been done for the comparison of $u_1(t)$ and $1-2t^2$, including the remark on the positiveness of the polynomial $-6t^4+6t^2-1$ on the interval $t \in \left(\sqrt{\tfrac{1}{2}-\tfrac{\sqrt{3}}{6}}, \tfrac{\sqrt{2}}{2}\right)$. Therefore, for t under consideration, we have

$$u_2(t) \geqslant 1-2t^2 \quad \Leftrightarrow \quad t \in \left[\sqrt{\tfrac{5-\sqrt{7}}{6}}, \sqrt{\tfrac{5+\sqrt{7}}{6}}\right] \bigcap \left(\sqrt{\tfrac{1}{2}-\tfrac{\sqrt{3}}{6}}, \tfrac{\sqrt{2}}{2}\right) = \left[\sqrt{\tfrac{5-\sqrt{7}}{6}}, \tfrac{\sqrt{2}}{2}\right),$$

$$u_2(t) < 1-2t^2 \quad \Leftrightarrow \quad t \in \left(\sqrt{\tfrac{1}{2}-\tfrac{\sqrt{3}}{6}}, \sqrt{\tfrac{5-\sqrt{7}}{6}}\right).$$

Unifying the obtained domains of the values of t, we finally get

$$u_2(t) \geqslant 1-2t^2 \text{ on the interval } t \in \left(0, \tfrac{\sqrt{3}}{2}\right) \quad \Leftrightarrow \quad \sqrt{\tfrac{5-\sqrt{7}}{6}} =: t_0 \leqslant t < \tfrac{\sqrt{3}}{2},$$

with equality attained only at the point $t=t_0$.

Taking into account that $u_2(t)$ is the global maximum point of the function $M_1(\,\cdot\,,t)$ for $0<t<\sqrt{3}/2$, and also that

$$M_1(1-2t^2,t)\Big|_{t=\sqrt{3}/2} = M_1\left(-\frac{1}{2}, \frac{\sqrt{3}}{2}\right),$$

we conclude that

$$\max_{-1<u<1-2t^2} M_1(u,t) = \begin{cases} M_1(u_2(t),t), & 0<t<t_0, \\ M_1(1-2t^2,t) \vee 1, & t_0 \leqslant t < \frac{\sqrt{3}}{2}, \\ M_1(1-2t^2,t), & \frac{\sqrt{3}}{2} \leqslant t < 1. \end{cases} \tag{32}$$

We now consider the behavior of the function $M_2(\,\cdot\,,t)$. Since both functions $\sqrt{1-v^2}/(v^2+1)$ and $v/(v^2+1)$ increase for $v \in (-1,0]$, $M_2(v,t)$ increases in $v \in (-1,0]$ for every $t \in (0,1)$.

The numerator of the derivative

$$\frac{\partial M_2(v,t)}{\partial v} = \frac{b(t)v(v^2-3)+2(1-v^2)^{3/2}}{\sqrt{1-v^2}\cdot(v^2+1)^2}$$

decreases on the interval $v \in (0,1)$ and takes the values $2 > 0$ and $-2b(t) < 0$ of different signs at the endpoints. Therefore, the equation $\frac{\partial M_2}{\partial v} = 0$, which is equivalent to

$$f(v) := \frac{2(1-v^2)^{3/2}}{v(3-v^2)} = b(t) \tag{33}$$

and coincides with (11), has a unique root on $(0,1)$, which is the maximum point of $M_2(v,t)$ on the interval $v \in [0,1]$. Since the function $f(v)$ is continuously differentiable and monotonically decreasing on the interval $v \in (0,1)$ with $f(+0) = +\infty$, $f(1-) = 0$, there exists an inverse function

$$f^{-1} : (0, +\infty) \to (0,1),$$

which is also continuously differentiable and monotonically decreasing. Furthermore, since the function $b(t)$ is continuously differentiable and monotonically increasing on the interval $t \in (0,1)$, Equation (33) has a unique root

$$v(t) = f^{-1}(b(t)),$$

on $v \in (0,1)$, which is the global maximum point of the function $M_2(\cdot, t)$ on the whole interval $(-1,1)$ (see the plots of the function $M_2(\cdot, t)$ for some t in Figure 8). Moreover, $v(t)$ is continuously differentiable and monotonically decreasing for $t \in (0,1)$, as a superposition of two continuously differentiable functions, one of which ($b(t)$) increases, whereas the other one ($f^{-1}(b)$) decreases. By conducting direct calculations we make sure that $b(0) = 0$, $b(1-) = +\infty$, and hence, $v(0+) = 1$, $v(1-) = 0$.

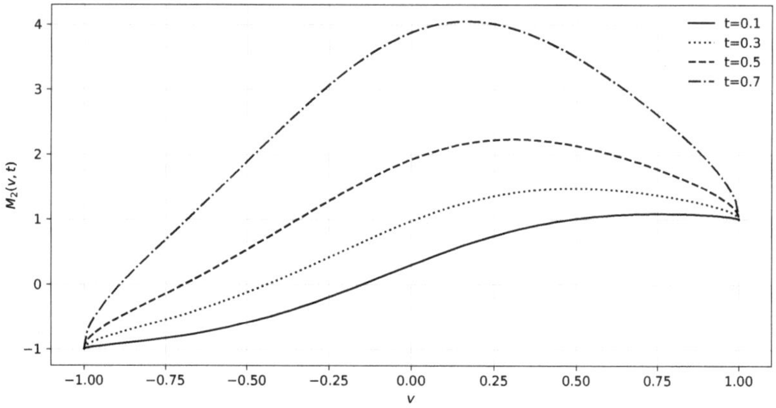

Figure 8. Plots of the function $M_2(\cdot, t)$ for some t.

So, for an arbitrary $s \in (-1,1)$, we have

$$\sup_{s \leqslant v < 1} M_2(v,t) = M_2(v(t) \vee s, t).$$

In particular, for $s = 1 - 2t^2$ we obtain

$$\sup_{1-2t^2 \leqslant v < 1} M_2(v,t) = M_2(v(t) \vee (1-2t^2), t).$$

Compare $v(t)$ and $1 - 2t^2$. Since $v(t) \in (0,1)$ for all $t \in (0,1)$ by definition, a fortiori $v(t) > 0 \geqslant 1 - 2t^2$ for $\frac{\sqrt{2}}{2} \leqslant t < 1$. On the interval $0 < t < \frac{\sqrt{2}}{2}$, we have

$$1 - 2t^2 \leqslant v(t) \quad \Leftrightarrow \quad f(1-2t^2) \geqslant f(v(t)) \equiv b(t) \quad \Leftrightarrow$$

$$\Leftrightarrow \quad \frac{8t^3(1-t^2)^{3/2}}{(2t^2-1)(2t^4-2t^2-1)} \geqslant \frac{t(3-2t^2)}{(1-t^2)^{3/2}} \quad \Leftrightarrow$$

$$\Leftrightarrow \quad 8t^2(1-t^2)^3 \geqslant (3-2t^2)(2t^2-1)(2t^4-2t^2-1) \quad \Leftrightarrow \quad 6t^4-10t^2+3 \leqslant 0$$

$$\Leftrightarrow \quad t \in \left[\sqrt{\tfrac{5-\sqrt{7}}{6}}, \sqrt{\tfrac{5+\sqrt{7}}{6}}\right] \cap \left(0, \tfrac{\sqrt{2}}{2}\right) = \left[\sqrt{\tfrac{5-\sqrt{7}}{6}}, \tfrac{\sqrt{2}}{2}\right) = [0.626\ldots, 0.707\ldots).$$

On the third step here we also took into account the fact that $2t^2-1<0$, $2t^4-2t^2-1<0$ in the domain of the values of t under consideration. Thus, unifying the obtained interval with the domain $t \geqslant \sqrt{2}/2$, we arrive at

$$v(t) \geqslant 1-2t^2 \text{ on the interval } t \in (0,1) \quad \Leftrightarrow \quad t_0 \leqslant t < 1,$$

with equality attained only at the point $t = t_0$.

So, for $s = 1-2t^2$ we finally obtain

$$\max_{1-2t^2 \leqslant v < 1} M_2(v,t) = \begin{cases} M_2(1-2t^2,t), & 0<t<t_0, \\ M_2(v(t),t), & t_0 \leqslant t < 1. \end{cases} \tag{34}$$

As a by-product we showed that

$$u_2(t_0) = v(t_0) = 1-2t_0^2 = \frac{\sqrt{7}-2}{3} = 0.21525\ldots. \tag{35}$$

In addition, note that the function

$$M_1(1-2t^2,t) = \frac{1}{(1-t^2)(2t^4-2t^2+1)} = M_2(1-2t^2,t), \quad t \in (0,1), \tag{36}$$

increases monotonically on the interval $t_0 \leqslant t \leqslant \frac{\sqrt{3}}{2}$.

Finally, from (29), (31), (32), (34), (36), it follows that

$$\widetilde{H}(t) = \sup_{-1<z<1} \widetilde{H}\left(\frac{1-z}{2}, t\right) = \max\left\{ \max_{-1<u<1-2t^2} M_1(u,t), \max_{1-2t^2 \leqslant v<1} M_2(v,t) \right\} =$$

$$= \begin{cases} M_1(u_2(t),t) \vee M_2(1-2t^2,t), & 0<t<t_0, \\ M_1(1-2t^2,t) \vee M_2(v(t),t) \vee 1, & t_0 \leqslant t < \frac{\sqrt{3}}{2}, \\ M_1(1-2t^2,t) \vee M_2(v(t),t), & \frac{\sqrt{3}}{2} \leqslant t < 1, \end{cases} =$$

$$= \begin{cases} M_1(u_2(t),t) \vee M_1(1-2t^2,t), & 0<t<t_0, \\ M_2(1-2t^2,t) \vee M_2(v(t),t) \vee 1, & t_0 \leqslant t < \frac{\sqrt{3}}{2}, \\ M_2(1-2t^2,t) \vee M_2(v(t),t), & \frac{\sqrt{3}}{2} \leqslant t < 1. \end{cases}$$

Taking into account that

$$M_1(1-2t_0^2,t_0) = M_2(1-2t_0^2,t_0) = \frac{54}{8\sqrt{7}-4} = 3.14575\ldots > 1,$$

we obtain

$$\widetilde{H}(t) = \begin{cases} M_1(u_2(t),t) \vee M_1(1-2t^2,t), & 0<t<t_0, \\ M_2(1-2t^2,t) \vee M_2(v(t),t), & t_0 \leqslant t < 1. \end{cases}$$

Recalling that $v(t)$ is the unique point of global maximum of $M_2(v,t)$ on the interval $v \in (-1,1)$, and $u_2(t)$ is the unique point of global maximum of $M_1(u,t)$ on the interval $u \in (-1,1)$ for $t \in (0,t_0] \subset \left(0, \frac{\sqrt{3}}{2}\right)$ (when $a(t) < 0$), we conclude that

$$\widetilde{H}(t) = \begin{cases} M_1(u_2(t),t), & 0 < t < t_0, \\ M_2(v(t),t), & t_0 \leqslant t < 1, \end{cases} \quad = \quad M(z(t),t).$$

Thus, the function $u_2(t)$ defined for $t \in (0, \sqrt{3}/2)$ (which corresponds to the case $a(t) < 0$) and monotonically decreasing in its domain, acts as the function $u(t)$ given in the formulation of Theorem 1 and the lemma being proved, whereas the role of the global maximum point $z(t)$ of the function $M(\,\cdot\,,t)$ is played by the functions $u(t) = u_2(t)$ for $t \in (0,t_0)$ and $v(t)$ for $t \in [t_0,1)$, which completely agrees with (9).

(b) The functions M_1 and M_2 are obviously differentiable in the domain $(z,t) \in (-1,1) \times (0,1)$ and have continuous partial derivatives there. It is easy to see from (27) and (28) that the function $\widetilde{H}(p,t)$ is differentiable in the domain $(p,t) \in (0,1) \times (0,1)$ and has continuous partial derivatives there. With the account of (31) we conclude that M is differentiable in the domain $(z,t) \in (-1,1) \times (0,1)$ and has continuous partial derivatives there.

(c) This statement can be verified directly.

(d) We show that $z(t)$ is continuously differentiable and decreases on the interval $t \in (0,1)$. Since $u_2(t)$ is continuously differentiable and monotonically decreasing on the interval $t \in \left(0, \frac{\sqrt{3}}{2}\right) \supset (0,t_0]$ and the function $v(t)$ is continuously differentiable and monotonically decreasing on the interval $t \in (0,1) \supset [t_0,1]$, with the account of (35), we conclude that the function $z(t)$ is continuous and monotonically decreasing on the interval $t \in (0,1)$. Furthermore, the function $z(t)$ is continuously differentiable on each of the intervals $(0,t_0)$ and $(t_0,1)$. In addition, we show that $u_2'(t_0) = v'(t_0)$, whence it will follow that the function z is continuously differentiable in the point t_0, and hence, on the whole, interval $t \in (0,1)$. In the neighborhood of t_0, we have

$$u_2(t_0) = g^{-1}(a(t_0)), \quad v(t_0) = f^{-1}(b(t_0)),$$

therefore,

$$u_2'(t_0) = \frac{a'(t_0)}{g'(u_2(t_0))}, \quad v'(t_0) = \frac{b'(t_0)}{f'(v(t_0))},$$

whence by virtue of (35), we obtain

$$u_2'(t_0) = \frac{a'(t_0)}{g'(1-2t_0^2)}, \quad v'(t_0) = \frac{b'(t_0)}{f'(1-2t_0^2)}.$$

By direct calculations, we make sure that

$$u_2'(t_0) = v'(t_0) = -2\sqrt{\tfrac{3-\sqrt{7}}{3}} = -0.687263\ldots.$$

Thus, the function $z(t)$ is differentiable on the interval $t \in (0,1)$.

Now to complete the proof of item **(d)**, it remains to recall that

$$z(0+) = u_2(0+) = \frac{\sqrt{3}}{3}, \quad z(1-) = v(1-) = 0, \quad z(t_0) = u_2(t_0) = v(t_0) = \frac{\sqrt{7}-2}{3},$$

and that (see the proof of item **(a)**) each of the equations

$$u_2(t) = 1 - 2t^2, \quad t \in (0, \sqrt{3}/2),$$

$$v(t) = 1 - 2t^2, \quad t \in (0,1),$$

has the unique root $t = t_0$. $\square$

5. Proofs of Main Results

Proof of Theorem 1. It is obvious that $H(0) = 1$ and H is an even function. Since $J(X)$ is invariant with respect to the scale transform of X, the single non-linear condition in (8) can be replaced by the two linear ones: $\mathbb{E}X = t$, $\mathbb{E}X^2 = 1$. Further, from Lemmas 3 and 4 **(a)**, **(d)**, it follows that for $t \in (0,1)$, we have

$$H(t) = M(z(t),t) = \begin{cases} M_1(z(t),t), & -1 < z(t) < 1 - 2t^2, \\ M_2(z(t),t), & 1 - 2t^2 \leqslant z(t) < 1, \end{cases} =$$

$$= \begin{cases} 1 + \dfrac{3t^2}{1-t^2} \cdot \dfrac{1 - z^2(t) - a(t)z(t)\sqrt{1-z^2(t)}}{1+z^2(t)}, & 0 < t < t_0, \\ \dfrac{b(t)\sqrt{1-z^2(t)} + 2z(t)}{z^2(t)+1}, & t_0 \leqslant t < 1. \end{cases}$$

By the definition of the function $z(t)$, we have

$$a(t) = \frac{4z(t)\sqrt{1-z^2(t)}}{3z^2(t)-1}, \quad 0 < t < t_0,$$

$$b(t) = \frac{2(1-z^2(t))^{3/2}}{z(t)(3-z^2(t))}, \quad t_0 \leqslant t < 1.$$

Hence,

$$H(t) = \begin{cases} 1 + \dfrac{3t^2}{1-t^2} \cdot \dfrac{1-z^2(t)}{1-3z^2(t)}, & 0 < t < t_0, \\ \dfrac{2}{z(t)(3-z^2(t))}, & t_0 \leqslant t < 1, \end{cases}$$

which coincides with (8). The form and uniqueness of the extreme distribution were proved in Lemma 4 **(a)**.

It remains to be proven that the function H is continuous and monotonically increasing on the interval $t \in [0,1)$ and that $H(1-) = +\infty$. By virtue of Lemma 4 **(a)** for $t \in (0,1)$, we have $H(t) = M(z(t),t)$, moreover, M is continuous in the domain $(z,t) \in (-1,1) \times (0,1)$, whereas z is continuous on the interval $t \in (0,1)$, whence $H(t)$ is continuous on the interval $t \in (0,1)$. Since

$$H(0+) = M(z(0+),0+) = 1 = H(0),$$

H is also continuous in zero.

Finally, prove that the function H is monotonically increasing. From the definition of the function $z(t)$, it follows that

$$\frac{1}{1-3z^2(t)} = \frac{3-4t^2}{12tz(t)\sqrt{(1-t^2)(1-z^2(t))}}, \quad t \in (0,t_0),$$

and hence, we can write

$$H(t) = \begin{cases} 1 + \dfrac{t(3-4t^2)\sqrt{1-z^2(t)}}{4z(t)(1-t^2)^{3/2}}, & 0 < t < t_0, \\ \dfrac{2}{z(t)(3-z^2(t))}, & t_0 \leqslant t < 1. \end{cases}$$

Note that the function $t(3-4t^2)(1-t^2)^{-3/2}$ is positive and monotonically increasing on the interval $0 < t < t_0$, whereas the function $z^{-1}\sqrt{1-z^2}$ is positive and monotonically decreasing on the interval $0 < z < 1$. Since the function $z(t)$ decreases on the interval

$0 < t < t_0$ as well, we conclude that H increases on the interval $(0, t_0)$ as a product of two positive monotonically increasing functions (up to an additive constant). Furthermore, since the function $2/\big(z(3-z^2)\big)$ decreases on the interval $0 < z < 1$ and the function $z(t)$ decreases on the interval $t_0 \leqslant t < 1$, the function $H(t)$ increases on the interval $t_0 \leqslant t < 1$, as a superposition of two decreasing functions. Finally, the existence of an infinite limit of $H(t)$, as $t \to 1-$, follows from that $z(t) \to 0+$, as $t \to 1-$. □

Proof of Proposition 1. By virtue of the continuity of H and $\hat{H}$, it suffices to prove inequality (15) only on the interval $(0, t_0)$. By the definition of $z(t)$ for $0 < t < t_0$, as a unique root of the equation

$$g(z) := \frac{4z\sqrt{1-z^2}}{3z^2-1} = \frac{4t^2-3}{3t\sqrt{1-t^2}} =: a(t),$$

on the interval $0 < z < \sqrt{3}/3$, we have

$$\lim_{t\to 0+} z(t) = \frac{\sqrt{3}}{3}, \quad \lim_{t\to 0+} z'(t) = \lim_{t\to 0+} \frac{a'(t)}{g'(z(t))} = -\frac{2\sqrt{6}}{9},$$

hence, by the Lagrange theorem,

$$z(t) = \tilde{z}(t) + o(t), \quad \tilde{z}(t) := \frac{\sqrt{3}}{3} - \frac{2\sqrt{6}}{9}t.$$

We show that $z(t) < \tilde{z}(t)$ for $0 < t < t_0$. By virtue of the monotonic decrease of $g(u)$ for $0 < u < \sqrt{3}/3$, we have

$$z(t) < \tilde{z}(t) \quad \Longleftrightarrow \quad g(z(t)) > g(\tilde{z}(t)) \quad \Longleftrightarrow$$

$$\Longleftrightarrow \quad -\frac{3-4t^2}{3t\sqrt{1-t^2}} > -\frac{\left(3\sqrt{2}-4t\right)\sqrt{-4t^2+6\sqrt{2}t+9}}{3t\left(3\sqrt{2}-2t\right)} \quad \Longleftrightarrow$$

$$\Longleftrightarrow \quad (3-4t^2)(3\sqrt{2}-2t) < (3\sqrt{2}-4t)\sqrt{(-4t^2+6\sqrt{2}+9)(1-t^2)} \quad \Longleftrightarrow$$

$$\Longleftrightarrow \quad 96\sqrt{2}t^5 + t^4\big(-328-96\sqrt{2}\big) + t^3\big(24\sqrt{2}+288\big) + t^2\big(306-12\sqrt{2}\big) +$$

$$+t\big(-288-108\sqrt{2}\big) + 108\sqrt{2} =: s(t) > 0.$$

We show that $s(t) > 0$ for $0 < t < t_0$. We have

$$s'(t) = 480\sqrt{2}t^4 + t^3\big(-1312-384\sqrt{2}\big) + t^2\big(72\sqrt{2}+864\big) + t\big(612-24\sqrt{2}\big) - 288 - 108\sqrt{2},$$

$$s''(t) = 1920\sqrt{2}t^3 + t^2\big(-3936-1152\sqrt{2}\big) + t\big(144\sqrt{2}+1728\big) - 24\sqrt{2} + 612,$$

$$s^{(3)}(t) = 5760\sqrt{2}t^2 + t\big(-7872-2304\sqrt{2}\big) + 144\sqrt{2} + 1728,$$

$$s^{(4)}(t) = 11520\sqrt{2}t - 7872 - 2304\sqrt{2} < 0, \quad t \in (0, t_0),$$

therefore, $s^{(3)}(t)$ decreases for $t \in (0, t_0)$. Since

$$s^{(3)}(0+) = 144\sqrt{2} + 1728 > 0, \quad s^{(3)}(t_0-) = -1844.1499\ldots < 0,$$

$s''(t)$ has a unique stationary point on the interval $t \in (0, t_0)$, namely, the local maximum point. Taking into account that

$$s''(0+) = 612 - 24\sqrt{2} > 0, \quad s''(t_0-) = 271.7769\ldots > 0,$$

we conclude that $s''(t) > 0$ for $t \in (0, t_0)$, and whence, $s'(t)$ increases for $t \in (0, t_0]$. Since $s'(t_0) = -51.1066 < 0,$, we have $s'(t) < 0$ for all $t \in (0, t_0]$ and hence, $s(t)$ decreases for

$t \in (0, t_0]$. Finally, $s(t_0) = 10.8876\ldots$, therefore, $s(t) > 0$ for $t \in (0, t_0]$. So, the inequality $z(t) < \widetilde{z}(t)$ is proved for $t \in (0, t_0)$.

Note that

$$H(t) = M(z(t), t) = 1 + \frac{3t^2}{1-t^2} \cdot \frac{1 - z^2(t)}{1 - 3z^2(t)}$$

for $0 < t < t_0$, moreover, the function $M(\cdot, t)$ increases on the interval $0 < z < \sqrt{3}/3$, therefore, taking into account that $0 < z(t) < \widetilde{z}(t) < \sqrt{3}/3$ and

$$\widetilde{z}^2(t) = \frac{1}{3} - \frac{4\sqrt{2}}{9}t + \frac{24}{81}t^2,$$

we obtain

$$H(t) \leqslant M(\widetilde{z}(t), t) = 1 + \frac{3t^2}{1-t^2} \cdot \frac{\frac{2}{3} + \frac{4\sqrt{2}}{9}t - \frac{24}{81}t^2}{\frac{4\sqrt{2}}{3}t - \frac{24}{27}t^2} = \frac{5t + 6\sqrt{2}}{2(1-t^2)(3\sqrt{2} - 2t)} = \hat{H}(t).$$

The function $\hat{H}(t)$ obviously increases on $(0, t_0)$. It now remains to note that, as $t \to 0$,

$$z^2(t) = \left(\frac{\sqrt{3}}{3} - \frac{2\sqrt{6}}{9}t + o(t)\right)^2 = \frac{1}{3} - \frac{4\sqrt{2}}{9}t + o(t) = \widetilde{z}^2(t),$$

$$\begin{aligned} H(t) - 1 = \frac{3t^2}{1-t^2} \cdot \frac{1 - z^2(t)}{1 - 3z^2(t)} &= \frac{3t^2}{1-t^2} \cdot \frac{\frac{2}{3} + \frac{4\sqrt{2}}{9}t + o(t)}{\frac{4\sqrt{2}}{3}t + o(t)} = \\ &= \frac{3t}{1-t^2} \cdot \frac{2 + o(1)}{4\sqrt{2} + o(1)} = \frac{3t^2}{1-t^2} \cdot \frac{1 - \widetilde{z}^2(t)}{1 - 3\widetilde{z}^2(t)} = \hat{H}(t) - 1, \end{aligned} \quad (37)$$

and hence,

$$\lim_{t \to 0+} \frac{\hat{H}(t) - 1}{H(t) - 1} = \lim_{t \to 0+} \frac{2 + o(1)}{4\sqrt{2} + o(1)} \cdot \frac{4\sqrt{2} + o(1)}{2 + o(1)} = 1.$$

□

Proof of Theorem 2. Lemma 4(**a**) implies that $H(t) = M(z(t), t)$, where $z(t)$, $t \in (0, 1)$, is the unique global maximum point of the function $M(\cdot, t)$, $t \in (0, 1)$. Moreover, the function $M(z, t)$ is differentiable in the domain $(z, t) \in (-1, 1) \times (0, 1)$ and has continuous partial derivatives there, whereas the function $z(t)$ is continuously differentiable on the interval $t \in (0, 1)$ and takes values from the interval $\left(0, \frac{\sqrt{3}}{3}\right)$. So,

$$\sup_{0<t<1} H(t)(1-t^2)^{3/2} = \sup_{0<t<1} h(t),$$

where $h(t) = M(z(t), t)(1-t^2)^{3/2}$, $t \in (0, 1)$. It is obvious that h is continuously differentiable on the interval $t \in (0, 1)$.

We find the stationary points of the function h on the interval $t \in (0, 1)$. We have

$$h'(t) = (1-t^2)^{3/2}(M(z(t), t))'_t - 3t\sqrt{1-t^2}M(z(t), t),$$

$$(M(z(t), t))'_t = M'_z(z, t)\big|_{z=z(t)} \cdot z'(t) + M'_t(z, t)\big|_{z=z(t)} = M'_t(z, t)\big|_{z=z(t)}.$$

For $t \in [t_0, 1)$, we have

$$\frac{1}{3}h'(t) = \frac{(1-2t^2)\sqrt{1-z^2(t)} - 2tz(t)\sqrt{1-t^2}}{z^2(t) + 1}.$$

In the domain $(z,t) \in \left(0, \frac{\sqrt{3}}{3}\right) \times [t_0, 1)$ the equation

$$(1-2t^2)\sqrt{1-z^2} - 2tz\sqrt{1-t^2} = 0$$

is only satisfied by the couples $(1-2t^2, t)$, $t \in \left[t_0, \frac{\sqrt{2}}{2}\right)$, whence with the account of the fact that $z(t) = 1-2t^2$ only for $t = t_0$ (see Lemma 4 (**d**)), we conclude that $t = t_0$ is the unique stationary point of the function h on the interval $[t_0, 1)$.

For $t \in (0, t_0]$, we have

$$\tfrac{1}{3}h'(t) = \frac{-2t^3 + t + z^2(t)(4t^2-3)t + z(t)(1-4t^2)\sqrt{1-t^2}\sqrt{1-z^2(t)}}{\sqrt{1-t^2}(z^2(t)+1)}.$$

Find the solutions to the equation

$$z(1-4t^2)\sqrt{1-t^2}\sqrt{1-z^2} = t(2t^2 - 1 - z^2(4t^2-3))$$

in the domain $(z,t) \in \left(0, \frac{\sqrt{3}}{3}\right) \times (0, t_0]$. Squaring both sides, we obtain

$$z^2(1-4t^2)^2(1-t^2)(1-z^2) = t^2(2t^2 - 1 - z^2(4t^2-3))^2,$$

which is equivalent to

$$(t-z)(t+z)(z-2t^2+1)(z+2t^2-1) = 0.$$

Therefore, the original equation can only be satisfied by the points

$$(t,t), \quad (-t,t), \quad (1-2t^2, t), \quad (-1+2t^2, t), \quad 0 < t < 1.$$

By direct calculations, we make sure that in the domain $(z,t) \in \left(0, \frac{\sqrt{3}}{3}\right) \times (0, t_0]$ the original equation is only satisfied by the couple $(1-2t^2, t)$, $t \in \left(\sqrt{\frac{3-\sqrt{3}}{6}}, t_0\right]$ and the couple $\left(\frac{1}{2}, \frac{1}{2}\right)$. Since $z(t) = 1-2t^2$ iff $t = t_0$, we conclude that $t = t_0$ is the stationary point of the function h, and h has no other stationary points except for $t = \frac{1}{2}$. We show that $z\left(\frac{1}{2}\right) \neq \frac{1}{2}$ and, hence, $t = \frac{1}{2}$ cannot be a stationary point of h. Recall (see Theorem 1), that $z(t)$ turns the equation

$$g(z) := \frac{4z\sqrt{1-z^2}}{3z^2-1} = \frac{4t^2-3}{3t\sqrt{1-t^2}}$$

into identity on the interval $t \in (0, t_0)$. By direct verification, we make sure that $(z,t) = \left(\frac{1}{2}, \frac{1}{2}\right)$ is not a root of this equation.

Thus, the function h has a unique stationary point $t = t_0$ on the interval $t \in (0,1)$. Moreover,

$$h(t_0) = \frac{\sqrt{1-t_0^2}}{1-2t_0^2+2t_0^4} = \frac{\sqrt{17+7\sqrt{7}}}{4} = 1.489971\ldots.$$

Also, note that

$$\lim_{t\to 0} h(t) = h(0) = 1 < h(t_0),$$

$$\lim_{t\to 1} h(t) = \frac{(1-t^2)^{3/2}(b(t)\sqrt{1-z^2(t)} + 2z)}{z^2(t)+1} =$$

$$= \lim_{t\to 1} \frac{t\sqrt{1-z^2(t)}(3-2t^2) + 2z(t)(1-t^2)^{\frac{3}{2}}}{z^2(t)+1} = 1 < h(t_0),$$

therefore, the point t_0 is the global maximum point of the function h on the interval $(0,1)$, and h increases on $[0,t_0]$ and decreases on $[t_0,1)$. The fact that the maximum is attained on the two-point distribution follows from Theorem 1. □

Proof of Proposition 2. Inequality (18) for $0 \leqslant t \leqslant t_0$ follows trivially from Proposition 1. Let us prove the equivalence of the left-hand and right-hand sides of this inequality as $t \to 0$. From the proof of Proposition 1 (see (37)), we have

$$H(t) = 1 + \frac{3t}{1-t^2} \cdot \frac{2+o(1)}{4\sqrt{2}+o(1)} = \hat{H}(t), \quad t \to 0,$$

whence with the account of the asymptotics $(1-t^2)^\alpha = 1+o(t), t \to 0, \alpha \in \mathbb{R}$, it follows that

$$H(t)(1-t^2)^{3/2} = (1-t^2)^{3/2} + 3t\sqrt{1-t^2}\frac{2+o(1)}{4\sqrt{2}+o(1)} =$$

$$= 1 + o(t) + 3t(1+o(t))(2+o(1))\Big(\tfrac{1}{4\sqrt{2}} + o(1)\Big) =$$

$$= 1 + o(t) + 3t\Big(\tfrac{2}{4\sqrt{2}} + o(1)\Big) = 1 + \tfrac{3\sqrt{2}}{4}t + o(t) = \hat{H}(t)(1-t^2)^{3/2},$$

and hence,

$$\lim_{t\to 0+} \frac{\hat{H}(t)(1-t^2)^{3/2}-1}{H(t)(1-t^2)^{3/2}-1} = \lim_{t\to 0+} \frac{\frac{3\sqrt{2}}{4}t + o(t)}{\frac{3\sqrt{2}}{4}t + o(t)} = 1.$$

The function

$$\hat{H}(t)(1-t^2)^{3/2} = \frac{\sqrt{1-t^2}(5t+6\sqrt{2})}{2(3\sqrt{2}-2t)} =: s(t)$$

is continuous on $[0,t_0]$ by virtue of the continuity of $\hat{H}$. To prove that $\hat{H}(t)(1-t^2)^{3/2}$ increases on $(0,t_0)$, consider the derivative

$$s'(t) = \frac{10t^3 - 30\sqrt{2}t^2 - 36t + 27\sqrt{2}}{2\sqrt{1-t^2}(2t-3\sqrt{2})^2}.$$

With the account of the positiveness of the denominator for $t \in (0,t_0)$, it suffices to prove that the numerator of $s'(t)$ is positive; that is,

$$s_1(t) := 10t^3 - 30\sqrt{2}t^2 - 36t + 27\sqrt{2} > 0, \quad t \in (0,t_0).$$

Since $5t^2 - 6 < -1$ for all $t \in (0,1)$,, we have

$$s_1'(t) = 6(5t^2 - 10\sqrt{2}t - 6) < 6(-1 - 10\sqrt{2}t) < 0, \quad t \in (0,t_0),$$

therefore, $s_1(t)$ decreases on the interval $t \in (0,t_0)$ and, hence, for all $t \in (0,t_0)$, we have

$$s_1(t) \geqslant s_1(t_0) = 1.4442\ldots > 0. \quad \square$$

Proof of Theorem 3. According to the Berry–Esseen inequality (1), the following estimate in terms of the non-central Lyapunov ratio holds:

$$\Delta_\lambda(X) \leqslant C_1 \cdot \frac{L_1(X)}{\sqrt{\lambda}}, \quad \lambda > 0.$$

From Theorem 2, it follows that for any $\mathscr{L}(X) \in \mathscr{P}$ with $\mathbb{E}X/\sqrt{\mathbb{E}X^2} = t \in (-1,1)$

$$\frac{L_1(X)}{L_0(X)} = \frac{\mathbb{E}|X|^3}{\mathbb{E}|X-\mathbb{E}X|^3}\left(\frac{\mathbb{D}X}{\mathbb{E}X^2}\right)^{3/2} = \frac{\mathbb{E}|X|^3(1-t^2)^{3/2}}{\mathbb{E}|X-\mathbb{E}X|^3} \leqslant H(t)\left(1-t^2\right)^{3/2} \leqslant \frac{\sqrt{17+7\sqrt{7}}}{4},$$

and hence,

$$\Delta_\lambda(X) \leqslant C_1 \cdot H(t)(1-t^2)^{3/2}\frac{L_0(X)}{\sqrt{\lambda}} \leqslant \frac{\sqrt{17+7\sqrt{7}}}{4}C_1 \cdot \frac{L_0(X)}{\sqrt{\lambda}},$$

that is, inequality (19) holds with $C_0(t) = C_1 \cdot H(t)\left(1-t^2\right)^{3/2} \leqslant \frac{\sqrt{17+7\sqrt{7}}}{4}C_1$. The estimate $C_1 \leqslant 0.3031$ was obtained in ([20], Theorem 4).

In Theorem 2, it was also shown that $H(t)\left(1-t^2\right)^{3/2}$ increases for $0 \leqslant t \leqslant t_0$ and decreases for $t_0 \leqslant t < 1$. Therefore,

$$C_0(t) \leqslant C_0(t \wedge t_0), \quad 0 \leqslant t < 1,$$

and the function $C_0(t \wedge t_0)$ does not decrease for $0 \leqslant t < 1$. Hence, for $|\mathbb{E}X|/\sqrt{\mathbb{E}X^2} = s \leqslant t$ in accordance with what has just been proven, we have

$$\Delta_\lambda(X) \leqslant C_0(s)\frac{L_0(X)}{\sqrt{\lambda}} \leqslant C_0(s \wedge t_0) \cdot \frac{L_0(X)}{\sqrt{\lambda}} \leqslant C_0(t \wedge t_0) \cdot \frac{L_0(X)}{\sqrt{\lambda}}.$$

Finally, the upper bound of $C_0(t)$ for $0 \leqslant t \leqslant t_0$ declared in the formulation of the theorem trivially follows from the inequality $H(t) \leqslant \hat{H}(t)$ obtained in Proposition 1 with the account of the particular upper bound 0.3031 for the constant C_1:

$$C_0(t) \leqslant C_1 \cdot \hat{H}(t)(1-t^2)^{3/2} \leqslant 0.3031 \cdot \frac{\sqrt{1-t^2}(5t+6\sqrt{2})}{2(3\sqrt{2}-2t)}, \quad 0 \leqslant t \leqslant t_0.$$

The monotonicity of these upper bounds follows from that of the function $\hat{H}(t)(1-t^2)^{3/2}$ proved in Proposition 2. □

6. Conclusions

In this paper, we posed and solved a new problem of a delicate comparison of Lyapunov ratios, where the word "delicate" addresses the presence of additional moment conditions (on the first two moments) in the originally [24] unconditional problem of optimization of the ratio of Lyapunov fractions.

The problem of comparison of Lyapunov fractions arises naturally in the construction of convergence rate estimates for random sums of independent random variables, in particular, compound Poisson random sums, as was observed in [24]. As a possible application of the results in Theorem 2, we introduced a new Berry–Esseen-type error bound for the accuracy of the normal approximation to distributions of Poisson random sums in terms of the classical central Lyapunov fraction whose factor depends on the value of the normalized expectation of random summands. The introduced error bound improves up to 1.5 times the best-known one [31], where the factor of the Lyapunov fraction was constant. In addition to an independent interest, the Berry–Esseen-type inequality (4), namely with the central Lyapunov fraction, plays an important role in the construction of moment-type estimates of the rate of convergence of random walks with equivalent elementary trends and variances to variance-mean mixtures of normal laws [25–29], including skew exponential power law, skew Student's law, and more generally, variance-generalized gamma law and generalized hyperbolic distributions. In addition, the introduction of the non-constant factor of the central Lyapunov fraction in this inequality, as proposed in Theorem 3, will allow, in particular, to improve the above-cited results considerably.

Author Contributions: Conceptualization, I.S.; methodology, I.S.; software, V.M.; validation, V.M., I.S.; formal analysis, V.M.; writing—original draft preparation, V.M.; writing—review and editing, V.M. and I.S.; visualization, V.M.; funding acquisition, V.M. and I.S. All authors have read and agreed to the published version of the manuscript.

Funding: Research supported by the Russian Science Foundation, project 22-11-00212 (Theorem 1 and Proposition 1), the President grant MD-5748.2021.1 (Theorem 2 and Proposition 2), and the Russian Ministry for Education and Science, agreement No. 075-15-2022-284 within the program of Moscow Center for Fundamental and Applied Mathematics (Theorem 3).

Institutional Review Board Statement: Not applicable.

Data Availability Statement: Not applicable.

Acknowledgments: The authors would like to express their sincere gratitude to Victor Korolev, who suggested constructing a simple majorant for the function H resulting in formulas (15) and (18) and translated the paper into English.

Conflicts of Interest: The authors declare no conflict of interest.

Abbreviations

The following abbreviations are used in this manuscript:

i.i.d.	independent and identically distributed
r.v.	random variable
iff	if and only if

References

1. Cramér, H. *Collective Risk Theory*; Skandia Jubilee Volume: Stockholm, Sweden, 1955.
2. Grandell, J. *Aspects of risk theory*; Springer: New York, NY, USA, 1991.
3. Gnedenko, B.V.; Korolev, V.Y. *Random Summation: Limit Theorems and Applications*; CRC Press: Boca Raton, FL, USA, 1996.
4. Bening, V.E.; Korolev, V.Y. *Generalized Poisson Models and Their Applications in Insurance and Finance*; VSP: Utrecht, The Netherlands, 2002.
5. Shevtsova, I.G. On the accuracy of the normal approximation to compound Poisson distributions. *Theory Probab. Appl.* **2014**, *58*, 138–158. [CrossRef]
6. Korolev, V.; Dorofeyeva, A. Bounds of the accuracy of the normal approximation to the distributions of random sums under relaxed moment conditions. *Lith. Math. J.* **2017**, *57*, 38–58. [CrossRef]
7. Kruglov, V.M.; Korolev, V.Y. *Limit Theorems for Random Sums*; Moscow University Press: Moscow, Russia, 1990.
8. Englund, G. A remainder term estimate in a random–sum central limit theorem. *Theory Probab. Appl.* **1984**, *28*, 149–157. [CrossRef]
9. Rotar, G.V. Some Problems of Planning of Reserve. Ph.D. Thesis, Central Institute of Economics and Mathematics, Moscow, Russia, 1972. (In Russian)
10. Rotar, G.V. On a problem of control of reserves. *Econ. Math. Methods* **1976**, *12*, 733–739. (In Russian)
11. Von Chossy, R.; Rappl, G. Some approximation methods for the distribution of random sums. *Insur. Math. Econ.* **1983**, *2*, 251–270. [CrossRef]
12. Berry, A.C. The accuracy of the Gaussian approximation to the sum of independent variates. *Trans. Am. Math. Soc.* **1941**, *49*, 122–136. [CrossRef]
13. Esseen, C.G. On the Liapounoff limit of error in the theory of probability. *Ark. Mat. Astron. Fys.* **1942**, *A28*, 1–19.
14. Michel, R. On Berry–Esseen results for the compound Poisson distribution. *Insur. Math. Econ.* **1993**, *13*, 35–37. [CrossRef]
15. Korolev, V.Y.; Shorgin, S.Y. On the absolute constant in the remainder term estimate in the central limit theorem for Poisson random sums. In Proceedings of the Probabilistic Methods in Discrete Mathematics, Proceedings of the Fourth International Petrozavodsk Conference, VSP, Petrozavodsk, Russia, 3–7 June 1997; pp. 305–308.
16. Korolev, V.Y.; Shevtsova, I.G. Sharpened upper bounds for the absolute constant in the Berry–Esseen inequality for mixed Poisson random sums. *Dokl. Math.* **2010**, *81*, 180–182. [CrossRef]
17. Esseen, C.G. A moment inequality with an application to the central limit theorem. *Skand. Aktuarietidskr.* **1956**, *39*, 160–170. [CrossRef]
18. Korolev, V.; Shevtsova, I. An improvement of the Berry–Esseen inequality with applications to Poisson and mixed Poisson random sums. *Scand. Actuar. J.* **2012**, *2012*, 81–105. [CrossRef]
19. Korolev, V.Y.; Bening, V.E.; Shorgin, S.Y. *Mathematical Foundations of Risk Theory*, 2nd ed.; Fizmatlit: Moscow, Russia, 2011. (In Russian)
20. Shevtsova, I.G. On the absolute constants in the Berry–Esseen-type inequalities. *Dokl. Math.* **2014**, *89*, 378–381. [CrossRef]

21. Nefedova, Y.S.; Shevtsova, I.G. On the accuracy of the normal approximation to distributions of Poisson random sums. *Inform. Its Appl.* **2011**, *5*, 39–45. (In Russian)
22. Shevtsova, I.G., On the absolute constants in Nagaev–Bikelis–type inequalities. In *Inequalities and Extremal Problems in Probability and Statistics*; Pinelis, I., Ed.; Elsevier: Amsterdam, The Netherlands, 2017; Chapter 3, pp. 47–102.
23. Shevtsova, I.G. On the asymptotically exact constants in the Berry–Esseen–Katz inequality. *Theory Probab. Appl.* **2011**, *55*, 225–252. Original Russian text: *Teor. Veroyatn. Primen.* **2010**, *55*, 271–304. [CrossRef]
24. Shorgin, S.Y. On the accuracy of the normal approximation to ditributions of random sums with infinitely divisible indices. *Theory Probab. Appl.* **1997**, *41*, 798–805. [CrossRef]
25. Korolev, V.Y. Generalized hyperbolic laws as limit distributions for random sums. *Theory Probab. Appl.* **2014**, *58*, 63–75. [CrossRef]
26. Zaks, L.M.; Korolev, V.Y. Variance-generalized-gamma-distributions as limit laws for random sums. *Inform. Its Appl.* **2013**, *7*, 105–115. (In Russian)
27. Grigor'eva, M.E.; Korolev, V.Y. On convergence of the distributions of random sums to skew exponential power laws. *Inform. Its Appl.* **2013**, *7*, 66–74. (In Russian)
28. Bening, V.E.; Zaks, L.M.; Korolev, V.Y. Estimates of the rate of convergence of the distributions of random sums to the skew Student distribution. *Sistemy i Sredstva Inform.* **2012**, *22*, 132–141. (In Russian)
29. Bening, V.E.; Zaks, L.M.; Korolev, V.Y. Estimates of the rate of convergence of the distributions of random sums to variance-gamma distributions. *Inform. Its Appl.* **2012**, *6*, 69–73. (In Russian)
30. Shorgin, S.Y. Approximation of generalized Poisson distributions: Comparison of Lyapunov fractions. In Proceedings of the 21st Seminar on Stability Problems for Stochastic Models, Eger, Hungary, 28 January–3 February 2001; Abstracts; House of University of Debrecen: Eger, Hungary, 2001; pp. 166–167.
31. Korolev, V.Y.; Shevtsova, I.G.; Shorgin, S.Y. On the Berry–Esseen type inequalities for Poisson random sums. *Inform. Its Appl.* **2011**, *5*, 64–66. (In Russian)
32. Hoeffding, W. The extrema of the expected value of a function of independent random variables. *Ann. Math. Statist.* **1955**, *26*, 268–275. [CrossRef]
33. Hoeffding, W.; Shrikhande, S.S. Bounds for the distribution function of a sum of independent, identically distributed random variables. *Ann. Math. Statist.* **1955**, *26*, 439–449. [CrossRef]
34. Mulholland, H.P.; Rogers, C.A. Representation theorems for distribution functions. *Proc. Lond. Math. Soc.* **1958**, *8*, 177–223. [CrossRef]
35. Zolotarev, V.M. Probability metrics. *Theory Probab. Appl.* **1984**, *28*, 278–302. [CrossRef]
36. Nefedova, Y.S.; Shevtsova, I.G. On non-uniform convergence rate estimates in the central limit theorem. *Theory Probab. Appl.* **2013**, *57*, 28–59. [CrossRef]
37. Pinelis, I., Optimal re-centering bounds, with applications to Rosenthal-type concentration of measure inequalities. In *High Dimensional Probability VI*; Progress in Probability; Houdré, C., Mason, D.M., Rosiński, J., Wellner, J.A., Eds.; Springer: Basel, Switzerland, 2013; Volume 66, pp. 81–93.
38. Shevtsova, I.G. A moment inequality with application to convergence rate estimates in the global CLT for Poisson–binomial random sums. *Theory Probab. Appl.* **2018**, *62*, 278–294. Original Russian text: *Teor. Veroyatn. Primen.* **2017**, *62*, 345–364. [CrossRef]
39. Richter, H. Parameterfreie Abschätzung und Realisierung von Erwartungswerten. Bl. Deutsch. Ges. Versicherungsmath. *Bl. Deutsch. Ges. Versicherungsmath.* **1957**, *3*, 147–162.

Article

Branching Random Walks with One Particle Generation Center and Possible Absorption at Every Point

Elena Filichkina [1,2,†] and Elena Yarovaya [1,*,†]

1. Department of Probability Theory, Lomonosov Moscow State University, 119234 Moscow, Russia
2. National Medical Research Center for Therapy and Preventive Medicine, 101990 Moscow, Russia
* Correspondence: yarovaya@mech.math.msu.su
† These authors contributed equally to this work.

Abstract: We consider a new model of a branching random walk on a multidimensional lattice with continuous time and one source of particle reproduction and death, as well as an infinite number of sources in which, in addition to the walk, only the absorption of particles can occur. The asymptotic behavior of the integer moments of both the total number of particles and the number of particles at a lattice point is studied depending on the relationship between the model parameters. In the case of the existence of an isolated positive eigenvalue of the evolution operator of the average number of particles, a limit theorem is obtained on the exponential growth of both the total number of particles and the number of particles at a lattice point.

Keywords: branching random walks; moments of particle numbers; evolution operator; Green's function

MSC: 60J27; 60J80; 05C81; 60J85

1. Introduction

We consider a continuous-time branching random walk (BRW) on the multidimensional lattice $\mathbb{Z}^d$, $d \in \mathbb{N}$, with one source of particle reproduction and death located at the origin and an infinite number of *absorbing* sources located at all other points of the lattice in which, in addition to walk, the particle can only disappear.

The behavior of a BRW with a single source of particle generation (*branching*) located at the origin and no absorption at other points under the assumption of a finite variance of jumps has been studied, for example, in [1], and with infinite variance in [2,3]. The random walk underlying the processes under consideration is defined using the transition intensity matrix $A = (a(x,y))_{x,y \in \mathbb{Z}^d}$ and satisfies conditions of regularity $a(x,y) \geq 0$ for $x \neq y$ and $a(x,x) < 0$, symmetry and spatial homogeneity $a(x,y) = a(y,x) = a(0, y-x) = a(y-x)$, where $\sum_z a(z) = 0$ (which allows us to consider $a(x,y)$ as a function of one argument $a(y-x)$), and irreducibility, i.e., for every $z \in \mathbb{Z}^d$ there exists a set of vectors $z_1, z_2, \ldots, z_k \in \mathbb{Z}^d$ such that $z - \sum_{i=1}^{k} z_i$ and $a(z_i) \neq 0$ for $i = 1, 2, \ldots, k$. In these models, the operator that specifies the evolution of the average number of particles has the form

$$\mathcal{H} = \mathcal{A} + \beta \Delta_0,$$

where the operator $\mathcal{A}: l^p(\mathbb{Z}^d) \to l^p(\mathbb{Z}^d)$ generated by the matrix A acts on the function $\varphi \in l^p(\mathbb{Z}^d)$ by the formula

$$(\mathcal{A}\varphi)(x) = \sum_{y \in \mathbb{Z}^d} a(x-y)\varphi(y), \qquad x \in \mathbb{Z}^d, \qquad (1)$$

Citation: Filichkina, E.; Yarovaya, E. Branching Random Walks with One Particle Generation Center and Possible Absorption at Every Point. *Mathematics* **2023**, *11*, 1676. https://doi.org/10.3390/math11071676

Academic Editors: Irina Shevtsova and Victor Korolev

Received: 11 February 2023
Revised: 24 March 2023
Accepted: 29 March 2023
Published: 31 March 2023

Copyright: © 2023 by the authors. Licensee MDPI, Basel, Switzerland. This article is an open access article distributed under the terms and conditions of the Creative Commons Attribution (CC BY) license (https://creativecommons.org/licenses/by/4.0/).

and the operator Δ_0 is defined by the equality $\Delta_0 = \delta_0\delta_0^T$, where $\delta_0 = \delta_0(\cdot)$ denotes a column-vector on the lattice taking the unit value at the point $0 \in \mathbb{Z}^d$ and vanishing at other points. The parameter β in the definition of the operator $\mathcal{H}$ is given by the equality $\beta := \sum_{n>1}(n-1)b_n - b_0$, where b_n is the intensity of occurrence of $n > 1$ descendants of the particle, including the particle itself, b_0 is the absorption intensity of the particle. Thus, the operator $\beta\Delta_0$ determines the process of particle branching at the origin.

As shown in [1], the operator $\mathcal{A}$ appears in the system of differential-difference equations (backward Kolmogorov equations) for the transition probability $p(t,x,y)$:

$$\frac{\partial p(t,x,y)}{\partial t} = \mathcal{A}p(t,x,y), \quad p(0,x,y) = \delta_y(x),$$

where $\delta_y(\cdot)$ is the Kronecker delta on $\mathbb{Z}^d$. Schur's lemma shows that the operator $\mathcal{A} : l^p(\mathbb{Z}^d) \to l^p(\mathbb{Z}^d)$, given by the Formula (1), is bounded linear operator in $l^p(\mathbb{Z}^d)$ for $1 \le p \le \infty$.

In a BRW with an infinite number of absorbing sources, the evolution operator of the average number of particles is modified as follows:

$$\mathcal{E} = \mathcal{A} + \beta^*\Delta_0 - b_0 I,$$

where I is the identity operator and the last term specifies the process of absorption of particles at every lattice point. Note that the parameter $\beta^* := \sum_{n>1}(n-1)b_n$ in the considered BRW differs from the parameter $\beta = \beta^* - b_0$ in that for $b_0 > 0$ the parameter β can take values from the interval $(-\infty, +\infty)$, while the parameter β^* is non-negative: $\beta^* \ge 0$.

Let the parameter β_c be determined by the formula $\beta_c := 1/G_0(0,0)$, where $G_\lambda(x,y)$ is the Green's function of the random walk. Many properties of the transition probabilities of a random walk $p(t,x,y)$, see details in Section 2, are expressed in terms of the Green's function, while the Green's function can be defined as the Laplace transform of the transition probability $p(t,x,y)$ by the formula:

$$G_\lambda(x,y) := \int_0^\infty e^{-\lambda t} p(t,x,y)\,dt, \quad \lambda \ge 0. \tag{2}$$

As shown, for example, in [1], when the relation $\beta^* > \beta_c$ holds, the operator $\mathcal{A} + \beta^*\Delta_0$ has an isolated positive eigenvalue λ_0, which is the solution of the equation $\beta^* G_\lambda(0,0) = 1$. The asymptotic behavior of the integer moments of the total number of particles and the number of particles at every point of the lattice in the process under consideration depends on the dimension of the lattice d, the relation between the parameters β^* and β_c, and for $\beta^* > \beta_c$ also on the relation between λ_0 and b_0.

In the case of $\beta > \beta_c$, a BRW with one source of particle generation and no absorbing sources is called *supercritical*. The operator $\mathcal{H}$ in this case has an isolated positive eigenvalue and there is an exponential growth in the number of particles at every point and in the total number of particles [1]. In the process under consideration, if the relation $\beta^* > \beta_c$ holds, the operator $\mathcal{E}$ has an isolated eigenvalue $\lambda_{\mathcal{E}} = \lambda_0 - b_0$, where $\lambda_0 > 0$ is an isolated eigenvalue of the operator $\mathcal{A} + \beta^*\Delta_0$. Note that the eigenvalue $\lambda_{\mathcal{E}}$ of the operator $\mathcal{E}$ is not always positive, so the behavior of the process differs significantly depending on the relation between the parameters λ_0 and b_0.

The structure of the paper is as follows. In Section 2, we give a formal description of a BRW with particle reproduction at the origin and absorption at every point of the lattice. Section 3 presents the key equations. Section 4 gives a complete classification of the asymptotic behavior of the first moments of particle numbers. In Section 5 the limit Theorem 7 is obtained, which states that despite the infinite number of absorbing sources, an exponential growth of both the total number of particles and the number of particles at every point can be observed in the considered BRW. This happens when $\lambda_{\mathcal{E}} > 0$, which is equivalent to $\lambda_0 > b_0$. In Section 6, we study the asymptotic behavior of the particle number moments for $\beta^* > \beta_c$ and $\lambda_{\mathcal{E}} = 0$ ($\lambda_0 = b_0$), and it is found that the integer moments of both the total number of particles and the number of particles at every point grow in a power-law manner as $t \to \infty$, with the first moments behaving as constants at infinity. In Section 7 we consider the remaining cases, that is, the case when $\beta^* > \beta_c$ and $\lambda_{\mathcal{E}} < 0$ ($\lambda_0 < b_0$), and also, when the operator $\mathcal{E}$ does not have an isolated eigenvalue, that is, when $\beta^* \leq \beta_c$. Theorems 9–11 are obtained, stating that the moments of particle numbers in these cases decrease exponentially as $t \to \infty$. It turned out that the results of Sections 5 and 6, as well as Theorem 9 of Section 7, do not depend on the conditions imposed on the variance of random walk jumps, while the behavior of the process for $\beta^* \leq \beta_c$ turns out to be different for the finite and infinite variance of jumps (Theorems 10 and 11).

We will call the considered BRW *supercritical* if $\beta^* > \beta_c$ and $\lambda_{\mathcal{E}} > 0$, *critical* if $\beta^* > \beta_c$ and $\lambda_{\mathcal{E}} = 0$ and *subcritical* if $\beta^* > \beta_c$ and $\lambda_{\mathcal{E}} < 0$ or $\beta^* \leq \beta_c$.

Note that there is no exponential decrease of moments in a BRW with a single source of particle generation (and the absence of other absorbing sources) [1]. The classification of the asymptotic behavior of the BRW with possible absorption of particles at every point $\mathbb{Z}^d$ turns out to be closer to the classification of the behavior of the Markov branching process $\mu(t)$ with continuous time, where the average number of particles $\mathsf{E}\mu(t) = e^{at}$. A branching process is called *supercritical* if $\mathsf{E}\mu(t) > 1$ ($a > 0$), *critical* if $\mathsf{E}\mu(t) = 1$ ($a = 0$) and *subcritical* if $\mathsf{E}\mu(t) < 1$ ($a < 0$), that is, the average number of particles in the supercritical branching process increases exponentially, in the critical it tends to a constant and in the subcritical it decreases exponentially [4].

The main results of the paper are Theorem 7 on the exponential growth of particle numbers in the supercritical case, as well as Theorem 8 and Theorems 9, 10, and 11 on the asymptotic behavior of the particle number moments in the critical and subcritical cases, respectively.

2. Description of the Model

Let us proceed to a formal description of the BRW with one source of particle reproduction and death located at the origin of the coordinates and an infinite number of absorbing sources located at the remaining points of the lattice $\mathbb{Z}^d$, $d \in \mathbb{N}$.

The random walk underlying the process is specified using the transition intensity matrix $A = (a(x,y))_{x,y \in \mathbb{Z}^d}$ and satisfies the conditions regularity, symmetry, spatial homogeneity (which allows us to consider $a(x,y)$ as a function of one argument $a(y-x)$), time homogeneity and irreducibility (a particle can be at any point of the lattice).

The transition probability of a random walk, that is, the probability that at time $t \geq 0$ the particle is at point y, provided that at time $t = 0$ it was at point x, is denoted by $p(t,x,y)$. Asymptotically for $h \to 0$ the transition probabilities are expressed in terms of the transition intensities as follows:

$$p(h,x,y) = a(x,y)h + o(h), \quad x \neq y,$$
$$p(h,x,x) = 1 + a(x,x)h + o(h).$$

Note that the condition for the finite variance of jumps in terms of the transition intensity matrix is written as $\sum_{z \in \mathbb{Z}^d} |z|^2 a(z) < \infty$. In situations where the finiteness of the variance of jumps turns out to be essential, we will separately consider the case when the function $a(z)$ has the following behavior at infinity:

$$a(z) \sim \frac{H(z/|z|)}{|z|^{d+\alpha}}, \quad |z| \to \infty, \tag{3}$$

where $|\cdot|$ is Euclidean norm on $\mathbb{R}^d$, $H(z/|z|) = H(-z/|z|)$ is a positive continuous function on $\mathbb{S}^{d-1} = \{z \in \mathbb{R}^d : |z| = 1\}$, $\alpha \in (0,2)$ and the symbol $\sim$ here and below will denote the asymptotic equivalence of functions. Under this assumption, the variance of jumps becomes infinite (see [5]). Random walks with an infinite variance of jumps are commonly referred to in the literature as random walks with heavy tails. We will consider the simplest case, when

$H(z/|z|) \equiv C > 0$, and use the results obtained in [2,3], where a BRW with one particle generation center and the absence of absorbing sources was considered under condition (3).

To describe the behavior of a random walk, it is convenient to use the Green's function $G_\lambda(x,y)$, which, as mentioned in the introduction, can be defined as the Laplace transform of the transition probability $p(t,x,y)$ by the Formula (2).

As in [1], we will call the random walk *recurrent* if $G_0(0,0) = \infty$ and *nonrecurrent* or *transient* if $G_0(0,0) < \infty$. In the case of a finite variance of jumps the random walk is transient for $d \geq 3$ and is recurrent for $d = 1,2$, while in the case of an infinite variance of jumps (when the condition (3) is satisfied) the transience of a random walk turns out to be possible in the dimension $d = 1$ for $\alpha \in (0,1)$ and in the dimension $d = 2$ for $\alpha \in (0,2)$.

The branching process at the particle generation center is specified using the infinitesimal generating function $f(u) = \sum_{n=0}^{\infty} b_n u^n$, $0 \leq u \leq 1$, where $b_n \geq 0$ for $n \neq 1$, $b_1 < 0$, $\sum_{n=0}^{\infty} b_n = 0$. The coefficients b_n determine the main linear part of the probability $p_*(h,n)$ of having n particles at time h provided that there was one particle at the initial time $t = 0$:

$$p_*(h,n) = b_n h + o(h) \text{ for } n \neq 1,$$
$$p_*(h,1) = 1 + b_1 h + o(h).$$

The coefficients b_n for $n \geq 1$ can be interpreted as the intensities of appearance of n descendants of the particle, including the particle itself, while b_0 is interpreted as the intensity of death, or absorption, of the particle. The generating function at other points of the lattice has a simpler form: $\overline{f}(u) = b_0 + \overline{b}_1 u = b_0(1-u)$. Further, we assume that the intensity of death is the same at all lattice points.

The evolution of particles in the system occurs as follows: a particle located at some time $t > 0$ at the point $x \in \mathbb{Z}^d$ in a short time $dt \to 0$ can either jump to the point $y \neq x, y \in \mathbb{Z}^d$, with probability $a(x,y)dt + o(dt)$, or die with probability $b_0 dt + o(dt)$. If the point x is the center of particle generation $(x = 0)$, then the particle can also produce $n > 1$ descendants, including itself, with probability $b_n dt + o(dt)$. Otherwise, with probability $1 + a(x,x)dt + \delta_0(x) b_1 dt + (1 - \delta_0(x))(-b_0 dt) + o(dt)$, the particle remains at the point x during the entire time interval $[t, t+dt]$. We assume that each new particle evolves according to the same law, independently of other particles and of the entire prehistory.

The main objects of study in BRW are the number of particles at the time $t \geq 0$ at the point $y \in \mathbb{Z}^d$ (the local number of particles), denoted by $\mu(t,y)$, the total number of particles (particle population), denoted by $\mu(t) = \sum_{y \in \mathbb{Z}^d} \mu(t,y)$, and their integer moments, which are denoted as $m_n(t,x,y) := \mathsf{E}_x \mu^n(t,y)$ and $m_n(t,x) := \mathsf{E}_x \mu^n(t)$, $n \in \mathbb{N}$, where E_x is the mean on condition $\mu(0,y) = \delta(x-y)$, $\delta(\cdot)$ is the Kronecker delta on $\mathbb{Z}^d$. We will assume that at the initial moment of time $t = 0$ the system consists of one particle located at the point $x \in \mathbb{Z}^d$, so the expectations of the local and total number of particles satisfy the initial conditions $m_1(0,x,y) = \delta_y(x)$ and $m_1(0,x) \equiv 1$, respectively.

3. Key Equations

Let us present the key equations that will be required to study the behavior of the considered BRW. The proofs of the theorems presented in this section are based on the methods developed in [1] and follow the same scheme, so the corresponding theorems will be presented below without proof.

We introduce the Laplace generating functions of the random variables $\mu(t,y)$ and $\mu(t)$ for $z \geq 0$:

$$F(z;t,x,y) := \mathsf{E}_x e^{-z\mu(t,y)}, \quad F(z;t,x) := \mathsf{E}_x e^{-z\mu(t)}.$$

Taking into account the evolution of particles in the system and using the Markov property of the process, the following statement can be proved for the generating functions.

Theorem 1. *The functions $F(z;t,x)$ and $F(z;t,x,y)$ are continuously differentiable with respect to t uniformly with respect to $x, y \in \mathbb{Z}^d$ for all $0 \le z \le \infty$. They are the solutions to the following Cauchy problems:*

$$\begin{aligned}
\partial_t F(z;t,x) &= (\mathcal{A}F(z;t,\cdot))(x) + \delta_0(x) f(F(z;t,x)) + \\
&\quad + (1-\delta_0(x)) b_0 (1 - F(z;t,x)), \\
\partial_t F(z;t,x,y) &= (\mathcal{A}F(z;t,\cdot,y))(x) + \delta_0(x) f(F(z;t,x,y)) + \\
&\quad + (1-\delta_0(x)) b_0 (1 - F(z;t,x,y))
\end{aligned}$$

with the initial conditions $F(z;0,x) = e^{-z}$ and $F(z;0,x,y) = e^{-z\delta_y(x)}$, respectively. Here, $\mathcal{A} : l^p(\mathbb{Z}^d) \to l^p(\mathbb{Z}^d)$, $1 \le p \le \infty$, is a walk operator that acts on the function $\varphi \in l^p(\mathbb{Z}^d)$ by the Formula (1).

Note that the proof of this theorem repeats the arguments from the proof of Lemma 1.2.1 in [1] and differs only in technical details.

The following theorem turns out to be true for the moments of particle numbers.

Theorem 2. *The moments $m_n(t,\cdot,y) \in l^2(\mathbb{Z}^d)$ and $m_n(t,\cdot) \in l^\infty(\mathbb{Z}^d)$ satisfy the following differential equations in the corresponding Banach spaces for all natural $n \ge 1$:*

$$\frac{dm_1}{dt} = \mathcal{E}m_1 = \mathcal{A}m_1 + \beta^* \Delta_0 m_1 - b_0 m_1, \tag{4}$$

$$\frac{dm_n}{dt} = \mathcal{E}m_n + \delta_0(\cdot) g_n(m_1, \dots, m_{n-1}), \quad n \ge 2, \tag{5}$$

with the initial conditions $m_n(0,\cdot,y) = \delta_y(\cdot)$ and $m_n(t,\cdot) \equiv 1$, respectively. Here, $\beta^* := \sum_{n>1}(n-1)b_n$, the operator $\mathcal{A} : l^p(\mathbb{Z}^d) \to l^p(\mathbb{Z}^d)$ is given by the Formula (1), the operator Δ_0 is defined by the equality $\Delta_0 = \delta_0 \delta_0^T$, where $\delta_0 = \delta_0(\cdot)$ denotes a column-vector on the lattice taking the unit value at the point $0 \in \mathbb{Z}^d$ and vanishing at other points and the function $g_n(m_1, \dots, m_{n-1})$ is given by the formula

$$g_n(m_1, \dots, m_{n-1}) := \sum_{r=2}^{n} \frac{\beta^{(r)}}{r!} \sum_{\substack{i_1,\dots,i_r > 0 \\ i_1 + \dots + i_r = n}} \frac{n!}{i_1! \cdots i_r!} m_{i_1} \cdots m_{i_r},$$

where $\beta^{(r)} := f^{(r)}(1)$.

The proof of this theorem repeats the argument of the proof of Theorem 1.3.1 from [1]. It also uses equations for generating functions, the Faà di Bruno's formula and the following property:

$$\begin{aligned}
m_n(t,x) &= (-1)^n \lim_{z \to 0+} \partial_z^n F(z;t,x), \\
m_n(t,x,y) &= (-1)^n \lim_{z \to 0+} \partial_z^n F(z;t,x,y).
\end{aligned}$$

Considering separately the case $\beta^* = 0$, this condition is equivalent to the fact that all b_n for $n > 1$ are equal to zero. That is, in this case the particle does not produce new descendants and only the death and movement of the particle along the lattice is possible. The operator describing the evolution of the average number of particles in this particular case has the form $\mathcal{E} = \mathcal{A} - b_0 I$ and the equations for the moments for all $n \in \mathbb{N}$ take the form

$$\partial_t m_n = \mathcal{A}m_n - b_0 m_n.$$

Making the change of variables $m_n = q_n e^{-b_0 t}$ in the last equation, we find that the functions q_n satisfy the equation

$$\partial_t q_n = \mathcal{A}q_n.$$

The equation for the transition probabilities of a random walk $p(t,x,y)$ has the same form, whence we find that

$$m_n(t,x,y) = e^{-b_0 t} p(t,x,y), \qquad m_n(t,x) = e^{-b_0 t},$$

for all $d, n \in \mathbb{N}$.

Further, we will assume that the parameter β^* is strictly positive (a particle in the generation source can produce at least one new particle).

Integral equations for the moments will play an important role in the further analysis, the derivation of which is carried out according to the same scheme as in (Theorem 1.4.1 [1]).

Theorem 3. *The moment $m_1(t,x,y)$ satisfies both integral equations*

$$m_1(t,x,y) = p(t,x,y) + \int_0^t (\beta^* p(t-s,x,0) - b_0 e^{\mathcal{A}(t-s)}) m_1(s,0,y)\, ds, \tag{6}$$

$$m_1(t,x,y) = p(t,x,y) + \int_0^t (\beta^* p(t-s,0,y) - b_0 e^{\mathcal{A}(t-s)}) m_1(s,x,0)\, ds. \tag{7}$$

The moment $m_1(t,x)$ satisfies both integral equations

$$\begin{aligned} m_1(t,x) &= 1 + \int_0^t (\beta^* p(t-s,x,0) - b_0 e^{\mathcal{A}(t-s)}) m_1(s,0)\, ds, \\ m_1(t,x) &= 1 + \int_0^t (\beta^* - b_0 e^{\mathcal{A}(t-s)}) m_1(s,x,0)\, ds. \end{aligned} \tag{8}$$

For $k > 1$, the moments $m_k(t,x,y)$ and $m_k(t,x)$ satisfy the equations

$$\begin{aligned} m_k(t,x,y) &= m_1(t,x,y) + \\ &\quad + \int_0^t m_1(t-s,x,0) g_k(m_1(s,0,y),\ldots,m_{k-1}(s,0,y))\, ds, \\ m_k(t,x) &= m_1(t,x) + \\ &\quad + \int_0^t m_1(t-s,x,0) g_k(m_1(s,0),\ldots,m_{k-1}(s,0))\, ds. \end{aligned} \tag{9}$$

Note that the derivation of the differential and integral equations presented in this section does not depend on the conditions imposed on the variance of random walk jumps, as noted, for example, in [2,6].

4. Classification of the Asymptotic Behavior of the First Moments

Let us first study the asymptotic behavior of the first moments. To do this, we pass from the functions $m_1(t,\cdot,y)$ and $m_1(t,\cdot)$ to the functions $q(t,\cdot,y)$ and $q(t,\cdot)$, making a change of variables $m_1 = qe^{-b_0 t}$. We obtain an equation for the functions $q(t,\cdot,y)$ and $q(t,\cdot)$ of the form

$$\frac{dq}{dt} = \mathcal{A}q + \beta^* \Delta_0 q$$

with the initial conditions $q(0,\cdot,y) = \delta_y(\cdot)$ and $q(0,\cdot) \equiv 1$, respectively.

Note that the resulting equation has exactly the same form as the equation for the first moments in the BRW without absorbing sources, considered in [1] (or in [3] for the case of heavy tails), which greatly simplifies the study. The classification of the asymptotic behavior of the first moments of the local number of particles and the total number of particles for arbitrary $d-$dimensional lattices in the considered BRW can be obtained using the classification of the asymptotic behavior for the functions $q(t,x,y)$ and $q(t,x)$, obtained in [1,3], and the relation $m_1 = qe^{-b_0 t}$.

As in [1] we denote $\beta_c := 1/G_0(0,0)$, where $G_\lambda(x,y)$ is the Green's function of the random walk. When $\beta^* > \beta_c$, the operator $\mathcal{A} + \beta^* \Delta_0$ has a single isolated positive eigenvalue λ_0, which is a solution of the equation $\beta^* G_\lambda(0,0) = 1$. However, the eigenvalue $\lambda_{\mathcal{E}}$ of the operator $\mathcal{E}$ that arises in this case is equal to $\lambda_0 - b_0$ and is not always positive, which complicates the problem. In contrast to the BRW considered in [1], the asymptotic behavior of the process considered in this paper differs significantly depending on the relation between the parameters λ_0 and b_0, namely, for $\lambda_0 > b_0$, $\lambda_0 = b_0$ and $\lambda_0 < b_0$.

So, in the case of a finite variance of jumps, we obtain the following classification of the asymptotic behavior of the first moments.

Theorem 4. *Let the variance of jumps of the random walk be finite, then for $t \to \infty$ the asymptotic behavior of the first moments can be represented as*

$$m_1(t,x,y) \sim C(x,y)u^*(t), \quad m_1(t,x) \sim C(x)v^*(t),$$

where $C(x,y), C(x)$ are some positive functions, whose explicit form was obtained in [1], and the functions $u^*(t)$ and $v^*(t)$ have the following form:

(a) *for $\beta^* > \beta_c$: $u^*(t) = e^{\lambda_{\mathcal{E}} t}$, $v^*(t) = e^{\lambda_{\mathcal{E}} t}$;*

(b) *for $\beta^* = \beta_c$:*

$$d = 3\colon u^*(t) = t^{-1/2} e^{-b_0 t},\ v^*(t) = t^{1/2} e^{-b_0 t};$$
$$d = 4\colon u^*(t) = (\ln t)^{-1} e^{-b_0 t},\ v^*(t) = t(\ln t)^{-1} e^{-b_0 t};$$
$$d \geq 5\colon u^*(t) = e^{-b_0 t},\ v^*(t) = t e^{-b_0 t};$$

(c) *for $\beta^* < \beta_c$, $d \geq 3$: $u^*(t) = t^{-d/2} e^{-b_0 t}$, $v^*(t) = e^{-b_0 t}$.*

Note that for a recurrent random walk $\beta_c = 0$, and since the parameter β^* is assumed to be positive, then assuming a finite variance of jumps for $d \leq 2$ the relation $\beta^* > \beta_c$ always holds, due to which in the above classification, in contrast to [1], there are no cases of $d = 1, 2$ for $\beta^* \leq \beta_c$.

We also note that for $\beta^* \leq \beta_c$ for all d, an exponential decrease in the first moments of both the local number and the total number of particles is observed.

Let us separately consider the result obtained for $\beta^* > \beta_c$. In this case, since $\lambda_{\mathcal{E}} = \lambda_0 - b_0$, the asymptotic behavior of the first moments depends on the relation between λ_0 and b_0: three different cases are possible. For $\lambda_0 > b_0$, an exponential growth of the first moments is observed, for $\lambda_0 = b_0$ the first moments tend to a constant and for $\lambda_0 < b_0$ an exponential decrease is observed, and these cases correspond to supercritical, critical and subcritical cases in the theory of branching processes [4].

The classification of the asymptotic behavior of the first moments in the case of heavy tails uses the classification of the behavior of the functions $q(t,x,y)$ and $q(t,x)$ obtained in [3].

Theorem 5. *Under the condition* (3), *the asymptotic behavior of the first moments for $\alpha \in (0,2)$ and $t \to \infty$ can be represented as*

$$m_1(t,x,y) \sim C(x,y)u^*(t), \quad m_1(t,x) \sim C(x)v^*(t),$$

where $C(x,y), C(x) > 0$ and the functions $u^*(t)$ and $v^*(t)$ have the following form:

(a) *for $\beta^* > \beta_c$: $u^*(t) = e^{\lambda_{\mathcal{E}} t}$, $v^*(t) = e^{\lambda_{\mathcal{E}} t}$;*

(b) *for $\beta^* = \beta_c$:*

$$u^*(t) = t^{d/\alpha - 2} e^{-b_0 t},\ v^*(t) = t^{d/\alpha - 1} e^{-b_0 t},\ \text{if } d/\alpha \in (1,2);$$
$$u^*(t) = (\ln t)^{-1} e^{-b_0 t},\ v^*(t) = t(\ln t)^{-1} e^{-b_0 t},\ \text{if } d/\alpha = 2;$$
$$u^*(t) = e^{-b_0 t},\ v^*(t) = t e^{-b_0 t},\ \text{if } d/\alpha \in (2, +\infty);$$

(c) *for $\beta^* < \beta_c$: $u^*(t) = t^{-d/\alpha} e^{-b_0 t}$, $v^*(t) = e^{-b_0 t}$, $d/\alpha \in (1, +\infty)$.*

Note that for $\beta^* > \beta_c$, the obtained asymptotic relations do not depend on the conditions imposed on the variance of random walk jumps (see [6]). In addition, $\beta^* > 0$, while $\beta_c = 0$ for $d/\alpha \in (1/2, 1]$, so in the above classification for $\beta^* \leq \beta_c$ there are no cases where $d/\alpha \in (1/2, 1]$, in contrast to the classification of the asymptotic behavior of the first moments in [3].

5. Supercritical Case

Theorem 6. *Let $\beta^* > \beta_c$ and $\lambda_{\mathcal{E}} > 0$. Then, for $t \to \infty$ and all $n \in \mathbb{N}$, the following statements hold:*

$$m_n(t,x,y) \sim C_n(x,y)e^{n\lambda_{\mathcal{E}}t}, \qquad m_n(t,x) \sim C_n(x)e^{n\lambda_{\mathcal{E}}t},$$

where

$$C_1(x,y) = \frac{G_{\lambda_0}(x,0)G_{\lambda_0}(0,y)}{\|G_{\lambda_0}(0,y)\|^2}, \qquad C_1(x) = \frac{G_{\lambda_0}(x,0)}{\lambda_0\|G_{\lambda_0}(0,0)\|^2},$$

and the functions $C_n(x,y), C_n(x) > 0$ for $n \geq 2$ are defined as follows:

$$C_n(x,y) = g_n(C_1(0,y),\dots,C_{n-1}(0,y))D_n(x),$$
$$C_n(x) = g_n(C_1(0),\dots,C_{n-1}(0))D_n(x),$$

where $D_n(x)$ are certain functions satisfying the estimate $|D_n(x)| \leq \frac{2}{n\lambda_{\mathcal{E}}}$ for $n \geq n_*$ and some $n_* \in \mathbb{N}$.

Proof. In the case under consideration, the operator $\mathcal{E}$ has an isolated positive eigenvalue $\lambda_{\mathcal{E}} = \lambda_0 - b_0$, where λ_0 is an isolated positive eigenvalue of the operator $\mathcal{H} = \mathcal{A} + \beta^*\Delta_0$.

For $n \in \mathbb{N}$, we consider the functions $\nu_n := \nu_n(t,x,y) = m_n(t,x,y)e^{-n\lambda_{\mathcal{E}}t}$. From Theorem 2, we obtain the following equations for ν_n:

$$\begin{cases} \partial_t\nu_1 &= \mathcal{E}\nu_1 - \lambda_{\mathcal{E}}\nu_1, \\ \partial_t\nu_n &= \mathcal{E}\nu_n - n\lambda_{\mathcal{E}}\nu_n + \delta_0(x)g_n(\nu_1,\dots,\nu_{n-1}), \quad n \geq 2 \end{cases}$$

with the initial conditions $\nu_n(0,\cdot,y) = \delta_y(\cdot)$, $n \in \mathbb{N}$.

We define the operator $\mathcal{E}_n$ by setting $\mathcal{E}_n := \mathcal{E} - n\lambda_{\mathcal{E}}I$. Since $\lambda_{\mathcal{E}}$ is the largest eigenvalue of $\mathcal{E}$, the spectrum of $\mathcal{E}_n$ for $n \geq 2$ is included into $(-\infty, -(n-1)\lambda_{\mathcal{E}}]$, that is, it is on the negative semiaxis, since $\lambda_{\mathcal{E}} > 0$.

Further, arguments similar to those given in [6] in the proof of a similar theorem remain valid.

The value of n_* from the statement of the theorem is determined by the formula $n_* := \frac{2\|\mathcal{E}\|}{\lambda_{\mathcal{E}}}$. The theorem is proved. □

For the number of particles in the case under consideration, the following limit theorem is true, the proof of which is carried out according to the scheme of proof of the limit theorem obtained in [6], so we present only the main parts of the proof.

Theorem 7. *Let $\beta^* > \beta_c$ and $\lambda_{\mathcal{E}} > 0$. If $\beta^{(r)} = O(r!r^{r-1})$ for all sufficiently large $r \in \mathbb{N}$, then the following statements hold in the sense of convergence in distribution*

$$\lim_{t\to\infty} \mu(t,y)e^{-\lambda_{\mathcal{E}}t} = \xi\psi(y), \qquad \lim_{t\to\infty} \mu(t)e^{-\lambda_{\mathcal{E}}t} = \xi,$$

where $\psi(y)$ is some non-negative function and ξ is a non-degenerate random variable.

Proof. Let us define the functions

$$m(n,x,y) := \lim_{t\to\infty} \frac{\mathsf{E}_x\mu^n(t,y)}{m_1^n(t,x,y)} = \lim_{t\to\infty} \frac{m_n(t,x,y)}{m_1^n(t,x,y)} = \frac{C_n(x,y)}{C_1^n(x,y)},$$
$$m(n,x) := \lim_{t\to\infty} \frac{\mathsf{E}_x\mu^n(t)}{m_1^n(t,x)} = \lim_{t\to\infty} \frac{m_n(t,x)}{m_1^n(t,x)} = \frac{C_n(x)}{C_1^n(x)}.$$

As shown, for example, in [6], the functions $C_n(x,y)$ and $C_n(x)$ for $\beta^* > \beta_c$ for all $n \in \mathbb{N}$ are related by the relation $C_n(x,y) = \psi^n(y)C_n(x)$, where $\psi(y)$ is some function, from which the next equalities follow:

$$m(n,x,y) = m(n,x) = \frac{C_n(x)}{C_1^n(x)} = \frac{C_n(x,y)}{C_1^n(x,y)}.$$

From Theorem 6, we have this theorem statements in terms of convergence of the moments of the random variables $\xi(y) = \psi(y)\xi$ and ξ.

The distributions of the limit random variables $\xi(y)$ and ξ are to be uniquely determined by their moments if the Carleman condition is satisfied.

$$\sum_{n=1}^{\infty} m(n,x,y)^{-1/(2n)} = \infty, \quad \sum_{n=1}^{\infty} m(n,x)^{-1/(2n)} = \infty.$$

Assuming $N = 1$ in the notation from [6] and defining n_* as in Theorem 6, we obtain $C_n(x) \leq \gamma^{n-1}n!n^n$, where γ is some constant, from here and from the estimate $n! \leq ((n+1)/2)^n$ we obtain

$$\sum_{n=1}^{\infty} m(n,x)^{-1/(2n)} = \sum_{n=1}^{\infty} \left(\frac{C_n(x)}{C_1^n(x)}\right)^{-1/(2n)} = \infty.$$

The proof for $m(n,x,y)$ is similar.

Thus, the Stieltjes moment problem has a unique solution, hence the relations from the formulation of the theorem are valid in terms of convergence in distribution. The theorem is proved. □

Note that the obtained limit theorem is true without restrictions on the variance of random walk jumps, see [6].

6. Moments in a Critical Case

Theorem 8. *Let $\beta^* > \beta_c$ and $\lambda_{\mathcal{E}} = 0$. Then, for $t \to \infty$ and all $n \in \mathbb{N}$ the following statements hold*

$$m_n(t,x,y) \sim J_n(x,y)t^{n-1}, \qquad m_n(t,x) \sim J_n(x)t^{n-1},$$

where $J_n(x,y)$ and $J_n(x)$ are some constants.

Proof. The proof will be carried out for $m_n(t,x,y)$ using the asymptotic relation for the first moment and the equations for the higher moments. The limit relations for $m_n(t,x)$ follow from the form of the integral Equation (3) and the asymptotics for $m_n(t,x,y)$.

In the case $\beta^* > \beta_c$, the operator $\mathcal{E}$ has a unique isolated eigenvalue $\lambda_{\mathcal{E}} = \lambda_0 - b_0$, which is zero in this case, consider its corresponding eigenfunction $f(x) \in l^2(\mathbb{Z}^d)$.

Consider first the second moment $m_2(t,x,y)$, which satisfies the equation

$$\partial_t m_2(t,x,y) = \mathcal{E}m_2(t,x,y) + \delta_0(x)g_2(m_1(t,x,y)).$$

Multiplying this equation scalarly by f, we obtain

$$\partial_t\langle f, m_2(t,x,y)\rangle = f(0)g_2(m_1(t,0,y)).$$

Denote $h(t,y) := \langle f, m_2(t,x,y)\rangle$, then the function $h(t,y)$ satisfies the equation

$$\partial_t h(t,y) = f(0)g_2(m_1(t,0,y))$$

with the initial condition

$$h(0,y) = \langle f, m_2(0,x,y)\rangle = \langle f, \delta_0(x-y)\rangle = f(y),$$

whose solution has the form

$$h(t,y) = f(y) + \int_0^t f(0)g_2(m_1(\tau,0,y))\,d\tau.$$

Since for $m_1(t,0,y)$ we have $m_1(t,0,y) \sim C(0,y)$ as $t \to \infty$, then for $h(t,y)$ as $t \to \infty$ the following limit relation holds:

$$h(t,y) \sim tf(0)g_2(C(0,y)).$$

Denote by E_f the eigensubspace of the operator $\mathcal{E}$ corresponding to the eigenvalue $\lambda_{\mathcal{E}}$, i.e., $E_f := \{tf : t \in \mathbb{R}\}$. Via $E_f^{\perp}$, we will further denote the orthogonal complement to the subspace E_f. Then, $l^2(\mathbb{Z}^d) = E_f \oplus E_f^{\perp}$, that is, for any $v \in l^2(\mathbb{Z}^d)$ there are unique $\alpha \in \mathbb{C}$ and $v_1 \in E_f^{\perp}$ such that $v = \alpha f + v_1$. Since f is an eigenfunction of the self-adjoint operator $\mathcal{E}$, then $E_f^{\perp}$ is an eigensubspace of the operator $\mathcal{E}$, that is, $\mathcal{E}E_f^{\perp} \subseteq E_f^{\perp}$.

Since $\lambda_{\mathcal{E}} = 0$ is a simple eigenvalue corresponding to the eigenfunction f, it is not a point of the spectrum of the operator $\mathcal{E}$ restricted to $E_f^{\perp}$, so the spectrum of this operator lies on the negative semiaxis and is separated from zero. Let us use the property, which was noted, for example, in [1]: if the spectrum of a self-adjoint continuous operator $\mathcal{H}$ on a Hilbert space is included into $(-\infty, -s]$, $s > 0$, and also $f(t) \to f_*$ as $t \to \infty$, then the solution of the equation

$$\frac{dv}{dt} = \mathcal{H}v + f(t)$$

satisfies $v(t) \to -\mathcal{H}^{-1}f_*$ condition.

Since $m_2(t,x,y)$ satisfies the equation

$$\partial_t m_2(t,x,y) = \mathcal{E}m_2(t,x,y) + \delta_0(x)g_2(m_1(t,x,y))$$

and for $t \to \infty$ we have the relation

$$\delta_0(x)g_2(m_1(t,x,y)) \sim \delta_0(x)g_2(C(x,y)),$$

we obtain the limit relation that holds on $E_f^{\perp}$:

$$m_2(t,x,y)) \sim -\mathcal{E}^{-1}(\delta_0(x)g_2(C(x,y))) =: v_1^*(x,y).$$

We have $m_2(t,x,y) = \alpha f + v_1$, where $\alpha = \frac{\langle f, m_2(t,x,y)\rangle}{\langle f,f\rangle} = \frac{h(t,y)}{\langle f,f\rangle}$ and $v_1 \sim v_1^*$. For $t \to \infty$ we obtain the relation

$$m_2(t,x,y) \sim \frac{tf(x)f(0)g_2(C(0,y))}{\langle f,f\rangle}.$$

Denoting $J_2(x,y) := \frac{f(x)f(0)g_2(C(0,y))}{\langle f,f\rangle}$, we find that $m_2(t,x,y) \sim J_2(x,y)t$.

Further, we continue similarly, using the asymptotics for the moments obtained at the previous step. On the subspace E_f, carrying out similar reasoning for $m_n(t,x,y)$, we obtain the asymptotics

$$m_n(t,x,y) \sim J_n^{(1)}t^{n-1},$$

where $J_n^{(1)}$ is some constant. On the subspace $E_f^{\perp}$ we use the following property: if the spectrum of a self-adjoint continuous operator $\mathcal{H}$ on a Hilbert space is included into $(-\infty, -s]$, $s > 0$, and $f(t) = P_n(t)$, where $P_n(t)$ is a polynomial of degree n, then the solution of the equation

$$\frac{dv}{dt} = \mathcal{H}v + f(t)$$

satisfies $v(t) = Q_n(t) + u(t)$ condition, where $Q_n(t)$ is a polynomial of degree n and $u(t)$ is a function that decreases exponentially in t. We find that on the subspace $E_f^{\perp}$ the asymptotics $m_n(t,x,y) \sim J_n^{(2)} t^{n-2}$ is true, where $J_n^{(2)}$ is some constant. So, for $m_n(t,x,y)$ we have

$$m_n(t,x,y) \sim J_n(x,y)t^{n-1}$$

as $t \to \infty$. The theorem is proved. □

7. Moments in a Subcritical Case

To study the asymptotic behavior of the particle number moments for $\lambda_{\mathcal{E}} < 0$, we need an auxiliary lemma.

Lemma 1. *If the spectrum of a self-adjoint continuous operator $\mathcal{H}$ on a Hilbert space is included into $(-\infty, -\sigma]$, $\sigma > 0$, and $f(t)$ is a function such that $\|f(t)\| < Ce^{-\alpha t}$, where $C, \alpha > 0$ are some constants, then the solution of the equation*

$$\frac{dv}{dt} = \mathcal{H}v + f(t)$$

satisfies $\|v\| \leq \widetilde{C}_1 e^{-\min(\alpha,\sigma)t}$ for $\alpha \neq \sigma$ and $\|v\| \leq \widetilde{C}_2 t e^{-\sigma t}$ otherwise, where $\widetilde{C}_1, \widetilde{C}_2$ are some constants.

Proof. The solution of the considered equation with the given initial condition $v(0) = v_0$ can be represented explicitly:

$$v(t) = e^{\mathcal{H}t}v_0 + \int_0^t e^{\mathcal{H}(t-s)} f(s)\, ds. \tag{10}$$

Let us estimate the norm of each of the terms. To estimate the norm of the first term, we recall some properties of the spectrum of a self-adjoint continuous operator on a Hilbert space, denoting the operator's spectrum as $\mathrm{spec}(\cdot)$.

1. Theorem 7.2.6 in [7]: for any self-adjoint operator $\mathcal{H}$ on a Hilbert space, the following equality holds

   $$\|\mathcal{H}\| = \sup\{|\lambda| : \lambda \text{ is the point of the spectrum } \mathcal{H}\}.$$

2. Corollary 7.8.10 in [7]: let $\mathcal{H}$ be a self-adjoint operator and f be a continuous complex function on $\mathrm{spec}(\mathcal{H})$. Then,

   $$\mathrm{spec}(f(\mathcal{H})) = f(\mathrm{spec}(\mathcal{H})).$$

   In particular, $\mathrm{spec}(e^{\mathcal{H}t}) = e^{\mathrm{spec}(\mathcal{H})t}$.

   Using these properties, we find that the first term in (10) satisfies the estimate $\|e^{\mathcal{H}t}v_0\| \leq \|e^{\mathcal{H}t}\|\|v_0\| = e^{-\sigma t}\|v_0\|$. Additionally, for the second term for $\alpha \neq \sigma$, we have:

$$\begin{aligned}
\left\| \int_0^t e^{\mathcal{H}(t-s)} f(s)\, ds \right\| &\leq \int_0^t \left\| e^{\mathcal{H}(t-s)} \right\| \|f(s)\|\, ds \leq \int_0^t e^{-\sigma(t-s)} C e^{-\alpha s}\, ds = \\
&= Ce^{-\sigma t} \int_0^t e^{(\sigma-\alpha)s}\, ds = \frac{Ce^{-\sigma t}}{\sigma - \alpha} e^{(\sigma-\alpha)s}\Big|_0^t = \\
&= \frac{Ce^{-\sigma t}}{-(\sigma-\alpha)}\left(1 - e^{(\sigma-\alpha)t}\right) = \frac{C}{-(\sigma-\alpha)}\left(e^{-\sigma t} - e^{-\alpha t}\right) \leq \\
&\leq \widehat{C} e^{-\min(\alpha,\sigma)t}.
\end{aligned}$$

In the case $\alpha > \sigma$, we set $\widetilde{C}_1 = \|v_0\| + \widehat{C}$ and in the case $\alpha < \sigma$: $\widetilde{C}_1 = \widehat{C}$. It remains to note that for $\alpha = \sigma$ the following equality holds

$$Ce^{-\sigma t} \int_0^t e^{(\sigma-\alpha)s}\, ds = Cte^{-\sigma t},$$

so we can put $\widetilde{C}_2 = \|v_0\| + C$, which completes the proof of Lemma 1. □

Theorem 9. *Let $\beta^* > \beta_c$ and $\lambda_{\mathcal{E}} < 0$. Then, for $t \to \infty$ and all $n \in \mathbb{N}$ the following statements hold:*

$$m_n(t,x,y) \sim D_n(x,y)e^{\lambda_{\mathcal{E}} t}, \qquad m_n(t,x) \sim D_n(x)e^{\lambda_{\mathcal{E}} t},$$

where $D_n(x,y)$ and $D_n(x)$ are some constants.

Proof. The proof will be carried out for $m_n(t,x,y)$. The limit relations for $m_n(t,x)$ follow from the form of the integral Equation (3) and the asymptotics for $m_n(t,x,y)$.

As in the proof of Theorem 8, we consider the eigenfunction $f(x) \in l^2(\mathbb{Z}^d)$ with the eigenvalue $\lambda_{\mathcal{E}}$ of the operator $\mathcal{E}$ and denote by $E_f^{\perp}$ the subspace in $l^2(\mathbb{Z}^d)$, which is orthogonal to the element f (see the corresponding definition in the proof of Theorem 8).

Multiplying the equation for $m_2(t,x,y)$ scalarly by f, we obtain

$$\partial_t \langle f, m_2(t,x,y)\rangle = \lambda_{\mathcal{E}} \langle f, m_2(t,x,y)\rangle + f(0)g_2(m_1(t,0,y)).$$

Let $h(t,y) := \langle f, m_2(t,x,y)\rangle$. This function satisfies the equation

$$\partial_t h(t,y) = \lambda_{\mathcal{E}} h(t,y) + f(0)g_2(m_1(t,0,y))$$

with the initial condition $h(0,y) = \langle f, m_2(0,x,y)\rangle = \langle f, \delta_0(x-y)\rangle = f(y)$, whose solution has the form

$$h(t,y) = e^{\lambda_{\mathcal{E}} t} f(y) + \int_0^t e^{\lambda_{\mathcal{E}}(t-s)} f(0) g_2(m_1(s,0,y))\, ds.$$

Since the relation $m_1(t,0,y) \sim C(0,y)e^{\lambda_{\mathcal{E}} t}$ holds for $m_1(t,0,y)$, and this and the explicit form of the function $g_2(m_1)$ imply the relation $g_2(m_1(t,0,y)) \sim \widetilde{K}e^{2\lambda_{\mathcal{E}} t}$, where $\widetilde{K}$ is some constant, then $h(t,y)$ satisfies the limit relation

$$h(t,y) \sim K_1(y)e^{\lambda_{\mathcal{E}} t} + K_2 e^{2\lambda_{\mathcal{E}} t},$$

where $K_1(y), K_2$ are constant.

Consider now the subspace $E_f^{\perp}$. The function $m_2(t,x,y)$ satisfies the equation

$$\partial_t m_2(t,x,y) = \mathcal{E} m_2(t,x,y) + \delta_0(x) g_2(m_1(t,x,y))$$

and the spectrum of the operator $\mathcal{E}$ restricted to $E_f^{\perp}$ is included into $(-\infty, -\sigma]$, $\sigma > 0$. Using Lemma 1, we find that on the subspace $E_f^{\perp}$ for $-2\lambda_{\mathcal{E}} \neq \sigma$ the following estimate holds

$$\|m_2(t,x,y)\| \leq \widetilde{C}_1 e^{-\min(-2\lambda_{\mathcal{E}},\sigma)t}$$

and $\|m_2(t,x,y)\| \leq \widetilde{C}_2 t e^{2\lambda_{\mathcal{E}} t}$ otherwise, with some constants $\widetilde{C}_1, \widetilde{C}_2$.

As in the proof of Theorem 8, taking into account the representation $l^2(\mathbb{Z}^d) = E_f \oplus E_f^{\perp}$, we find for $m_2(t,x,y)$ as $t \to \infty$ the relation

$$m_2(t,x,y) \sim D_2(x,y)e^{\lambda_{\mathcal{E}} t}.$$

It remains to be noted that for all $n \geq 2$ and $t \to \infty$ the relation $g_n(m_1, \ldots, m_{n-1}) \sim \widetilde{K}_n e^{2\lambda_{\mathcal{E}} t}$ holds, where $\widetilde{K}_n$ is some constant. This follows from the explicit form of the function $g_n(m_1, \ldots, m_{n-1})$. Additionally, the above reasoning remains true for $m_n(t,x,y)$ for all $n \in \mathbb{N}$.

So, for $m_n(t,x,y)$ for all $n \in \mathbb{N}$ and for $t \to \infty$, we have

$$m_n(t,x,y) \sim D_n(x,y)e^{\lambda_{\mathcal{E}} t}.$$

The theorem is proved. □

Note that in proving Theorems 8 and 9 in addition to the asymptotic behavior of the first moments, which for $\beta^* > \beta_c$ does not depend on the variance of jumps of the random walk, we also use differential equations for higher moments, which, as noted above, also do not depend on the conditions imposed on the variance of jumps. Consequently, all the results obtained for the case $\beta^* > \beta_c$ do not depend on the variance of jumps of the random walk.

To study the asymptotic behavior of the particle number moments in the case $\beta^* \leq \beta_c$, when there is no isolated eigenvalue $\lambda_{\mathcal{E}}$, we need the following auxiliary lemma.

Lemma 2. *Let continuous functions $\varphi(t), \chi(t) \geq 0$, $t \geq 0$, satisfy the following asymptotic relations as $t \to \infty$*

$$\varphi(t) \sim \varphi_0 t^{\alpha} (\ln t)^{\beta} e^{-b_0 t}, \qquad \chi(t) \sim \chi_0 t^{2\alpha} (\ln t)^{2\beta} e^{-2b_0 t},$$

where $\alpha, \beta \in \mathbb{R}$, $b_0 \in \mathbb{R}_+$ and let $W(t) := \int_0^t \varphi(t-s)\chi(s)\,ds$. Then, for $W(t)$ the following asymptotic relation holds as $t \to \infty$

$$W(t) \sim W_0 t^{\alpha} (\ln t)^{\beta} e^{-b_0 t}.$$

Proof. It follows from the form of the asymptotics for the functions $\varphi(t)$ and $\chi(t)$, that for any $\varepsilon > 0$ there exists $\delta > 0$ such that the following relations hold for $t \geq \delta$

$$(1-\varepsilon) t^{\alpha} (\ln t)^{\beta} e^{-b_0 t} \leq \varphi(t) \leq (1+\varepsilon) t^{\alpha} (\ln t)^{\beta} e^{-b_0 t},$$
$$(1-\varepsilon) t^{2\alpha} (\ln t)^{2\beta} e^{-2b_0 t} \leq \chi(t) \leq (1+\varepsilon) t^{2\alpha} (\ln t)^{2\beta} e^{-2b_0 t}.$$

We choose $t \geq 2\delta$ and represent the function $W(t)$ as a sum

$$W(t) = W_{1,\delta}(t) + W_{2,\delta}(t),$$

where

$$W_{1,\delta}(t) = \int_0^{t-\delta} \varphi(t-s)\chi(s)\,ds, \qquad W_{2,\delta}(t) = \int_{t-\delta}^{t} \varphi(t-s)\chi(s)\,ds.$$

To estimate $W_{1,\delta}(t)$, note that for $0 \leq s \leq t-\delta$ the inequality $t-s \geq \delta$ holds. Hence, we find that

$$\int_0^{t-\delta} (1-\varepsilon)(t-s)^{\alpha} (\ln(t-s))^{\beta} e^{-b_0(t-s)} \chi(s)\,ds \leq W_{1,\delta}(t) \leq$$
$$\leq \int_0^{t-\delta} (1+\varepsilon)(t-s)^{\alpha} (\ln(t-s))^{\beta} e^{-b_0(t-s)} \chi(s)\,ds.$$

Note that

$$\int_0^{t-\delta} (t-s)^{\alpha} (\ln(t-s))^{\beta} e^{-b_0(t-s)} \chi(s)\,ds =$$
$$= e^{-b_0 t} t^{\alpha} (\ln t)^{\beta} \int_0^{t-\delta} (1-s/t)^{\alpha} \left(\frac{\ln t + \ln(1-s/t)}{\ln t} \right)^{\beta} e^{b_0 s} \chi(s)\,ds,$$

in this case the functions $(1-s/t)^{\alpha}$ and $\left(\frac{\ln t + \ln(1-s/t)}{\ln t}\right)^{\beta}$ tend monotonically to 1 as $t \to \infty$ and $e^{b_0 s}\chi(s) \sim \chi_0 s^{2\alpha} (\ln s)^{2\beta} e^{-b_0 s}$ as $s \to \infty$, i.e., $e^{b_0 s}\chi(s) \in L[0, +\infty)$.

So, we obtain

$$\int_0^{t-\delta} (t-s)^{\alpha} (\ln(t-s))^{\beta} e^{-b_0(t-s)} \chi(s)\,ds = e^{-b_0 t} t^{\alpha} (\ln t)^{\beta} \left(\int_0^{+\infty} e^{b_0 s} \chi(s)\,ds + o(1) \right).$$

Consider now $W_{2,\delta}(t)$. Since $t \geq 2\delta$, we have

$$\begin{aligned} W_{2,\delta}(t) &= \int_{t-\delta}^{t} \varphi(t-s)\chi(s)\,ds \leq \\ &\leq (1+\varepsilon)(t-\delta)^{2\alpha}(\ln(t-\delta))^{2\beta}e^{-2b_0(t-\delta)} \int_0^{\delta} \varphi(s)\,ds = \\ &= e^{-b_0 t} t^{\alpha}(\ln t)^{\beta} o(1). \end{aligned}$$

Finally, denoting $W_0 := \int_0^{+\infty} e^{b_0 s}\chi(s)\,ds$, we obtain the required asymptotic relation and Lemma 2 is proved. □

Theorem 10. *Let the variance of jumps of the random walk be finite, then for $t \to \infty$ and all $n \in \mathbb{N}$, the following statements hold:*

(a) *for $\beta^* = \beta_c$:*

$d = 3$: $m_n(t,x,y) \sim A_n(x,y)t^{-1/2}e^{-b_0 t}$, $m_n(t,x) \sim A_n(x)t^{1/2}e^{-b_0 t}$,
$d = 4$: $m_n(t,x,y) \sim B_n(x,y)(\ln t)^{-1}e^{-b_0 t}$, $m_n(t,x) \sim B_n(x)t(\ln t)^{-1}e^{-b_0 t}$,
$d \geq 5$: $m_n(t,x,y) \sim C_n(x,y)e^{-b_0 t}$, $m_n(t,x) \sim C_n(x)te^{-b_0 t}$,

(b) *for $\beta^* < \beta_c$:*

$d \geq 3$: $m_n(t,x,y) \sim D_n(x,y)t^{-d/2}e^{-b_0 t}$, $m_n(t,x) \sim D_n(x)e^{-b_0 t}$,

where $A_n(x,y)$, $A_n(x)$, $B_n(x,y)$, $B_n(x)$, $C_n(x,y)$, $C_n(x)$, $D_n(x,y)$ and $D_n(x)$ are some constants.

Proof. The limit relations for the first moments are obtained in Theorem 4. The second moments are expressed in terms of the first moments and their convolutions with the functions $g_2(m_1(t,0,y))$ and $g_2(m_1(t,0))$ using Theorem 3. Note that the asymptotic relations for the first moments for all d in the case $\beta^* \leq \beta_c$ have the form $m_1 \sim \widetilde{C}_1 t^{\alpha}(\ln t)^{\beta}e^{-b_0 t}$ and for the functions $g_2(m_1)$ the following asymptotic relations hold: $g_2(m_1) \sim \widetilde{G}_2 t^{2\alpha}(\ln t)^{2\beta}e^{-2b_0 t}$, where $\widetilde{G}_2$ is some constant and α and β are the same, as in the asymptotics of the corresponding first moment m_1. Using Lemma 2 for the functions m_1 and g_2, we find that

$$\int_0^t m_1(t-s)g_2(m_1(s))\,ds \sim W_0 t^{\alpha}(\ln t)^{\beta}e^{-b_0 t}.$$

Finally, we find that for the second moments the relation $m_2 \sim \widetilde{C}_2 t^{\alpha}(\ln t)^{\beta}e^{-b_0 t}$ holds, i.e., the second moments behave at infinity in the same way as the corresponding first moments, up to a constant.

To complete the proof, we note that for all $n \geq 2$ the following relation will hold $g_n(m_1, \ldots, m_{n-1}) \sim \widetilde{G}_n t^{2\alpha}(\ln t)^{2\beta}e^{-2b_0 t}$, where $\widetilde{G}_n$ is some constant. This means that for all $n \in \mathbb{N}$ and $t \to \infty$ the following limit relations will hold: $m_n \sim \widetilde{C}_n t^{\alpha}(\ln t)^{\beta}e^{-b_0 t}$. The theorem is proved. □

When the condition (3) is satisfied, which leads to an infinite variance of jumps, the following theorem turns out to be true.

Theorem 11. *Under the condition (3) for $t \to \infty$ and all $n \in \mathbb{N}$, the following statements hold:*

(a) *for $\beta^* = \beta_c$:*

$$m_n(t,x,y) \sim B_{n,d/\alpha}(x,y)u^*(t), \quad m_n(t,x) \sim B_{n,d/\alpha}(x)v^*(t),$$

where $B_{n,d/\alpha}(x,y)$, $B_{n,d/\alpha}(x) > 0$ and

$u^*(t) = t^{d/\alpha-2}e^{-b_0 t}$, $v^*(t) = t^{d/\alpha-1}e^{-b_0 t}$, *if $d/\alpha \in (1,2)$;*
$u^*(t) = (\ln t)^{-1}e^{-b_0 t}$, $v^*(t) = t(\ln t)^{-1}e^{-b_0 t}$, *if $d/\alpha = 2$;*
$u^*(t) = e^{-b_0 t}$, $v^*(t) = te^{-b_0 t}$, *if $d/\alpha \in (2,+\infty)$;*

(b) *for* $\beta^* < \beta_c$:

$$m_n(t,x,y) \sim A_n(x,y)u^*(t), \quad m_n(t,x) \sim A_n(x)v^*(t),$$

where $A_n(x,y)$, $A_n(x) > 0$, $u^*(t) = t^{-d/\alpha}e^{-b_0 t}$, $v^*(t) = e^{-b_0 t}$.

Proof. Asymptotic relations for the first moments in the case of the condition (3) are obtained in Theorem 5. Note that for all possible values of the parameter d/α for $\beta^* \le \beta_c$ these relations have the form

$$m_1 \sim Ct^{\alpha}(\ln t)^{\beta}e^{-b_0 t},$$

where α and β are some known constants.

Furthermore, carrying out the arguments from the proof of the Theorem 10 without changes, we find that all integer moments in the case under consideration behave at infinity in the same way as the corresponding first moments, up to a constant. The theorem is proved. □

8. Conclusions

We study a model of a BRW, apparently not previously considered, with one branching source and possible absorption at every point of the lattice. The possibility of particle absorption at every point makes the model more realistic for some applications compared to the process considered in [1–3], where there is one branching source and at other points only particle movement is possible.

One of the main results is Theorem 7, which states that, despite the possible absorption at every point, an exponential growth of both the total number of particles and the number of particles at a lattice point can be observed. Also in the process under consideration, an exponential decrease in the moments of the particle numbers can be observed, which distinguishes it from the previously considered BRWs. The resulting classification of the behavior of the moments of particle numbers turned out to be close to the classification of the behavior of a Markov branching process with continuous time [4].

As is well-known, an irregular growth of moments characterizes such a phenomenon as the intermittency of the field of particles intensively studied in different areas of physics [8], in particular in hydrodynamics [9]. We established that in the supercritical case for our model, the intermittency of the particle field is not observed, see Theorem 7. However, the proposed model can be developed for further study of BRW models with the so-called random potential, which find numerous applications in statistical physics. As a rule, such a phenomenon occurs in BRW models under assumption that the intensities of particle birth and death are random, i.e., the operator $\mathcal{A}$ is perturbed by a random potential.

In conclusion, we note that in addition to the method of moments, a martingale approach can be used to prove the limit theorems on the behavior of particle numbers at lattice points for some BRW models, which allows us to establish the convergence of the limiting process in the mean square [10].

Author Contributions: Conceptualization, E.Y.; formal analysis, E.F.; funding acquisition, E.Y.; investigation, E.F. and E.Y.; methodology, E.Y.; visualization, E.F.; writing—original draft, E.F.; writing, review and editing, E.Y. All authors have read and agreed to the published version of the manuscript.

Funding: This research was funded by the Russian Foundation for the Basic Research (RFBR), grant number 20-01-00487.

Acknowledgments: The authors thank the anonymous reviewers for numerous valuable comments which, we hope, have substantially improved the presentation.

Conflicts of Interest: The authors declare no conflict of interest.

References

1. Yarovaya, E.B. *Branching Random Walks in a Heterogeneous Environment*; Center of Applied Investigations of the Faculty of Mechanics and Mathematics of the Moscow State University: Moscow, Russia, 2007. (In Russian)
2. Rytova, A.; Yarovaya, E. Heavy-tailed branching random walks on multidimensional lattices. A moment approach. *Proc. R. Soc. Edinb. Sect. A Math.* **2021**, *151*, 971–992. [CrossRef]
3. Rytova, A.I.; Yarovaya, E.B. Moments of particle numbers in a branching random walk with heavy tails. *Russ. Math. Surv.* **2019**, *74*, 1126–1128. [CrossRef]
4. Sevast'yanov, B.A. *Vetvyashchiesya Protsessy*; Izdat. "Nauka": Moscow, Russia, 1971; p. 436. (In Russian)
5. Yarovaya, E. Branching random walks with heavy tails. *Comm. Statist. Theory Methods* **2013**, *42*, 3001–3010. [CrossRef]
6. Khristolyubov, I.I.; Yarovaya, E.B. A Limit Theorem for Supercritical Random Branching Walks with Branching Sources of Varying Intensity. *Theory Probab. Appl.* **2019**, *64*, 365–384. [CrossRef]
7. Bogachev, V.I.; Smolyanov, O.G. *Dejstvitel'nyj i Funkcional'nyj Analiz: Universitetskij Kurs*; NIC Regulyarnaya i Haoticheskaya Dinamika: Moscow, Russia, 2009; p. 729. (In Russian)
8. Boldrighini, C.; Molchanov, S.; Pellegrinotti, A. Anderson Parabolic Model for a Quasi-Stationary Medium. *J. Stat. Phys.* **2007**, *129*, 151–169. [CrossRef]
9. Gärtner, J.; Molchanov, S.A. Parabolic problems for the Anderson model. Intermittency and related topics. *Comm. Math. Phys.* **1990**, 132, 613–655. [CrossRef]
10. Smorodina, N.V.; Yarovaya, E.B. Martingale method for investigation of branching random walks. *Uspekhi Mat. Nauk* **2022**, *77*, 193–194. [CrossRef]

mathematics

Article

Limit Distributions for the Estimates of the Digamma Distribution Parameters Constructed from a Random Size Sample

Alexey Kudryavtsev [1,2,*] and Oleg Shestakov [1,2,3,*]

1 Faculty of Computational Mathematics and Cybernetics, M. V. Lomonosov Moscow State University, Moscow 119991, Russia
2 Moscow Center for Fundamental and Applied Mathematics, Moscow 119991, Russia
3 Federal Research Center "Computer Science and Control" of the Russian Academy of Sciences, Moscow 119333, Russia
* Correspondence: aakudryavtsev@cs.msu.ru (A.K.); oshestakov@cs.msu.ru (O.S.)

Abstract: In this paper, we study a new type of distribution that generalizes distributions from the gamma and beta classes that are widely used in applications. The estimators for the parameters of the digamma distribution obtained by the method of logarithmic cumulants are considered. Based on the previously proved asymptotic normality of the estimators for the characteristic index and the shape and scale parameters of the digamma distribution constructed from a fixed-size sample, we obtain a statement about the convergence of these estimators to the scale mixtures of the normal law in the case of a random sample size. Using this result, asymptotic confidence intervals for the estimated parameters are constructed. A number of examples of the limit laws for sample sizes with special forms of negative binomial distributions are given. The results of this paper can be widely used in the study of probabilistic models based on continuous distributions with an unbounded non-negative support.

Keywords: parameter estimation; digamma distribution; mixed distributions; generalized gamma distribution; generalized beta distribution; method of moments; cumulants; transfer theorem

MSC: 62F12

Citation: Kudryavtsev, A.; Shestakov, O. Limit Distributions for the Estimates of the Digamma Distribution Parameters Constructed from a Random Size Sample. *Mathematics* **2023**, *11*, 1778. https://doi.org/10.3390/math11081778

Academic Editor: Christophe Chesneau

Received: 9 March 2023
Revised: 31 March 2023
Accepted: 6 April 2023
Published: 7 April 2023

1. Introduction

Distributions belonging to beta and gamma classes play an essential role in probability theory and mathematical statistics. Such distributions have proven themselves as convenient and efficient tools in modeling a large number of real processes and phenomena [1–6]. Special cases of the generalized beta distribution of the second kind and the generalized gamma distribution can have the properties of infinite divisibility and stability, which makes it possible to use them as asymptotic approximations in various limit theorems. Ref. [7] proposed a new probability distribution closely related to both beta and gamma classes.

Definition 1. *We say that the random variable ζ has the digamma distribution $DiG(r,\nu,p,q,\delta)$ with a characteristic index $r \in \mathbb{R}$ and the parameters of shape $\nu \neq 0$, concentration $p,q > 0$, and scale $\delta > 0$, if its Mellin transform is*

$$\mathcal{M}_\zeta(z) = \frac{\delta^z \Gamma(p + z/\nu)\Gamma(q - rz/\nu)}{\Gamma(p)\Gamma(q)}, \quad p + \frac{\mathrm{Re}(z)}{\nu} > 0, \quad q - \frac{r\mathrm{Re}(z)}{\nu} > 0, \tag{1}$$

where $\mathrm{Re}(z)$ is the real part of a complex number z, and $\Gamma(z)$ is Euler's gamma function.

Particular types of digamma distribution include the generalized gamma distribution (also known as the Amoroso distribution with zero shift) [8], the generalized beta distribution of the second kind (also known as the McDonald distribution) [9], and the gamma-exponential distribution [10].

The digamma distribution (1) can be represented as a scale mixture of two generalized gamma-distributed random variables, i.e., for $\zeta \sim DiG(r, \nu, p, q, \delta)$ and independent random variables $\lambda \sim \Gamma(p, 1)$ and $\mu \sim \Gamma(q, 1)$ with gamma distributions

$$\zeta \stackrel{d}{=} \delta \left(\frac{\lambda}{\mu^r} \right)^{1/\nu}. \tag{2}$$

This representation makes it possible [11] to use the digamma distribution for an adequate description of the Bayesian balance models proposed in [12].

Assuming that the process is modeled using the digamma distribution, the problem of statistical estimation of its unknown parameters inevitably arises [5,13,14]. As shown in Ref. [7], the density of the digamma distribution is expressed in terms of the special Fox's H-function. This significantly complicates the application of the maximum likelihood method. The form of the Mellin transform (1) of the digamma distribution also indicates the infeasibility of using the direct method of moments. Refs. [15–17] originally proposed a modified method for estimating the parameters of the gamma-exponential distribution based on logarithmic moments and cumulants. Due to the fact that the digamma distribution and the gamma-exponential distribution have the Mellin transform of the same type (up to the range of the parameter r), all previously obtained conclusions about the form of estimates by the method of logarithmic cumulants for the gamma-exponential distribution automatically remain valid for the digamma distribution, taking into account the formal expansion of the characteristic index range from a unit interval to the entire real line.

In today's rapidly changing world, it is quite problematic to use the traditional statistical approach based on the analysis of fixed-size samples. Thus, in the context of the global crisis caused by the COVID-19 epidemic, it is necessary to have a mechanism to respond to negative impacts using only the currently available data. Since the accumulation of a sufficient fixed amount of statistics can often take an indefinite time, it makes sense to strive for the possession of methods that allow one to draw adequate conclusions based on an a priori indefinite number of observations. This approach inevitably leads to the consideration of models with randomized sample sizes and is usually found not only in medicine but also in other fields in situations where the accumulation of statistical data continues not up to a certain amount but, rather, over a given period of time. For example, a similar situation can be observed in insurance when a different number of insurance events (insurance payments and/or insurance contracts) occur during different reporting periods of the same length (say, months), etc. Due to these circumstances, it becomes quite natural to study the asymptotic behavior of distributions of fairly general statistics based on the random size samples. When replacing a non-random sample size with a random variable, the asymptotic properties of statistics can radically change. This fact was apparently first noted by B.V. Gnedenko in 1989 [18,19]. It was shown that if the sample size is a geometrically distributed random variable, then instead of the normal law expected in accordance with the classical theory, a Student distribution with two degrees of freedom arises as an asymptotic distribution for the sample median, whose tails are so heavy that it does not have second-order moments. The "heaviness" of the tails of asymptotic distributions is of critical importance, in particular, in problems of testing hypotheses.

The distributions from the gamma class and their derivatives have become very popular for modeling random non-negative parameters, and, when modeling a random number of events and studying an a priori unknown number of observations, their discrete analogs are widely used, which are mixed Poisson distributions with corresponding continuous structural distributions.

The discrete analog of the gamma distribution $\Gamma(p,\delta)$ is the negative binomial distribution, whose partial probabilities for $n = 0, 1, \ldots$ are

$$\mathsf{P}(N=n) = \int\limits_0^\infty \frac{\lambda^{n+p-1}e^{-(1+1/\delta)\lambda}}{\delta^p\Gamma(p)n!}\,d\lambda = \frac{\Gamma(n+p)}{\Gamma(n+1)\Gamma(p)}\left(\frac{\delta}{\delta+1}\right)^n\left(\frac{1}{\delta+1}\right)^p. \tag{3}$$

A natural generalization of the distribution (3) is the mixed Poisson distribution whose structure is given by the generalized gamma distribution $GG(\nu,p,\delta)$ with the density

$$f(x) = \frac{|\nu|x^{\nu p-1}e^{-(x/\delta)^\nu}}{\delta^{\nu p}\Gamma(p)}, \quad \nu \neq 0, \; p > 0, \; x > 0. \tag{4}$$

Such distributions are called generalized negative binomial distributions and are widely used in insurance, financial mathematics, physics, and other fields [20–24].

The purpose of this article is to study the asymptotic behavior of digamma distribution parameter estimates under conditions of an a priori unknown sample size.

The article has the following structure. Section 2 describes a method for obtaining digamma distribution parameter estimates; auxiliary relations are given. Section 3 contains the main statement of this paper on the asymptotic behavior of the digamma distribution parameter estimates constructed from random size samples. Section 4 discusses special cases of limit distributions. This paper also contains a section with our conclusions.

2. Auxiliary Relations

This section describes a method based on logarithmic cumulants for obtaining estimators for the parameters r, ν, and δ of the digamma distribution (1) with fixed concentration parameters p and q and a sample of a non-random size n. Estimating the parameters p and q is a separate problem due to the analytical complexity of inverting the polygamma function.

The results and relations of this section were published in Ref. [17] and are provided as auxiliary statements.

To obtain an explicit form of theoretical logarithmic cumulants, consider the polygamma functions

$$\psi(z) = \frac{d}{dz}\ln\Gamma(z), \;\; \psi^{(m)}(z) = \frac{d^{m+1}}{dz^{m+1}}\ln\Gamma(z), \;\; m = 1, 2, \ldots$$

The theoretical cumulants of the random variable $\ln\zeta$ for $\zeta \sim DiG(r,\nu,p,q,\delta)$ have the form

$$\kappa_1(r,\nu,\delta) = \mathsf{E}\ln\zeta = \frac{\nu\ln\delta + \psi(p) - r\psi(q)}{\nu};$$

$$\kappa_m(r,\nu) = (-i)^m\frac{d^m}{dy^m}\ln\mathsf{E}\zeta^{iy}\Big|_{y=0} = \frac{\psi^{(m-1)}(p) + (-r)^m\psi^{(m-1)}(q)}{\nu^m}, \quad m > 1.$$

The moments of the random variable $\ln\zeta$ can be represented as [25]

$$\mu_m(r,\nu,\delta) \equiv \mathsf{E}\ln^m\zeta = B_m(\kappa_1(r,\nu,\delta),\kappa_2(r,\nu),\ldots,\kappa_m(r,\nu)), \tag{5}$$

where B_m is a complete (exponential) Bell polynomial that can be recurrently defined as

$$B_{m+1}(x_1,\ldots,x_{m+1}) = \sum_{k=0}^m C_m^k B_{m-k}(x_1,\ldots,x_{m-k})x_{k+1}, \;\; B_0 = 1.$$

An explicit form of the necessary relations connecting moments and cumulants can be found in Ref. [25].

In addition, we will need the following moment characteristics of the logarithm of a random variable with a digamma distribution:

$$\sigma_m^2(r,\nu,\delta) \equiv \mathsf{D}\ln^m\zeta = \mu_{2m}(r,\nu,\delta) - \mu_m^2(r,\nu,\delta);$$
$$\sigma_{ml}(r,\nu,\delta) \equiv \mathsf{cov}(\ln^m\zeta, \ln^l\zeta) = \mu_{m+l}(r,\nu,\delta) - \mu_m(r,\nu,\delta)\mu_l(r,\nu,\delta). \quad (6)$$

To define the sample logarithmic cumulants, we introduce a notation for the sample logarithmic moments of the random variable ζ:

$$L_m(\mathbb{X}_n) = \frac{1}{n}\sum_{i=1}^{n}\ln^m X_i,$$

where $\mathbb{X}_n = (X_1, \ldots, X_n)$ is a sample from the distribution ζ of non-random size n.

Let us denote $l = (l_1, l_2, l_3, l_4)$. Consider the functions

$$K_1(l) \equiv K_1(l_1) = (\psi(q))^{-1}l_1;$$

$$K_2(l) \equiv K_2(l_1, l_2) = (\psi'(q))^{-1}(l_2 - l_1^2);$$
$$K_3(l) \equiv K_3(l_1, l_2, l_3) = (\psi''(q))^{-1}(l_3 - 3l_2l_1 + 2l_1^3);$$
$$K_4(l) \equiv K_4(l_1, l_2, l_3, l_4) = (\psi'''(q))^{-1}(l_4 - 4l_3l_1 - 3l_2^2 + 12l_2l_1^2 - 6l_1^4).$$

Consider the statistics

$$K_1(\mathbb{X}_n) \equiv K_1(L_1(\mathbb{X}_n));$$

$$K_2(\mathbb{X}_n) \equiv K_2(L_1(\mathbb{X}_n), L_2(\mathbb{X}_n)); \quad (7)$$
$$K_3(\mathbb{X}_n) \equiv K_3(L_1(\mathbb{X}_n), L_2(\mathbb{X}_n), L_3(\mathbb{X}_n));$$

$$K_4(\mathbb{X}_n) \equiv K_4(L_1(\mathbb{X}_n), L_2(\mathbb{X}_n), L_3(\mathbb{X}_n), L_4(\mathbb{X}_n)). \quad (8)$$

Note that the statistics $\psi^{(m-1)}(q)K_m(\mathbb{X}_n)$ are the m-th sample logarithmic cumulants of the digamma distribution.

The method for estimating the unknown parameters considered in this paper is based on solving the system for logarithmic cumulants:

$$\kappa_m(r,\nu,\delta) = \psi^{(m-1)}(q)K_m(\mathbb{X}_n), \quad m = 1,2,3,4.$$

To describe the solution of this system, we introduce a number of functions of sample logarithmic cumulants with the arguments $k = (k_1, k_2, k_3, k_4)$:

$$\phi_m = \frac{\psi^{(m)}(p)}{\psi^{(m)}(q)}; \quad \tau(k) \equiv \tau(k_2, k_4) = \phi_1^2 k_4 + \phi_3\left(k_4 - k_2^2\right); \quad (9)$$

$$R_\pm(k) \equiv R_\pm(k_2, k_4) = \sqrt{\frac{\phi_1 k_4 \pm k_2\sqrt{\tau(k)}}{k_2^2 - k_4}};$$
$$V_\pm(k) \equiv V_\pm(k_2, k_4) = \sqrt{\frac{\phi_1 k_2 \pm \sqrt{\tau(k)}}{k_2^2 - k_4}};$$
$$D_\pm(k) \equiv D_\pm(k_1, k_2, k_4) = \exp\left\{\psi(q)k_1 + \frac{\psi(q)R_\pm(k) - \psi(p)}{V_\pm(k)}\right\}. \quad (10)$$

In what follows, we will need the derivatives of functions (10), expressed in terms of the functions ϕ_m and τ, defined in (9). Note that

$$R_{k_2,\pm}(k) \equiv \frac{\partial R_\pm}{\partial k_2}(k_2,k_4) = \mp\frac{k_4\left(\phi_1^2k_2^2+\tau(k)\pm 2\phi_1k_2\sqrt{\tau(k)}\right)}{2\left(k_2^2-k_4\right)^{3/2}\sqrt{\tau(k)}\sqrt{\phi_1k_4\pm k_2\sqrt{\tau(k)}}};$$

$$R_{k_4,\pm}(k) \equiv \frac{\partial R_\pm}{\partial k_4}(k_2,k_4) = \pm\frac{k_2\left(\phi_1^2k_2^2+\tau(k)\pm 2\phi_1k_2\sqrt{\tau(k)}\right)}{4(k_2^2-k_4)^{3/2}\sqrt{\tau(k)}\sqrt{\phi_1k_4\pm k_2\sqrt{\tau(k)}}};$$

$$V_{k_2,\pm}(k) \equiv \frac{\partial V_\pm}{\partial k_2}(k_2,k_4) = \mp\frac{k_2(\phi_1^2k_4+\tau(k))\pm\phi_1(k_2^2+k_4)\sqrt{\tau(k)}}{2(k_2^2-k_4)^{3/2}\sqrt{\tau(k)}\sqrt{\phi_1k_2\pm\sqrt{\tau(k)}}};$$

$$V_{k_4,\pm}(k) \equiv \frac{\partial V_\pm}{\partial k_4}(k_2,k_4) = \pm\frac{\phi_1^2k_2^2+\tau(k)\pm 2\phi_1k_2\sqrt{\tau(k)}}{4(k_2^2-k_4)^{3/2}\sqrt{\tau(k)}\sqrt{\phi_1k_2\pm\sqrt{\tau(k)}}};$$

$$D_{k_1,\pm}(k) \equiv \frac{\partial D_\pm}{\partial k_1}(k_1,k_2,k_4) = \psi(q)\exp\left\{\psi(q)k_1+\frac{\psi(q)R_\pm(k)-\psi(p)}{V_\pm(k)}\right\};$$

$$D_{k_2,\pm}(k) \equiv \frac{\partial D_\pm}{\partial k_2}(k_1,k_2,k_4) = \exp\left\{\psi(q)k_1+\frac{\psi(q)R_\pm(k)-\psi(p)}{V_\pm(k)}\right\}\times$$
$$\times\frac{\psi(p)V_{k_2,\pm}(k)+\psi(q)R_{k_2,\pm}(k)V_\pm(k)-\psi(q)R_\pm(k)V_{k_2,\pm}(k)}{V_\pm^2(k)};$$

$$D_{k_4,\pm}(k) \equiv \frac{\partial D_\pm}{\partial k_4}(k_1,k_2,k_4) = \exp\left\{\psi(q)k_1+\frac{\psi(q)R_\pm(k)-\psi(p)}{V_\pm(k)}\right\}\times$$
$$\times\frac{\psi(p)V_{k_4,\pm}(k)+\psi(q)R_{k_4,\pm}(k)V_\pm(k)-\psi(q)R_\pm(k)V_{k_4,\pm}(k)}{V_\pm^2(k)}.$$

Using the formula for the derivative of a composite function, we obtain

$$\frac{\partial R_\pm}{\partial l_1}(l) = -\frac{2l_1}{\psi'(q)}R_{k_2,\pm}(K_2(l),K_4(l)) - \frac{4l_3-24l_2l_1+24l_1^3}{\psi'''(q)}R_{k_4,\pm}(K_2(l),K_4(l));$$

$$\frac{\partial R_\pm}{\partial l_2}(l) = \frac{1}{\psi'(q)}R_{k_2,\pm}(K_2(l),K_4(l)) - \frac{6l_2-12l_1^2}{\psi'''(q)}R_{k_4,\pm}(K_2(l),K_4(l));$$

$$\frac{\partial R_\pm}{\partial l_3}(l) = -\frac{4l_1}{\psi'''(q)}R_{k_4,\pm}(K_2(l),K_4(l));$$

$$\frac{\partial R_\pm}{\partial l_4}(l) = \frac{1}{\psi'''(q)}R_{k_4,\pm}(K_2(l),K_4(l));$$

$$\frac{\partial V_\pm}{\partial l_1}(l) = -\frac{2l_1}{\psi'(q)} V_{k_2,\pm}(K_2(l), K_4(l)) - \frac{4l_3 - 24l_2l_1 + 24l_1^3}{\psi'''(q)} V_{k_4,\pm}(K_2(l), K_4(l));$$
$$\frac{\partial V_\pm}{\partial l_2}(l) = \frac{1}{\psi'(q)} V_{k_2,\pm}(K_2(l), K_4(l)) - \frac{6l_2 - 12l_1^2}{\psi'''(q)} V_{k_4,\pm}(K_2(l), K_4(l));$$
$$\frac{\partial V_\pm}{\partial l_3}(l) = -\frac{4l_1}{\psi'''(q)} V_{k_4,\pm}(K_2(l), K_4(l));$$
$$\frac{\partial V_\pm}{\partial l_4}(l) = \frac{1}{\psi'''(q)} V_{k_4,\pm}(K_2(l), K_4(l));$$
$$\frac{\partial D_\pm}{\partial l_1}(l) = \frac{1}{\psi(q)} D_{k_1,\pm}(K_1(l), K_2(l), K_4(l)) - \frac{2l_1}{\psi'(q)} D_{k_2,\pm}(K_1(l), K_2(l), K_4(l)) - \\ - \frac{4l_3 - 24l_2l_1 + 24l_1^3}{\psi'''(q)} D_{k_4,\pm}(K_1(l), K_2(l), K_4(l));$$
$$\frac{\partial D_\pm}{\partial l_2}(l) = \frac{1}{\psi'(q)} D_{k_2,\pm}(K_1(l), K_2(l), K_4(l)) - \frac{6l_2 - 12l_1^2}{\psi'''(q)} D_{k_4,\pm}(K_1(l), K_2(l), K_4(l));$$
$$\frac{\partial D_\pm}{\partial l_3}(l) = -\frac{4l_1}{\psi'''(q)} D_{k_4,\pm}(K_1(l), K_2(l), K_4(l));$$
$$\frac{\partial D_\pm}{\partial l_4}(l) = \frac{1}{\psi'''(q)} D_{k_4,\pm}(K_1(l), K_2(l), K_4(l)). \quad (11)$$

To formulate the statement about the asymptotic normality of estimators for the parameters r, ν, and δ with fixed concentration parameters p and q for a fixed sample size n, we introduce some notations. Let

$$\Sigma = \begin{pmatrix} \sigma_1^2(r,\nu,\delta) & \sigma_{12}(r,\nu,\delta) & \sigma_{13}(r,\nu,\delta) & \sigma_{14}(r,\nu,\delta) \\ \sigma_{12}(r,\nu,\delta) & \sigma_2^2(r,\nu,\delta) & \sigma_{23}(r,\nu,\delta) & \sigma_{24}(r,\nu,\delta) \\ \sigma_{13}(r,\nu,\delta) & \sigma_{23}(r,\nu,\delta) & \sigma_3^2(r,\nu,\delta) & \sigma_{34}(r,\nu,\delta) \\ \sigma_{14}(r,\nu,\delta) & \sigma_{24}(r,\nu,\delta) & \sigma_{34}(r,\nu,\delta) & \sigma_4^2(r,\nu,\delta) \end{pmatrix};$$
$$d_{R_\pm} = \left(\frac{\partial R_\pm}{\partial l_1}(l)\Big|_{l=\mu}, \frac{\partial R_\pm}{\partial l_2}(l)\Big|_{l=\mu}, \frac{\partial R_\pm}{\partial l_3}(l)\Big|_{l=\mu}, \frac{\partial R_\pm}{\partial l_4}(l)\Big|_{l=\mu} \right);$$
$$d_{V_\pm} = \left(\frac{\partial V_\pm}{\partial l_1}(l)\Big|_{l=\mu}, \frac{\partial V_\pm}{\partial l_2}(l)\Big|_{l=\mu}, \frac{\partial V_\pm}{\partial l_3}(l)\Big|_{l=\mu}, \frac{\partial V_\pm}{\partial l_4}(l)\Big|_{l=\mu} \right);$$
$$d_{D_\pm} = \left(\frac{\partial D_\pm}{\partial l_1}(l)\Big|_{l=\mu}, \frac{\partial D_\pm}{\partial l_2}(l)\Big|_{l=\mu}, \frac{\partial D_\pm}{\partial l_3}(l)\Big|_{l=\mu}, \frac{\partial D_\pm}{\partial l_4}(l)\Big|_{l=\mu} \right), \quad (12)$$

where the variances $\sigma_m^2(r,\nu,\delta)$ and the covariances $\sigma_{ml}(r,\nu,\delta)$ are defined in the relations (6), the partial derivatives $\partial R_\pm/\partial l_k(l)$, $\partial V_\pm/\partial l_k(l)$, and $\partial D_\pm/\partial l_k(l)$ are defined in (11), and $\mu = (\mu_1, \mu_2, \mu_3)$ is the vector of moments (5).

Previously, in Ref. [17], the following result was obtained for the gamma-exponential distribution.

Theorem 1. *Let $0 \le r < 1$ and $\nu > 0$. Assume that the concentration parameters p and q of the digamma distribution $DiG(r,\nu,p,q,\delta)$ are fixed. Then, for $r > \sqrt{\phi_3/\phi_1}$, the estimators $\hat{r}(\mathbb{X}_n) = R_+(K_2(\mathbb{X}_n), K_4(\mathbb{X}_n))$ for the unknown characteristic index r, $\hat{\nu}(\mathbb{X}_n) = V_+(K_2(\mathbb{X}_n), K_4(\mathbb{X}_n))$ for the unknown shape parameter ν and $\hat{\delta}(\mathbb{X}_n) = D_+(K_1(\mathbb{X}_n), K_2(\mathbb{X}_n), K_4(\mathbb{X}_n))$ for the unknown scale parameter δ have the property of asymptotic normality when $n \to \infty$:*

$$\sqrt{n}\frac{\hat{r}(\mathbb{X}_n) - r}{\sqrt{d_{R_+}\Sigma d_{R_+}^T}} \Longrightarrow N(0,1), \quad \sqrt{n}\frac{\hat{\nu}(\mathbb{X}_n) - \nu}{\sqrt{d_{V_+}\Sigma d_{V_+}^T}} \Longrightarrow N(0,1); \quad \sqrt{n}\frac{\hat{\delta}(\mathbb{X}_n) - \delta}{\sqrt{d_{D_+}\Sigma d_{D_+}^T}} \Longrightarrow N(0,1). \quad (13)$$

Remark 1. *In addition to the property of asymptotic normality, the estimators listed in Theorem 1 have the property of strong consistency [16].*

Remark 2. *In Theorem 1, if* $0 \leq r < \sqrt{\phi_3/\phi_1}$*, then one should choose the statistics* $\hat{r}(\mathbb{X}_n) = R_-(K_2(\mathbb{X}_n), K_4(\mathbb{X}_n))$, $\hat{v}(\mathbb{X}_n) = V_-(K_2(\mathbb{X}_n), K_4(\mathbb{X}_n))$*, and* $\hat{\delta}(\mathbb{X}_n) = D_-(K_1(\mathbb{X}_n), K_2(\mathbb{X}_n), K_4(\mathbb{X}_n))$ *with a corresponding modification of the normalizing constants in (13) [17].*

Remark 3. *In Theorem 1, if* $v < 0$*, then one should choose as an estimator for the unknown parameter* v *the statistics* $\hat{v}(\mathbb{X}_n) = -V_+(K_2(\mathbb{X}_n), K_4(\mathbb{X}_n))$ *if* $r > \sqrt{\phi_3/\phi_1}$*, and* $\hat{v}(\mathbb{X}_n) = -V_-(K_2(\mathbb{X}_n), K_4(\mathbb{X}_n))$ *if* $0 \leq r < \sqrt{\phi_3/\phi_1}$.

Remark 4. *Since the gamma-exponential distribution and the digamma distribution have the Mellin transform of the same type (1), the results of Theorem 1 and Remark 1 remain valid for all* $r \geq 0$*. In the case when* $r < 0$*, one should consider as an estimator for the parameter* r *the statistics* $\hat{r}(\mathbb{X}_n) = -R_+(K_2(\mathbb{X}_n), K_4(\mathbb{X}_n))$ *for* $r < -\sqrt{\phi_3/\phi_1}$ *and* $\hat{r}(\mathbb{X}_n) = -R_-(K_2(\mathbb{X}_n), K_4(\mathbb{X}_n))$ *for* $-\sqrt{\phi_3/\phi_1} < r \leq 0$.

Remark 5. *When processing real data, one should first choose one of the statistics* $\pm R_\pm(K_2(\mathbb{X}_n), K_4(\mathbb{X}_n))$*, and* $\pm V_\pm(K_2(\mathbb{X}_n), K_4(\mathbb{X}_n))$ *as the estimators* $\hat{r}(\mathbb{X}_n)$ *and* $\hat{v}(\mathbb{X}_n)$*, using the algorithm for eliminating unnecessary solutions described in Ref. [17]. The estimator for the unknown parameter* δ *is always defined by the formula*

$$\hat{\delta}(\mathbb{X}_n) = \exp\left\{\psi(q)K_1(\mathbb{X}_n) + \frac{\psi(q)\hat{r}(\mathbb{X}_n) - \psi(p)}{\hat{v}(\mathbb{X}_n)}\right\}.$$

3. Main Result

Everywhere below we will assume that the sample size is random. To obtain asymptotic approximations, it is reasonable to consider a situation in which the random size of the sample increases in some sense. We will consider a sequence N_n such that $N_n \longrightarrow \infty$ in probability as $n \to \infty$.

Let the non-random size sample $\mathbb{X}_n = (X_1, \ldots, X_n)$ and the random size sample $\mathbb{X}_{N_n} = (X_1, \ldots, X_{N_n})$ be from the digamma distribution $DiG(r, v, p, q, \delta)$ with the known concentration parameters p and q.

Using the Functions (7) and (8), we construct the statistics

$$K_2(\mathbb{X}_{N_n}) \equiv K_2(L_1(\mathbb{X}_{N_n}), L_2(\mathbb{X}_{N_n}));$$

$$K_4(\mathbb{X}_{N_n}) \equiv K_4(L_1(\mathbb{X}_{N_n}), L_2(\mathbb{X}_{N_n}), L_3(\mathbb{X}_{N_n}), L_4(\mathbb{X}_{N_n})),$$

based on sample logarithmic moments

$$L_m(\mathbb{X}_{N_n}) = \frac{1}{N_n}\sum_{i=1}^{N_n} \ln^m X_i.$$

Let N_n be a sequence of natural-valued random variables independent of $X_1, X_2, \ldots$, for each n, and let N_n tend toward infinity in probability as $n \to \infty$.

The following statement holds.

Theorem 2. *Let* $r > \sqrt{\phi_3/\phi_1}$ *and* $v > 0$*. Suppose that the concentration parameters* p *and* q *of the digamma distribution* $DiG(r, v, p, q, \delta)$ *are fixed. Assume that there exists a numerical sequence* $\{b_n > 0\}$ *and a random variable* U *such that*

$$\frac{N_n}{b_n} \Longrightarrow U \tag{14}$$

when $n \to \infty$*. Then, the estimators* $\hat{r}(\mathbb{X}_{N_n}) = R_+(K_2(\mathbb{X}_{N_n}), K_4(\mathbb{X}_{N_n}))$ *for the unknown characteristic index* r, $\hat{v}(\mathbb{X}_{N_n}) = V_+(K_2(\mathbb{X}_{N_n}), K_4(\mathbb{X}_{N_n}))$ *for the unknown shape parameter* v*, and* $\hat{\delta}(\mathbb{X}_{N_n}) = D_+(K_1(\mathbb{X}_{N_n}), K_2(\mathbb{X}_{N_n}), K_4(\mathbb{X}_{N_n}))$ *for the unknown scale parameter* δ *converge in distribution when* $n \to \infty$:

$$\sqrt{b_n}\frac{\hat{r}(\mathbb{X}_{N_n})-r}{\sqrt{d_{R_+}\Sigma d_{R_+}^T}} \Longrightarrow \frac{Y}{\sqrt{U}}, \quad \sqrt{b_n}\frac{\hat{v}(\mathbb{X}_{N_n})-v}{\sqrt{d_{V_+}\Sigma d_{V_+}^T}} \Longrightarrow \frac{Y}{\sqrt{U}}, \quad \sqrt{b_n}\frac{\hat{\delta}(\mathbb{X}_{N_n})-\delta}{\sqrt{d_{D_+}\Sigma d_{D_+}^T}} \Longrightarrow \frac{Y}{\sqrt{U}}, \tag{15}$$

where Y has a standard normal distribution, and U can be considered independent of Y.

Proof of Theorem 2. We consider the statement of the theorem for estimating the characteristic index r. The argument is based on the method proposed in Ref. [26].

Denote

$$a_n = \frac{\sqrt{d_{R_+}\Sigma d_{R_+}^T}}{\sqrt{b_n}}, \quad c_n = \frac{\sqrt{d_{R_+}\Sigma d_{R_+}^T}}{\sqrt{n}}.$$

Let $h_n(t)$ be the characteristic function of a random variable

$$Y_n \equiv \sqrt{n}\frac{\hat{r}(\mathbb{X}_n)-r}{\sqrt{d_{R_+}\Sigma d_{R_+}^T}} \equiv \frac{\hat{r}(\mathbb{X}_n)-r}{c_n};$$

and $f_n(t)$ be the characteristic function of

$$Z_n \equiv \sqrt{b_n}\frac{\hat{r}(\mathbb{X}_{N_n})-r}{\sqrt{d_{R_+}\Sigma d_{R_+}^T}} \equiv \frac{\hat{r}(\mathbb{X}_{N_n})-r}{a_n}.$$

Theorem 1 implies that when $n \to \infty$

$$Y_n \Longrightarrow Y \sim N(0,1).$$

Denote by $h(t)$ the characteristic function of a standard normal random variable Y. Define the random variables

$$U_n \equiv \frac{c_{N_n}}{a_n}.$$

Let

$$g_n(t) = \mathsf{E}h(tU_n).$$

Let us show that for any $t \in \mathbb{R}$

$$\lim_{n\to\infty} |f_n(t) - g_n(t)| = 0.$$

For some positive number γ and positive integer m, we define

$$K_{1,n} \equiv K_{1,n}(\gamma) = \{m \mid c_m \le \gamma a_n\}, \quad K_{2,n} \equiv K_{2,n}(\gamma) = \{m \mid c_m > \gamma a_n\}.$$

For $t = 0$, the statement is obvious. Fix an arbitrary $t \neq 0$. Then,

$$|f_n(t) - g_n(t)| = |\mathsf{E}\exp\{itZ_n\} - \mathsf{E}h(tU_n)| =$$

$$= \left|\sum_{m=1}^{\infty} \mathsf{P}(N_n = m)\left[\mathsf{E}\exp\left\{it\frac{\hat{r}(\mathbb{X}_m)-r}{a_n}\right\} - h\left(t\frac{c_m}{a_n}\right)\right]\right| =$$

$$= \left|\sum_{m=1}^{\infty} \mathsf{P}(N_n = m)\left[\mathsf{E}\exp\left\{it\frac{c_m}{a_n}\cdot\frac{\hat{r}(\mathbb{X}_m)-r}{c_m}\right\} - h\left(t\frac{c_m}{a_n}\right)\right]\right| =$$

$$= \left|\sum_{m=1}^{\infty} \mathsf{P}(N_n = m)\left[h_m\left(t\frac{c_m}{a_n}\right) - h\left(t\frac{c_m}{a_n}\right)\right]\right| \le \sum_{m\in K_{1,n}} \mathsf{P}(N_n = m)\left|h_m\left(t\frac{c_m}{a_n}\right) - h\left(t\frac{c_m}{a_n}\right)\right| +$$

$$+\sum_{m\in K_{2,n}} \mathsf{P}(N_n=m)\left|h_m\left(t\frac{c_m}{a_n}\right)-h\left(t\frac{c_m}{a_n}\right)\right| = I_1+I_2.$$

Fix an arbitrary $\epsilon > 0$. Consider I_2.

$$I_2 = \sum_{m\in K_{2,n}} \mathsf{P}(N_n=m)\left|h_m\left(t\frac{c_m}{a_n}\right)-h\left(t\frac{c_m}{a_n}\right)\right| \leq 2\sum_{m\in K_{2,n}} \mathsf{P}(N_n=m) = 2\mathsf{P}(U_n>\gamma) < \epsilon/2$$

for all $\gamma > \gamma_2(\epsilon)$, due to the convergence $U_n \Longrightarrow 1/\sqrt{U}$.

Now, consider I_1. Let $\gamma > \gamma_2(\epsilon)$. Since $|tc_m/a_n| \leq |t|\gamma$,

$$I_1 = \sum_{m\in K_{1,n}} \mathsf{P}(N_n=m)\left|h_m\left(t\frac{c_m}{a_n}\right)-h\left(t\frac{c_m}{a_n}\right)\right| \leq$$

$$\leq \sum_{m=1}^{\infty} \mathsf{P}(N_n=m) \sup_{|\tau|\leq\gamma|t|} |h_m(\tau)-h(\tau)| = \mathsf{E}\sup_{|\tau|\leq\gamma|t|} |h_{N_n}(\tau)-h(\tau)|.$$

Due to the uniform convergence of the sequence of characteristic functions $h_n(t)$ to $h(t)$ on any finite interval and the convergence $N_n \longrightarrow \infty$ in probability,

$$\mathsf{E}\sup_{|\tau|\leq\gamma|t|} |h_{N_n}(\tau)-h(\tau)| < \epsilon/2$$

starting from some n.

Since $I_1 + I_2 < \epsilon$ starting from some n, we conclude that for any t

$$\lim_{n\to\infty} |f_n(t)-g_n(t)| = 0.$$

Note that the function

$$\phi_t(x) = h(tx)$$

is bounded and continuous. Therefore, the weak convergence condition $U_n \Longrightarrow 1/\sqrt{U}$ implies

$$\lim_{n\to\infty} \mathsf{E}\phi_t(U_n) = \mathsf{E}\phi_t(1/\sqrt{U}) = \mathsf{E}h(t/\sqrt{U}).$$

By the Fubini theorem, the right-hand side of the last equality is the characteristic function of the random variable $Y/\sqrt{U}$ for a copy of the standard normal random variable Y independent of U.

Since

$$|f_n(t)-\mathsf{E}h(t/\sqrt{U})| \leq |f_n(t)-g_n(t)| + |g_n(t)-\mathsf{E}h(t/\sqrt{U})| < 2\epsilon$$

for all $\epsilon > 0$ starting from some n,

$$\lim_{n\to\infty} f_n(t) = \mathsf{E}h(t/\sqrt{U}),$$

which completes the proof of the theorem for the estimator of the characteristic index r.

The statements of the theorem for the estimators of the form parameter ν and the scale parameter δ are proved in a completely similar way. The theorem is proved. □

Remark 6. *Similarly to Remarks 2–5, the statement of Theorem 2 remains valid in the cases* $r < -\sqrt{\phi_3/\phi_1}$, $-\sqrt{\phi_3/\phi_1} < r \leq 0$, $0 \leq r < \sqrt{\phi_3/\phi_1}$ *and* $\nu < 0$ *for the estimators* $\hat{r}(\mathbb{X}_{N_n}) = \pm R_\pm(K_2(\mathbb{X}_{N_n}), K_4(\mathbb{X}_{N_n}))$ *and* $\hat{\nu}(\mathbb{X}_{N_n}) = \pm V_\pm(K_2(\mathbb{X}_{N_n}), K_4(\mathbb{X}_{N_n}))$ *with the corresponding modification of the normalizing constants in (15). The choice of the "correct" signs of the estimators is carried out using the algorithm for eliminating unnecessary solutions from Ref. [17]. The estimator for the unknown parameter* δ *is always defined by the formula*

$$\hat{\delta}(\mathbb{X}_{N_n}) = \exp\left\{\psi(q)K_1(\mathbb{X}_{N_n}) + \frac{\psi(q)\hat{r}(\mathbb{X}_{N_n}) - \psi(p)}{\hat{\nu}(\mathbb{X}_{N_n})}\right\}.$$

Let us introduce additional notation

$$s_{mm}(\mathbb{X}_{N_n}) \equiv \sigma_m^2(\hat{r}(\mathbb{X}_{N_n}), \hat{\nu}(\mathbb{X}_{N_n}), \hat{\delta}(\mathbb{X}_{N_n}));$$
$$s_{ml}(\mathbb{X}_{N_n}) = s_{lm}(\mathbb{X}_{N_n}) \equiv \sigma_{ml}(\hat{r}(\mathbb{X}_{N_n}), \hat{\nu}(\mathbb{X}_{N_n}), \hat{\delta}(\mathbb{X}_{N_n}));$$
$$d_r^{[m]}(\mathbb{X}_{N_n}) \equiv \frac{\partial \hat{r}(\mathbb{X}_{N_n})}{\partial l_m};\ d_\nu^{[m]}(\mathbb{X}_{N_n}) \equiv \frac{\partial \hat{\nu}(\mathbb{X}_{N_n})}{\partial l_m};\ d_\delta^{[m]}(\mathbb{X}_{N_n}) \equiv \frac{\partial \hat{\delta}(\mathbb{X}_{N_n})}{\partial l_m}, \tag{16}$$

where $\sigma_m^2(r,\nu,\delta)$ and $\sigma_{ml}(r,\nu,\delta)$ are defined in (6) and $\hat{r}(\mathbb{X}_{N_n})$, $\hat{\nu}(\mathbb{X}_{N_n})$, and $\hat{\delta}(\mathbb{X}_{N_n})$ satisfy the conditions of Theorem 2.

Theorem 2 implies a statement about the form of the asymptotic confidence intervals for unknown parameters of the digamma distribution. Denote by u_γ the $(1+\gamma)/2$-quantile of the limiting random variable $Y/\sqrt{U}$.

Corollary 1. *Suppose that the conditions of Theorem 2 are met; then the asymptotic confidence intervals with a confidence level γ based on the estimators $\hat{r}(\mathbb{X}_{N_n})$, $\hat{\nu}(\mathbb{X}_{N_n})$, and $\hat{\delta}(\mathbb{X}_{N_n})$ for the unknown parameters r, ν, and δ have the form*

$$(A_r(\mathbb{X}_{N_n}), B_r(\mathbb{X}_{N_n})) = \left(\hat{r}(\mathbb{X}_{N_n}) - \frac{u_\gamma}{\sqrt{n}}C_r(\mathbb{X}_{N_n}), \hat{r}(\mathbb{X}_{N_n}) + \frac{u_\gamma}{\sqrt{n}}C_r(\mathbb{X}_{N_n})\right);$$

$$(A_\nu(\mathbb{X}_{N_n}), B_\nu(\mathbb{X}_{N_n})) = \left(\hat{\nu}(\mathbb{X}_{N_n}) - \frac{u_\gamma}{\sqrt{n}}C_\nu(\mathbb{X}_{N_n}), \hat{\nu}(\mathbb{X}_{N_n}) + \frac{u_\gamma}{\sqrt{n}}C_\nu(\mathbb{X}_{N_n})\right);$$

$$(A_\delta(\mathbb{X}_{N_n}), B_\delta(\mathbb{X}_{N_n})) = \left(\hat{\delta}(\mathbb{X}_{N_n}) - \frac{u_\gamma}{\sqrt{n}}C_\delta(\mathbb{X}_{N_n}), \hat{\delta}(\mathbb{X}_{N_n}) + \frac{u_\gamma}{\sqrt{n}}C_\delta(\mathbb{X}_{N_n})\right),$$

where

$$C_r(\mathbb{X}_{N_n}) = \sqrt{\sum_{m=1}^{4}\sum_{l=1}^{4} d_r^{[m]}(\mathbb{X}_{N_n})s_{ml}(\mathbb{X}_{N_n})d_r^{[l]}(\mathbb{X}_{N_n})};$$

$$C_\nu(\mathbb{X}_{N_n}) = \sqrt{\sum_{m=1}^{4}\sum_{l=1}^{4} d_\nu^{[m]}(\mathbb{X}_{N_n})s_{ml}(\mathbb{X}_{N_n})d_\nu^{[l]}(\mathbb{X}_{N_n})};$$

$$C_\delta(\mathbb{X}_{N_n}) = \sqrt{\sum_{m=1}^{4}\sum_{l=1}^{4} d_\delta^{[m]}(\mathbb{X}_{N_n})s_{ml}(\mathbb{X}_{N_n})d_\delta^{[l]}(\mathbb{X}_{N_n})},$$

and $s_{ml}(\mathbb{X}_{N_n})$, $d_r^{[m]}(\mathbb{X}_{N_n})$, $d_\nu^{[m]}(\mathbb{X}_{N_n})$, $d_\delta^{[m]}(\mathbb{X}_{N_n})$ are defined in (16).

The proof is completely analogous to the proof of Corollary 2 from Ref. [17].

4. Examples of Limit Distributions

Let us give a number of examples of possible limit distributions in Theorem 2.

As noted in Section 1, special forms of the negative binomial distribution have gained great popularity in modeling a random number of events. Since the negative binomial distribution is concentrated on non-negative integers, it cannot be directly used as a random sample size. We will consider such distributions with a shift by one, which will ensure the natural value of the sample size. According to the generalized Slutsky theorem, all conclusions concerning the asymptotic behavior of "shifted" distributions are equivalent to the statements about the asymptotics for sequences of random variables that have a classical negative binomial distribution or a mixed Poisson distribution with a structural gamma distribution.

Note that the gamma distribution belongs to the class of distributions with a scale parameter. It means that if $\Lambda \sim \Gamma(s,\theta)$, then $\hat{\Lambda}\stackrel{d}{=}\Lambda/\theta \sim \Gamma(s,1)$. The following statements are based on the fact that for a standard Poisson process $N_1(t)$ independent of the random variable Λ,

$$\frac{N_1(\Lambda n)}{\theta n} \Longrightarrow \hat{\Lambda}, \quad n \to \infty.$$

Note also that if a random variable ξ has a generalized gamma distribution $GG(v,s,\theta)$ with the density (4), then

$$\frac{1}{\sqrt{\xi}} \sim GG\left(-2v, s, \frac{1}{\sqrt{\theta}}\right).$$

Denote by $\Pi(\Lambda)$ the mixed Poisson distribution whose structure is given by the random variable Λ. To specify particular cases of Theorem 2, we consider the distribution $D(\theta)$ degenerate at the point θ, the gamma distribution $\Gamma(s,\theta)$, the exponential distribution $E(\theta) \equiv \Gamma(1,\theta)$, and the scaled χ^2-distribution $\chi^2(k,\theta) \equiv \Gamma(k/2,\theta)$, $k \in \mathbb{N}$ as the structural one. To determine the corresponding mixed Poisson distributions, consider the negative binomial distribution $NB(p, 1/(1+\theta))$ whose partial probabilities are given by (3), and the geometric distribution $G(1/(1+\theta)) \equiv NB(1, 1/(1+\theta))$. To determine the limit distributions, consider the type VII Pearson distribution $P7(m,\alpha)$, $m \geq 1/2$, $\alpha > 0$, with the density

$$f_{P7}(x) = \frac{\alpha^{2m-1}}{B(m-1/2, 1/2)}(\alpha^2 + x^2)^{-m};$$

the Student distribution $St(n) \equiv P7((n+1)/2, \sqrt{n})$; and the Cauchy distribution $K(\alpha) \equiv P7(1,\alpha)$.

For $b_n = \theta n$, let us list several examples of limit distributions of the random variable $Y/\sqrt{U}$ from (15).

Let $N_n - 1\stackrel{d}{=}N_1(\Lambda n) \sim \Pi(\Lambda n)$. Then, the limit random variable U in (14) coincides in distribution with $\hat{\Lambda}$, and the distributions of the random variable $Y/\sqrt{U}$ have the form shown in Table 1.

Table 1. Special cases of the limit distribution.

$\Lambda \sim$	$\Pi(\Lambda n)$	$Y/\sqrt{U} \sim$
$D(\theta)$	$\Pi(\theta n)$	$N(0,1)$
$E(\theta)$	$G\left(\frac{1}{1+\theta n}\right)$	$St(2)$
$\chi^2(1,\theta)$	$NB\left(\frac{1}{2}, \frac{1}{1+\theta n}\right)$	$K\left(\sqrt{2}\right)$
$\Gamma(s,\theta)$	$NB\left(s, \frac{1}{1+\theta n}\right)$	$P7\left(s+\frac{1}{2}, \sqrt{2}\right)$

Let us give some numerical examples of calculating the estimates of the parameters r, ν, and δ of the digamma distribution $DiG(r,\nu,p,q,\delta)$ from the model samples. The concentration parameters p and q are fixed. The data given in Table 2 are obtained using the algorithm described in Ref. [17].

The pseudorandom sample size N_n for each n is generated for the distributions $\Pi(\Lambda n)$ from Table 1. The simulation of pseudorandom samples from the digamma distribution is based on Relation (2).

Table 2 lists the values of the estimates $\hat{r}(\mathbb{X}_{N_n})$, $\hat{\nu}(\mathbb{X}_{N_n})$, and $\hat{\delta}(\mathbb{X}_{N_n})$ of the parameters r, ν, and δ, obtained by simulating a sample from the digamma distribution $DiG(0.5; 2.5; 2.4; 1.9; 1.0)$, and the corresponding boundaries of the confidence intervals. The distributions of the random sample size are taken from Table 1 with $\theta = 1$ and $s = 2$.

Table 2. Examples of parameter estimates and boundaries of confidence intervals for a model distribution for $r = 0.5$, $\nu = 2.5$, and $\delta = 1.0$.

$N_n - 1 \sim$	$\hat{r}(\mathbb{X}_{N_n})$	$A_r(\mathbb{X}_{N_n})$	$B_r(\mathbb{X}_{N_n})$	$\hat{\nu}(\mathbb{X}_{N_n})$	$A_\nu(\mathbb{X}_{N_n})$	$B_\nu(\mathbb{X}_{N_n})$	$\hat{\delta}(\mathbb{X}_{N_n})$	$A_\delta(\mathbb{X}_{N_n})$	$B_\delta(\mathbb{X}_{N_n})$
$\Pi(10^4)$	0.5754	0.0458	1.1051	2.5877	1.8475	3.3278	1.0159	0.8915	1.1403
$\Pi(10^5)$	0.4693	0.3526	0.5859	2.4633	2.3205	2.6061	0.9912	0.9630	1.0195
$\Pi(10^6)$	0.5032	0.4631	0.5433	2.5039	2.4525	2.5554	1.0005	0.9909	1.0101
$G\left(\frac{1}{1+10^4}\right)$	0.4073	−0.2401	1.0549	2.3678	1.6620	3.0735	0.9767	0.8180	1.1355
$G\left(\frac{1}{1+10^5}\right)$	0.5613	0.1982	0.9243	2.5793	2.077	3.0808	1.0140	0.9284	1.0995
$G\left(\frac{1}{1+10^6}\right)$	0.4942	0.4392	0.5493	2.4927	2.4229	2.5626	0.9985	0.9853	1.0118
$NB\left(\frac{1}{2}, \frac{1}{1+10^4}\right)$	0.4575	−2.9511	3.8662	2.4297	−1.6338	6.4933	0.9884	0.1551	1.8217
$NB\left(\frac{1}{2}, \frac{1}{1+10^5}\right)$	0.4137	−0.7791	1.6065	2.4056	1.0728	3.7384	0.9780	0.6893	1.2668
$NB\left(\frac{1}{2}, \frac{1}{1+10^6}\right)$	0.5107	0.2524	0.7690	2.5133	2.1781	2.8485	1.0024	0.9404	1.0644
$NB\left(2, \frac{1}{1+10^4}\right)$	0.5700	0.2545	0.8855	2.5935	2.1529	3.0341	1.0148	0.9407	1.0888
$NB\left(2, \frac{1}{1+10^5}\right)$	0.5317	0.3867	0.6767	2.5418	2.3483	2.7353	1.0079	0.9733	1.0424
$NB\left(2, \frac{1}{1+10^6}\right)$	0.5052	0.4848	0.5256	2.5056	2.4793	2.5319	1.0009	0.9960	1.0058

5. Conclusions

This paper has considered the problem of estimating the parameters of the digamma distribution with a random sample size. The consideration of a random sample size is very important since the accumulation of a sufficient fixed amount of statistical data can often take an indefinite amount of time, and, sometimes, it is impossible, in principle. Therefore, it becomes natural to study the asymptotic behavior of statistics based on random size samples.

The digamma distribution is a generalization of popular distributions from the gamma and beta classes, as well as the gamma-exponential distribution. This paper has discussed a method for estimating unknown parameters of the digamma distribution based on the logarithmic cumulants. Assuming that the sample size is random, the weak convergence of the studied estimators to the scale mixtures of the normal law is proved. This result allows for the construction of asymptotic confidence intervals for the estimated parameters. It is shown that the asymptotic properties of the statistics can change radically when passing from a fixed sample size to a random one. In particular, it leads to heavier tails of the limit distribution. For example, the type VII Pearson distribution may appear to be a limiting distribution whose representatives may not have a mathematical expectation.

The results proposed in this paper concern the estimation of the characteristic index and the shape and scale parameters of the digamma distribution assuming that the concentration parameters are known. Naturally, the question arises about the form of statistical estimates in the case in which all five parameters are unknown. The equations for constructing the estimates contain polygamma functions with arguments depending on the concentration parameters. Theoretical methods for inverting polygamma functions are being actively developed at the present time, but, apparently, there are currently no effective tools suitable for use in the method under consideration. At the same time, polygamma functions have nice properties that make their inversion easy using numerical methods. The authors plan to continue their studies in this direction.

Author Contributions: Conceptualization, A.K. and O.S.; methodology, A.K. and O.S.; formal analysis, A.K. and O.S.; investigation, A.K. and O.S.; writing—original draft preparation, A.K. and O.S.; writing—review and editing, A.K. and O.S.; supervision, A.K. and O.S.; funding acquisition, O.S. All authors have read and agreed to the published version of the manuscript.

Funding: This research was supported by the Russian Science Foundation, project no. 22-11-00212.

Data Availability Statement: Data sharing not applicable.

Conflicts of Interest: The authors declare no conflict of interest.

References

1. Feng, M.; Qu, H.; Yi, Z.; Kurths, J. Subnormal Distribution Derived From Evolving Networks With Variable Elements *IEEE Trans. Cybern.* **2018**, *48*, 2556–2568.
2. Iriarte, Y.A.; Varela, H.; Gómez, H.J.; Gómez, H.W. A Gamma-Type Distribution with Applications. *Symmetry* **2020**, *12*, 870. [CrossRef]
3. Feng, M.; Deng, L.-J.; Chen, F.; Perc, M.; Kurths, J. The accumulative law and its probability model: An extension of the Pareto distribution and the log-normal distribution. *Proc. R. Soc.* **2020**, *476*, 20200019. [CrossRef] [PubMed]
4. Barranco-Chamorro, I.; Iriarte, Y.A.; Gómez, Y.M.; Astorga, J.M.; Gómez, H.W. A Generalized Rayleigh Family of Distributions Based on the Modified Slash Model. *Symmetry* **2021**, *13*, 1226. [CrossRef]
5. López-Rodríguez, F.; García-Sanz-Calcedo, J.; Moral-García, F.J.; García-Conde, A.J. Statistical Study of Rainfall Control: The Dagum Distribution and Applicability to the Southwest of Spain. *Water* **2019**, *11*, 453. [CrossRef]
6. Santoro, K.I.; Gómez, H.J.; Barranco-Chamorro, I.; Gómez, H.W. Extended Half-Power Exponential Distribution with Applications to COVID-19 Data. *Mathematics* **2022**, *10*, 942. [CrossRef]
7. Kudryavtsev, A.A.; Nedolivko, Y.N.; Shestakov, O.V. Main Probabilistic Characteristics of the Digamma Distribution and the Method of Estimating Its Parameters. *Moscow Univ. Comput. Math. Cybern.* **2022**, *46*, 79–86. [CrossRef]
8. Amoroso, L. Ricerche intorno alla curva dei redditi. *Ann. Mat. Pura Appl.* **1925**, *21*, 123–159. [CrossRef]
9. McDonald, J.B. Some Generalized Functions for the Size Distribution of Income. *Econometrica* **1984**, *52*, 647–665. [CrossRef]
10. Kudryavtsev, A.A. On the representation of gamma-exponential and generalized negative binomial distributions. *Inform. Appl.* **2019**, *13*, 78–82.
11. Kudryavtsev, A.A.; Shestakov, O.V. Digamma Distribution as a Limit for the Integral Balance Index. *Moscow Univ. Comput. Math. Cybern.* **2022**, *46*, 133–139. [CrossRef]
12. Kudryavtsev, A.A. Bayesian balance models. *Inform. Appl.* **2018**, *12*, 18–27.
13. Combes, C.; Ng, H.K.T. On parameter estimation for Amoroso family of distributions. *Math. Comp. Sim.* **2021**, *191*, 309–327. [CrossRef]
14. Liu, S.; Gui, W. Estimating the Parameters of the Two-Parameter Rayleigh Distribution Based on Adaptive Type II Progressive Hybrid Censored Data with Competing Risks. *Mathematics* **2020**, *8*, 1783. [CrossRef]
15. Kudryavtsev, A.; Shestakov, O. Asymptotically Normal Estimators for the Parameters of the Gamma-Exponential Distribution. *Mathematics* **2021**, *9*, 273. [CrossRef]
16. Kudryavtsev, A.A.; Shestakov, O.V. A Method for Estimating Bent, Shape and Scale Parameters of the Gamma-Exponential Distribution. *Inform. Appl.* **2021**, *15*, 57–62.
17. Kudryavtsev, A.; Shestakov, O. The Estimators of the Bent, Shape and Scale Parameters of the Gamma-Exponential Distribution and their Asymptotic Normality. *Mathematics* **2022**, *10*, 619. [CrossRef]
18. Korolev, V.Y. Product representations for random variables with Weibull distributions and their applications. *J. Math. Sci.* **2016**, *218*, 298–313. [CrossRef]
19. Gnedenko, B.V. On the estimation of unknown distribution parameters with a random number of independent observations. *Tr. Tbilis. Mat. Inst.* **1989**, *92*, 146–150.
20. Korolev, V.Y.; Zeifman, A.I. Generalized negative binomial distributions as mixed geometric laws and related limit theorems. *Lith. Math. J.* **2019**, *59*, 366–388. [CrossRef]
21. Wang, X.; Zhao, X.; Sun, J. A compound negative binomial distribution with mutative termination conditions based on a change point. *J. Comput. Appl. Math.* **2019**, *351*, 237–249. [CrossRef]
22. Bhati, D.; Ahmed, I.S. On uniform-negative binomial distribution including Gauss hypergeometric function and its application in count regression modeling. *Commun. Stat. Theory Methods* **2021**, *50*, 3106–3122. [CrossRef]
23. Zhang, J.; Wang, D.; Yang, K. A study of RCINAR(1) process with generalized negative binomial marginals. *Commun. Stat. B Simul. Comput.* **2020**, *49*, 1487–1510. [CrossRef]
24. Mangiola, S.; Thomas, E.A.; Modrák, M.; Vehtari, A.; Papenfuss, A.T. Probabilistic outlier identification for RNA sequencing generalized linear models. *NAR Genom. Bioinform.* **2021**, *3*, lqab005. [CrossRef]
25. Kendall, M.G.; Stuart, A. *The Advanced Theory of Statistics*, 3rd ed.; Griffin: London, UK, 1969; Volume 1.
26. Korolev, V.Y.; Zeifman, A.I. On Convergence of the Distributions of Random Sequences with Independent Random Indexes to Variance–Mean Mixtures. *Stoch. Models.* **2016**, *32*, 414–432. [CrossRef]

mathematics

MDPI

Article

Quick and Complete Convergence in the Law of Large Numbers with Applications to Statistics

Alexander G. Tartakovsky

AGT StatConsult, 71 Cypress Way, Rolling Hills Estates, CA 90274, USA; alexg.tartakovsky@gmail.com;
Tel.: +1-310-292-7847

Abstract: In the first part of this article, we discuss and generalize the complete convergence introduced by Hsu and Robbins in 1947 to the r-complete convergence introduced by Tartakovsky in 1998. We also establish its relation to the r-quick convergence first introduced by Strassen in 1967 and extensively studied by Lai. Our work is motivated by various statistical problems, mostly in sequential analysis. As we show in the second part, generalizing and studying these convergence modes is important not only in probability theory but also to solve challenging statistical problems in hypothesis testing and changepoint detection for general stochastic non-i.i.d. models.

Keywords: complete convergence; r-quick convergence; sequential analysis; hypothesis testing; changepoint detection.

MSC: 60F15; 60G35; 60G40; 60J05; 62L10; 62C10; 62C20; 62F03; 62H15; 62M02; 62P30

Citation: Tartakovsky, A.G. Quick and Complete Convergence in the LLN with Applications to Statistics. *Mathematics* **2023**, *11*, 2687. https://doi.org/10.3390/math11122687

Academic Editors: Irina Shevtsova and Victor Korolev

Received: 11 May 2023
Revised: 6 June 2023
Accepted: 7 June 2023
Published: 13 June 2023

1. Introduction

In [1], Hsu and Robbins introduced the notion of complete convergence which is stronger than almost sure (a.s.) convergence. Hsu and Robbins used this notion to discuss certain aspects of the law of large numbers (LLN). In particular, let $X_1, X_2, \dots$ be independent and identically distributed (i.i.d.) random variables with the common mean $\mu = \mathsf{E}[X_1]$. Hsu and Robbins proved that, while in Kolmogorov's strong law of large numbers (SLLN), only the first moment condition is needed for the sample mean $n^{-1}\sum_{t=1}^{n} X_t$ to converge to μ as $n \to \infty$, the complete version of the SLLN requires the second-moment condition $\mathsf{E}|X_1|^2 < \infty$ (finiteness of variance). Later, Baum and Katz [2], working on the rate of convergence in the LLN established that the second-moment condition is not only necessary but also sufficient for complete convergence. Strassen [3] introduced another mode of convergence, the r-quick convergence. When $r = 1$, these two modes of convergence are closely related. In the case of i.i.d. random variables and the sample mean $n^{-1}\sum_{t=1}^{n} X_t$, they are identical. This fact and certain statistical applications motivated Tartakovsky [4] (see also Tartakovsky [5] and Tartakovsky et al. [6]) to introduce a natural generalization of complete convergence—the r-complete convergence, which turns out to be identical to the r-quick convergence in the i.i.d. case.

The goal of this overview paper is to discuss the importance of quick and complete convergence concepts for several challenging statistical applications. These modes of convergence are discussed in detail in the first part of this paper. Statistical applications, which constitute the second part of this paper, include such fields as sequential hypothesis testing and changepoint detection in general non-i.i.d. stochastic models when observations can be dependent and highly non-stationary. Specifically, in the second part, we first address near optimality of Wald's sequential probability ratio test (SPRT) for testing two hypotheses regarding the distributions of non-i.i.d. data. We discuss Lai's results in his fundamental paper [7], which was the first publication that used the r-quick convergence of the log-likelihood ratio processes to establish the asymptotic optimality of the SPRT as probabilities of errors go to zero. We then go on to tackle the much more difficult multi-decision problem of testing multiple hypotheses and show that certain multi-hypothesis sequential tests asymptotically minimize moments of the stopping time distribution up to the order r when properly normalized log-likelihood ratio processes between hypotheses converge r-quickly or r-completely to finite positive numbers. These results can be established based on the former works of the author (see, e.g., Tartakovsky [4,5] and Tartakovsky et al. [6]). The second challenging application is the quickest change detection when it is necessary to detect a change that occurs at an unknown point in time as rapidly as possible. We show, using the works of the author (see, e.g., [5,6] and the references therein), that certain popular changepoint detection procedures such as CUSUM, Shiryaev, and Shiryaev–Roberts procedures are asymptotically optimal as the false alarm rate is low when the normalized log-likelihood ratio processes converge r-completely to finite numbers.

The rest of the paper is organized as follows. Section 2 discusses pure probabilistic issues related to r-complete convergence and r-quick convergence. Section 3 explores statistical applications in sequential hypothesis testing and changepoint detection. Section 4 outlines sufficient conditions for the r-complete convergence for Markov and hidden Markov models, which is needed to establish the optimality properties of sequential hypothesis tests and changepoint detection procedures. Section 5 provides a final discussion and concludes the paper.

2. Modes of Convergence and the Law of Large Numbers

We begin by listing some standard definitions in probability theory. Let $(\Omega, \mathscr{F})$ be a measurable space, i.e., Ω is a set of elementary events ω and $\mathscr{F}$ is a sigma-algebra (a system of subsets of Ω satisfying standard conditions). A probability space is a triple $(\Omega, \mathscr{F}, \mathsf{P})$, where P is a probability measure (completely additive measure normalized to 1) defined on the sets from the sigma-algebra $\mathscr{F}$. More specifically, by Kolmogorov's axioms, probability P satisfies: $\mathsf{P}(\mathcal{A}) \geq 0$ for any $\mathcal{A} \in \mathscr{F}$; $\mathsf{P}(\Omega) = 1$; and $\mathsf{P}(\cup_{i=1}^{\infty} \mathcal{A}_i) = \sum_{i=1}^{\infty} \mathsf{P}(\mathcal{A}_i)$ for $\mathcal{A}_i \in \mathscr{F}$, $\mathcal{A}_i \cap \mathcal{A}_j = \varnothing, i \neq j$, where $\varnothing$ is an empty set.

A function $X = X(\omega)$ defined on $(\Omega, \mathscr{F})$ with values in $\mathscr{X}$ is called a random variable if it is $\mathscr{F}$-measurable, i.e., $\{\omega : X(\omega) \in B\}$ belongs to the sigma-algebra $\mathscr{F}$. The function $F(x) = \mathsf{P}(\omega : X(\omega) \leq x)$ is the distribution function of X. It is also referred to as a cumulative distribution function (cdf). The real-valued random variables $X_1, X_2, \dots$ are independent if the events $\{X_1 \leq x_1\}, \{X_2 \leq x_2\}, \dots$ are independent for every sequence $x_1, x_2, \dots$ of real numbers. In what follows, we shall deal with real-valued random variables unless specified otherwise.

2.1. Standard Modes of Convergence

Let X be a random variable and let $\{X_n\}_{n \in \mathbb{Z}_+}$ ($\mathbb{Z}_+ = \{0, 1, 2, \dots\}$) be a sequence of random variables, both defined on the probability space $(\Omega, \mathscr{F}, \mathsf{P})$. We now give several standard definitions and results related to the law of large numbers.

Convergence in Distribution (Weak Convergence). Let $F_n(x) = \mathsf{P}(\omega : X_n \leq x)$ be the cdf of X_n and let $F(x) = \mathsf{P}(\omega : X \leq x)$ be the cdf of X. We say that the sequence $\{X_n\}_{n \in \mathbb{Z}_+}$ converges to X in distribution (or in law or weakly) as $n \to \infty$ and write $X_n \xrightarrow[n \to \infty]{\text{law}} X$ if

$$\lim_{n \to \infty} F_n(x) = F(x)$$

at all continuity points of $F(x)$.

Convergence in Probability. We say that the sequence $\{X_n\}_{n \in \mathbb{Z}_+}$ converges to X in probability as $n \to \infty$ and write $X_n \xrightarrow[n \to \infty]{\mathsf{P}} X$ if

$$\lim_{n \to \infty} \mathsf{P}(|X_n - X| > \varepsilon) = 0 \quad \text{for every } \varepsilon > 0.$$

Almost Sure Convergence. We say that the sequence $\{X_n\}_{n\in\mathbb{Z}_+}$ converges to X almost surely (a.s.) or with probability 1 (w.p. 1) as $n \to \infty$ under probability measure P and write $X_n \xrightarrow[n\to\infty]{\mathsf{P}-\text{a.s.}} X$ if

$$\mathsf{P}\Big(\omega : \lim_{n\to\infty} X_n = X\Big) = 1. \tag{1}$$

It is easily seen that (1) is equivalent to the condition

$$\lim_{n\to\infty} \mathsf{P}\left(\omega : \sum_{t=n}^{\infty} |X_t - X| > \varepsilon\right) = 0 \quad \text{for every } \varepsilon > 0,$$

and that the a.s. convergence implies convergence in probability, and the convergence in probability implies convergence in distribution, while the converse statements are not generally true.

The following double implications that establish necessary and sufficient conditions (i.e., equivalences) for the a.s. convergence are useful:

$$X_n \xrightarrow[n\to\infty]{\text{a.s.}} X \iff \mathsf{P}\left(\sup_{t\geq n} |X_t - X| > \varepsilon\right) \xrightarrow[n\to\infty]{} 0 \quad \text{for all } \varepsilon > 0. \tag{2}$$

The following result is often useful.

Lemma 1. *Let $f(t)$ be a non-negative increasing function, $\lim_{t\to\infty} f(t) = \infty$. If*

$$\frac{X_n}{f(n)} \xrightarrow[n\to\infty]{\mathsf{P}-a.s.} 0,$$

then

$$\lim_{n\to\infty} \mathsf{P}\left(\frac{1}{f(n)} \max_{0\leq t\leq n} X_t > \varepsilon\right) = 0 \quad \text{for every } \varepsilon > 0. \tag{3}$$

Proof. For any $\varepsilon > 0$, $n_0 > 0$ and $n > n_0$, we have

$$\begin{aligned}\mathsf{P}\left(\frac{1}{f(n)} \max_{0\leq t\leq n} X_t > \varepsilon\right) &\leq \mathsf{P}\left(\frac{1}{f(n)} \max_{0\leq t\leq n_0} X_t > \varepsilon\right) + \mathsf{P}\left(\frac{1}{f(n)} \max_{n_0< t\leq n} X_t > \varepsilon\right) \\ &\leq \mathsf{P}\left(\frac{1}{f(n)} \max_{0\leq t\leq n_0} X_t > \varepsilon\right) + \mathsf{P}\left(\sup_{t>n_0} \frac{X_t}{f(t)} > \varepsilon\right).\end{aligned}$$

Letting $n \to \infty$ and taking into account that

$$\lim_{n\to\infty} \mathsf{P}\left(\frac{1}{f(n)} \max_{0\leq t\leq n_0} X_t > \varepsilon\right) = 0,$$

we obtain

$$\limsup_{n\to\infty} \mathsf{P}\left(\frac{1}{f(n)} \max_{0\leq t\leq n} X_t > \varepsilon\right) \leq \mathsf{P}\left(\sup_{t>n_0} \frac{X_t}{f(t)} > \varepsilon\right).$$

Since n_0 can be arbitrarily large, we can let $n_0 \to \infty$ and since, by assumption, $X_n/f(n) \xrightarrow[n\to\infty]{\text{a.s.}} 0$, it follows from (2) that the upper bound approaches 0 as $n_0 \to \infty$. This completes the proof. □

Random Walk. Let $X_0, X_1, X_2, \ldots$ be i.i.d. random variables with the mean $\mathsf{E}[X_n] = \mu$ for $n \geq 1$ and the initial condition $X_0 = x$. Then, $S_n = \sum_{t=0}^{n} X_t$ is called a random walk with the mean $x + \mu\, n$.

In what follows, in the case where $X_1, X_2, \dots$ are i.i.d. random variables and $S_n = \sum_{t=0}^{n} X_t$, we prefer to formulate the results in terms of the random walk $\{S_n\}_{n \in \mathbb{Z}_+}$ (typically but not necessarily $S_0 = 0$).

We now recall the two strong law of large numbers (SLLN). Write $S_n = X_0 + X_1 + \dots + X_n$ for the partial sum ($X_0 = S_0 = 0$), so that $\{S_n\}_{n \in \mathbb{Z}_+}$ is a random walk with an initial condition of zero as long as $X_1, X_2, \dots$ are i.i.d. with mean μ.

Kolmogorov's SLLN. Let $\{S_n\}_{n \in \mathbb{Z}_+}$ be a random walk under probability measure P. If $\mathsf{E}[S_1]$ exists, then the sample mean S_n/n converges to the mean value $\mathsf{E}[S_1]$ w.p. 1, i.e.,

$$n^{-1} S_n \xrightarrow[n \to \infty]{\mathsf{P}-\text{a.s.}} \mathsf{E}[S_1]. \tag{4}$$

Conversely, if $n^{-1} S_n \xrightarrow[n \to \infty]{\mathsf{P}-\text{a.s.}} \mu$, where $|\mu| < \infty$, then $\mathsf{E}[S_1] = \mu$.

Marcinkiewicz–Zygmund's SLLN. Let $\{S_n\}_{n \in \mathbb{Z}_+}$ be a zero-mean random walk under probability measure P. The two following statements are equivalent:

(i) $\mathsf{E}|S_1|^p < \infty$ for $0 < p < 2$;

(ii) $n^{-1/p} S_n \xrightarrow[n \to \infty]{\mathsf{P}-\text{a.s.}} 0$.

2.2. Complete and r-Complete Convergence

We begin with discussing the issue of rates of convergence in the LLN.

Rates of Convergence. Let $\{X_n\}_{n \in \mathbb{Z}_+}$ be a sequence of random variables and assume that X_n converges to 0 w.p. 1 as $n \to \infty$. The question asks what the rate of convergence is. In other words, we are concerned with the speed at which the tail probability $\mathsf{P}(|X_n| > \varepsilon)$ decays to zero. This question can be answered by analyzing the behavior of the sums

$$\Sigma(r, \varepsilon) := \sum_{n=1}^{\infty} n^{r-1} \mathsf{P}(|X_n| > \varepsilon) \quad \text{for some } r > 0 \text{ and all } \varepsilon > 0.$$

More specifically, if $\Sigma(r, \varepsilon)$ is finite for every $\varepsilon > 0$, then the tail probability $\mathsf{P}(|X_n| > \varepsilon)$ decays with a rate faster than $1/n^r$, so that $n^r \mathsf{P}(|X_n| > \varepsilon) \to 0$ for all $\varepsilon > 0$ as $n \to \infty$.

To answer this question, we now consider modes of convergence that strengthen the almost sure convergence and therefore help determine the rate of convergence in the SLLN. Historically, this issue was first addressed in 1947 by Hsu and Robbins [1], who introduced the new mode of convergence which they called *complete convergence*.

Complete Convergence. The sequence $\{X_n\}_{n \in \mathbb{Z}_+}$ converges to 0 *completely* if

$$\lim_{n \to \infty} \sum_{i=n}^{\infty} \mathsf{P}(|X_t| > \varepsilon) = 0 \quad \text{for every } \varepsilon > 0, \tag{5}$$

which is equivalent to

$$\Sigma(1, \varepsilon) = \sum_{n=1}^{\infty} \mathsf{P}(|X_n| > \varepsilon) < \infty \quad \text{for every } \varepsilon > 0$$

Let $\{S_n\}_{n \in \mathbb{Z}_+}$ be a random walk with a mean of $\mathsf{E}[S_n] = \mu\, n$. Kolmogorov's SLLN (4) implies that the sample mean S_n/n converges to μ w.p. 1. Hsu and Robbins [1] proved that, under the same assumptions (i.e., under the only first-moment condition $\mathsf{E}|S_1| < \infty$) the sequence $\{n^{-1} S_n\}_{n \geq 1}$ does not need to completely converge to μ, but it will do so under the further second-moment condition $\mathsf{E}|S_1|^2 < \infty$. Thus, the finiteness of variance is a sufficient condition for complete convergence in the SLLN. They conjectured that the second-moment condition is not only sufficient but also necessary for complete convergence. Thus, it follows from these results that, if the variance is finite, then the rate of convergence in Kolmogorov's SLLN is $\lim_{n \to \infty} n\, \mathsf{P}(|S_n/n - \mu| > \varepsilon) = 0$ for all $\varepsilon > 0$.

In 1965, Baum and Katz [2] made a further step towards this issue. In particular, the following result follows from Theorem 3 in [2] for the zero-mean random walk $\{S_n\}_{n\in\mathbb{Z}_+}$.

Theorem 1. *Let $r > 0$ and $\alpha > 1/2$. If $\{S_n\}_{n\in\mathbb{Z}_+}$ is a zero-mean random walk, then the following statements are equivalent:*

$$\begin{aligned} \mathsf{E}[|S_1|^{(r+1)/\alpha}] < \infty &\iff \sum_{n=1}^{\infty} n^{r-1}\mathsf{P}\{n^{-\alpha}|S_n| > \varepsilon\} < \infty \textit{ for all } \varepsilon > 0 \\ &\iff \sum_{n=1}^{\infty} n^{r-1}\mathsf{P}\left\{\sup_{k\geq n}\frac{1}{k^\alpha}|S_k| > \varepsilon\right\} < \infty \textit{ for all } \varepsilon > 0. \end{aligned} \tag{6}$$

Setting $r = 1$ and $\alpha = 1$ in (6), we obtain the following equivalence

$$\mathsf{E}[|S_1|^2] < \infty \iff \sum_{n=1}^{\infty} \mathsf{P}\left\{|n^{-1}S_n| > \varepsilon\right\} < \infty \text{ for all } \varepsilon > 0,$$

which shows that the conjecture of Hsu and Robbins is correct—the second-moment condition $\mathsf{E}|S_1|^2 < \infty$ is both necessary and sufficient for complete convergence

$$n^{-1}S_n \xrightarrow[n\to\infty]{\mathsf{P}-\text{completely}} 0.$$

Furthermore, if for some $r > 0$, the $(r+1)$-th moment is finite, $\mathsf{E}|S_1|^{r+1} < \infty$, then the rate of convergence in the SLLN is $\lim_{n\to\infty} n^r\, \mathsf{P}(|n^{-1}S_n| > \varepsilon) = 0$ for all $\varepsilon > 0$.

Previous results suggest that it is reasonable to generalize the notion of complete convergence into the following mode of convergence that we will refer to as *r-complete convergence*, which is also related to the so-called r-quick convergence that we will discuss later on (see Section 2.3).

Definition 1 (*r-Complete Convergence*). *Let $r > 0$. We say that the sequence of random variables $\{X_n\}_{n\in\mathbb{Z}_+}$ converges to X as $n \to \infty$ r-completely under probability measure P and write $X_n \xrightarrow[n\to\infty]{\mathsf{P}-r-completely} X$ if*

$$\Sigma(r,\varepsilon) := \sum_{n=1}^{\infty} n^{r-1}\mathsf{P}(|X_n - X| > \varepsilon) < \infty \quad \textit{for every } \varepsilon > 0. \tag{7}$$

Note that the a.s. convergence of $\{X_n\}$ to X can be equivalently written as

$$\lim_{n\to\infty} \mathsf{P}\left(\sum_{t=n}^{\infty} |X_t - X| > \varepsilon\right) = 0 \quad \text{for every } \varepsilon > 0,$$

so that the r-complete convergence with $r \geq 1$ implies the a.s. convergence, but the converse is not true in general.

Suppose that X_n converges a.s. to X. If $\Sigma(r,\varepsilon)$ is finite for every $\varepsilon > 0$, then

$$\lim_{n\to\infty} \sum_{t=n}^{\infty} t^{r-1}\mathsf{P}(|X_t - X| > \varepsilon) = 0 \quad \text{for every } \varepsilon > 0$$

and probability $\mathsf{P}(|X_n - X| > \varepsilon)$ goes to 0 as $n \to \infty$ with the rate faster than $1/n^r$. Hence, as already mentioned above, the r-complete convergence allows one to determine the rate of convergence of X_n to X, i.e., to answer the question of how fast the tail probability $\mathsf{P}(|X_n - X| > \varepsilon)$ decays to zero.

The following result provides a very useful implication of complete convergence.

Theorem 2. *Let $\{X_n\}_{n\in\mathbb{Z}_+}$ and $\{Y_n\}_{n\in\mathbb{Z}_+}$ be two arbitrary, possibly dependent sequences of random variables. Assume that there are positive and finite numbers μ_1 and μ_2 such that*

$$\sum_{n=1}^{\infty} \mathsf{P}\left(\left|\frac{1}{n}X_n - \mu_1\right| > \varepsilon\right) < \infty \quad \text{for every } \varepsilon > 0 \tag{8}$$

and

$$\sum_{n=1}^{\infty} \mathsf{P}\left(\left|\frac{1}{n}Y_n - \mu_2\right| > \varepsilon\right) < \infty \quad \text{for every } \varepsilon > 0, \tag{9}$$

i.e., $n^{-1}X_n \xrightarrow[n\to\infty]{\mathsf{P}-completely} \mu_1$ *and* $n^{-1}Y_n \xrightarrow[n\to\infty]{\mathsf{P}-completely} \mu_2$. *If* $\mu_1 \geq \mu_2$, *then for any random time* T

$$\mathsf{P}(X_T < b,\, Y_{T+1} \geq b(1+\delta)) \longrightarrow 0 \quad \text{as } b \to \infty \quad \text{for any } \delta > 0. \tag{10}$$

Proof. Fix $\delta > 0$, $c \in (0, \delta)$ and let $N_b = \lceil (1+c)b/\mu_2 \rceil$ be the smallest integer that is larger than or equal to $(1+c)b/\mu_2$. Observe that

$$\begin{aligned}\mathsf{P}(X_T < b,\, Y_{T+1} \geq b(1+\delta)) &\leq \mathsf{P}(X_T \leq b,\, T \geq N_b) + \mathsf{P}(Y_{T+1} \geq (1+\delta)b,\, T < N_b) \\ &\leq \mathsf{P}(X_T \leq b,\, T \geq N_b) + \mathsf{P}\left(\max_{1\leq n\leq N_b} Y_n \geq (1+\delta)b\right).\end{aligned}$$

Thus, to prove (10), it suffices to show that the two terms on the right-hand side go to 0 as $b \to \infty$.

For the first term, we notice that, for any $n \geq N_b$,

$$\frac{b}{n} \leq \frac{b}{N_b} \leq \frac{\mu_2}{1+c} \leq \frac{\mu_1}{1+c} < \mu_1,$$

so that

$$\begin{aligned}\mathsf{P}(X_T \leq b,\, T \geq N_b) &= \sum_{n=N_b}^{\infty} \mathsf{P}(X_n \leq b,\, T = n) \leq \sum_{n=N_b}^{\infty} \mathsf{P}\left(\frac{X_n}{n} \leq \frac{b}{n}\right) \\ &\leq \sum_{n=N_b}^{\infty} \mathsf{P}\left(\frac{X_n}{n} \leq \frac{\mu_1}{1+c}\right) = \sum_{n=N_b}^{\infty} \mathsf{P}\left(\frac{X_n}{n} - \mu_1 \leq -\frac{c}{1+c}\mu_1\right).\end{aligned}$$

Since $N_b \to \infty$ as $b \to \infty$, the upper bound goes to 0 as $b \to \infty$ due to condition (8).

Next, since $c \in (0, \delta)$, there exists $\varepsilon' > 0$ such that

$$\frac{(1+\delta)b}{N_b} = \frac{(1+\delta)b}{\lceil b(1+c)/\mu_2 \rceil} \geq (1+\varepsilon')\mu_2.$$

As a result,

$$\mathsf{P}\left(\max_{1\leq n\leq N_b} Y_n \geq (1+\delta)b\right) \leq \mathsf{P}\left(\frac{1}{N_b}\max_{1\leq n\leq N_b} Y_n \geq (1+\epsilon')\mu_2\right),$$

where the upper bound goes to 0 as $b \to \infty$ by condition (9) (see Lemma 1). □

Remark 1. *The proof suggests that the assertion* (10) *of Theorem 2 holds under the following one-sided conditions*

$$\mathsf{P}\left(n^{-1}\max_{1\leq s\leq n} Y_s - \mu_2 > \varepsilon\right) \xrightarrow[n\to\infty]{} 0, \quad \sum_{n=1}^{\infty} \mathsf{P}\left(n^{-1}X_n - \mu_1 < -\varepsilon\right) < \infty.$$

Complete convergence conditions (8) *and* (9) *guarantee both these conditions.*

Remark 2. *Theorem 2 can be applied to the overshoot problem. Indeed, if $X_n = Y_n = Z_n$ and the random time T is the first time n when Z_n exceeds the level b, $T = \inf\{n \ge 1 : Z_n > b\}$, then Theorem 2 shows that the relative excess of boundary crossing (overshoot) $(Z_T - b)/b$ converges to 0 in probability as $b \to \infty$ when Z_n/n completely converges as $n \to \infty$ to a positive number μ.*

2.3. *r*-Quick Convergence

In 1967, Strassen [3] introduced the notion of r-quick limit points of a sequence of random variables. The r-quick convergence has been further addressed by Lai [7,8], Chow and Lai [9], Fuh and Zhang [10], and Tartakovsky [4,5] (see certain details in Section 2.4).

We define r-quick convergence in a way suitable for this paper. Let $\{X_n\}_{n\in\mathbb{Z}_+}$ be a sequence of real-valued random variables and let X be a random variable defined on the same probability space $(\Omega, \mathscr{F}, \mathsf{P})$.

Definition 2 (*r*-Quick Convergence). *Let $r > 0$ and for $\varepsilon > 0$, let*

$$L_\varepsilon = \sup\{n \ge 1 : |X_n - X| > \varepsilon\} \quad (\sup\{\varnothing\} = 0)$$

be the last entry time of X_n in the region $(X + \varepsilon, \infty) \cup (-\infty, X - \varepsilon)$. We say that the sequence $\{X_n\}_{n\in\mathbb{Z}_+}$ converges to X r-quickly as $n \to \infty$ under the probability measure P and write $X_n \xrightarrow[n\to\infty]{\mathsf{P}-r-quickly} X$ if and only if

$$\mathsf{E}[L_\varepsilon^r] < \infty \quad \textit{for every } \varepsilon > 0, \tag{11}$$

where E is the operator of expectation under probability P.

This definition can be generalized to random variables X, $\{X_n\}_{n\in\mathbb{Z}_+}$ taking values in a metric space $(\mathscr{X}, d)$ with distance d: $X_n \xrightarrow[n\to\infty]{r-\text{quickly}} X$ if

$$\mathsf{E}\big[(\sup\{n \ge 1 : d(X, X_n) > \varepsilon\})^r\big] < \infty \quad \text{for every } \varepsilon > 0.$$

Note that the a.s. convergence $X_n \to \mu$ ($|\mu| < \infty$) as $n \to \infty$ to a constant μ can be expressed as $\mathsf{P}(L_\varepsilon(\mu) < \infty) = 1$, where $L_\varepsilon(\mu) = \sup\{n \ge 1 : |X_n - \mu| > \varepsilon\}$. Therefore, the r-quick convergence implies the convergence w.p. 1 but not conversely.

Also, in general, r-quick convergence is stronger than r-complete convergence. Specifically, the following lemma shows that

$$\max_{1\le i\le n} X_t \xrightarrow[n\to\infty]{r-\text{completely}} \mu \implies X_n \xrightarrow[n\to\infty]{r-\text{quickly}} \mu \implies X_n \xrightarrow[n\to\infty]{r-\text{completely}} \mu. \tag{12}$$

Lemma 2. *Let $\{X_n\}_{n\in\mathbb{Z}_+}$ be a sequence of random variables. Let $f(t)$ be a non-negative increasing function, $f(0) = 0$, $\lim_{t\to\infty} f(t) = +\infty$, and let for $\varepsilon > 0$*

$$L_\varepsilon(f) = \sup\{n \ge 1 : |X_n| > \varepsilon f(n)\} \quad (\sup\{\varnothing\} = 0)$$

be the last time that X_n leaves the interval $[-\varepsilon f(n), +\varepsilon f(n)]$.

(i) For any $r > 0$ and any $\varepsilon > 0$, the following inequalities hold:

$$r\sum_{n=1}^{\infty} n^{r-1}\mathsf{P}\{|X_n| \ge \varepsilon f(n)\} \le \mathsf{E}\big[L_\varepsilon(f)^r\big] \le r\sum_{n=1}^{\infty} n^{r-1}\mathsf{P}\left\{\sup_{t\ge n}\frac{|X_t|}{f(t)} \ge \varepsilon\right\}. \tag{13}$$

Therefore,

$$\sum_{n=1}^{\infty} n^{r-1}\mathsf{P}\left\{\sup_{t\ge n}\frac{|X_t|}{f(t)} \ge \varepsilon\right\} < \infty \quad \textit{for all } \varepsilon > 0 \implies X_n \xrightarrow[n\to\infty]{r-quickly} 0.$$

(ii) *If $f(t)$ is a power function, $f(t) = t^\gamma$, $\gamma > 0$, then the finiteness of*

$$\sum_{n=1}^{\infty} n^{r-1} \mathsf{P}\Big\{ \max_{1 \le t \le n} X_t \ge \varepsilon n^\gamma \Big\}$$

for some $r > 0$ and every $\varepsilon > 0$ implies the r-quick convergence of X_n to 0:

$$\left\{ \sum_{n=1}^{\infty} n^{r-1} \mathsf{P}\Big(\max_{1 \le t \le n} X_t \ge \varepsilon n^\gamma \Big) < \infty \, \forall \, \varepsilon > 0 \right\} \implies \{ \mathsf{E}[L_\varepsilon(\gamma)^r] < \infty \, \forall \, \varepsilon > 0 \}, \tag{14}$$

where $L_\varepsilon(\gamma) = \sup\{n \ge 1 : |X_n| > \varepsilon n^\gamma\}$.

Proof. Proof of (i). Obviously,

$$\mathsf{P}\{|X_n| \ge \varepsilon f(n)\} \le \mathsf{P}\{L_\varepsilon(f) \ge n\} \le \mathsf{P}\left\{ \sup_{t \ge n} \tfrac{1}{f(t)} |X_t| \ge \varepsilon \right\}$$

from which the inequalities (13) follow immediately.

Proof of (ii). Write $M_u = \max_{1 \le n \le \lceil u \rceil} |X_n|$, where $\lceil u \rceil$ is a smallest integer greater or equal to u. We have the following chain of inequalities and equalities:

$$\begin{aligned}
\mathsf{E}\big[L_{2\varepsilon}(\gamma)^r\big] &\le r \int_0^\infty t^{r-1} \mathsf{P}\left\{ \sup_{u \ge t} u^{-\gamma} |X_u| \ge 2\varepsilon \right\} \mathrm{d}t \\
&\le r \int_0^\infty t^{r-1} \mathsf{P}\left\{ \sup_{u \ge t} \big[|X_u| - \varepsilon u^\gamma\big] \ge \varepsilon t^\gamma \right\} \mathrm{d}t \\
&\le r \int_0^\infty t^{r-1} \mathsf{P}\left\{ \sup_{u > 0} \big[|X_u| - \varepsilon u^\gamma\big] \ge \varepsilon t^\gamma \right\} \mathrm{d}t \\
&\le r \sum_{n=1}^{\infty} \int_0^\infty t^{r-1} \mathsf{P}\left\{ \sup_{(2^{n-1}-1)t^\gamma < u^\gamma \le (2^n-1)t^\gamma} \big[|X_u| - \varepsilon u^\gamma\big] \ge \varepsilon t^\gamma \right\} \mathrm{d}t \\
&\le r \sum_{n=1}^{\infty} \int_0^\infty t^{r-1} \mathsf{P}\left\{ \sup_{u^\gamma \le 2^n t^\gamma} |X_u| \ge 2^{n-1} \varepsilon t^\gamma \right\} \mathrm{d}t \\
&= r \sum_{n=1}^{\infty} \int_0^\infty t^{r-1} \mathsf{P}\left\{ M_{2^{n/\gamma} u} \ge 2^{n-1} \varepsilon t^\gamma \right\} \mathrm{d}t \\
&= r \left[\sum_{n=1}^{\infty} 2^{-n/\gamma} \right] \int_0^\infty u^{r-1} \mathsf{P}\{M_u \ge (\varepsilon/2) u^\gamma\} \, \mathrm{d}u.
\end{aligned}$$

It follows that

$$\begin{aligned}
\mathsf{E}\big[L_{2\varepsilon}(\gamma)^r\big] &\le r(2^{1/\gamma} - 1)^{-1} \int_0^\infty u^{r-1} \mathsf{P}\{M_u \ge (\varepsilon/2) u^\gamma\} \, \mathrm{d}u \le \\
&< r(2^{1/\gamma} - 1)^{-1} \sum_{n=1}^{\infty} n^{r-1} \mathsf{P}\left\{ \max_{1 \le t \le n} X_n \ge c n^\gamma \right\}
\end{aligned}$$

which yields the implication (14) and completes the proof. □

The following theorem shows that, in the i.i.d. case, the implications in (12) become equivalences.

Theorem 3. *Let $\{S_n\}_{n \in \mathbb{Z}_+}$ be a zero-mean random walk. The following statements are equivalent*

$$\mathsf{E}|S_1|^{r+1} < \infty \iff n^{-1} S_n \xrightarrow[n \to \infty]{r\text{-completely}} 0, \tag{15}$$

$$\mathsf{E}|S_1|^{r+1} < \infty \Longleftrightarrow n^{-1}S_n \xrightarrow[n\to\infty]{r-quickly} 0, \tag{16}$$

$$\mathsf{E}|S_1|^{r+1} \Longleftrightarrow \sum_{n=1}^{\infty} n^{r-1}\mathsf{P}\left\{\sup_{t\geq n}\frac{1}{t}|S_t| > \varepsilon\right\} < \infty \quad \textit{for all } \varepsilon > 0. \tag{17}$$

Proof. By Theorem 1, in the i.i.d. case,

$$\mathsf{E}|S_1|^{r+1} < \infty \Longleftrightarrow \sum_{n=1}^{\infty} n^{r-1}\mathsf{P}\left(\frac{1}{n}|S_n| > \varepsilon\right) < \infty \quad \forall \varepsilon > 0 \tag{18}$$

and

$$\mathsf{E}|S_1|^{r+1} < \infty \Longleftrightarrow \sum_{n=1}^{\infty} n^{r-1}\mathsf{P}\left(\sup_{t\geq n}\frac{1}{t}|S_t| > \varepsilon\right) < \infty \quad \forall \varepsilon > 0, \tag{19}$$

so that assertion (15) follows from (18) and (17) from (19).

Next, let

$$L_\varepsilon = \sup\{n \geq 1 : |S_n| \geq n\,\varepsilon\} \quad (\sup \varnothing = 0).$$

By Lemma 2(i),

$$\mathsf{E}[L_\varepsilon^r] \leq r\sum_{n=1}^{\infty} n^{r-1}\mathsf{P}\left\{\sup_{t\geq n}(|S_t|/t) \geq \varepsilon\right\} \quad \forall \varepsilon > 0, \tag{20}$$

which, along with (19), implies (16). □

2.4. Further Remarks on r-Complete Convergence, r-Quick Convergence, and Rates of Convergence in SLLN

Let $\{S_n\}_{n\in\mathbb{Z}_+}$ be a random walk. Without loss of generality, let $S_0 = 0$ and $\mathsf{E}[S_1] = 0$.

1. Strassen [3] proved, in particular, that if $f(n) = (2n\log n)^{1/2}$ in Lemma 2, then for $r > 0$

$$\limsup_{n\to\infty}\frac{S_n}{\sqrt{2n\log n}} = \sqrt{r\,\mathsf{E}[S_1^2]} \quad r-\text{quickly} \tag{21}$$

whenever $\mathsf{E}|S_1|^p < \infty$ for $p > (2r+1)$. He also proved the functional form of the law of the iterated logarithm.

2. Lai [8] improved this result, showing that Strassen's moment condition $\mathsf{E}|S_1|^p < \infty$ for $p > (2r+1)$ can be relaxed. Specifically, he showed that a weaker condition

$$\mathsf{E}\left[|S_1|^{2(r+1)}(\log^+|S_1|+1)^{-(r+1)})\right] < \infty \quad \text{for } r > 0 \tag{22}$$

is the best one can do (i.e., both necessary and sufficient):

$$\mathsf{E}\left[|S_1|^{2(r+1)}(\log^+|S_1|+1)^{-(r+1)}\right] < \infty \Longleftrightarrow \limsup_{n\to\infty}\frac{S_n}{\sqrt{2n\log n}} < \infty \ r-\text{quickly},$$

in which case equality (21) holds.

Note, however, that for $r = 0$, in terms of the a.s. convergence,

$$\mathsf{E}\left[|S_1|^2\right] < \infty \Longleftrightarrow \limsup_{n\to\infty}\frac{S_n}{\sqrt{2n\log\log n}} = \sqrt{\mathsf{E}[|S_1|^2]} \text{ a.s.}$$

but under condition (22) for all $r > 0$

$$\limsup_{n\to\infty}\frac{S_n}{\sqrt{2n\log\log n}} = \infty \ r-\text{quickly}.$$

3. Let $\alpha > 1/2$ and $r > 0$. Chow and Lai [9] established the following one-sided inequality for tail probabilities:

$$\sum_{n=1}^{\infty} n^{r-1} \mathsf{P}\Big(\max_{1\le t\le n} S_t \ge n^{\alpha}\Big) \le C_{r,\alpha}\Big\{\mathsf{E}\Big[(S_1^+)^{(r+1)/\alpha}\Big] + \Big(\mathsf{E}[S_1^2]\Big)^{r/(2\alpha-1)}\Big\} \tag{23}$$

whenever $\mathsf{E}|S_1|^2 < \infty$. Under the same hypotheses, this one-sided inequality implies the two-sided one:

$$\sum_{n=1}^{\infty} n^{r-1} \mathsf{P}\Big(\max_{1\le t\le n} |S_t| \ge n^{\alpha}\Big) \le C_{r,\alpha}\Big\{\mathsf{E}\Big[|S_1|^{(r+1)/\alpha}\Big] + \Big(\mathsf{E}[S_1^2]\Big)^{r/(2\alpha-1)}\Big\}. \tag{24}$$

The upper bound in (24) turns out to be sharp since the lower bound also holds:

$$\sum_{n=1}^{\infty} n^{r-1} \mathsf{P}\Big(\max_{1\le t\le n} |S_t| \ge n^{\alpha}\Big) \ge 1 + B_{r,\alpha}\Big\{\mathsf{E}\Big[|S_1|^{(r+1)/\alpha}\Big] + \Big(\mathsf{E}[S_1^2]\Big)^{r/(2\alpha-1)}\Big\}.$$

Here, the constants $C_{r,\alpha}$ and $B_{r,\alpha}$ are universal only depending on r, α.

The results of Chow and Lai [9] provide one-sided analogues of the results of Baum and Katz [2] as well as extend their results. Indeed, the one-sided inequality (23) implies that the following statements are equivalent for the zero-mean random walk $\{S_n\}_{n\in\mathbb{N}}$:

(i) $\mathsf{E}[(S_1^+)^{(r+1)/\alpha}] < \infty$;
(ii) $\sum_{n=1}^{\infty} n^{r-1}\mathsf{P}(n^{-\alpha}S_n \ge \varepsilon) < \infty$ for all $\varepsilon > 0$;
(iii) $\sum_{n=1}^{\infty} n^{r-1}\mathsf{P}\Big(\sup_{k\ge n} k^{-\alpha}S_k \ge \varepsilon\Big) < \infty$ for all $\varepsilon > 0$,

where $\alpha > 1/2$.

Clearly, the two-sided inequality (24) yields the assertions of Theorem 1.

4. The Marcinkiewicz–Zygmund SLLN states that, for $\alpha > 1/2$, the following implications hold:

$$\mathsf{E}|S_1|^{1/\alpha} < \infty \Longleftrightarrow n^{-\alpha}S_n \xrightarrow[n\to\infty]{\text{a.s.}} 0. \tag{25}$$

The strengthened r-quick equivalent of this SLLN is: for any $r > 0$ and $\alpha > 1/2$, the following statements are equivalent,

$$\begin{aligned}\mathsf{E}[|S_1|^{(r+1)/\alpha}] < \infty &\Longleftrightarrow \sum_{i=1}^{\infty} n^{r-1}\mathsf{P}\Big\{\frac{1}{n^{\alpha}}|S_n| > \varepsilon\Big\} < \infty \text{ for all } \varepsilon > 0\\ &\Longleftrightarrow \sum_{n=1}^{\infty} n^{r-1}\mathsf{P}\Big\{\sup_{k\ge n}\frac{1}{k^{\alpha}}|S_k| > \varepsilon\Big\} < \infty \text{ for all } \varepsilon > 0\\ &\Longleftrightarrow n^{-\alpha}S_n \xrightarrow[n\to\infty]{r-\text{quickly}} 0.\end{aligned} \tag{26}$$

Implications (26) follow from Theorem 1, Theorem 3 and inequality (24). The proof is almost obvious and omitted.

3. Applications of *r*-Complete and *r*-Quick Convergences in Statistics

In this section, we outline certain statistical applications which show the usefulness of r-complete and r-quick versions of the SLLN.

3.1. Sequential Hypothesis Testing

We begin by formulating the following multi-hypothesis testing problem for a general non-i.i.d. stochastic model. Let $(\Omega, \mathscr{F}, \mathscr{F}_n, \mathsf{P})$, $n \in \mathbb{Z}_+ = \{0,1,2,\dots\}$ be a filtered probability space with standard assumptions about the monotonicity of the sub-σ-algebras $\mathscr{F}_n$. The sub-σ-algebra $\mathscr{F}_n = \sigma(\mathbf{X}^n)$ of $\mathscr{F}$ is assumed to be generated by the sequence $\mathbf{X}^n = \{X_t, 1 \le t \le n\}$ observed up to time n, which is defined on the space $(\Omega, \mathscr{F})$. The hypotheses are $\mathsf{H}_i: \mathsf{P} = \mathsf{P}_i$, $i = 0, 1, \dots, N$, where $\mathsf{P}_0, \mathsf{P}_1, \dots, \mathsf{P}_N$ are given probability measures assumed to be locally mutually absolutely continuous, i.e., their restrictions P_i^n and P_j^n to $\mathscr{F}_n$ are equivalent for all $1 \le n < \infty$ and all $i, j = 0, 1, \dots, N, i \neq j$. Let Q^n be a restriction to $\mathscr{F}_n$ of a σ-finite measure Q on $(\Omega, \mathscr{F})$. Under P_i, the sample $\mathbf{X}^n = (X_1, \dots, X_n)$ has a joint density $p_{i,n}(\mathbf{X}^n)$ with respect to the dominating measure Q^n for all $n \in \mathbb{N}$, which can be written as

$$p_{i,n}(\mathbf{X}^n) = \prod_{t=1}^{n} f_{i,t}(X_t | \mathbf{X}^{t-1}), \tag{27}$$

where $f_{i,n}(X_n | \mathbf{X}^{n-1}), n \ge 1$ are corresponding conditional densities.

For $n \in \mathbb{N}$, define the likelihood ratio (LR) process between the hypotheses H_i and H_j

$$\Lambda_{ij}(n) = \frac{\mathrm{d}\mathsf{P}_i^n}{\mathrm{d}\mathsf{P}_j^n}(\mathbf{X}^n) = \frac{p_{i,n}(\mathbf{X}^n)}{p_{j,n}(\mathbf{X}^n)} = \prod_{t=1}^{n} \frac{f_{i,t}(X_t | \mathbf{X}^{t-1})}{f_{j,t}(X_t | \mathbf{X}^{t-1})}$$

and the log-likelihood ratio (LLR) process

$$\lambda_{ij}(n) = \log \Lambda_{ij}(n) = \sum_{t=1}^{n} \log \left[\frac{f_{i,t}(X_t | \mathbf{X}^{t-1})}{f_{j,t}(X_t | \mathbf{X}^{t-1})} \right].$$

A multi-hypothesis sequential test is a pair $\delta = (d, T)$, where T is a stopping time with respect to the filtration $\{\mathscr{F}_n\}_{n \in \mathbb{Z}_+}$ and $d = d(\mathbf{X}^T)$ is an $\mathscr{F}_T$-measurable terminal decision function with values in the set $\{0, 1, \dots, N\}$. Specifically, $d = i$ means that the hypothesis H_i is accepted upon stopping, i.e., $\{d = i\} = \{T < \infty, \delta \text{ accepts } \mathsf{H}_i\}$. Let $\alpha_{ij}(\delta) = \mathsf{P}_i(d = j)$, $i \neq j$, $i, j = 0, 1, \dots, N$ denote the error probabilities of the test δ, i.e., the probabilities of accepting the hypothesis H_j when H_i is true.

Introduce the class of tests with probabilities of errors $\alpha_{ij}(\delta)$ that do not exceed the prespecified numbers $0 < \alpha_{ij} < 1$:

$$\mathbb{C}(\boldsymbol{\alpha}) = \{\delta : \alpha_{ij}(\delta) \le \alpha_{ij} \text{ for } i, j = 0, 1, \dots, N, \ i \neq j\}, \tag{28}$$

where $\boldsymbol{\alpha} = (\alpha_{ij})$ is a matrix of given error probabilities that are positive numbers less than 1.

Let E_i denote the expectation under the hypothesis H_i (i.e., under the measure P_i). The goal of a statistician is to find a sequential test that would minimize the expected sample sizes $\mathsf{E}_i[T]$ for all hypotheses H_i, $i = 0, 1, \dots, N$ at least approximately, say asymptotically for small probabilities of errors, i.e., as $\alpha_{ij} \to 0$.

3.1.1. Asymptotic Optimality of Walds's SPRT

First, assume that $N = 1$, i.e., that we are dealing with two hypotheses H_0 and H_1. In the mid-1940s, Wald [11,12] introduced the *sequential probability ratio test* (SPRT) for the sequence of i.i.d. observations $X_1, X_2, \dots$, in which case $f_{i,t}(X_t | \mathbf{X}^{t-1}) = f_i(X_t)$ in (27) and the LR $\Lambda_{1,0}(n) = \Lambda_n$ is

$$\Lambda_n = \prod_{t=1}^{n} \frac{f_1(X_t)}{f_0(X_t)}.$$

After n observations have been made, Wald's SPRT prescribes for each $n \ge 1$:

$$\begin{aligned} \text{stop and accept } H_1 \quad &\text{if} \quad \Lambda_n \ge A_1; \\ \text{stop and accept } H_0 \quad &\text{if} \quad \Lambda_n \le A_0; \\ \text{continue sampling} \quad &\text{if} \quad A_0 < \Lambda_n < A_1, \end{aligned}$$

where $0 < A_0 < 1 < A_1$ are two thresholds.

Let $Z_t = \log[f_1(X_t)/f_0(X_t)]$ be the LLR for the observation X_t, so the LLR for the sample $\mathbf{X}^n$ is the sum

$$\lambda_{10}(n) = \lambda_n = \sum_{t=1}^{n} Z_t, \quad n = 1, 2, \dots$$

Let $a_0 = -\log A_0 > 0$ and $a_1 = \log A_1 > 0$. The SPRT $\delta_*(a_0, a_1) = (d_*, T_*)$ can be represented in the form

$$T_*(a_0, a_1) = \inf\{n \ge 1 : \lambda_n \notin (-a_0, a_1)\}, \quad d_*(a_0, a_1) = \begin{cases} 1 & \text{if } \lambda_{T_*} \ge a_1 \\ 0 & \text{if } \lambda_{T_*} \le -a_0. \end{cases} \tag{29}$$

In the case of two hypotheses, the class of tests (28) is of the form

$$\mathbb{C}(\alpha_0, \alpha_1) = \{\delta : \alpha_0(\delta) \le \alpha_0 \text{ and } \alpha_1(\delta) \le \alpha_1\}.$$

That is, it includes hypothesis tests with upper bounds α_0 and α_1 on the probabilities of errors of Type 1 (false positive) $\alpha_0(\delta) = \alpha_{0,1}(\delta)$ and Type 2 (false negative) $\alpha_1(\delta) = \alpha_{1,0}(\delta)$, respectively.

Wald's SPRT has an extraordinary optimality property: it minimizes both expected sample sizes $\mathsf{E}_0[T]$ and $\mathsf{E}_1[T]$ in the class of sequential (and non-sequential) tests $\mathbb{C}(\alpha_0, \alpha_1)$ with given error probabilities as long as the observations are i.i.d. under both hypotheses. More specifically, Wald and Wolfowitz [13] proved, using a Bayesian approach, that if $\alpha_0 + \alpha_1 < 1$ and thresholds $-a_0$ and a_1 can be selected in such a way that $\alpha_0(\delta_*) = \alpha_0$ and $\alpha_1(\delta_*) = \alpha_1$, then the SPRT δ_* is strictly optimal in class $\mathbb{C}(\alpha_0, \alpha_1)$. A rigorous proof of this fundamental result is tedious and involves several delicate technical details. Alternative proofs can be found in [14–18].

Regardless of the strict optimality of SPRT which holds if and only if thresholds are selected so that the probabilities of errors of SPRT are exactly equal to the prescribed values α_0, α_1, which is usually impossible, suppose that thresholds a_0 and a_1 are so selected that

$$a_0 \sim \log(1/\alpha_1) \quad \text{and} \quad a_1 \sim \log(1/\alpha_0) \quad \text{as } \alpha_{\max} \to 0. \tag{30}$$

Then

$$\mathsf{E}_1[T_*] \sim \frac{|\log \alpha_0|}{I_1}, \quad \mathsf{E}_0[T_*] \sim \frac{|\log \alpha_1|}{I_0} \quad \text{as } \alpha_{\max} \to 0, \tag{31}$$

where $I_1 = \mathsf{E}_1[Z_1]$ and $I_0 = \mathsf{E}_0[-Z_1]$ are Kullback–Leibler (K-L) information numbers so that the following asymptotic lower bounds for expected sample sizes are attained by SPRT:

$$\inf_{\delta \in \mathbb{C}(\alpha_0, \alpha_1)} \mathsf{E}_1[T] \ge \frac{|\log \alpha_0|}{I_1} + o(1), \quad \inf_{\delta \in \mathbb{C}(\alpha_0, \alpha_1)} \mathsf{E}_0[T] \ge \frac{|\log \alpha_1|}{I_0} + o(1) \quad \text{as } \alpha_{\max} \to 0$$

(cf. [6]). Hereafter, $\alpha_{\max} = \max(\alpha_0, \alpha_1)$.

The following inequalities for the error probabilities of the SPRT hold in the most general non-i.i.d. case

$$\alpha_1(\delta_*) \le \exp\{-a_0\}[1 - \alpha_0(\delta_*)], \quad \alpha_0(\delta_*) \le \exp\{-a_1\}[1 - \alpha_1(\delta_*)]. \tag{32}$$

These bounds can be used to guarantee asymptotic relations (30).

In the i.i.d. case, by the SLLN, the LLR λ_n has the following stability property

$$n^{-1}\lambda_n \xrightarrow[n\to\infty]{\mathsf{P}_1-\text{a.s.}} I_1, \quad n^{-1}(-\lambda_n) \xrightarrow[n\to\infty]{\mathsf{P}_0-\text{a.s.}} I_0. \tag{33}$$

This allows one to conjecture that, if in the general non-i.i.d. case, the LLR is also stable in the sense that the almost sure convergence conditions (33) are satisfied with some positive and finite numbers I_1 and I_0, then the asymptotic formulas (31) still hold. In the general case, these numbers represent the local K-L information in the sense that often (while not always) $I_1 = \lim_{n\to\infty} n^{-1}\mathsf{E}_1[\lambda_n]$ and $I_0 = \lim_{n\to\infty} n^{-1}\mathsf{E}_0[-\lambda_n]$. Note, however, that in the general non-i.i.d. case, the SLLN does not even guarantee the finiteness of the expected sample sizes $\mathsf{E}_i[T_*]$ of the SPRT, so some additional conditions are needed, such as a certain rate of convergence in the strong law, e.g., complete or quick convergence.

In 1981, Lai [7] was the first to prove the asymptotic optimality of Wald's SPRT in a general non-i.i.d. case as $\alpha_{\max} = \max(\alpha_0, \alpha_1) \to 0$. While the motivation was the near optimality of invariant SPRTs with respect to nuisance parameters, Lai proved a more general result using the r-quick convergence concept.

Specifically, for $0 < I_0 < \infty$ and $0 < I_1 < \infty$, define

$$L_1(\varepsilon) = \sup\Big\{n \ge 1 : |n^{-1}\lambda_n - I_1| \ge \varepsilon\Big\} \quad \text{and} \quad L_0(\varepsilon) = \sup\Big\{n \ge 1 : |n^{-1}\lambda_n + I_0| \ge \varepsilon\Big\}$$

($\sup\{\varnothing\} = 0$) and suppose that $\mathsf{E}_i[L_i(\varepsilon)^r] < \infty$ ($i = 0,1$) for some $r > 0$ and every $\varepsilon > 0$, i.e., that the normalized LLR converges r-quickly to I_1 under P_1 and to $-I_0$ under P_0:

$$n^{-1}\lambda_n \xrightarrow[n\to\infty]{\mathsf{P}_1-r-\text{quickly}} I_1 \quad \text{and} \quad n^{-1}\lambda_n \xrightarrow[n\to\infty]{\mathsf{P}_0-r-\text{quickly}} -I_0. \tag{34}$$

Strengthening the a.s. convergence (33) into the r-quick version (34), Lai [7] established the first-order asymptotic optimality of Wald's SPRT for moments of the stopping time distribution up to order r: If thresholds $a_1(\alpha_0, \alpha_1)$ and $-a_0(\alpha_0, \alpha_1)$ in the SPRT are so selected that $\delta_*(a_0, a_1) \in \mathbb{C}(\alpha_0, \alpha_1)$ and asymptotics (30) hold, then as $\alpha_{\max} \to 0$,

$$\begin{aligned} \inf_{\delta \in \mathbb{C}(\alpha_0,\alpha_1)} \mathsf{E}_1[T^r] &\sim \left(\frac{|\log \alpha_0|}{I_1}\right)^r \sim \mathsf{E}_1[T_*^r], \\ \inf_{\delta \in \mathbb{C}(\alpha_0,\alpha_1)} \mathsf{E}_0[T^r] &\sim \left(\frac{|\log \alpha_1|}{I_0}\right)^r \sim \mathsf{E}_0[T_*^r]. \end{aligned} \tag{35}$$

Wald's ideas have been generalized in many publications to construct sequential tests of composite hypotheses with nuisance parameters when these hypotheses can be reduced to simple ones by the principle of invariance. If M_n is the maximal invariant statistic and $p_i(M_n)$ is the density of this statistic under hypothesis H_i, then the invariant SPRT is defined as in (29) with the LLR $\lambda_n = \log[p_1(M_n)/p_0(M_n)]$. However, even if the observations $X_1, X_2, \dots$ are i.i.d. the invariant LLR statistic λ_n is not a random walk anymore and Wald's methods cannot be applied directly. Lai [7] has applied the asymptotic optimality property (35) of Wald's SPRT in the non-i.i.d. case to investigate the optimality properties of several classical invariant SPRTs such as the sequential t-test, the sequential T^2-test, and Savage's rank-order test.

In the sequel, we will call the case where the a.s. convergence in the non-i.i.d. model (33) holds with the rate $1/n$ *asymptotically stationary*. Assume now that (33) is generalized to

$$\lambda_n/\psi(n) \xrightarrow[n\to\infty]{\mathsf{P}_1-\text{a.s.}} I_1, \quad (-\lambda_n)/\psi(n) \xrightarrow[n\to\infty]{\mathsf{P}_0-\text{a.s.}} I_0, \tag{36}$$

where $\psi(t)$ is a positive increasing function. If $\psi(t)$ is not linear, then this case will be referred to as *asymptotically non-stationary*.

A simple example where this generalization is needed is testing H_0 versus H_1 regarding the mean of the normal distribution:

$$X_n = i\,S_n + \xi_n, \quad n \in \mathbb{Z}_+, \quad i = 0,1,$$

where $\{\xi_n\}_{n\ge1}$ is a zero-mean i.i.d. standard Gaussian sequence $\mathcal{N}(0,1)$ and $S_n = \sum_{j=0}^k c_j n^j$ is a polynomial of order $k \ge 1$. Then,

$$\lambda_n = \sum_{t=1}^n S_t X_t - \frac{1}{2}\sum_{t=1}^n S_t^2,$$

$\mathsf{E}_1[\lambda_n] = -\mathsf{E}_0[\lambda_n] = \frac{1}{2}\sum_{t=1}^n S_t^2 \sim c_k^2 n^{2k}$ for a large n, so $\psi(n) = n^{2k}$ and $I_1 = I_0 = c_k^2/2$ in (36). This example is of interest for certain practical applications, in particular, for the recognition of ballistic objects and satellites.

Tartakovsky et al. ([6] Section 3.4) generalized Lai's results for the asymptotically non-stationary case. Write $\Psi(t)$ for the inverse function of $\psi(t)$.

Theorem 4 (*SPRT asymptotic optimality*)**.** *Let $r \geq 1$. Assume that there exist finite positive numbers I_0 and I_1 and an increasing non-negative function $\psi(t)$ such that the r-quick convergence conditions*

$$\frac{\lambda_n}{\psi(n)} \xrightarrow[n\to\infty]{\mathsf{P}_1-r-quickly} I_1, \quad \frac{-\lambda_n}{\psi(n)} \xrightarrow[n\to\infty]{\mathsf{P}_0-r-quickly} I_0$$

hold. If thresholds $-a_0(\alpha_0, \alpha_1)$ and $a_1(\alpha_0, \alpha_1)$ are selected so that $\delta_*(a_0, a_1) \in \mathbb{C}(\alpha_0, \alpha_1)$ and $a_0 \sim |\log \alpha_1|$ and $a_1 \sim |\log \alpha_0|$, then, as $\alpha_{\max} \to 0$,

$$\begin{aligned} \inf_{\delta \in \mathbb{C}(\alpha_0,\alpha_1)} \mathsf{E}_1[T^r] &\sim \left[\Psi\left(\frac{|\log \alpha_0|}{I_1}\right)\right]^r \sim \mathsf{E}_1[T_*^r], \\ \inf_{\delta \in \mathbb{C}(\alpha_0,\alpha_1)} \mathsf{E}_0[T^r] &\sim \left[\Psi\left(\frac{|\log \alpha_1|}{I_0}\right)\right]^r \sim \mathsf{E}_0[T_*^r]. \end{aligned} \tag{37}$$

This theorem implies that the SPRT asymptotically minimizes the moments of the stopping time distribution up to order r.

The proof of this theorem is performed in two steps which are related to our previous discussion of the rates of convergence in Section 2. The first step is to obtain the asymptotic lower bounds in class $\mathbb{C}(\alpha_0, \alpha_1)$:

$$\liminf_{\alpha_{\max}\to 0} \frac{\inf_{\delta \in \mathbb{C}(\alpha_0,\alpha_1)} \mathsf{E}_1[T^r]}{[\Psi(|\log \alpha_0|/I_1)]^r} \geq 1, \quad \liminf_{\alpha_{\max}\to 0} \frac{\inf_{\delta \in \mathbb{C}(\alpha_0,\alpha_1)} \mathsf{E}_0[T^r]}{[\Psi(|\log \alpha_1|/I_0)]^r} \geq 1.$$

These bounds hold whenever the following right-tail conditions for the LLR are satisfied:

$$\begin{aligned} \lim_{M\to\infty} \mathsf{P}_1\left\{\frac{1}{\psi(M)} \max_{1\leq n\leq M} \lambda_n \geq (1+\varepsilon)I_1\right\} &= 1, \\ \lim_{M\to\infty} \mathsf{P}_0\left\{\frac{1}{\psi(M)} \max_{1\leq n\leq M} (-\lambda_n) \geq (1+\varepsilon)I_0\right\} &= 1. \end{aligned}$$

Note that, by Lemma 1, these conditions are satisfied when the SLLN (36) holds so that the almost sure convergence (36) is sufficient. However, as we already mentioned, the SLLN for the LLR is not sufficient to guarantee even the finiteness of the SPRT stopping time.

The second step is to show that the lower bounds are attained by the SPRT. To do so, it suffices to impose the following additional left-tail conditions:

$$\sum_{n=1}^{\infty} n^{r-1} \mathsf{P}_1\{\lambda_n \leq (I_1 - \varepsilon)\psi(n)\} < \infty, \quad \sum_{n=1}^{\infty} n^{r-1} \mathsf{P}_0\{-\lambda_n \leq (I_0 - \varepsilon)\psi(n)\} < \infty$$

for all $0 < \varepsilon < \min(I_0, I_1)$. Since both right-tail and left-tail conditions hold if the LLR converges r-completely to I_i,

$$\sum_{n=1}^{\infty} n^{r-1} \mathsf{P}_1\left\{\left|\frac{\lambda_n}{\psi(n)} - I_1\right| \geq \varepsilon\right\} < \infty, \quad \sum_{n=1}^{\infty} n^{r-1} \mathsf{P}_0\left\{\left|\frac{\lambda_n}{\psi(n)} + I_0\right| \geq \varepsilon\right\} < \infty,$$

and since r-quick convergence implies r-complete convergence (see (12)), we conclude that the assertions (37) hold.

Remark 3. *In the i.i.d. case, Wald's approach allows us to establish asymptotic equalities (37) with $I_1 = \mathsf{E}_1[\lambda_1]$ and $I_0 = -\mathsf{E}_0[\lambda_1]$ being K-L information numbers under the only condition of finiteness I_i. However, Wald's approach breaks down in the non-i.i.d. case. Certain generalizations in the case of independent but non-identically and substantially non-stationary observations, extending Wald's ideas, were considered in [19–21]. Theorem 4 covers all these non-stationary models.*

Fellouris and Tartakovsky [22] extended previous results on the asymptotic optimality of the SPRT to the case of the multistream hypothesis testing problem when the observations are sequentially acquired in multiple data streams (or channels or sources). The problem is to test the null hypothesis H_0 that none of the N streams are affected against the composite hypothesis H_B that a subset $B \subset \{1, \dots, N\}$ is affected. Write P_B and E_B for the distribution of observations and expectation under hypothesis H_B. Let $\mathscr{P}$ denote a class of subsets of $\{1, \dots, N\}$ that incorporates prior information which is available regarding the subset of affected streams, e.g., not more than $K < N$ streams can be affected. (In many practical problems, K is substantially smaller than the total number of streams N, which can be very large.)

Two sequential tests were studied in [22]—the generalized sequential likelihood ratio test and the mixture sequential likelihood ratio test. It has been shown that both tests are first-order asymptotically optimal, minimizing the moments of the sample size $\mathsf{E}_0[T^r]$ and $\mathsf{E}_B[T^r]$ for all $B \in \mathscr{P}$ up to order r as $\max(\alpha_0, \alpha_1) \to 0$ in the class of tests

$$\mathbb{C}_{\mathscr{P}}(\alpha_0, \alpha_1) = \left\{\delta : \mathsf{P}_0(d = 1) \le \alpha_0 \text{ and } \max_{B \in \mathscr{P}} \mathsf{P}_B(d = 0) \le \alpha_1\right\}, \quad 0 < \alpha_i < 1.$$

The proof is essentially based on the concept of r-complete convergence of LLR with the rate $1/n$. See also Chapter 1 in [5].

3.1.2. Asymptotic Optimality of the Multi-hypothesis SPRT

We now return to the multi-hypothesis model with $N > 1$ that we started to discuss at the beginning of this section (see (27) and (28)). The problem of the sequential testing of many hypotheses is substantially more difficult than that of testing two hypotheses. For multiple-decision testing problems, it is usually very difficult, if even possible, to obtain optimal solutions. Finding an optimal non-Bayesian test in the class of tests (28) that minimizes expected sample sizes $\mathsf{E}_i[T]$ for all hypotheses H_i, $i = 0, 1, \dots, N$ is not manageable even in the i.i.d. case. For this reason, a substantial part of the development of sequential multi-hypothesis testing in the 20th century has been directed towards the study of certain combinations of one-sided sequential probability ratio tests when observations are i.i.d. (see, e.g., [23–28]).

We will focus on the following first-order asymptotic criterion: Find a multi-hypothesis test $\delta_*(\boldsymbol{\alpha}) = (d_*(\boldsymbol{\alpha}), T_*(\boldsymbol{\alpha}))$ such that, for some $r \ge 1$,

$$\lim_{\alpha_{\max} \to 0} \frac{\inf_{\delta \in \mathbb{C}(\boldsymbol{\alpha})} \mathsf{E}_i[T^r]}{\mathsf{E}_i[T_*(\boldsymbol{\alpha})^r]} = 1 \quad \text{for all } i = 0, 1, \dots, N, \tag{38}$$

where $\alpha_{\max} = \max_{0 \le i,j \le N, i \ne j} \alpha_{ij}$.

In 1998, Tartakovsky [4] was the first who considered the sequential multiple hypothesis testing problems for general non-i.i.d. stochastic models following Lai's idea of exploiting the r-quick convergence in the SLLN for two hypotheses. The results were obtained for both discrete and continuous-time scenarios and for the asymptotically non-stationary case where the LLR processes between hypotheses converge to finite numbers with the rate $1/\psi(t)$. Two multi-hypothesis tests were investigated: (1) the *rejecting* test, which rejects the hypotheses one by one, and the last hypothesis, which is not rejected, is accepted; and (2) the *matrix accepting* test that accepts a hypothesis for which all component SPRTs that involve this hypothesis vote for accepting it.

We now proceed with introducing this accepting test which we will refer to as the *matrix SPRT* (MSPRT). In the present article, we do not consider the continuous-time scenarios. Those who are interested in continuous time are referred to [4,6,19,21,29].

Write $\mathcal{N} = \{0, 1, \ldots, N\}$. For a threshold matrix $(A_{ij})_{i,j\in\mathcal{N}}$, with $A_{ij} > 0$ and the A_{ii} being immaterial (say 0), define the matrix SPRT $\delta_*^N = (T_*^N, d_*^N)$, built on $(N+1)N/2$ one-sided SPRTs between the hypotheses H_i and H_j, as follows:

$$\text{Stop at the first } n \geq 1 \text{ such that, for some } i,\ \Lambda_{ij}(n) \geq A_{ji} \text{ for all } j \neq i, \tag{39}$$

and accept the unique H_i that satisfies these inequalities. Note that, for $N = 1$, the MSPRT coincides with Wald's SPRT.

In the following, we omit the superscript N in $\delta_*^N = (T_*^N, d_*^N)$ for brevity. Obviously, with $a_{ji} = \log A_{ji}$, the MSPRT in (39) can be written as

$$T_* = \inf\{n \geq 1 : \lambda_{ij}(n) \geq a_{ji} \ \text{ for all } j \neq i \text{ and some } i\}, \tag{40}$$

$$d_* = i \ \text{ for which (40) holds.} \tag{41}$$

Introducing the Markov accepting times for the hypotheses H_i as

$$T_i = \inf\left\{ n \geq 1 : \lambda_{i0}(n) \geq \max_{\substack{1\leq j\leq N \\ j\neq i}} [\lambda_{j0}(n) + a_{ji}] \right\}, \quad i = 0, 1, \ldots, N, \tag{42}$$

the test in (40), (41) can be also written in the following form:

$$T_* = \min_{0\leq j\leq N} T_j, \qquad d_* = i \quad \text{if} \quad T_* = T_i. \tag{43}$$

Thus, in the MSPRT, each component SPRT is extended until, for some $i \in \mathcal{N}$, all N SPRTs involving H_i accept H_i.

Using Wald's likelihood ratio identity, it is easily shown that $\alpha_{ij}(\delta_*) \leq \exp(-a_{ij})$ for $i, j \in \mathcal{N}, i \neq j$, so selecting $a_{ji} = |\log \alpha_{ji}|$ implies that $\delta_* \in \mathbb{C}(\boldsymbol{\alpha})$. These inequalities are similar to Wald's ones in the binary hypothesis case and are very imprecise. In his ingenious paper, Lorden [27] showed that, with a very sophisticated design that includes the accurate estimation of thresholds accounting for overshoots, the MSPRT is nearly optimal in the third-order sense, i.e., it minimizes the expected sample sizes for all hypotheses up to an additive disappearing term: $\inf_{\delta\in\mathbb{C}(\boldsymbol{\alpha})} \mathsf{E}_i[T] = \mathsf{E}_i[T_*] + o(1)$ as $\alpha_{\max} \to 0$. This result only holds for i.i.d. models with the finite second moment $\mathsf{E}_i[\lambda_{ij}(1)^2] < \infty$. In the non-i.i.d. case (and even in the i.i.d. case for higher moments $r > 1$), there is no way to obtain such a result, so we focus on the first-order optimality (38).

The following theorem establishes asymptotic operating characteristics and the optimality of MSPRT under the r-quick convergence of $\lambda_{ij}(n)/\psi(n)$ to finite K-L-type numbers I_{ij}, where $\psi(n)$ is a positive increasing function, $\psi(\infty) = \infty$.

Theorem 5 (*MSPRT asymptotic optimality* [4]). *Let $r \geq 1$. Assume that there exist finite positive numbers I_{ij}, $i, j = 0, 1, \ldots, N$, $i \neq j$ and an increasing non-negative function $\psi(t)$ such that, for some $r > 0$,*

$$\frac{\lambda_{ij}(n)}{\psi(n)} \xrightarrow[n\to\infty]{\mathsf{P}_i-r-\text{quickly}} I_{ij} \quad \text{for all } i, j = 0, 1, \ldots, N, i \neq j. \tag{44}$$

Then, the following assertions are true.

(i) *For $i - 0, 1, \ldots, N$,*

$$\mathsf{E}_i[T_*^r] \sim \left[\Psi\left(\max_{\substack{0\leq j\leq N \\ j\neq i}} \frac{a_{ji}}{I_{ij}}\right)\right]^r \quad \text{as} \ \min_{j,i} a_{ji} \to \infty. \tag{45}$$

(ii) *If the thresholds are so selected that* $\alpha_{ij}(\delta^*) \le \alpha_{ij}$ *and* $a_{ji} \sim |\log \alpha_{ji}|$*, particularly as* $a_{ji} = |\log \alpha_{ji}|$*, then for all* $i = 0, 1, \dots, N$

$$\inf_{\delta \in \mathbb{C}(\boldsymbol{\alpha})} \mathsf{E}_i[T^r] \sim \left[\Psi\left(\max_{\substack{0 \le j \le N \\ j \ne i}} \frac{|\log \alpha_{ji}|}{I_{ij}}\right)\right]^r \sim \mathsf{E}_i[T_*^r] \quad \text{as } \alpha_{\max} \to 0. \tag{46}$$

Assertion (ii) implies that the MSPRT asymptotically minimizes the moments of the stopping time distribution up to order r for all hypotheses $\mathsf{H}_0, \mathsf{H}_1, \dots, \mathsf{H}_N$ in the class of tests $\mathbb{C}(\boldsymbol{\alpha})$.

Remark 4. *Both assertions of Theorem 5 are correct under the r-complete convergence*

$$\frac{\lambda_{ij}(n)}{\psi(n)} \xrightarrow[n\to\infty]{\mathsf{P}_i - r-\text{complete}} I_{ij} \quad \text{for all } i, j = 0, 1, \dots, N, i \ne j,$$

i.e., when

$$\sum_{n=1}^{\infty} n^{r-1} \mathsf{P}_i\left\{\left|\frac{1}{\psi(n)}\lambda_{ij}(n) - I_{ij}\right| > \varepsilon\right\} < \infty \quad \text{for all } \varepsilon > 0.$$

While this statement has not been proven anywhere to date, it can be easily proven using the methods developed for multistream hypothesis testing and changepoint detection ([5] Ch 1, Ch 6).

Remark 5. *As shown in the example given in Section 3.4.3 of [6], the r-quick convergence conditions in Theorem 5 (or corresponding r-complete convergence conditions for LLR processes) cannot be generally relaxed into the almost sure convergence*

$$\frac{\lambda_{ij}(n)}{\psi(n)} \xrightarrow[n\to\infty]{\mathsf{P}_i - a.s.} I_{ij} \quad \text{for all } i, j = 0, 1, \dots, N, i \ne j. \tag{47}$$

However, the following weak asymptotic optimality result holds for the MSPRT under the a.s. convergence: if the a.s. convergence (47) *holds with the power function* $\psi(t) = t^k$, $k > 0$*, then, for every* $0 < \varepsilon < 1$,

$$\inf_{\delta \in \mathbb{C}(\boldsymbol{\alpha})} \mathsf{P}_i(T > \varepsilon T_*) \to 1 \quad \text{as } \alpha_{\max} \to 0 \text{ for all } i = 0, 1, \dots, N \tag{48}$$

whenever thresholds a_{ji} *are selected as in Theorem 5 (ii).*

Note that several interesting statistical and practical applications of these results to invariant sequential testing and multisample slippage scenarios are discussed in Sections 4.5 and 4.6 of Tartakovsky et al. [6] (see Mosteller [30] and Ferguson [16] for terminology regarding multisample slippage problems).

3.2. Sequential Changepoint Detection

Sequential (or quickest) changepoint detection is an important subfield of sequential analysis. The observations are made one at a time and as long as their behavior suggests that the process of interest is in control (i.e., in a normal state), the process is allowed to continue. If the state is believed to have lost control, the goal is to detect the change in distribution as rapidly as possible. Quickest change detection problems have an enormous number of important applications, e.g., object detection in noise and clutter, industrial quality control, environment surveillance, failure detection, navigation, seismology, computer network security, genomics, and epidemiology (see, e.g., [31–40]). Many challenging application areas are discussed in the books by Tartakovsky, Nikiforov, and Basseville ([6] Ch 11) and Tartakovsky ([5] Ch 8).

3.2.1. Changepoint Models

The probability distribution of the observations $\mathbf{X} = \{X_n\}_{n\in\mathbb{N}}$ is subject to a change at an unknown point in time $\nu \in \{0,1,2,\dots\} = \mathbb{Z}_+$ so that $X_1,\dots,X_\nu$ are generated by one stochastic model and $X_{\nu+1}, X_{\nu+2},\dots$ are generated by another model. A sequential detection rule is a stopping time T for an observed sequence $\{X_n\}_{n\geq 1}$, i.e., T is an integer-valued random variable such that the event $\{T = n\}$ belongs to the sigma-algebra $\mathscr{F}_n = \sigma(X_1,\dots,X_n)$ generated by observations $X_1,\dots,X_n$.

Let P_∞ denote the probability measure corresponding to the sequence of observations $\{\mathbf{X}_n\}_{n\geq 1}$ when there is never a change ($\nu = \infty$) and, for $k = 0,1,2,\dots$, let P_k denote the measure corresponding to the sequence $\{\mathbf{X}_n\}_{n\geq 1}$ when $\nu = k < \infty$. We denote the hypothesis that the change never occurs by $\mathsf{H}_\infty : \nu = \infty$ and we denote the hypothesis that the change occurs at time $0 \leq k < \infty$ by $\mathsf{H}_k : \nu = k$.

First consider a general non-i.i.d. model assuming that the observations may have a very general stochastic structure. Specifically, if we let, as before, $\mathbf{X}^n = (X_1,\dots,X_n)$ denote the sample of size n, then when $\nu = \infty$ (there is no change), the conditional density of X_n given $\mathbf{X}^{n-1}$ is $g_n(X_n|\mathbf{X}^{n-1})$ for all $n \geq 1$ and when $\nu = k < \infty$, then the conditional density is $g_n(X_n|\mathbf{X}^{n-1})$ for $n \leq k$ and $f_n(X_n|\mathbf{X}^{n-1})$ for $n > k$. Thus, for the general non-i.i.d. changepoint model, the joint density $p(\mathbf{X}^n|\mathsf{H}_k)$ under hypothesis H_k can be written as follows

$$p(\mathbf{X}^n|\mathsf{H}_k) = \begin{cases} \prod_{t=1}^n g_t X_t|\mathbf{X}^{t-1}) & \text{for } \nu = k \geq n, \\ \prod_{t=1}^k g_t(\mathbf{X}_t|\mathbf{X}^{t-1}) \times \prod_{t=k+1}^n f_t(X_t|\mathbf{X}^{t-1}) & \text{for } \nu = k < n, \end{cases} \tag{49}$$

where $g_n(X_n|\mathbf{X}^{n-1})$ is the pre-change conditional density and $f_n(X_n|\mathbf{X}^{n-1})$ is the post-change conditional density which may depend on ν, $f_n(X_n|\mathbf{X}^{n-1}) = f_n^{(\nu)}(X_n|\mathbf{X}^{n-1})$, but we will omit the superscript ν for brevity.

The classical changepoint detection problem deals with the i.i.d. case where there is a sequence of observations $X_1, X_2,\dots$ that are identically distributed with a probability density function (pdf) $g(x)$ for $n \leq \nu$ and with a pdf $f(x)$ for $n > \nu$. That is, in the i.i.d. case, the joint density of the vector $\mathbf{X}^n = (X_1,\dots,X_n)$ under hypothesis H_k has the form

$$p(\mathbf{X}^n|\mathsf{H}_k) = \begin{cases} \prod_{t=1}^n g(X_t) & \text{for } \nu = k \geq n, \\ \prod_{t=1}^k g(X_t) \times \prod_{t=k+1}^n f(X_t) & \text{for } \nu = k < n. \end{cases} \tag{50}$$

Note that, as discussed in [5,6], in applications, there are two different kinds of changes—additive and non-additive. Additive changes lead to a change in the mean value of the sequence of observations. Non-additive changes are typically produced by a change in variance or covariance, i.e., these are spectral changes.

We now proceed by discussing the models for the change point ν. The change point ν may be considered either as an unknown deterministic number or as a random variable. If the change point is treated as a random variable, then the model has to be supplied with the *prior distribution* of the change point. There may be several changepoint mechanisms, and, as a result, a random variable ν may be dependent on or independent of the observations. In particular, Moustakides [41] assumed that ν can be a $\{\mathscr{F}_n\}$-adapted stopping time. In this article, we will not discuss Moustakides's concept by allowing the prior distribution to depend on some additional information available to "Nature" (see [5] for a detailed discussion); rather, when considering a Bayesian approach, we will assume that the prior distribution of the unknown change point is independent of the observations.

3.2.2. Popular Changepoint Detection Procedures

Before formulating the criteria of optimality in the next subsection, we begin by defining the three most popular and common change detection procedures, which are either optimal or nearly optimal in different settings. To define these procedures, we need to introduce the partial likelihood ratio and the corresponding log-likelihood ratio

$$\mathsf{LR}_t = \frac{f_t(X_t|\mathbf{X}^{t-1})}{g_t(X_t|\mathbf{X}^{t-1})}, \quad Z_t = \log\frac{f_t(X_t|\mathbf{X}^{t-1})}{g_t(X_t|\mathbf{X}^{t-1})}, \quad t = 1, 2, \dots$$

It is worth iterating that, for general non-i.i.d. models, the post-change density often depends on the point of change, $f_t(X_t|\mathbf{X}^{t-1}) = f_t^{(\nu)}(X_t|\mathbf{X}^{t-1})$, so in general $\mathsf{LR}_t = \mathsf{LR}_t^{(\nu)}$ and $Z_t = Z_t^{(\nu)}$ also depend on the change point ν. However, this is not the case for the i.i.d. model (50).

The CUSUM Procedure

We now introduce the *Cumulative Sum* (CUSUM) algorithm, which was first proposed by Page [42] for the i.i.d. model (50). Recall that we consider the changepoint detection problem as a problem of testing two hypotheses: H_ν that the change occurs at a fixed-point $0 \le \nu < \infty$ against the alternative H_∞ that the change never occurs. The LR between these hypotheses is $\Lambda_n^\nu = \prod_{t=\nu+1}^n \mathsf{LR}_t$ for $\nu < n$ and 1 for $\nu \ge n$. Since the hypothesis H_ν is composite, we may apply the generalized likelihood ratio (GLR) approach maximizing the LR Λ_n^ν over ν to obtain the GLR statistic

$$V_n = \max_{0 \le \nu < n} \prod_{t=\nu+1}^{n} \mathsf{LR}_t, \quad n \ge 1.$$

It is easy to verify that this statistic follows the recursion

$$V_n = \max\{1, V_{n-1}\}\mathsf{LR}_n, \quad n \ge 1, \ V_0 = 1 \tag{51}$$

as long as the partial LR LR_n does not depend on the change point, i.e., the post-change conditional density $f_n(X_n|\mathbf{X}^{n-1})$ does not depend on ν. This is always the case for i.i.d. models (50) when $f_n(X_n|\mathbf{X}^{n-1}) = f(X_n)$. However, as we already mentioned, for non-i.i.d. models, $f_n(X_n|\mathbf{X}^{n-1}) = f_n^{(\nu)}(X_n|\mathbf{X}^{n-1})$ often depends on the change point ν, so $\mathsf{LR}_n = \mathsf{LR}_n^{(\nu)}$, in which case the recursion (51) does not hold.

The logarithmic version of V_n, $W_n = \log V_n$, is related to Page's CUSUM statistic G_n introduced by Page [42] in the i.i.d. case as $G_n = \max(0, W_n)$. The statistic G_n can also be obtained via the GLR approach by maximizing the LLR $\lambda_n^\nu = \log \Lambda_n^\nu$ over $0 \le \nu < \infty$. However, since the hypotheses H_∞ and H_ν are indistinguishable for $\nu \ge n$, the maximization over $\nu \ge n$ does not make very much sense. Note also that, in contrast to Page's CUSUM statistic G_n, the statistic W_n may take values smaller than 0, so the CUSUM procedure

$$\mathsf{T}_{\mathsf{CS}} = \inf\{n \ge 1 : W_n \ge a\} \tag{52}$$

makes sense even for negative values of the threshold a. Thus, it is more general than Page's CUSUM. Note the recursions

$$W_n = W_{n-1}^+ + Z_n, \quad n \ge 1, \ W_0 = 0 \tag{53}$$

and

$$G_n = (G_{n-1} + Z_n)^+, \quad n \ge 1, \ G_0 = 0$$

in cases where $Z_n = \log[f_n(X_n|\mathbf{X}^{n-1})/g_n(X_n|\mathbf{X}^{n-1})]$ does not depend on ν.

Shiryaev's Procedure

In the i.i.d. case and for the zero-modified geometric prior distribution of the change point, Shiryaev [43] introduced the change detection procedure that prescribes the thresholding of the posterior probability $\mathsf{P}(\nu < n|\mathbf{X}^n)$. Introducing the statistic

$$\mathsf{S}_n^\pi = \frac{\mathsf{P}(\nu < n|\mathbf{X}^n)}{1 - \mathsf{P}(\nu < n|\mathbf{X}^n)}$$

one can write the stopping time of the Shiryaev procedure in the general non-i.i.d. case and for an arbitrary prior π as

$$\mathsf{T}_{\mathsf{SH}} = \inf\{n \geq 1 : \mathsf{S}_n^\pi \geq A\}, \tag{54}$$

where A ($A > 0$) is a threshold controlling for the false alarm risk. The statistic S_n^π can be written as

$$\begin{aligned} \mathsf{S}_n^\pi &= \frac{1}{\mathsf{P}(\nu \geq n)} \sum_{k=0}^{n-1} \pi_k \Lambda_n^k \\ &= \frac{1}{\mathsf{P}(\nu \geq n)} \sum_{k=0}^{n-1} \pi_k \prod_{t=k+1}^{n} \mathsf{LR}_t, \quad n \geq 1, \quad \mathsf{S}_0^\pi = 0, \end{aligned} \tag{55}$$

where the product $\prod_{t=i}^{j} \mathsf{LR}_t = 1$ for $j < i$.

Often (following Shiryaev's assumptions), it is supposed that the change point ν is distributed according to the geometric distribution Geometric(ϱ)

$$\mathsf{P}(\nu = k) = \varrho(1-\varrho)^k \quad \text{for } k = 0, 1, 2, \dots, \tag{56}$$

where $\varrho \in (0,1)$.

If LR_n does not depend on the change point ν and the prior distribution is geometric (56), then the statistic $\widetilde{\mathsf{S}}_n^\varrho = \mathsf{S}_n^\pi/\varrho$ can be rewritten in the recursive form

$$\widetilde{\mathsf{S}}_n^\varrho = \left(1 + \widetilde{\mathsf{S}}_{n-1}^\varrho\right) \frac{\mathsf{LR}_n}{1-\varrho}, \quad n \geq 1, \ \widetilde{\mathsf{S}}_0^\varrho = 0. \tag{57}$$

However, as mentioned above, this may not be the case for non-i.i.d. models, since LR_n often depends on ν.

Shiryaev–Roberts Procedure

The generalized Shiryaev–Roberts (SR) change detection procedure is based on the thresholding of the generalized SR statistic

$$\mathsf{R}_n^{r_0} = r_0 \Lambda_n^0 + \sum_{k=0}^{n-1} \Lambda_n^k = r_0 \prod_{t=1}^{n} \mathsf{LR}_t + \sum_{k=0}^{n-1} \prod_{t=k+1}^{n} \mathsf{LR}_t, \quad n \geq 1, \tag{58}$$

with a non-negative head-start $\mathsf{R}_0 = r_0$, $r_0 \geq 0$, i.e., the stopping time of the SR procedure is given by

$$\mathsf{T}_{\mathsf{SR}}^{r_0} = \inf\{n \geq 1 : \mathsf{R}_n^{r_0} \geq A\}, \quad A > 0. \tag{59}$$

This procedure is usually referred to as the SR-r detection procedure in contrast to the standard SR procedure $\mathsf{T}_{\mathsf{SR}} \equiv \mathsf{T}_{\mathsf{SR}}^{r_0}$, $r_0 = 0$ that starts with a zero initial condition $r_0 = 0$. In the i.i.d. case (50), this modification of the SR procedure was introduced and studied in detail in [44,45].

If LR_n does not depend on the change point ν, then the SR-r detection statistic satisfies the recursion

$$\mathsf{R}_n^{r_0} = (1 + \mathsf{R}_{n-1}^{r_0})\mathsf{LR}_n, \quad n \geq 1, \quad \mathsf{R}_0^{r_0} = r_0.$$

Note that, as the parameter of the geometric prior distribution $\varrho \to 0$, the Shiryaev statistic $\widetilde{S}_n^{\varrho}$ converges to the SR statistic $R_n^{r_0=0}$.

3.2.3. Optimality Criteria

The goal of online change detection is to detect the change with the smallest delay controlling for a false alarm rate at a given level. Tartakovsky et al. [6] suggested several changepoint problem settings, including Bayesian, minimax, and uniform (pointwise) approaches.

Let E_k denote the expectation with respect to measure P_k when the change occurs at $\nu = k < \infty$ and E_∞ with respect to P_∞ when there is no change.

In 1954, Page [42] suggested measuring the risk due to a false alarm by the mean time to false alarm $\mathsf{E}_\infty[T]$ and the risk associated with a true change detection by the mean time to detection $\mathsf{E}_0[T]$ when the change occurs at the very beginning. He called these performance characteristics the *average run length* (ARL). Page also introduced the now most famous change detection procedure—the CUSUM procedure (see (52) with W_n replaced by G_n)—and analyzed it using these operating characteristics in the i.i.d. case.

While the false alarm rate can be reasonably measure by the ARL to false alarm

$$\mathsf{ARL2FA}(T) = \mathsf{E}_\infty[T],$$

as Figure 1 suggests, the risk due to a true change detection can be reasonably measured by the conditional expected delay to detection

$$\mathsf{CEDD}_\nu(T) = \mathsf{E}_\nu[T - \nu | T > \nu], \quad \nu = 0, 1, 2, \ldots$$

for any possible change point $\nu \in \mathbb{Z}_+ = \{0, 1, 2, \ldots\}$ but not necessarily by the ARL to detection $\mathsf{E}_0[T] \equiv \mathsf{CEDD}_0(T)$. A good detection procedure has to guarantee small values of the expected detection delay $\mathsf{CEDD}_\nu(T)$ for all change points $\nu \in \mathbb{Z}_+$ when $\mathsf{ARL2FA}(T)$ is set at a certain level. However, if the false alarm risk is measured in terms of the ARL to false alarm, i.e., it is required that $\mathsf{ARL2FA}(T) \geq \gamma$ for some $\gamma \geq 1$, then a procedure that minimizes the conditional expected delay to detection $\mathsf{CEDD}_\nu(T)$ uniformly over all ν does not exist. For this reason, we must resort to different optimality criteria, e.g., to Bayesian and minimax criteria.

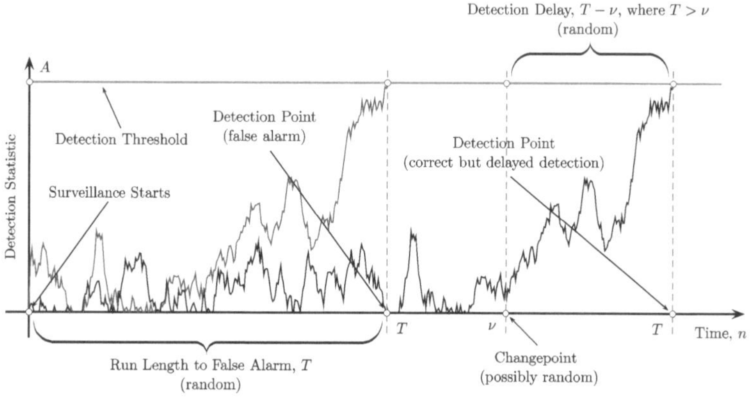

Figure 1. Illustration of a single-run sequential changepoint detection. Two possibilities in the detection process: false alarm (**left**) and correct detection (**right**).

Minimax Changepoint Optimization Criteria

There are two popular minimax criteria. The first one was introduced by Lorden [46]:

$$\inf_T \sup_{\nu \in \mathbb{Z}_+} \operatorname{ess\,sup} \mathsf{E}_\nu[T - \nu \mid T > \nu, \mathscr{F}_\nu] \quad \text{subject to } \mathsf{ARL2FA}(T) \geq \gamma.$$

This requires minimizing the conditional expected delay to detection $\mathsf{E}_\nu[T-\nu \mid T>\nu, \mathscr{F}_\nu]$ in the worst-case scenario with respect to both the change point ν and the trajectory $(X_1, \dots, X_\nu)$ of the observed process in the class of detection procedures

$$\mathbb{C}_{\mathrm{ARL}}(\gamma) = \{T : \mathsf{ARL2FA}(T) \geq \gamma\}, \quad \gamma \geq 1,$$

for which the ARL to false alarm exceeds the prespecified value $\gamma \in [1, \infty)$. Let $\mathsf{ESADD}(T) = \sup_{\nu \geq 0} \operatorname{ess\,sup} \mathsf{E}_\nu[T-\nu \mid T>\nu, \mathscr{F}_\nu]$ denote Lorden's speed detection measure. Under Lorden's minimax approach, the goal is to find a stopping time $T_{\mathrm{opt}} \in \mathbb{C}_{\mathrm{ARL}}(\gamma)$ such that

$$\mathsf{ESADD}(T_{\mathrm{opt}}) = \inf_{T \in \mathbb{C}_{\mathrm{ARL}}(\gamma)} \mathsf{ESADD}(T) \quad \text{for any } \gamma \geq 1.$$

In the classical i.i.d. scenario (50), Lorden [46] proved that the CUSUM detection procedure (52) is asymptotically first-order minimax optimal as $\gamma \to \infty$, i.e.,

$$\inf_{T \in \mathbb{C}_{\mathrm{ARL}}(\gamma)} \mathsf{ESADD}(T) = \mathsf{ESADD}(\mathsf{T}_{\mathsf{CS}})(1+o(1)), \quad \gamma \to \infty.$$

Later on, Moustakides [47], using optimal stopping theory, in his ingenious paper, established the exact optimality of CUSUM for any ARL to the false alarm $\gamma \geq 1$.

Another popular, less pessimistic minimax criterion is from Pollak [48]:

$$\inf_T \sup_{\nu \in \mathbb{Z}_+} \mathsf{CEDD}_\nu(T) \quad \text{subject to } \mathsf{ARL2FA}(T) \geq \gamma,$$

which requires minimizing the conditional expected delay to detection $\mathsf{CEDD}_\nu(T) = \mathsf{E}_\nu[T-\nu \mid T>\nu]$ in the worst-case scenario with respect to the change point ν in class $\mathbb{C}_{\mathrm{ARL}}(\gamma)$. Under Pollak's minimax approach, the goal is to find a stopping time $T_{\mathrm{opt}} \in \mathbb{C}_{\mathrm{ARL}}(\gamma)$ such that

$$\sup_{\nu \in \mathbb{Z}_+} \mathsf{CEDD}_\nu(T_{\mathrm{opt}}) = \inf_{T \in \mathbb{C}_{\mathrm{ARL}}(\gamma)} \sup_{\nu \in \mathbb{Z}_+} \mathsf{CEDD}_\nu(T) \quad \text{for any } \gamma \geq 1.$$

For the i.i.d. model (50), Pollak [48] showed that the modified SR detection procedure that starts from the quasi-stationary distribution of the SR statistic (i.e., the head-start r_0 in the SR-r procedure is a specific random variable) is third-order asymptotically optimal as $\gamma \to \infty$, i.e., the best one can attain up to an additive term $o(1)$:

$$\inf_{T \in \mathbb{C}_{\mathrm{ARL}}(\gamma)} \sup_{\nu \in \mathbb{Z}_+} \mathsf{CEDD}_\nu(T) = \sup_{\nu \in \mathbb{Z}_+} \mathsf{CEDD}_\nu(\mathsf{T}_{\mathsf{SR}}^{\mathsf{r}_0}) + o(1), \quad \gamma \to \infty,$$

where $o(1) \to 0$ as $\gamma \to \infty$. Later, Tartakovsky et al. [49] proved that this is also true for the SR-r procedure (59) that starts from the fixed but specially designed point $r_0 = r_0(\gamma)$ that depends on γ, which was first introduced and thoroughly studied by Moustakides et al. [44]. See also Polunchenko and Tartakovsky [50] on the exact optimality of the SR-r procedure.

Bayesian Changepoint Optimization Criterion

In Bayesian problems, the point of change ν is treated as random with a prior distribution $\pi_k = \mathsf{P}(\nu = k)$, $k \in \mathbb{Z}_+$. Define the probability measure on the Borel σ-algebra $\mathscr{B}$ in $\mathbb{R}^\infty \times \mathbb{Z}_+$ as

$$\mathsf{P}^\pi(\mathcal{A} \times \mathcal{K}) = \sum_{k \in \mathcal{K}} \pi_k \mathsf{P}_k(\mathcal{A}), \quad \mathcal{A} \subset \mathscr{B}(\mathbb{R}^\infty), \quad \mathcal{K} \subset \mathbb{Z}_+.$$

Under measure P^π, the change point ν has a distribution $\pi = \{\pi_k\}$ and the model for the observations is given in (49).

From the Bayesian point of view, it is reasonable to measure the false alarm risk with the *weighted probability of false alarm* (PFA) defined as

$$\mathsf{PFA}^{\pi}(T) := \mathsf{P}^{\pi}(T \le \nu) = \sum_{k=0}^{\infty} \pi_k \mathsf{P}_k(T \le k) = \sum_{k=0}^{\infty} \pi_k \mathsf{P}_{\infty}(T \le k). \tag{60}$$

The last equality follows from the fact that $\mathsf{P}_k(T \le k) = \mathsf{P}_{\infty}(T \le k)$ because the event $\{T \le k\}$ depends on the first k observations which under measure P_k correspond to the no-change hypothesis H_{∞}. Thus, for $\alpha \in (0,1)$, introduce the class of changepoint detection procedures

$$\mathbb{C}_{\pi}(\alpha) = \{T : \mathsf{PFA}^{\pi}(T) \le \alpha\} \tag{61}$$

for which the weighted PFA does not exceed a prescribed level α.

Let E^{π} denote the expectation with respect to the measure P^{π}.

Shiryaev [18,43] introduced the Bayesian optimality criterion

$$\inf_{T \in \mathbb{C}_{\pi}(\alpha)} \mathsf{E}^{\pi}[(T-\nu)^{+}],$$

which is equivalent to minimizing the conditional expected detection delay $\mathsf{EDD}^{\pi}(T) = \mathsf{E}^{\pi}[T-\nu | T > \nu]$

$$\inf_{T} \mathsf{EDD}^{\pi}(T) \quad \text{subject to } \mathsf{PFA}^{\pi}(T) \le \alpha.$$

Under the Bayesian approach, the goal is to find a stopping time $T_{\rm opt} \in \mathbb{C}_{\pi}(\alpha)$ such that

$$\mathsf{EDD}^{\pi}(T_{\rm opt}) = \inf_{T \in \mathbb{C}_{\pi}(\alpha)} \mathsf{EDD}^{\pi}(T) \quad \text{for any } \alpha \in (0,1). \tag{62}$$

For the i.i.d. model (50) and for the geometric prior distribution Geometric(ϱ) of the changepoint ν (see (56)), this problem was solved by Shiryaev [18,43]. Shiryaev [18,43,51] proved that the detection procedure given by the stopping time $\mathsf{T}_{\mathsf{SH}}(A)$ defined in (54) is strictly optimal in class $\mathbb{C}_{\pi}(\alpha)$ if $A = A_{\alpha}$ in (54) can be selected in such a way that $\mathsf{PFA}^{\pi}(\mathsf{T}_{\mathsf{SH}}(A_{\alpha})) = \alpha$, that is

$$\inf_{T \in \mathbb{C}_{\pi}(\alpha)} \mathsf{EDD}^{\pi}(T) = \mathsf{EDD}^{\pi}(\mathsf{T}_{\mathsf{SH}}(A_{\alpha})) \text{ for any } \alpha \in (0,1).$$

Uniform Pointwise Optimality Criterion

In many applications, the most reasonable optimality criterion is the pointwise uniform criterion of minimizing the conditional expected detection delay $\mathsf{CEDD}_{\nu}(T) = \mathsf{E}_{\nu}[T - \nu | T \ge \nu]$ for all $\nu \in \mathbb{Z}_{+}$ when the false alarm risk is fixed at a certain level. However, as we already mentioned, if it is required that $\mathsf{ARL2FA}(T) \ge \gamma$ for some $\gamma \ge 1$, then a procedure that minimizes $\mathsf{CEDD}_{\nu}(T)$ for all ν does not exist. More importantly, as discussed in ([5] Section 2.3), the requirement of having large values of the $\mathsf{ARL2FA}(T)$ generally does not guarantee small values of the maximal local probability of false alarm $\mathsf{MLPFA}(T) = \sup_{\ell \ge 0} \mathsf{P}_{\infty}(T \le \ell + m | T > \ell)$ in a time window of a length $m \ge 1$, while the opposite is always true (see Lemmas 2.1–2.2 in [5]). Hence, the constraint $\mathsf{MLPFA}(T) \le \beta$ is more stringent than $\mathsf{ARL2FA}(T) \ge \gamma$.

Another reason for considering the MLPFA constraint instead of the ARL to false alarm constraint is that the latter one makes sense if and only if the P_{∞}-distribution of stopping times are geometric or at least close to geometric, which is often the case for many popular detection procedures such as CUSUM and SR in the i.i.d. case. However, for general non-i.i.d. models, this is not necessarily true (see [5,52] for a detailed discussion).

For these reasons, introduce the most stringent class of change detection procedures for which the $\mathsf{MLPFA}(T)$ is upper-bounded by the prespecified level $\beta \in (0,1)$:

$$\mathbb{C}_{\mathrm{PFA}}(m,\beta) = \left\{ T : \sup_{\ell \geq 0} \mathsf{P}_\infty(T \leq \ell + m | T > \ell) \leq \beta \right\}. \tag{63}$$

The goal is to find a stopping time $T_{\mathrm{opt}} \in \mathbb{C}_{\mathrm{PFA}}(m,\beta)$ such that

$$\mathsf{CEDD}_\nu(T_{\mathrm{opt}}) = \inf_{T \in \mathbb{C}_{\mathrm{PFA}}(m,\beta)} \mathsf{CEDD}_\nu(T) \quad \text{for all } \nu \in \mathbb{Z}_+ \text{ and any } 0 < \beta < 1. \tag{64}$$

3.2.4. Asymptotic Optimality for General Non-i.i.d. Models via r-Quick and r-Complete Convergence

Complete Convergence and General Bayesian Changepoint Detection Theory

First consider the Bayesian problem assuming that the change point ν is a random variable independent of the observations with a prior distribution $\pi = \{\pi_k\}$. Unfortunately, in the general non-i.i.d. case and for an arbitrary prior π, the Bayesian optimization problem (62) is intractable for arbitrary values of PFA $\alpha \in (0,1)$. For this reason, we will consider the first-order asymptotic problem assuming that the given PFA α approaches zero. To be specific, the goal is to design such a detection procedure T^* that asymptotically minimizes the expected detection delay $\mathsf{EDD}^\pi(T)$ to first order as $\alpha \to 0$:

$$\inf_{T \in \mathbb{C}_\pi(\alpha)} \mathsf{EDD}^\pi(T) = \mathsf{EDD}^\pi(T^*)(1 + o(1)) \quad \text{as } \alpha \to 0, \tag{65}$$

where $o(1) \to 0$ as $\alpha \to 0$. It turns out that, in the asymptotic setting, it is also possible to find a procedure that minimizes the conditional expected detection delay $\mathsf{EDD}_k(T) = \mathsf{E}_k[T - k \,|\, T > k]$ uniformly for all possible values of the change point $\nu = k \in \mathbb{Z}_+$, i.e.,

$$\lim_{\alpha \to 0} \frac{\inf_{T \in \mathbb{C}_\pi(\alpha)} \mathsf{EDD}_k(T)}{\mathsf{EDD}_k(T^*)} = 1 \quad \text{for all } k \in \mathbb{Z}_+. \tag{66}$$

Furthermore, asymptotic optimality results can also be established for higher moments of the detection delay of the order of $r > 1$

$$\mathsf{E}_k[(T-k)^r \,|\, T > k] \quad \text{and} \quad \mathsf{E}^\pi[(T-\nu)^r \,|\, T > \nu].$$

Since the Shiryaev procedure $\mathsf{T_{SH}}(A)$, which was defined in (54), (55), is optimal for the i.i.d. model and Geometric(ϱ) prior, it is reasonable to assume that it is asymptotically optimal for the more general prior and the non-i.i.d model. However, to study asymptotic optimality, we need certain constraints imposed on the prior distribution and on the asymptotic behavior of the decision statistics as the sample size increases, i.e., on the general stochastic model (49).

Assume that the prior distribution $\{\pi_k\}$ is fully supported, i.e., $\pi_k > 0$ for all $k \in \mathbb{Z}_+$ and $\pi_\infty = 0$ and that the following condition holds:

$$\lim_{n \to \infty} \frac{1}{n} \left| \log \sum_{k=n+1}^{\infty} \pi_k \right| = \mu \quad \text{for some } 0 \leq \mu < \infty. \tag{67}$$

Obviously, if $\mu > 0$, then the prior π has an exponential right tail (e.g., the geometric distribution Geometric(ϱ), in which case $\mu = |\log(1-\varrho)|$). If $\mu = 0$, then it has a heavier tail than an exponential tail. In this case, we will refer to it as a heavy-tailed distribution.

Define the LLR of the hypotheses H_k and H_∞

$$\lambda_n^k = \log \frac{d\mathsf{P}_k^n}{d\mathsf{P}_\infty^n} = \sum_{t=k+1}^{n} \frac{f_t(X_t|\mathbf{X}^t)}{g_t(X_t|\mathbf{X}^t)}, \quad n > k$$

($\lambda_n^k = 0$ for $n \le k$). To obtain asymptotic optimality results, the general non-i.i.d. model for observations is restricted to the case that the normalized LLR $n^{-1}\lambda_{k+n}^k$ obeys the SLLN as $n \to \infty$ with a finite and positive number I under the probability measure P_k and its r-complete strengthened version

$$\sum_{n=1}^{\infty} n^{r-1} \sup_{k \in \mathbb{Z}_+} \mathsf{P}_k\Big\{|n^{-1}\lambda_{k+n}^k - I| > \varepsilon\Big\} < \infty \quad \text{for every } \varepsilon > 0. \tag{68}$$

It follows from Lemma 7.2.1 in [6] that, for any $A > 0$,

$$\mathsf{PFA}^{\pi}(\mathsf{T_{SH}}(A)) \le (1+A)^{-1},$$

so that $\mathsf{T_{SH}}(A_\alpha) \in \mathbb{C}_\pi(\alpha)$ if $A = A_\alpha = (1-\alpha)/\alpha$.

The following theorem that can be deduced from Theorem 3.7 in [5] shows that the Shiryaev detection procedure is asymptotically optimal if the normalized LLR $n^{-1}\lambda_{k+n}^k$ converges r-completely to a positive and finite number I and the prior distribution satisfies condition (67).

Theorem 6. *Suppose that the prior distribution $\pi = \{\pi_k\}_{k \in \mathbb{Z}_+}$ of the change point satisfies condition (67) with some $0 \le \mu < \infty$. Assume that there exists some number $0 < I < \infty$ such that the LLR process $n^{-1}\lambda_{k+n}^k$ converges to I uniformly r-completely as $n \to \infty$ under P_k, i.e., condition (68) holds for some $r \ge 1$. If threshold $A = A_\alpha$ in the Shiryaev procedure is so selected that $\mathsf{PFA}^{\pi}(\mathsf{T_{SH}}(A_\alpha)) \le \alpha$ and $\log A_\alpha \sim |\log \alpha|$ as $\alpha \to 0$, e.g., as $A = (1-\alpha)/\alpha$, then as $\alpha \to 0$*

$$\inf_{T \in \mathbb{C}_\pi(\alpha)} \mathsf{E}_k[(T-k)^r \,|\, T > k] \sim \left(\frac{|\log \alpha|}{I+\mu}\right)^r \sim \mathsf{E}_k[(\mathsf{T_{SH}}-k)^r \,|\, \mathsf{T_{SH}} > k] \quad \textit{for all } k \in \mathbb{Z}_+$$

and

$$\inf_{T \in \mathbb{C}_\pi(\alpha)} \mathsf{E}^{\pi}[(T-\nu)^r \,|\, T > \nu] \sim \left(\frac{|\log \alpha|}{I+\mu}\right)^r \sim \mathsf{E}^{\pi}[(\mathsf{T_{SH}}-\nu)^r \,|\, \mathsf{T_{SH}} > \nu].$$

Therefore, the Shiryaev procedure $\mathsf{T_{SH}}(A_\alpha)$ is first-order asymptotically optimal as $\alpha \to 0$ in class $\mathbb{C}_\pi(\alpha)$, minimizing the moments of the detection delay up to order r whenever the r-complete version of the SLLN (68) holds for the LLR process.

For $r = 1$, the assertions of this theorem imply the asymptotic optimality of the Shiryaev procedure for the expected detection delays (65) and (66) as well as asymptotic approximations for the expected detection delays.

Remark 6. *The results of Theorem 6 can be generalized to the asymptotically non-stationary case where $\lambda_{k+n}^k/\psi(n)$ converges to I uniformly r-completely as $n \to \infty$ under P_k with a non-linear function $\psi(n)$ similarly to the hypothesis testing problem discussed in Section 3.1. See also the recent paper [53] for the minimax change detection problem with independent but substantially non-stationary post-change observations.*

It is also interesting to see how two other most popular changepoint detection procedures—the SR and CUSUM—perform in the Bayesian context.

Consider the SR procedure defined by (58), (59). By Lemma 3.4 (p. 100) in [5],

$$\mathsf{PFA}^{\pi}(\mathsf{T}_{\mathsf{SR}}^{r_0}(A)) \le \frac{r_0 \sum_{k=1}^{\infty} \pi_k + \sum_{k=1}^{\infty} k\pi_k}{A} \quad \text{for every } A > 0,$$

and therefore, setting $A = A_\alpha = \alpha^{-1}(r_0 + \sum_{k=1}^{\infty} k\pi_k)$ implies that $\mathsf{T}_{\mathsf{SR}}^{\mathsf{r}_0}(A_\alpha) \in \mathbb{C}_\pi(\alpha)$. If threshold $A = A_\alpha$ in the SR procedure is so selected that $\mathsf{PFA}_\pi(\mathsf{T}_{\mathsf{SR}}^{\mathsf{r}_0}(A_\alpha)) \le \alpha$ and $\log A_\alpha \sim |\log \alpha|$ as $\alpha \to 0$, e.g., as $A_\alpha = \alpha^{-1}(r_0 + \sum_{k=1}^{\infty} k\pi_k)$, then as $\alpha \to 0$

$$\mathsf{E}_k\left[(\mathsf{T}_{\mathsf{SR}}^{\mathsf{r}_0} - k)^r \mid \mathsf{T}_{\mathsf{SR}}^{\mathsf{r}_0} > k\right] \sim \left(\frac{|\log \alpha|}{I}\right)^r \quad \text{for all } k \in \mathbb{Z}_+ \tag{69}$$

and

$$\mathsf{E}^\pi\left[(\mathsf{T}_{\mathsf{SR}}^{\mathsf{r}_0} - \nu)^r \mid \mathsf{T}_{\mathsf{SR}}^{\mathsf{r}_0} > \nu\right] \sim \left(\frac{|\log \alpha|}{I}\right)^r \tag{70}$$

whenever the uniform r-complete convergence condition (68) holds. Therefore, the SR procedure $\mathsf{T}_{\mathsf{SR}}^{\mathsf{r}_0}(A_\alpha)$ is first-order asymptotically optimal as $\alpha \to 0$ in class $\mathbb{C}_\pi(\alpha)$, minimizing the moments of the detection delay up to order r, when the prior distribution π is heavy-tailed (i.e., when $\mu = 0$) and the r-complete version of the SLLN holds. In the case where $\mu > 0$ (i.e., the prior distribution has an exponential tail), the SR procedure is not optimal. This can be expected since it uses the improper uniform prior in the detection statistic.

The same asymptotic results (69), (70) are true for the CUSUM procedure $\mathsf{T}_{\mathsf{CS}}(a)$ defined in (52) if threshold $a = a_\alpha$ is so selected that $\mathsf{PFA}_\pi(\mathsf{T}_{\mathsf{CS}}(a_\alpha)) \le \alpha$ and $a_\alpha \sim |\log \alpha|$ as $\alpha \to 0$ and the uniform r-complete convergence condition (68) holds.

Hence, the r-complete convergence of the LLR process is the sufficient condition for the uniform asymptotic optimality of several popular change detection procedures in class $\mathbb{C}_\pi(\alpha)$.

Complete Convergence and General Non-Bayesian Changepoint Detection Theory

Consider the non-Bayesian problem where the change point ν is an unknown deterministic number. We focus on the most interesting for a variety of applications uniform optimality criterion (64) that requires minimizing the conditional expected delay to detection $\mathsf{CEDD}_\nu(T) = \mathsf{E}_\nu[T - \nu | T > \nu]$ for all values of the change point $\nu \in \mathbb{Z}_+$ in the class of change detection procedures $\mathbb{C}_{\mathrm{PFA}}(m, \beta)$ defined in (63). Recall that this class includes change detection procedures with the maximal local probability of false alarm in the time window m,

$$\mathsf{MLPFA}(T) = \sup_{\ell \ge 0} \mathsf{P}_\infty(T \le \ell + m | T > \ell),$$

which does not exceed the prescribed value $\beta \in (0, 1)$. However, the exact solution to this challenging problem is unknown even in the i.i.d. case.

Instead consider the following asymptotic problem assuming that the given MLPFA β goes to zero: find a change detection procedure $T^\star$ which asymptotically minimizes the expected detection delay $\mathsf{E}_\nu[T - \nu | T > \nu]$ to the first order as $\beta \to 0$. That is, the goal is to design such a detection procedure $T^\star$ that

$$\inf_{T \in \mathbb{C}_{\mathrm{PFA}}(m,\beta)} \mathsf{E}_\nu[T - \nu | T > \nu] = \mathsf{E}_\nu[T^\star - \nu | T^\star > \nu](1 + o(1)) \quad \text{for all } \nu \in \mathbb{Z}_+ \text{ as } \beta \to 0.$$

More generally, we may focus on the asymptotic problem of minimizing the moments of the detection delay of order $r \ge 1$:

$$\inf_{T \in \mathbb{C}_{\mathrm{PFA}}(m,\beta)} \mathsf{E}_\nu[(T - \nu)^r | T > \nu] = \mathsf{E}_\nu[(T^\star - \nu)^r | T^\star > \nu](1 + o(1)) \quad \text{for all } \nu \in \mathbb{Z}_+ \text{ as } \beta \to 0.$$

To solve this problem, we need to assume that the window length $m = m_\beta$ is a function of the MLPFA constraint β and that m_β goes to infinity as $\beta \to 0$ with a certain appropriate rate. Using [54], the following results can be established.

Consider the SR procedure defined by (58), (59) with $r_0 = 0$, in which case write $\mathsf{T}_{\mathsf{SR}}^{\mathsf{r}_0}(A) = \mathsf{T}_{\mathsf{SR}}(A)$. Let $r \ge 1$ and assume that the r-complete version of the SLLN holds with some number $0 < I < \infty$, i.e., $n^{-1}\lambda_{\nu+n}^{\nu}$ converges to I uniformly r-completely as

$n \to \infty$ under P_ν. If $m_\beta = O(|\log \beta|^2)$ as $\beta \to \infty$ and threshold $A = A_\beta$ in the SR procedure is so selected that $\mathsf{MLPFA}(\mathsf{T_{SR}}(A_\beta)) \le \beta$ and $\log A_\beta \sim |\log \beta|$ as $\beta \to 0$, e.g., as defined in [54], then as $\beta \to 0$

$$\inf_{T \in \mathbb{C}_{\mathrm{PFA}}(m_\beta,\beta)} \mathsf{E}_\nu[(T-\nu)^r \mid T > \nu] \sim \left(\frac{|\log \beta|}{I}\right)^r \sim \mathsf{E}_\nu[(\mathsf{T_{SR}}-\nu)^r \mid \mathsf{T_{SR}} > \nu] \quad \text{for all } \nu \in \mathbb{Z}_+.$$

A similar result also holds for the CUSUM procedure $\mathsf{T_{CS}}(a)$ if threshold $a = a_\beta$ is selected so that $\mathsf{MLPFA}(\mathsf{T_{CS}}(a_\beta)) \le \beta$ and $a_\beta \sim |\log \beta|$ as $\beta \to 0$ and the r-complete version of the SLLN holds for the normalized LLR $n^{-1}\lambda^\nu_{\nu+n}$ as $n \to \infty$.

Hence, the r-complete convergence of the LLR process is the sufficient condition for the uniform asymptotic optimality of SR and CUSUM change detection procedures with respect to the moments of the detection delay of order r in class $\mathbb{C}_{\mathrm{PFA}}(m_\beta, \beta)$.

4. Quick and Complete Convergence for Markov and Hidden Markov Models

Usually, in particular problems, the verification of the SLLN for the LLR process is relatively easy. However, in practice, verifying the strengthened r-complete or r-quick versions of the SLLN, i.e., checking condition (68), can cause some difficulty. Many interesting examples where this verification was performed can be found in [5,6]. However, it is interesting to find sufficient conditions for the r-complete convergence for a relatively large class of stochastic models.

In this section, we outline this issue for Markov and hidden Markov models based on the results obtained by Pergamenchtchikov and Tartakovsky [54] for ergodic Markov processes and by Fuh and Tartakovsky [55] for hidden Markov models (HMM). See also Tartakovsky ([5] Ch 3).

Let $\{X_n\}_{n \in \mathbb{Z}_+}$ be a time-homogeneous Markov process with values in a measurable space $(\mathscr{X}, \mathscr{B})$ with the transition probability $P(x, A)$ with density $p(y|x)$. Let E_x denote the expectation with respect to this probability. Assume that this process is geometrically ergodic, i.e., there exist positives constants $0 < R < \infty$, $\kappa > 0$, and probability measure $\varkappa$ on $(\mathscr{X}, \mathscr{B})$ and the Lyapunov $\mathscr{X} \to [1, \infty)$ function V with $\varkappa(V) < \infty$ such that

$$\sup_{n \in \mathbb{Z}_+} e^{\kappa n} \sup_{0 < \psi \le V} \sup_x \frac{1}{V(x)} |\mathsf{E}_x[\psi(X_n)] - \varkappa(\psi)| \le R.$$

In the change detection problem, the sequence $\{X_n\}_{n \in \mathbb{Z}_+}$ is a Markov process, such that $\{X_n\}_{1 \le n \le \nu}$ is a homogeneous process with the transition density $g(y|x)$ and $\{X_n\}_{n > \nu}$ is homogeneous positive ergodic with the transition density $f(y|x)$ and the ergodic (stationary) distribution $\varkappa$. In this case, the LLR process λ^k_n can be represented as

$$\lambda^k_n = \sum_{t=k+1}^{n} G(X_t, X_{t-1}), \quad n > k,$$

where $G(y, x) = \log[f(y|x)/g(y|x)]$.

Define

$$I = \int_{\mathscr{X}} \left\{ \int_{\mathscr{X}} G(y, x)\, f(y|x)\, \mathrm{d}y \right\} \varkappa(\mathrm{d}x).$$

Under a set of quite sophisticated sufficient conditions, the LLR λ^n_{k+n}/n converges to I as $n \to \infty$ r-completely (cf. [54]). We omit the details and only mention that the main condition is the finiteness of $(r+1)$-th moment of the LLR increment, $\mathsf{E}_0[(G(X_1, X_0))^{r+1}] < \infty$.

Now consider the HMM with finite state space. Then again, as in the pure Markov case, the main condition for the r-complete convergence of λ^n_{k+n}/n to I, where I is specified in Fuh and Tartakovsky [55], is $\mathsf{E}_0[(\lambda^0_1)^{r+1}] < \infty$. Further details can be found in [55].

Similar results for Markov and hidden Markov models hold for the hypothesis testing problem considered in Section 3.1. Specifically, if in the Markov case we assume that the observed Markov process $\{X_n\}_{n\in\mathbb{Z}_+}$ is a time-homogeneous geometrically ergodic with a transition density $f_i(y|x)$ under hypothesis H_i $(i = 0, 1, \dots, N)$ and invariant distribution $\varkappa_i$, then the LLR processes are

$$\lambda_{ij}(n) = \sum_{t=1}^{n} G_{ij}(X_t, X_{t-1}), \quad i, j = 0, 1, \dots, N, \ i \neq j,$$

where $G_{ij}(y, x) = \log[f_i(y|x)/f_j(y|x)]$. If $\mathsf{E}_i[(G_{ij}(X_1, X_0))^{r+1}] < \infty$, then the LLR $n^{-1}\lambda_{ij}(n)$ converges r-completely to a finite number

$$I_{ij} = \int_{\mathcal{X}} \left\{ \int_{\mathcal{X}} G_{ij}(y, x) f_i(y|x)\, \mathrm{d}y \right\} \varkappa_i(\mathrm{d}x).$$

5. Discussion and Conclusions

The purpose of this article is to provide an overview of two modes of convergence in the LLN—r-quick and r-complete convergences. These strengthened versions of the SLLN are often neglected in the theory of probability. In the first part of this paper (Section 2), we discussed in detail these two modes of convergence and corresponding strengthened versions of the SLLN. The main motivation was the fact that both r-quick and r-complete versions of the SLLN can be effectively used for establishing near optimality results in sequential analysis, in particular, in sequential hypothesis testing and quickest changepoint detection problems for very general stochastic models of dependent and non-stationary observations. These models are not limited to Markov and hidden Markov models. The results presented in the second part of this paper (Section 3) show that the constraints imposed on the models for observations can be formulated in terms of either the r-quick or r-complete convergence of properly normalized log-likelihood ratios between hypotheses to finite numbers, which can be interpreted as local Kullback–Leibler information numbers. This is natural and can be intuitively expected since optimal or nearly optimal decision-making rules are typically based on a combination of log-likelihood ratios. Therefore, if one is interested in the asymptotic optimality properties of decision-making rules, the asymptotic behavior of log-likelihood ratios as the sample size goes to infinity not only matters but provides the main contribution.

The results presented in this article allow us to conclude that the strengthened r-quick and r-complete versions of the SLLN are useful tools for many statistical problems for general non-i.i.d. stochastic models. In particular, r-quick and r-complete convergences for log-likelihood ratio processes are sufficient for the near optimality of sequential hypothesis tests and changepoint detection procedures for models with dependent and non-identically distributed observations. Such non-i.i.d. models are typical for modern large-scale information and physical systems that produce big data in numerous practical applications. Readers interested in specific applications may find detailed discussions in [4–7,21,22,33,35,37,53–58].

Funding: This article received no external funding.

Data Availability Statement: No real data were used in this research.

Conflicts of Interest: The author declares no conflict of interest.

References

1. Hsu, P.L.; Robbins, H. Complete convergence and the law of large numbers. *Proc. Natl. Acad. Sci. USA* **1947**, *33*, 25–31. [CrossRef] [PubMed]
2. Baum, L.E.; Katz, M. Convergence rates in the law of large numbers. *Trans. Am. Math. Soc.* **1965**, *120*, 108–123. [CrossRef]
3. Strassen, V. Almost sure behavior of sums of independent random variables and martingales. In *Proceedings of the Fifth Berkeley Symposium on Mathematical Statistics and Probability, San Diego, CA, USA, 21 June–18 July 1965 and 27 December 1965–7 January 1966*; Le Cam, L.M., Neyman, J., Eds.; Vol. 2: Contributions to Probability Theory. Part 1; University of California Press: Berkeley, CA, USA, 1967; pp. 315–343.

4. Tartakovsky, A.G. Asymptotic optimality of certain multihypothesis sequential tests: Non-i.i.d. case. *Stat. Inference Stoch. Process.* **1998**, *1*, 265–295. [CrossRef]
5. Tartakovsky, A.G. *Sequential Change Detection and Hypothesis Testing: General Non-i.i.d. Stochastic Models and Asymptotically Optimal Rules*; Monographs on Statistics and Applied Probability 165; Chapman & Hall/CRC Press, Taylor & Francis Group: Boca Raton, FL, USA; London, UK; New York, NY, USA, 2020.
6. Tartakovsky, A.G.; Nikiforov, I.V.; Basseville, M. *Sequential Analysis: Hypothesis Testing and Changepoint Detection*; Monographs on Statistics and Applied Probability 136; Chapman & Hall/CRC Press, Taylor & Francis Group: Boca Raton, FL, USA; London, UK; New York, NY, USA, 2015.
7. Lai, T.L. Asymptotic optimality of invariant sequential probability ratio tests. *Ann. Stat.* **1981**, *9*, 318–333. [CrossRef]
8. Lai, T.L. On *r*-quick convergence and a conjecture of Strassen. *Ann. Probab.* **1976**, *4*, 612–627. [CrossRef]
9. Chow, Y.S.; Lai, T.L. Some one-sided theorems on the tail distribution of sample sums with applications to the last time and largest excess of boundary crossings. *Trans. Am. Math. Soc.* **1975**, *208*, 51–72. [CrossRef]
10. Fuh, C.D.; Zhang, C.H. Poisson equation, moment inequalities and quick convergence for Markov random walks. *Stoch. Process. Their Appl.* **2000**, *87*, 53–67. [CrossRef]
11. Wald, A. Sequential tests of statistical hypotheses. *Ann. Math. Stat.* **1945**, *16*, 117–186. [CrossRef]
12. Wald, A. *Sequential Analysis*; John Wiley & Sons, Inc.: New York, NY, USA, 1947.
13. Wald, A.; Wolfowitz, J. Optimum character of the sequential probability ratio test. *Ann. Math. Stat.* **1948**, *19*, 326–339. [CrossRef]
14. Burkholder, D.L.; Wijsman, R.A. Optimum properties and admissibility of sequential tests. *Ann. Math. Stat.* **1963**, *34*, 1–17. [CrossRef]
15. Matthes, T.K. On the optimality of sequential probability ratio tests. *Ann. Math. Stat.* **1963**, *34*, 18–21. [CrossRef]
16. Ferguson, T.S. *Mathematical Statistics: A Decision Theoretic Approach*; Probability and Mathematical Statistics; Academic Press: Cambridge, MA, USA, 1967.
17. Lehmann, E.L. *Testing Statistical Hypotheses*; John Wiley & Sons, Inc.: New York, NY, USA, 1968.
18. Shiryaev, A.N. *Optimal Stopping Rules*; Series on Stochastic Modelling and Applied Probability; Springer: New York, NY, USA, 1978; Volume 8.
19. Golubev, G.K.; Khas'minskii, R.Z. Sequential testing for several signals in Gaussian white noise. *Theory Probab. Appl.* **1984**, *28*, 573–584. [CrossRef]
20. Tartakovsky, A.G. Asymptotically optimal sequential tests for nonhomogeneous processes. *Seq. Anal.* **1998**, *17*, 33–62. [CrossRef]
21. Verdenskaya, N.V.; Tartakovskii, A.G. Asymptotically optimal sequential testing of multiple hypotheses for nonhomogeneous Gaussian processes in an asymmetric situation. *Theory Probab. Appl.* **1991**, *36*, 536–547. [CrossRef]
22. Fellouris, G.; Tartakovsky, A.G. Multichannel sequential detection–Part I: Non-i.i.d. data. *IEEE Trans. Inf. Theory* **2017**, *63*, 4551–4571. [CrossRef]
23. Armitage, P. Sequential analysis with more than two alternative hypotheses, and its relation to discriminant function analysis. *J. R. Stat. Soc.-Ser. Methodol.* **1950**, *12*, 137–144. [CrossRef]
24. Chernoff, H. Sequential design of experiments. *Ann. Math. Stat.* **1959**, *30*, 755–770. [CrossRef]
25. Kiefer, J.; Sacks, J. Asymptotically optimal sequential inference and design. *Ann. Math. Stat.* **1963**, *34*, 705–750. [CrossRef]
26. Lorden, G. Integrated risk of asymptotically Bayes sequential tests. *Ann. Math. Stat.* **1967**, *38*, 1399–1422. [CrossRef]
27. Lorden, G. Nearly-optimal sequential tests for finitely many parameter values. *Ann. Stat.* **1977**, *5*, 1–21. [CrossRef]
28. Pavlov, I.V. Sequential procedure of testing composite hypotheses with applications to the Kiefer-Weiss problem. *Theory Probab. Appl.* **1990**, *35*, 280–292. [CrossRef]
29. Baron, M.; Tartakovsky, A.G. Asymptotic optimality of change-point detection schemes in general continuous-time models. *Seq. Anal.* **2006**, *25*, 257–296. [CrossRef]
30. Mosteller, F. A *k*-sample slippage test for an extreme population. *Ann. Math. Stat.* **1948**, *19*, 58–65. [CrossRef]
31. Bakut, P.A.; Bolshakov, I.A.; Gerasimov, B.M.; Kuriksha, A.A.; Repin, V.G.; Tartakovsky, G.P.; Shirokov, V.V. *Statistical Radar Theory*; Tartakovsky, G.P., Ed.; Sovetskoe Radio: Moscow, Russia, 1963; Volume 1. (In Russian)
32. Basseville, M.; Nikiforov, I.V. *Detection of Abrupt Changes—Theory and Application*; Information and System Sciences Series; Prentice-Hall, Inc.: Englewood Cliffs, NJ, USA, 1993.
33. Jeske, D.R.; Steven, N.T.; Tartakovsky, A.G.; Wilson, J.D. Statistical methods for network surveillance. *Appl. Stoch. Model. Bus. Ind.* **2018**, *34*, 425–445. [CrossRef]
34. Jeske, D.R.; Steven, N.T.; Wilson, J.D.; Tartakovsky, A.G. Statistical network surveillance. In *Wiley StatsRef: Statistics Reference Online*; Wiley: New York, NY, USA, 2018; pp. 1–12. [CrossRef]
35. Tartakovsky, A.G.; Brown, J. Adaptive spatial-temporal filtering methods for clutter removal and target tracking. *IEEE Trans. Aerosp. Electron. Syst.* **2008**, *44*, 1522–1537. [CrossRef]
36. Szor, P. *The Art of Computer Virus Research and Defense*; Addison-Wesley Professional: Upper Saddle River, NJ, USA, 2005.
37. Tartakovsky, A.G. Rapid detection of attacks in computer networks by quickest changepoint detection methods. In *Data Analysis for Network Cyber-Security*; Adams, N., Heard, N., Eds.; Imperial College Press: London, UK, 2014; pp. 33–70.
38. Tartakovsky, A.G.; Rozovskii, B.L.; Blažek, R.B.; Kim, H. Detection of intrusions in information systems by sequential change-point methods. *Stat. Methodol.* **2006**, *3*, 252–293. [CrossRef]

39. Tartakovsky, A.G.; Rozovskii, B.L.; Blaźek, R.B.; Kim, H. A novel approach to detection of intrusions in computer networks via adaptive sequential and batch-sequential change-point detection methods. *IEEE Trans. Signal Process.* **2006**, *54*, 3372–3382. [CrossRef]
40. Siegmund, D. Change-points: From sequential detection to biology and back. *Seq. Anal.* **2013**, *32*, 2–14. [CrossRef]
41. Moustakides, G.V. Sequential change detection revisited. *Ann. Stat.* **2008**, *36*, 787–807. [CrossRef]
42. Page, E.S. Continuous inspection schemes. *Biometrika* **1954**, *41*, 100–114. [CrossRef]
43. Shiryaev, A.N. On optimum methods in quickest detection problems. *Theory Probab. Appl.* **1963**, *8*, 22–46. [CrossRef]
44. Moustakides, G.V.; Polunchenko, A.S.; Tartakovsky, A.G. A numerical approach to performance analysis of quickest change-point detection procedures. *Stat. Sin.* **2011**, *21*, 571–596. [CrossRef]
45. Moustakides, G.V.; Polunchenko, A.S.; Tartakovsky, A.G. Numerical comparison of CUSUM and Shiryaev–Roberts procedures for detecting changes in distributions. *Commun. Stat.-Theory Methods* **2009**, *38*, 3225–3239. [CrossRef]
46. Lorden, G. Procedures for reacting to a change in distribution. *Ann. Math. Stat.* **1971**, *42*, 1897–1908. [CrossRef]
47. Moustakides, G.V. Optimal stopping times for detecting changes in distributions. *Ann. Stat.* **1986**, *14*, 1379–1387. [CrossRef]
48. Pollak, M. Optimal detection of a change in distribution. *Ann. Stat.* **1985**, *13*, 206–227. [CrossRef]
49. Tartakovsky, A.G.; Pollak, M.; Polunchenko, A.S. Third-order asymptotic optimality of the generalized Shiryaev–Roberts changepoint detection procedures. *Theory Probab. Appl.* **2012**, *56*, 457–484. [CrossRef]
50. Polunchenko, A.S.; Tartakovsky, A.G. On optimality of the Shiryaev–Roberts procedure for detecting a change in distribution. *Ann. Stat.* **2010**, *38*, 3445–3457. [CrossRef]
51. Shiryaev, A.N. The problem of the most rapid detection of a disturbance in a stationary process. *Sov. Math.–Dokl.* **1961**, *2*, 795–799; Translation from *Doklady Akademii Nauk SSSR* **1961**, *138*, 1039–1042.
52. Tartakovsky, A.G. Discussion on "Is Average Run Length to False Alarm Always an Informative Criterion?" by Yajun Mei. *Seq. Anal.* **2008**, *27*, 396–405. [CrossRef]
53. Liang, Y.; Tartakovsky, A.G.; Veeravalli, V.V. Quickest change detection with non-stationary post-change observations. *IEEE Trans. Inf. Theory* **2023**, *69*, 3400–3414. [CrossRef]
54. Pergamenchtchikov, S.; Tartakovsky, A.G. Asymptotically optimal pointwise and minimax quickest change-point detection for dependent data. *Stat. Inference Stoch. Process.* **2018**, *21*, 217–259. [CrossRef]
55. Fuh, C.D.; Tartakovsky, A.G. Asymptotic Bayesian theory of quickest change detection for hidden Markov models. *IEEE Trans. Inf. Theory* **2019**, *65*, 511–529. [CrossRef]
56. Kolessa, A.; Tartakovsky, A.; Ivanov, A.; Radchenko, V. Nonlinear estimation and decision-making methods in short track identification and orbit determination problem. *IEEE Trans. Aerosp. Electron. Syst.* **2020**, *56*, 301–312. [CrossRef]
57. Tartakovsky, A.; Berenkov, N.; Kolessa, A.; Nikiforov, I. Optimal sequential detection of signals with unknown appearance and disappearance points in time. *IEEE Trans. Signal Process.* **2021**, *69*, 2653–2662. [CrossRef]
58. Pergamenchtchikov, S.M.; Tartakovsky, A.G.; Spivak, V.S. Minimax and pointwise sequential changepoint detection and identification for general stochastic models. *J. Multivar. Anal.* **2022**, *190*, 104977. [CrossRef]

Σ *mathematics*

MDPI

Article

Analytic and Asymptotic Properties of the Generalized Student and Generalized Lomax Distributions

Victor Korolev [1,2,3]

[1] Faculty of Computational Mathematics and Cybernetics, Lomonosov Moscow State University, 119991 Moscow, Russia; vkorolev@cs.msu.ru
[2] Moscow Center for Fundamental and Applied Mathematics, 119991 Moscow, Russia
[3] Federal Research Center "Computer Science and Control", Russian Academy of Sciences, 119333 Moscow, Russia

Abstract: Analytic and asymptotic properties of the generalized Student and generalized Lomax distributions are discussed, with the main focus on the representation of these distributions as scale mixtures of the laws that appear as limit distributions in classical limit theorems of probability theory, such as the normal, folded normal, exponential, Weibull, and Fréchet distributions. These representations result in the possibility of proving some limit theorems for statistics constructed from samples with random sizes in which the generalized Student and generalized Lomax distributions are limit laws. An overview of known properties of the generalized Student distribution is given, and some simple bounds for its tail probabilities are presented. An analog of the 'multiplication theorem' is proved, and the identifiability of scale mixtures of generalized Student distributions is considered. The normal scale mixture representation for the generalized Student distribution is discussed, and the properties of the mixing distribution in this representation are studied. Some simple general inequalities are proved that relate the tails of the scale mixture with that of the mixing distribution. It is proved that for some values of the parameters, the generalized Student distribution is infinitely divisible and admits a representation as a scale mixture of Laplace distributions. Necessary and sufficient conditions are presented that provide the convergence of the distributions of sums of a random number of independent random variables with finite variances and other statistics constructed from samples with random sizes to the generalized Student distribution. As an example, the convergence of the distributions of sample quantiles in samples with random sizes is considered. The generalized Lomax distribution is defined as the distribution of the absolute value of the random variable with the generalized Student distribution. It is shown that the generalized Lomax distribution can be represented as a scale mixture of folded normal distributions. The convergence of the distributions of maximum and minimum random sums to the generalized Lomax distribution is considered. It is demonstrated that the generalized Lomax distribution can be represented as a scale mixture of Weibull distributions or that of Fréchet distributions. As a consequence, it is demonstrated that the generalized Lomax distribution can be limiting for extreme statistics in samples with random size. The convergence of the distributions of mixed geometric random sums to the generalized Lomax distribution is considered, and the corresponding extension of the famous Rényi theorem is proved. The law of large numbers for mixed Poisson random sums is presented, in which the limit random variable has a generalized Lomax distribution.

Keywords: generalized Student distribution; generalized Lomax distribution; exponential power distribution; scale mixture; limit theorem; random sum; statistic constructed from sample with random size

MSC: 60F05; 60G50; 60G55; 62E20; 62G30

Citation: Korolev, V. Analytic and Asymptotic Properties of the Generalized Student and Generalized Lomax Distributions. *Mathematics* **2023**, *11*, 2890. https://doi.org/10.3390/math11132890

Academic Editor: Jose Luis Vicente Villardon

Received: 22 May 2023
Revised: 24 June 2023
Accepted: 26 June 2023
Published: 27 June 2023

1. Introduction

1.1. History of the Problem and Motivation

The t-distribution, which is more often called the Student distribution, was proposed in 1908 in the fundamental paper [1] by William Sealy Gosset published in *Biometrika* under the pseudonym 'Student'. Originally, this distribution played only a technical role in the so-called theory of errors. In the paper [2], R. Fisher gave a detailed description of the application of the Student distribution in problems related to the statistical analysis of normal samples. However, when, in the middle of the 20th century, it was noticed that the distributions of various financial data (e.g., increments of stock prices) do not meet the normal model and have noticeably heavier tails with power-type decreases, some specialists turned to the Student distribution as a heavy-tailed alternative to the normal distribution. Now, the Student distribution is one of the most popular models for economic and financial data [3]. In the paper [4], an attempt was made to explain the adequacy of the Student model from the viewpoint of limit theorems of probability theory, and it was demonstrated that, in descriptive statistics, this distribution can be used as an asymptotic approximation since it appears as the limit law for statistics constructed from samples when the sample size obeys the negative binomial distribution.

In recent years, many generalizations of the Student distribution have been proposed, including those that are purely analytic [5] and purely artificial [6]. A comprehensive review of generalizations of the Student distribution was presented in [3]. Unfortunately, many generalizations are in some sense formal, not-so-well theoretically justified, and are based on the reasons of convenience of fitting to particular data. In the present paper, primary attention is paid to the generalization of the Student distribution that is based on the representation of a so-distributed random variable as a quotient of two independent random variables. The numerator in this quotient is the random variable with the exponential power distribution, whereas the denominator is the power of a gamma-distributed random variable with identical shape and scale parameters. This generalization is due to Mcdonald and Newey [7] (see also [8,9]), who noticed that the generalized Student distribution as defined can be obtained as the scale mixture of a power exponential distribution where the mixing law is the inverse generalized gamma distribution. The scale mixture representation opens the way to construct rather simple asymptotic settings in which the appropriately defined generalized Student distribution appears as a limit law. Consequently, the generalized Student distribution obtains a theoretic foundation as an asymptotic approximation. Apparently, it is this property that makes the generalized Student distribution an attractive model for financial data [10–13]. This approach is also very promising for the construction of multivariate and asymmetric generalizations, e.g., see [14].

Since heavy-tailed distributions are widely encountered in many practical problems, they are under serious theoretic study. For example, there are developments in the context of the Tsallis entropy that result in power-law distributions and fractional differential operators. In both cases, we also have a connection with stable distributions and Lévy processes (see, e.g., [15]). Although stable Lévy processes with power-type tails have very serious theoretic grounds, they are not so easily statistically treated because, with four rather trivial exceptions, stable densities cannot be represented in terms of elementary functions. Simple representations for the generalized Student densities make them promising alternatives to stable laws. Moreover, the analytic properties (e.g., the infinite divisibility) of the generalized Student distributions and limit theorems for sums of independent random variables with the generalized Student distributions as the limit laws presented below, together with the functional limit theorems for compound Cox processes proved in [16], guarantee the possibility to construct a Lévy process (more exactly, a subordinated Wiener process) whose finite-dimensional distributions are of the generalized Student type.

Another benefit of the approach based off the scale mixture representation is that it makes it possible to easily trace the relationship of the generalized Student distribution with the generalized Lomax distribution, which is a popular power-type heavy-tailed model that was used in many applied problems after it was introduced in [17], where it was used to analyze business failure data. The Lomax distribution appeared to be a convenient heavy-tailed alternative to exponential, gamma, and Weibull distributions [18]. Possible applications of the Lomax distribution and its generalizations involve many fields, from modelling business records [19] to reliability and lifetime testing [20]. An extensive bibliography can be found in [21]. Various generalizations of the Lomax distribution were used in [22–26] and many other studies; see the extensive bibliography in [21].

In accordance with the approach that is used in the present paper, the generalized Lomax distribution is just the distribution of the absolute value of a random variable with the generalized Student distribution. This definition makes it possible to study the important analytic properties of the so-generalized Lomax distribution, such as its infinite divisibility, identifiability, and mixture representability. In turn, these properties open the way to proving limit theorems in rather simple asymptotic settings in which the generalized Lomax distribution appears to be the limit law. These limit theorems may serve as a theoretical foundation for the adequacy of the generalized Lomax distribution as an asymptotic approximation in descriptive statistics and an explanation of the excellent fit of this distribution to real data in many cases.

In the present paper, we study analytic and asymptotic properties of the generalized Student and generalized Lomax distributions, paying main attention to the representation of these distributions as scale mixtures of the laws that appear as limit distributions in classical limit theorems of probability theory, such as the normal, folded normal, exponential, Weibull, and Fréchet distributions. These representations result in the possibility of proving some limit theorems for statistics constructed from samples with random sizes in which the generalized Student and generalized Lomax distributions are limit laws. Unlike the conventional analytical approach used in most papers on generalized Student or generalized Lomax distributions, in the present paper, we use a kind of 'arithmetic' way of reasoning within the space of random variables. According to this approach, instead of the operation of scale mixing distributions, we consider the operation of multiplication of random variables, provided the multipliers are independent. Nevertheless, speaking of random variables, we actually deal with their distributions. This approach makes the reasoning substantially simpler, the proofs shorte, and reveals some general features of the distributions under consideration.

The paper is organized as follows. Section 1.2 contains auxiliary definitions and introduces some basic properties of the distributions involved in the subsequent reasoning. In Section 2.1, an overview of known the properties of the generalized Student distribution is given, and some simple bounds for its tail probabilities are presented; furthermore, an analog of the 'multiplication theorem' is proved, and the identifiability of scale mixtures of generalized Student distributions is considered. In Section 2.2, the normal scale mixture representation for the generalized Student distribution is discussed, and the properties of the mixing distribution in this representation are studied. In particular, in order to study the tail probabilities of the mixing distributions, some simple general inequalities are proved here that relate the tails of the scale mixture with those of the mixing distribution. It is proved here that for some values of the parameters, the generalized Student distribution is infinitely divisible and admits a representation as a scale mixture of Laplace distributions. In Section 2.3, necessary and sufficient conditions are presented that provide the convergence of the distributions of sums of a random number of independent random variables with finite variances to the generalized Student distribution. Section 2.4 presents necessary and sufficient conditions that provide the convergence of the distributions of 'asymptotically normal' statistics constructed from samples with random sizes to the generalized Student distribution. As an example, the convergence of the distributions of sample quantiles in samples with random sizes is considered. Section 3.1 contains the definition and basic properties of the generalized Lomax distribution. In Section 3.2, it is shown that the generalized Lomax distribution can be represented as a scale mixture of the folded normal distribution (the distribution of the maximum of the standard Wiener process on the unit interval). In Section 3.3, the convergence of the distributions of maximum and minimum random sums to the generalized Lomax distribution is considered. In Section 3.4, it is demonstrated that the generalized Lomax distribution can be represented as a scale mixture of Weibull distributions or as a mixture of Fréchet distributions. These representations make it possible to demonstrate in Section 3.5 that the generalized Lomax distribution can be limiting for extreme statistics in samples with a random size. Finally, in Section 3.6, the convergence of the distributions of mixed geometric random sums to the generalized Lomax distribution is considered, and the corresponding extension of the famous Rényi theorem is proved.

1.2. Auxiliary Definitions and Notation

All the random variables are assumed to be defined on one and the same probability space $(\Omega, \mathcal{A}, \mathsf{P})$.

The product of *independent*random elements will be denoted by the symbol $\circ$. The symbols $\stackrel{d}{=}$ and $\Longrightarrow$ will stand for the coincidence of distributions and convergence in distribution, respectively. The symbol $\square$ marks the end of the proof. The indicator function of a set A will be denoted $\mathbb{I}_A(z)$: if $z \in A$, then $\mathbb{I}_A(z) = 1$; otherwise, $\mathbb{I}_A(z) = 0$.

A random variable with the standard exponential distribution will be denoted W_1, as follows:

$$\mathsf{P}(W_1 < x) = \big[1 - e^{-x}\big]\mathbb{I}_{[0,\infty)}(x).$$

For $x > 0$ and $r > 0$, the (lower) incomplete gamma function will be denoted as $\Gamma(r;x)$:

$$\Gamma(r;x) = \int_0^x z^{r-1}e^{-z}dz.$$

Let $\Gamma(r) \stackrel{\text{def}}{=} \Gamma(r;\infty)$ be the 'usual' Euler's gamma function.

A random variable having a gamma distribution with a shape parameter $r > 0$ and a scale parameter $\lambda > 0$ will be denoted as $G_{r,\lambda}$, where

$$\mathsf{P}(G_{r,\lambda} < x) = \int_0^x g(z;r,\lambda)dz, \;\; \text{with} \;\; g(x;r,\lambda) = \frac{\lambda^r}{\Gamma(r)}x^{r-1}e^{-\lambda x}\mathbb{I}_{[0,\infty)}(x),$$

Obviously, in this notation, $G_{1,1}$ is a random variable with the standard exponential distribution $G_{1,1} = W_1$.

A generalized gamma distribution is an absolutely continuous distribution defined by the density

$$gg_{r,\alpha,\mu}(x) = \frac{|\alpha|\mu^r}{\Gamma(r)}x^{\alpha r-1}e^{-\mu x^{\alpha}}\mathbb{I}_{[0,\infty)}(x)$$

with $\alpha \in \mathbb{R}$, $\mu > 0$, and $r > 0$. A random variable with the density $gg_{r,\alpha,\mu}(x)$ will be denoted as $\overline{G}_{r,\alpha,\mu}$. It is easy to see that

$$\overline{G}_{r,\alpha,\mu} \stackrel{d}{=} G_{r,\mu}^{1/\alpha} \stackrel{d}{=} \mu^{-1/\alpha}G_{r,1}^{1/\alpha} \stackrel{d}{=} \mu^{-1/\alpha}\overline{G}_{r,\alpha,1}. \tag{1}$$

Let $\gamma > 0$. The distribution of the random variable W_γ:

$$\mathsf{P}(W_\gamma < x) = \big[1 - e^{-x^{\gamma}}\big]\mathbb{I}_{[0,\infty)}(x),$$

is called the Weibull distribution with a shape parameter γ. It is easy to see that

$$W_1^{1/\gamma} \stackrel{d}{-} W_\gamma \stackrel{d}{=} \overline{G}_{1,\gamma,1}. \tag{2}$$

The random variable W_α^{-1} is said to have an inverse Weibull or Fréchet distribution, as follows:

$$\mathsf{P}(W_\alpha^{-1} < x) = \mathsf{P}(W_\alpha \geq \tfrac{1}{x}) = \exp\{x^{-\alpha}\}, \;\; x \geq 0.$$

The standard normal distribution function and its density will be denoted by $\Phi(x)$ and $\phi(x)$, where

$$\phi(x) = \frac{1}{\sqrt{2\pi}}e^{-x^2/2}, \quad \Phi(x) = \int_{-\infty}^{x} \phi(z)dz,$$

respectively. A random variable with the standard normal distribution will be denoted by X.

A random variable with the strictly stable characteristic function

$$\mathfrak{g}_{\alpha,\theta}(t) = \exp\Big\{ -|t|^{\alpha} \exp\Big\{ -\frac{i\pi\theta\alpha}{2}\mathrm{sign}t\Big\}\Big\}, \quad t \in \mathbb{R}, \tag{3}$$

where $0 < \alpha \leq 2$, $|\theta| \leq \theta_\alpha = \min\{1, \frac{2}{\alpha} - 1\}$, will be denoted by $S_{\alpha,\theta}$. The probability density of the random variable $S_{\alpha,\theta}$ will be denoted by $s_{\alpha,\theta}$. For the properties of stable distributions with characteristic functions (3), see, e.g., [15,27,28].

It is easy to see that $S_{2,0} \stackrel{d}{=} \sqrt{2}X$.

If $\theta = 1$ and $0 < \alpha \leq 1$, the corresponding strictly stable random variable takes only nonnegative values. If $\alpha = 1$ and $\theta = \pm 1$, then the corresponding stable distributions are degenerate in ± 1, respectively. All the other strictly stable distributions are absolutely continuous. There are no explicit representations for stable distributions in terms of elementary functions with four exceptions: the normal distribution ($\alpha = 2, \theta = 0$), the Cauchy distribution ($\alpha = 1, \theta = 0$), the Lévy distribution ($\alpha = \frac{1}{2}, \theta = 1$) and the distribution symmetric to the Lévy law ($\alpha = \frac{1}{2}, \theta = -1$). Expressions for stable densities in terms of generalized Meijer G-functions (Fox functions) can be found in [29,30].

According to the 'multiplication theorem' (see, e.g., Theorem 3.3.1 in [27]), for any admissible pair of parameters (α, θ) and any $\alpha' \in (0, 1]$, the product representation

$$S_{\alpha\alpha',\theta} \stackrel{d}{=} S_{\alpha',1}^{1/\alpha} \circ S_{\alpha,\theta}$$

holds. In particular, for any $\alpha \in (0, 2]$,

$$S_{\alpha,0} \stackrel{d}{=} \sqrt{2S_{\alpha/2,1}} \circ X,$$

that is, any symmetric strictly stable distribution is a scale mixture of the normal distributions.

Let $\alpha > 0$. The symmetric exponential power distribution is an absolutely continuous distribution defined by its Lebesgue probability density

$$p_\alpha(x) = \frac{\alpha}{2\Gamma(\frac{1}{\alpha})} \cdot e^{-|x|^\alpha}, \quad -\infty < x < \infty. \tag{4}$$

To simplify the notation and calculation, here and in what follows, we will use a single parameter α in Representation (4) since this parameter is, in some sense, characteristic of and determines the shape of the distribution (4). With $\alpha = 1$, Relationship (4) defines the classical Laplace distribution as

$$p_1(x) = \tfrac{1}{2}e^{-|x|}, \quad x \in \mathbb{R}$$

with zero mean and a variance of 2. With $\alpha = 2$, Relationship (4) defines the normal (Gaussian) distribution with a zero mean and a variance of $\frac{1}{2}$. Any random variable with a probability density $p_\alpha(x)$ will be denoted by Q_α.

The class of distributions (4) was introduced and studied in 1923 in the paper [31] by M. T. Subbotin. For more details concerning the properties of exponential power distributions, see [32,33] and the references therein.

It is easy to make sure that

$$|Q_\alpha|^\alpha \stackrel{d}{=} G_{1/\alpha,1}. \tag{5}$$

In our further reasoning, we will exploit the following properties of exponential power distributions. For convenience, we present them as lemmas.

Lemma 1 (e.g., see [32]). *For $\delta > -1$, we have*

$$\mathsf{E}|Q_\alpha|^\delta = \frac{\alpha}{\Gamma(\frac{1}{\alpha})}\int_0^\infty x^\delta e^{-x^\alpha}dx = \frac{\Gamma(\frac{\delta+1}{\alpha})}{\Gamma(\frac{1}{\alpha})}.$$

Lemma 2 ([32]). *Let $\alpha \in (0,2]$, $\alpha' \in (0,1]$. Then,*

$$Q_{\alpha\alpha'} \stackrel{d}{=} Q_\alpha \circ U_{\alpha,\alpha'}^{-1/\alpha}, \tag{6}$$

where $U_{\alpha,\alpha'}$ is a random variable such that if $\alpha' = 1$, then $U_{\alpha,\alpha'} = 1$ for any $\alpha \in (0,2]$, and if $0 < \alpha' < 1$, then $U_{\alpha,\alpha'}$ is absolutely continuous with a probability density

$$u_{\alpha,\alpha'}(x) = \frac{\alpha'\Gamma(\frac{1}{\alpha})}{\Gamma(\frac{1}{\alpha\alpha'})} \cdot \frac{s_{\alpha',1}(x)}{x^{1/\alpha}} \cdot \mathbb{I}_{(0,\infty)}(x).$$

Corollary 1 ([34]). *Any symmetric exponential power distribution with $\alpha \in (0,2]$ is a scale mixture of normal laws:*

$$Q_\alpha \stackrel{d}{=} \sqrt{\tfrac{1}{2}U_{2,\alpha/2}^{-1}} \circ X.$$

Corollary 2 (e.g., see [32]). *Any symmetric exponential power distribution with $\alpha \in (0,1]$ is a scale mixture of Laplace laws:*

$$Q_\alpha \stackrel{d}{=} U_{1,\alpha}^{-1} \circ Q_1.$$

Lemma 3 ([32]). *For any $\alpha \in (0,1]$, the distribution of the random variable $U_{2,\alpha/2}^{-1}$ is a mixed exponential:*

$$U_{2,\alpha/2}^{-1} \stackrel{d}{=} 4U_{1,\alpha}^{-2} \circ W_1.$$

Recall that a distribution function $F(x)$ whose characteristic function is denoted $f(t)$ is infinitely divisible if, for each $n \in \mathbb{N}$, there exists a characteristic function $f_n(t)$ such that $f(t) = f_n^n(t)$ and $t \in \mathbb{R}$. In terms of random variables (if the probability space $(\Omega, \mathcal{A}, \mathsf{P})$ is rich enough), this means that for each $n \in \mathbb{N}$, there exist independent identically distributed random variables $Y_{n,1}, Y_{n,2}, \ldots, Y_{n,n}$ such that a random variable Y whose distribution function is $F(x)$ admits the representation $Y = Y_{n,1} + Y_{n,2} + \ldots + Y_{n,n}$. The property of infinite divisibility is very important in some problems. For example, infinite divisible distributions exist, and only they can be limiting for sums of independent asymptotically negligible (in particular, identically distributed) random variables (see [35]. Moreover, this is crucial in the construction of Lévy processes (see, e.g., [15,16]).

Corollary 3 ([32]). *For any $\alpha \in (0,1]$, the distribution of the random variable $U_{2,\alpha/2}^{-1}$ is infinitely divisible.*

In the present paper, we consider the generalizations of the Student and Lomax distributions.

The Student distributionwas introduced in [1] and is defined as the distribution of the random variable

$$T_r \stackrel{d}{=} X \circ G_{r,r}^{-1/2},$$

where $r > 0$ is the shape parameter usually called 'the degrees of freedom'. The probability density of the Student distribution, up to scale and location transformation, has the form

$$f_r(x) = \frac{\Gamma(r+\frac{1}{2})}{\sqrt{\pi r}\Gamma(r)}\Big(1+\frac{x^2}{r}\Big)^{-(r+1/2)}, \quad x \in \mathbb{R}.$$

The Lomax distribution, also called the Pareto Type II distribution, was introduced in [17]. The probability density of the Lomax distribution, up to scale and location transformation, has the form

$$f_r^*(x) = \frac{r}{(1+x)^{r+1}}, \quad x \geq 0,$$

where $r > 0$ is the shape parameter.

2. The Generalized Student Distribution

2.1. The Definition and Elementary Properties of the Generalized Student Distribution

Let $\alpha \in (0,2]$ and $r \in \mathbb{R}$ be such that $\alpha r \geq 1$. Assume that the random variables Q_α and $G_{r,r}$ are independent. Consider the random variable $T_{r,\alpha}$, defined as the product

$$T_{r,\alpha} \stackrel{\text{def}}{=} Q_\alpha \circ G_{r,r}^{-1/\alpha}. \tag{7}$$

The distribution of the random variable $T_{r,\alpha}$ will be called a generalized Student distribution with parameters α and r. (It should be noted that in [14], instead of $-\frac{1}{\alpha}$, the exponent of $G_{r,r}$ is $-\frac{1}{2}$, which does not restrict generality but leads to more complicated notation).

Find the probability density function $f_{r,\alpha}(x)$ of $T_{r,\alpha}$. Since Q_α and $G_{r,r}$ are independent, by the Fubini theorem, we have

$$f_{r,\alpha}(x) = \frac{\alpha r^r}{2\Gamma(r)\Gamma(\frac{1}{\alpha})}\int_0^\infty u^{1/\alpha}e^{-u|x|^\alpha}u^{r-1}e^{-ru}du =$$

$$= \frac{\alpha r^r}{2\Gamma(r)\Gamma(\frac{1}{\alpha})(r+|x|^\alpha)^{r+1/\alpha}}\int_0^\infty u^{r+1/\alpha-1}e^{-u}du =$$

$$= \frac{\alpha\Gamma(r+\frac{1}{\alpha})}{2r^{1/\alpha}\Gamma(r)\Gamma(\frac{1}{\alpha})}\Big(1+\frac{|x|^\alpha}{r}\Big)^{-(r+1/\alpha)} = \frac{\alpha}{2r^{1/\alpha}\mathrm{B}(r,\frac{1}{\alpha})}\Big(1+\frac{|x|^\alpha}{r}\Big)^{-(r+1/\alpha)}, \quad x \in \mathbb{R}. \tag{8}$$

Here and in what follows, $\mathrm{B}(a,b)$ is the beta-function:

$$\mathrm{B}(a,b) = \frac{\Gamma(a)\Gamma(b)}{\Gamma(a+b)}, \quad a>0,\ b>0.$$

It is easily seen that with $\alpha = 2$, the generalized Student distribution turns into the classical Student distribution up to the re-parametrization. If, in addition, $r = 1$, the generalized Student distribution is a Cauchy distribution.

When $\alpha = 1$, the generalized Student distribution turns into a two-sided Lomax distribution.

We see that the family of generalized Student distributions is wide enough and contains popular power-type-tailed laws.

Moreover, this family is flexible enough since it contains distributions with various shapes of their vertices. Consider this variety in more detail. First, from (8), it follows that the densities of all the generalized Student distributions are finite:

$$\max_x f_{r,\alpha}(x) = f_{r,\alpha}(0) = \frac{\alpha\mathrm{B}(r,\frac{1}{\alpha})}{2r^{1/\alpha}}.$$

Second, consider the behavior of the derivative of the density $f_{r,\alpha}(x)$ in the neighborhood of zero. Since $f_{r,\alpha}(x)$ is symmetric, it suffices to consider $x > 0$. For such x, we have

$$\frac{d}{dx}f_{r,\alpha}(x) = -\frac{\alpha^2 \mathrm{B}(r,\frac{1}{\alpha})x^{\alpha-1}}{2r^{1/\alpha}}\Big(1+\frac{x^\alpha}{r}\Big)^{-(r+1)}.$$

Therefore, if $\alpha > 1$, then

$$\lim_{x\to 0+}\frac{d}{dx}f_{r,\alpha}(x) = 0;$$

that is, the vertex of $f_{r,\alpha}(x)$ is smooth and rather flat.

If $\alpha = 1$, then

$$\lim_{x\to 0+}\frac{d}{dx}f_{r,\alpha}(x) = -\frac{\alpha^2}{2r^{1/\alpha}\mathrm{B}(r,\frac{1}{\alpha})};$$

that is, the vertex of $f_{r,\alpha}(x)$ looks like a non-zero angle.

If $\alpha < 1$, then

$$\lim_{x\to 0+}\frac{d}{dx}f_{r,\alpha}(x) = -\infty;$$

that is, in this case, the vertex of $f_{r,\alpha}(x)$ is 'infinitely' sharp.

The two last cases noticeably differ from the traditional Student density shape.

As is demonstrated by the two following statements, when r increases, the tails of a generalized Student distribution become less heavy, so that finally, a generalized Student distribution turns into an exponential power distribution.

Proposition 1. *The following asymptotic relationship holds:*

$$\lim_{r\to\infty}\sup_x \Big|f_{r,\alpha}(x) - \frac{\alpha e^{-|x|^\alpha}}{2\Gamma(\frac{1}{\alpha})}\Big| = 0. \tag{9}$$

Proof. Note that the relationships

$$\lim_{r\to\infty}\Big(1+\frac{|x|^\alpha}{r}\Big)^r = e^{|x|^\alpha} \quad \text{and} \quad \lim_{r\to\infty}\frac{\Gamma(r+\frac{1}{\alpha})}{r^{1/\alpha}\Gamma(r)} = 1$$

imply the point-wise convergence of the densities. Since the limit exponential power density function is monotone on each semi-axis, as well as bounded and continuous, by the Dini theorem, the convergence is uniform in $x \in \mathbb{R}$. □

This property of the generalized Student distributions can be mathematically formulated in terms of distribution functions as well. For $\alpha \in (0,2]$ and $r > 0$, denote $F_{r,\alpha}(x) = \mathsf{P}(T_{r,\alpha} < x)$, $x \in \mathbb{R}$,

$$H_\alpha(x) \stackrel{\text{def}}{=} \mathsf{P}(Q_\alpha < x) = \begin{cases} \dfrac{1}{2} + \dfrac{\Gamma(\frac{1}{\alpha}; x^\alpha)}{2\Gamma(\frac{1}{\alpha})}, & x \geq 0, \\[2ex] \dfrac{1}{2} - \dfrac{\Gamma(\frac{1}{\alpha}; |x|^\alpha)}{2\Gamma(\frac{1}{\alpha})}, & x < 0. \end{cases}$$

Corollary 4. *For any $\alpha \in (0,2]$, as $r \to \infty$, the distribution functions of the random variables $T_{r,\alpha}$ converge to the exponential power distribution function $H_\alpha(x)$ uniformly in $x \in \mathbb{R}$:*

$$\lim_{r\to\infty}\sup_x |F_{r,\alpha}(x) - H_\alpha(x)| = 0.$$

Proof. This statement follows from Proposition 4 by the Lebesgue-dominated convergence theorem and the Dini theorem mentioned above.

Another way of proving this result is as follows. Let $[a]$ and $\{a\}$, correspondingly, denote the integer part and the fractional part of a real number a. Represent r as $r = [r] + \{r\}$. Then, the random variable $G_{r,r}$ can be represented as

$$G_{r,r} \stackrel{d}{=} \tfrac{1}{r}G_{r,1} \stackrel{d}{=} \frac{1}{r}\sum_{j=1}^{[r]} G_{1,1} + \frac{G_{\{r\},1}}{r}.$$

As $r \to \infty$, the first summand on the right-hand side of this relation almost surely converges to 1 by the strong law of large numbers, whereas the second summand almost surely converges to zero. This means that $G_{r,r} \longrightarrow 1$ almost surely converges to 1. Now, by the Slutsky theorem [36] (see also [37], Sect. 20.6), it follows from the definition of $T_{r,\alpha}$ that $T_{r,\alpha} \Longrightarrow Q_\alpha$. Since the limit function $H_\alpha(x)$ is monotone, bounded, and continuous, by the Dini theorem, the convergence of distribution functions is uniform in $x \in \mathbb{R}$. □

Now consider the moments of the generalized Student distribution.

Proposition 2. *For any $\delta \in (-1, \alpha r)$*

$$\mathsf{E}|T_{r,\alpha}|^\delta = \mathsf{E}G_{r,r}^{-\delta/\alpha} \cdot \mathsf{E}|Q_\alpha|^\delta = \frac{r^{\delta/\alpha}\Gamma(r - \frac{\delta}{\alpha})\Gamma(\frac{\delta+1}{\alpha})}{\Gamma(r)\Gamma(\frac{1}{\alpha})}.$$

Proof. This relationship follows from (7) and Lemma 1. □

The distribution function of $T_{r,\alpha}$, in general, cannot be expressed in terms of elementary functions. The integral of $f_{r,\alpha}(x)$ can be written (e.g., see [38], item 3.194) in terms of the hypergeometric function ${}_2F_1(\cdot,\cdot,\cdot,\cdot)$ (e.g., see [38], item 9.111):

$$F_{r,\alpha}(x) = \begin{cases} \dfrac{1}{2} + \dfrac{\alpha x}{2r^{1/\alpha}\mathrm{B}(r, \frac{1}{\alpha})} {}_2F_1\left(r + \frac{1}{\alpha}, \frac{1}{\alpha}; 1 + \frac{1}{\alpha}; -\frac{x^\alpha}{r}\right), & x \geq 0, \\ \dfrac{1}{2} - \dfrac{\alpha|x|}{2r^{1/\alpha}\mathrm{B}(r, \frac{1}{\alpha})} {}_2F_1\left(r + \frac{1}{\alpha}, \frac{1}{\alpha}; 1 + \frac{1}{\alpha}; -\frac{|x|^\alpha}{r}\right), & x < 0. \end{cases}$$

Nevertheless, we can obtain very simple two-sided bounds for the tail probabilities of $T_{r,\alpha}$.

Proposition 3. *For any $x > 0$, we have*

$$\frac{r^{r-1}}{\mathrm{B}(r, \frac{1}{\alpha})x^{\alpha r}} \cdot \frac{x^{\alpha r+1}}{(r + x^\alpha)^{r+1/\alpha}} \leq \mathsf{P}(|T_{r,\alpha}| \geq x) \leq \frac{r^{r-1}}{\mathrm{B}(r, \frac{1}{\alpha})x^{\alpha r}}.$$

Proof. For any $x > 0$, we obviously have

$$\mathsf{P}(|T_{r,\alpha}| \geq x) = 2\int_x^\infty f_{r,\alpha}(y)dy = \frac{\alpha}{r^{1/\alpha}\mathrm{B}(r, \frac{1}{\alpha})}\int_x^\infty \left(1 + \frac{|y|^\alpha}{r}\right)^{-(r+1/\alpha)} dy. \quad (10)$$

For the integral on the right-hand side of (10), we easily obtain the following lower bound:

$$\int_x^\infty \left(1 + \frac{|y|^\alpha}{r}\right)^{-(r+1/\alpha)} dy = r^{r+1/\alpha}\int_x^\infty \left(\frac{r}{y^\alpha} + 1\right)^{-(r+1/\alpha)} \frac{dy}{y^{\alpha r+1}} \geq$$

$$\geq \frac{r^{r+1/\alpha}x^{\alpha r+1}}{(r + x^\alpha)^{r+1/\alpha}}\int_x^\infty \frac{dy}{y^{\alpha r+1}} = \frac{r^{r+1/\alpha-1}}{\alpha x^{\alpha r}} \cdot \frac{x^{\alpha r+1}}{(r + x^\alpha)^{r+1/\alpha}}. \quad (11)$$

The upper bound for this integral is obvious:

$$\int_x^\infty \left(1+\frac{|y|^\alpha}{r}\right)^{-(r+1/\alpha)} dy = r^{r+1/\alpha} \int_x^\infty \left(\frac{r}{y^\alpha}+1\right)^{-(r+1/\alpha)} \frac{dy}{y^{\alpha r+1}} \leq$$

$$\leq r^{r+1/\alpha} \int_x^\infty \frac{dy}{y^{\alpha r+1}} = \frac{r^{r+1/\alpha-1}}{\alpha x^{\alpha r}}. \quad (12)$$

Now, the desired statement easily follows from (11), (12), and (10). □

Since

$$\lim_{x\to\infty} \frac{x^{\alpha r+1}}{(r+x^\alpha)^{r+1/\alpha}} = 1, \quad (13)$$

we immediately obtain the following statement.

Corollary 5. *The tailprobabilities of $T_{r,\alpha}$ satisfy the following asymptotic relation:*

$$\lim_{x\to\infty} x^{\alpha r} \mathsf{P}(|T_{r,\alpha}| \geq x) = \frac{r^{r-1}}{\mathrm{B}(r, \frac{1}{\alpha})}.$$

Lemma 2 was proved in [32] with the application of the 'multiplication theorem' for stable distributions (Theorem 3.3.1 in [27]). Therefore, this lemma can be regarded as a 'multiplication theorem' for exponential power distributions. This lemma can be used to establish a kind of an analog of 'multiplication theorem' for generalized Student distributions.

Proposition 4. *For any $0 < \alpha \leq \beta \leq 2$ and any $r > \frac{1}{\beta}$, we have*

$$G_{r,r}^{-1/\beta} \circ T_{r,\alpha} \stackrel{d}{=} G_{r,r}^{-1/\alpha} \circ T_{r,\beta} \circ U_{\beta,\alpha/\beta}^{-1/\beta}.$$

Proof. The assertion of Lemma 2 can be rewritten as

$$Q_\alpha \stackrel{d}{=} Q_\beta \circ U_{\beta,\alpha/\beta}^{-1/\beta}.$$

Now, the desired statement follows from the definition of $T_{r,\alpha}$. □

One more representation of a random variable with the generalized Student distribution is possible.

Proposition 5. *The following relationship holds:*

$$T_{r,\alpha} \stackrel{d}{=} r^{1/\alpha} Q_\alpha \circ |Q_{1/r}|^{-1/\alpha r}.$$

Proof. According to (5), we have

$$G_{r,r} \stackrel{d}{=} \tfrac{1}{r} G_{r,1} \stackrel{d}{=} \tfrac{1}{r} |Q_{1/r}|^{1/r},$$

whence follows the desired result. □

Now consider the property of the identifiability of scale mixtures of generalized Student distributions. Recall the definition of the identifiability of scale mixtures. Let T be a random variable with the distribution function $F_T(x)$ and let V_1 and V_2 be two nonnegative random variables. The family of scale mixtures of F_T is said to be identifiable if the equality $T \circ V_1 \stackrel{d}{=} T \circ V_2$ implies $V_1 \stackrel{d}{=} V_2$.

Proposition 6. *For any fixed $\alpha \in (0,2]$ and $r > \frac{1}{\alpha}$, the family of scale mixtures of generalized Student distributions is identifiable; that is, if V_1 and V_2 are two nonnegative random variables, then the equality $T_{r,\alpha} \circ V_1 \stackrel{d}{=} T_{r,\alpha} \circ V_2$ implies $V_1 \stackrel{d}{=} V_2$.*

Proof. In [32], it was proved that the family of scale mixtures of exponential power distributions is identifiable. Hence, if V_1 and V_2 are two nonnegative random variables, then the equality $T_{r,\alpha} \circ V_1 \stackrel{d}{=} T_{r,\alpha} \circ V_2$ implies $V_1 \circ G_{r,r}^{-1/\alpha} \stackrel{d}{=} V_2 \circ G_{r,r}^{-1/\alpha}$ or, which is the same, $G_{r,1} \circ V_1^{-\alpha} \stackrel{d}{=} G_{r,1} \circ V_2^{-\alpha}$. As was proved in [39], the family of scale mixtures of gamma distributions is identifiable. Hence, the last relationship implies $V_1^{-\alpha} \stackrel{d}{=} V_2^{-\alpha}$ or $V_1 \stackrel{d}{=} V_2$, which is the same. □

2.2. Mixture Representation for the Generalized Student Distribution and Related Topics

2.2.1. Normal Mixture Representation

Proposition 7. *For any $\alpha \in (0,2]$ and any $r > \frac{1}{\alpha}$ the generalized Student distribution is a scale mixture of normal distributions:*

$$T_{r,\alpha} \stackrel{d}{=} \sqrt{D_{r,\alpha}} \circ X, \tag{14}$$

where

$$D_{r,\alpha} \stackrel{\text{def}}{=} \tfrac{1}{2}\big(U_{2,\alpha/2} \circ G_{r,r}^{2/\alpha}\big)^{-1} \stackrel{d}{=} \tfrac{1}{2}\big(U_{2,\alpha/2} \circ \overline{G}_{r,\alpha/2,r}\big)^{-1},$$

so that

$$\mathsf{P}(T_{r,\alpha} < x) = \int_0^\infty \Phi\Big(\frac{x}{\sqrt{y}}\Big) d\mathsf{P}(D_{r,\alpha} < y). \tag{15}$$

This statement directly follows from (7) and Corollary 1.

In accordance with Lemma 2, for $\alpha \in (0,2)$, the probability density $u^*_{2,\alpha/2}(x)$ of the random variable $U^{-1}_{2,\alpha/2}$ has the form

$$u^*_{2,\alpha/2}(x) = \frac{\alpha\sqrt{\pi}}{2\Gamma(\frac{1}{\alpha})} \cdot \frac{s_{\alpha/2,1}(\frac{1}{x})}{x^{3/2}}, \quad x > 0.$$

If $\alpha = 2$, then the distribution of $U^{-1}_{2,\alpha/2}$ is degenerate at Point 1.

The generalized gamma probability density $gg_{r,\alpha/2,r}(x)$ of the random variable $G_{r,r}^{2/\alpha}$ has the form

$$gg_{r,\alpha/2,r}(x) = \frac{r^r}{\Gamma(r)} u^{\alpha(r+1)/2-2} e^{-ru^{\alpha/2}}, \quad x > 0.$$

Therefore, the mixing random variable $D_{r,\alpha}$ in (15) has the probability density

$$q_{r,\alpha}(x) = \frac{r^r \alpha\sqrt{2\pi}}{\Gamma(\frac{1}{\alpha})\Gamma(r)x^{3/2}} \int_0^\infty s_{\alpha/2,1}\big(\tfrac{2}{ux}\big) u^{\alpha(r+1)/2-5/2} e^{-ru^{\alpha/2}} du, \quad x > 0.$$

This expression is cumbersome and can hardly be used either for the purpose of clarifying the analytic and asymptotic properties of the mixing distribution or its statistical analysis. However, as will be shown in the next subsection, it is possible to obtain rather accurate (asymptotic) two-sided bounds for the tail probability of the distribution of $D_{r,\alpha}$.

2.2.2. The Properties of the Mixing Distribution And Inequalities for the Tail Probabilities

Proposition 8. *There exist finite positive constants $\underline{C} = \underline{C}(r,\alpha)$ and $\overline{C} = \overline{C}(r,\alpha)$ such that for any $\delta \in (0,1)$*

$$\liminf_{x\to\infty} x^{\alpha r/2+\delta} \mathsf{P}(D_{r,\alpha} \geq x) \geq \underline{C} \tag{16}$$

and

$$\limsup_{x\to\infty} x^{\alpha r/2} \mathsf{P}(D_{r,\alpha} \geq x) \leq \overline{C}. \tag{17}$$

For example, as $\underline{C}$ and $\overline{C}$, one can take

$$\underline{C} = \frac{r^{r-1}}{\mathsf{B}(r, \frac{1}{\alpha})}, \quad \overline{C} = \frac{r^{r-1}}{2\mathsf{B}(r, \frac{1}{\alpha})[1 - \Phi(1)]}.$$

Roughly speaking, Proposition 8 states that the distribution of the mixing random variable $D_{r,\alpha}$ in Proposition 4 has the power-type tails decreasing such that $O(x^{-\alpha r/2})$ as $x \to \infty$.

In order to prove this proposition, we need to formulate and prove some general inequalities relating the tails of a scale mixture with that of the mixing distribution. These inequalities will be formulated as lemmas.

Lemma 4. *Let Y be a random variable with a symmetric distribution. Let U be a positive random variable. Then, for any $x > 0$ and $u > 0$,*

$$\mathsf{P}(|Y \circ U| > x) \geq \mathsf{P}\Big(|Y| > \frac{x}{u}\Big)\mathsf{P}(U > u).$$

Proof. Denote the distribution function of Y as $F(x)$. Then, for any $x > 0$ and $u > 0$, due to the monotonicity of F, we have

$$\mathsf{P}(|Y \circ U| > x) = 2\int_0^\infty \Big[1 - F\Big(\frac{x}{y}\Big)\Big] d\mathsf{P}(U < y) \geq 2\int_u^\infty \Big[1 - F\Big(\frac{x}{y}\Big)\Big] d\mathsf{P}(U < y) \geq$$

$$\geq 2\Big[1 - F\Big(\frac{x}{u}\Big)\Big]\int_u^\infty d\mathsf{P}(U < y) = \mathsf{P}\Big(|Y| > \frac{x}{u}\Big)\mathsf{P}(U \geq u).$$

□

Now, if we set $Y = X$ (that is, $F = \Phi$), $U = \sqrt{D_{r,\alpha}}$, and $u = x^\epsilon$ with arbitrary $\epsilon \in [0, 2]$, then for any $x > 0$, Proposition 2, Lemma 4, and Proposition 3 yield the bound

$$\frac{r^{r-1}}{\mathsf{B}(r, \frac{1}{\alpha})x^{\alpha r}} \geq \mathsf{P}(|T_{r,\alpha}| > x) \geq \mathsf{P}(D_{r,\alpha} \geq x^\epsilon)\mathsf{P}(|X| \geq x^{1-\epsilon/2}). \tag{18}$$

Additionally, if $\epsilon = 2$, then (18), in turn, implies

$$x^{\alpha r}\mathsf{P}(D_{r,\alpha} \geq x^2) \leq \frac{r^{r-1}}{2\mathsf{B}(r, \frac{1}{\alpha})[1 - \Phi(1)]}, \tag{19}$$

thus proving (17).

Lemma 4 generalizes a result of [40].

Lemma 5. *Let Y be a random variable independent of a positive random variable U. Then, for any $x > 0$ and $\delta \in (0, 1)$,*

$$\mathsf{P}(|Y \circ U| \geq x) \leq \mathsf{P}(|Y| \geq x^{1-\delta}) + \mathsf{P}(U \geq x^\delta)\mathsf{P}(|Y| < x^{1-\delta}) =$$

$$= \mathsf{P}(|Y| \geq x^{1-\delta})\mathsf{P}(U < x^\delta) + \mathsf{P}(U \geq x^\delta) \leq \mathsf{P}(|Y| \geq x^{1-\delta}) + \mathsf{P}(U \geq x^\delta).$$

Proof. It is not difficult to verify that for any $\delta \in (0, 1)$,

$$\{\omega : \ln|Y(\omega)| + \ln U(\omega) \geq \ln x\} \subseteq \{\omega : \ln|Y(\omega)| \geq (1 - \delta)\ln x\} \cup \{\omega : \ln U(\omega) \geq \delta \ln x\}.$$

Therefore,

$$\mathsf{P}(|Y \circ U| \geq x) = \mathsf{P}(\ln|Y \circ U| \geq \ln x) = \mathsf{P}(\ln|Y| + \ln U \geq \ln x) \leq$$

$$\leq \mathsf{P}(\{\ln|Y| \geq (1 - \delta)\ln x\} \cup \{\ln U \geq \delta \ln x\})\} =$$

$$= \mathsf{P}(\ln|Y| \geq (1-\delta)\ln x) + \mathsf{P}(\ln U \geq \delta \ln x) - \mathsf{P}(\ln|Y| \geq (1-\delta)\ln x) \cdot \mathsf{P}(\ln U \geq \delta \ln x) \leq$$
$$= \mathsf{P}(|Y| \geq x^{1-\delta}) + \mathsf{P}(U \geq x^{\delta}) - \mathsf{P}(|Y| \geq x^{1-\delta}) \cdot \mathsf{P}(U \geq x^{\delta})\} =$$
$$= \mathsf{P}(|Y| \geq x^{1-\delta}) + \mathsf{P}(U \geq x^{\delta})\mathsf{P}(|Y| < x^{1-\delta}) = \mathsf{P}(|Y| \geq x^{1-\delta})\mathsf{P}(U < x^{\delta}) + \mathsf{P}(U \geq x^{\delta}) \leq$$
$$\leq \mathsf{P}(|Y| \geq x^{1-\delta}) + \mathsf{P}(U \geq x^{\delta}).$$

The lemma is proved. □

It should be noted that in Lemma 5, no conditions were imposed on the distribution of the random variable Y.

Now, if we set $Y = X$ (that is, $F = \Phi$) and $U = \sqrt{D_{r,\alpha}}$, then for any $x > 0$ and $\epsilon \in (0,2)$, Proposition 4 and Lemma 5 yield the bound

$$\mathsf{P}(|T_{r,\alpha}| > x) \leq \mathsf{P}(|X| \geq x^{1-\epsilon/2}) + \mathsf{P}(D_{r,\alpha} \geq x^{\epsilon}),$$

which is valid for any $\epsilon \in (0,2)$. Hence, in turn, it follows that

$$\frac{\mathsf{P}(D_{r,\alpha} \geq x^{\epsilon})}{\mathsf{P}(|T_{r,\alpha}| > x)} \geq 1 - \frac{\mathsf{P}(|X| \geq x^{1-\epsilon/2})}{\mathsf{P}(|T_{r,\alpha}| > x)}. \tag{20}$$

It is well-known that for any $y > 0$,

$$\mathsf{P}(|X| \geq y) \leq \frac{\sqrt{2}}{\sqrt{\pi} y} \exp\Big\{-\frac{y^2}{2}\Big\}. \tag{21}$$

From the left inequality of Proposition 3 and (21), it follows that for any $\epsilon \in (0,2)$,

$$\lim_{x\to\infty} \frac{\mathsf{P}(|X| \geq x^{1-\epsilon/2})}{\mathsf{P}(|T_{r,\alpha}| > x)} \leq \frac{\sqrt{2}\mathrm{B}(r, \frac{1}{\alpha})}{\sqrt{\pi} r^{r-1}} \cdot \lim_{x\to\infty} (r + x^{\alpha})^{r+1/\alpha} x^{\epsilon/2-2} \exp\Big\{-\frac{x^{2-\epsilon}}{2}\Big\} = 0.$$

Hence, with the account of (13), from (20) and the left inequality of Proposition 3, it follows that for any $\epsilon \in (0,2)$

$$\liminf_{x\to\infty} x^{\alpha r} \mathsf{P}(D_{r,\alpha} \geq x^{\epsilon}) \geq \frac{r^{r-1}}{\mathrm{B}(r, \frac{1}{\alpha})},$$

thus proving (35). Thus, Proposition 8 is completely proved. □

Proposition 9. *If $\alpha \in (0,1]$ and $r > \frac{1}{\alpha}$, then the random variable $D_{r,\alpha}$ has the mixed exponential distribution*

$$D_{r,\alpha} \stackrel{d}{=} 2\big(G_{r,r}^{1/\alpha} \circ U_{1,\alpha}\big)^{-2} \circ W_1.$$

Proof. From Corollary 1, Lemma 3, and the definition of the generalized Student distribution, we obtain the representation

$$T_{r,\alpha} \stackrel{d}{=} Q_{\alpha} \circ G_{r,r}^{-1/\alpha} \stackrel{d}{=} \sqrt{2\big(G_{r,r}^{1/\alpha} \circ U_{1,\alpha}\big)^{-2} \circ W_1} \circ X.$$

Now the desired result follows from the identifiability of scale mixtures of normal distributions (see, e.g., [39]). □

Corollary 6. *For $\alpha \in (0,1] \cup \{2\}$ and any $r > \frac{1}{\alpha}$, the generalized Student distribution is infinitely divisible.*

Proof. According to Proposition 6, for $\alpha \in (0,1]$ in Representation (14), the scaling (mixing) distribution is mixed exponential and, hence, in accordance with the result of [41], infinitely divisible. In turn, if the mixing distribution in a normal scale mixture is infinitely divisible, then, in accordance with [42], Ch. XVII, Sect. 3, the normal scale mixture is infinitely divisible itself.

In the case that $\alpha = 2$, the infinite divisibility of the generalized Student distribution (in this case, the conventional Student distribution) for any $r > 0$ was proved in [43]. □

Proposition 10. *If $\alpha \in (0,1]$ and $r > \frac{1}{\alpha}$, then the generalized Student distribution is a scale mixture of the Laplace laws,*

$$T_{r,\alpha} \stackrel{d}{=} Y_{r,\alpha} \circ Q_1,$$

where

$$Y_{r,\alpha} \stackrel{d}{=} \left(G_{r,r}^{1/\alpha} \circ U_{1,\alpha}\right)^{-1}.$$

Proof. This statement follows from Corollary 2 and the definition of the random variable $T_{r,\alpha}$. □

2.3. Convergence of the Distributions of Random Sums to the Generalized Student Law

In applied probability, it is a convention, probably based on some topics of [35], that to make sure that a probability distribution can serve as a well-justified model of a real phenomenon, one should construct a limit setting where this distribution is a limit distribution or asymptotic approximation (say, a scheme of maximum or summation of random variables). The existence of such a limit setting with specific conditions providing the convergence to the assumed distribution can provide a better understanding of real mechanisms that generate observed statistical regularities.

The representation for the generalized Student distribution as a scale mixture of normals obtained in Proposition 4 opens the way for the construction in this section of an 'if and only if' version of the random-sum central limit theorem with the generalized Student distribution as the limit law.

Consider independent not necessarily identically distributed random variables $X_1, X_2, \ldots$ with $\mathsf{E}X_i = 0$ and $0 < \sigma_i^2 = \mathsf{E}X_i^2 < \infty$, $i \geq 1$. For $n \in \mathbb{N}$, denote

$$S_n = X_1 + \ldots + X_n, \quad B_n^2 = \sigma_1^2 + \ldots + \sigma_n^2.$$

Assume that the random variables $X_1, X_2, \ldots$ satisfy the Lindeberg condition such that for any $\tau > 0$,

$$\lim_{n\to\infty} \frac{1}{B_n^2} \sum_{i=1}^{n} \int_{|x|\geq \tau B_n} x^2 d\mathsf{P}(X_i < x) = 0. \tag{22}$$

It is well-known that under these assumptions,

$$\mathsf{P}\big(S_n < B_n x\big) \Longrightarrow \Phi(x)$$

(this is the classical central limit theorem due to Lindeberg).

Let $N_1, N_2, \ldots$ be a sequence of integer-valued nonnegative random variables defined on the same probability space so that for each $n \in \mathbb{N}$, the random variable N_n is independent of the sequence $X_1, X_2, \ldots$. Denote $S_{N_n} = X_1 + \ldots + X_{N_n}$. For definiteness, in what follows, we assume that $\sum_{j=1}^{0} = 0$. In what follows, the convergence will be meant as $n \to \infty$.

Recall that a random sequence $N_1, N_2, \ldots$ is said to be infinitely increasing in probability if $\mathsf{P}(N_n \leq m) \longrightarrow 0$ for any $m \in (0, \infty)$.

Let $\{d_n\}_{n\geq 1}$ be an infinitely increasing sequence of positive numbers.

The following version of the central limit theorem for random sums is the base for the proof of the main result of this section.

Lemma 6 ([44])**.** *Assume that the random variables $X_1, X_2, \ldots$ and $N_1, N_2, \ldots$ satisfy the conditions specified above. In particular, let the Lindeberg condition* (22) *hold. Moreover, let $N_n \to \infty$ in* *probability. The distribution functions of appropriately normalized random sums* S_{N_n} *converge to some distribution function* $F(x)$,

$$\mathsf{P}\Big(\frac{S_{N_n}}{d_n} < x\Big) \Longrightarrow F(x),$$

if and only if there exists a distribution function $H(x)$ *satisfying the conditions*

$$H(0) = 0, \quad F(x) = \int_0^\infty \Phi\Big(\frac{x}{\sqrt{y}}\Big) dH(y), \quad x \in \mathbb{R},$$

and $\mathsf{P}(B_{N_n}^2 < xd_n^2) \Longrightarrow H(x)$.

Proof. This statement is a particular case of a result proved in [44]; also see Theorem 3.3.2 in [45]. □

The main result of this section is the following statement presenting *necessary and sufficient* conditions for the convergence of the distributions of random sums of independent random variables with finite variances to the generalized Student distribution.

Proposition 11. *Let* $\alpha \in (0,2]$, $r > \frac{1}{\alpha}$. *Assume that the random variables* $X_1, X_2, \dots$ *and* $N_1, N_2, \dots$ *satisfy the conditions specified above. In particular, let the Lindeberg condition (22) hold. Moreover, let* $N_n \to \infty$ *in probability. Then, the distributions of the normalized random sums* S_{N_n} *converge to the generalized Student law with parameters* r *and* α*; that is,*

$$\frac{S_{N_n}}{d_n} \Longrightarrow T_{r,\alpha}$$

with some $d_n > 0$, $d_n \to \infty$, *if and only if*

$$\frac{B_{N_n}^2}{d_n^2} \Longrightarrow D_{r,\alpha} \stackrel{d}{=} \tfrac{1}{2}\big(U_{2,\alpha/2} \circ \overline{G}_{r,\alpha/2,r}\big)^{-1}. \tag{23}$$

Proof. This statement is a direct consequence of Lemma 4 with $H(x) = \mathsf{P}(D_{r,\alpha} < x)$ and Proposition 4. □

Note that if the random variables $X_1, X_2, \dots$ are identically distributed, then $\sigma_i = \sigma$, $i \in \mathbb{N}$, and the Lindeberg condition holds automatically. In this case, it is reasonable to take $d_n = \sigma\sqrt{n}$. Hence, from Proposition 11, in this case, it follows that for the convergence

$$\frac{S_{N_n}}{\sigma\sqrt{n}} \Longrightarrow T_{r,\alpha}$$

to take place, it is necessary and sufficient that

$$\frac{N_n}{n} \Longrightarrow D_{r,\alpha}. \tag{24}$$

It should be especially noted that despite the requirement that the summands in the sum have finite variances, the resulting generalized Student distribution in Proposition 11 may have *arbitrarily heavy* tails. The parameters of the limit-generalized Student distribution are entirely defined by the asymptotic behavior of the random index N_n (see Relationship (24)).

One more remark concerns the curious form of the random variable $D_{r,\alpha}$ due to which the realization of Conditions (23) and (24) in practical situations may seem doubtful. However, in many practical problems, the flow of informative events producing observations can be successfully modelled by a doubly stochastic Poisson process (also called a Cox process). Such a process is defined as a Poisson process with stochastic intensity.

Namely, a doubly stochastic Poisson process is a stochastic point process of the form $N(t) \stackrel{\text{def}}{=} \Pi(L(t))$, where $\Pi(t)$, where $t \geq 0$, is a homogeneous Poisson process with unit intensity, and the stochastic process $L(t)$, where $t \geq 0$, is independent of $\Pi(t)$ and possesses the following properties: $L(0) = 0$, $\mathsf{P}(L(t) < \infty) = 1$ for any $t > 0$, and the sample paths of $L(t)$ do not decrease and are right-continuous. In this context, the Cox process $N(t)$ is said to be lead by the process $L(t)$. For more details concerning Cox and more general subordinated processes, see, e.g., [46–48].

In real problems, the process $L(t)$ characterizing the cumulative intensity of the flow of informative events depends on many factors whose influence is hardly predictable, and it is quite likely that the statistical regularities in its behavior can be approximated by the distribution of the random variable $D_{r,\alpha}$. Now, if $N_n \stackrel{\text{def}}{=} N(n)$, then for Condition (24) to hold, it is necessary and sufficient that $n^{-1}L(n) \Longrightarrow D_{r,\alpha}$ [49]. This means that actually, Conditions (23) and (24) are not as artificial as it may seem at the first sight.

2.4. Convergence of the Distributions of Statistics Constructed from Samples with Random Sizes to the Generalized Student Distribution

In practice, rather often, the data are collected or registered during a certain period of time so that the sequence (flow) of informative events, each of which brings the next observation, is a random point process. Hence, the number of available observations may be unknown until the termination of the process of their registration. Therefore, the number of accumulated observations (sample size) should also be treated as a (random) observation. This means that the problems and results of the classical mathematical statistics, in which the size of the available sample is usually assumed to be deterministic, deals with conditional distributions given the concrete value of the sample size. In the asymptotic settings, this value plays the role of an infinitely increasing known parameter. However, the asymptotic behavior of the (unconditional) distributions of statistics constructed from samples with random sizes noticeably differs from that of the distributions of statistics in the classical case, which are actually conditional distributions given the particular value of the sample size. For a more detailed motivation for the consideration of statistics constructed from samples with random sizes, see, e.g., [32].

The randomness of the sample size usually leads to the limit distributions for the corresponding statistics being heavy-tailed, even in situations where the conditional distributions of the same statistics given a non-random sample size are asymptotically normal; see, e.g., [4,45,50].

Consider a traditional setting of mathematical statistics. As in the preceding section, consider the random variables $N_1, N_2, \ldots, X_1, X_2, \ldots$ defined on one and the same probability space so that for each $n \geq 1$, the random variable N_n takes only natural values and is independent of the 'observations' $X_1, X_2, \ldots$. Let $t_n = t_n(X_1, \ldots, X_n)$ be a statistic, that is, a measurable function of $X_1, \ldots, X_n$. For every $n \geq 1$ and $\omega \in \Omega$, define the random variable $t_{N_n} = t_{N_n(\omega)}(\omega)$ as

$$t_{N_n} = t_{N_n(\omega)}\Big(X_1(\omega), \ldots, X_{N_n(\omega)}(\omega)\Big).$$

A statistic t_n is said to be *asymptotically normal* if there exist $\delta > 0$ and $\theta \in \mathbb{R}$ such that

$$\mathsf{P}(\delta\sqrt{n}(t_n - \theta) < x) \Longrightarrow \Phi(x). \tag{25}$$

Lemma 7 ([51]). *Assume that $N_n \longrightarrow \infty$ in probability and the statistic t_n is asymptotically normal in the sense of* (25)*. A distribution function $F(x)$ such that*

$$\mathsf{P}(\delta\sqrt{n}(t_{N_n} - \theta) < x) \Longrightarrow F(x),$$

exists if and only if there exists a distribution function $H(x)$ satisfying the conditions

$$H(0) = 0, \quad F(x) = \int_0^\infty \Phi(x\sqrt{y})dH(y), \quad x \in \mathbb{R}, \quad \mathsf{P}(N_n < nx) \Longrightarrow H(x).$$

The following theorem presents necessary and sufficient conditions for the convergence of the distributions of statistics, which are suggested to be asymptotically normal in the traditional sense but are constructed from samples with random sizes, to the generalized Student distribution.

Proposition 12. *Let $\alpha \in (0,2]$, $r > \frac{1}{\alpha}$. Assume that the random variables $X_1, X_2, \ldots$ and $N_1, N_2, \ldots$ satisfy the conditions specified above. Moreover, let $N_n \to \infty$ in probability and let the statistic t_n be asymptotically normal in the sense of (25). Then, the distribution of the statistic t_{N_n} constructed from samples with random sizes N_n converges to the generalized Student law $F_{r,\alpha}(x)$; that is,*

$$\mathsf{P}\big(\delta\sqrt{n}(t_{N_n} - \theta) < x\big) \Longrightarrow F_{r,\alpha}(x),$$

if and only if

$$\frac{N_n}{n} \Longrightarrow D_{r,\alpha}^{-1} \stackrel{d}{=} 2U_{2,\alpha/2} \circ \overline{G}_{r,\alpha/2,r}. \tag{26}$$

Proof. This statement is a direct consequence of (14) and Lemma 7 with $H(x) = \mathsf{P}(D_{r,\alpha}^{-1} < x)$. □

As an example of an application of Proposition 12, consider the following statement establishing necessary and sufficient conditions for the sample quantiles to have the generalized Student asymptotic distribution.

In addition to the notation introduced above, for each $n \in \mathbb{N}$, let $X_{(1)}, X_{(2)}, \ldots, X_{(n)}$ be order statistics constructed from the sample $X_1, X_2, \ldots, X_n$ so that $X_{(1)} \le X_{(2)} \le \ldots \le X_{(n)}$. Assume that the common distribution of X_j is absolutely continuous and denote the corresponding probability density as $p(x)$. Let $q \in (0,1)$. The quantile of order q of the random variable X_1 will be denoted ξ_q. For a fixed $n \in \mathbb{N}$, define the sample quantile as $X_{([nq]+1)}$, where $[a]$ stands for the integer part of a real number a. The following Lemma is a particular case of a result from [52].

Lemma 8. *Assume that the density $p(x)$ is differentiable in the neighborhood of ξ_q and $p(\xi_q) \neq 0$. Then, as $n \to \infty$,*

$$\frac{p(\xi_q)}{\sqrt{q(1-q)}} \cdot \sqrt{n}\big(X_{([nq]+1)} - \xi_q\big) \Longrightarrow X.$$

This statement means that the sample quantile $X_{([nq]+1)}$ is asymptotically normal in the sense of (25) with $\delta = p(\xi_q)/\sqrt{q(1-q)}$ and $\theta = \xi_q$.

In [4], an example was presented of the convergence of the distributions of some statistics constructed from samples with random sizes to the classical Student distribution. In that paper, it was assumed that the sample size had a negative binomial distribution. Here, we will present a generalization of this result. As is known, the negative binomial distribution considered in [4] is a mixed Poisson distribution with a mixing gamma distribution. A random variable N with a negative binomial distribution can be represented as $N = \Pi(G_{r,\lambda})$, where $r > 0$, $\lambda > 0$, and $\Pi(t)$ is the Poisson process with the unit intensity independent of the gamma-distributed random variable $G_{r,\lambda}$. Here, we will use the same construction and assume that for each $n \in \mathbb{N}$, the random sample size N_n has the mixed Poisson distribution of the form

$$N_n = \Pi(nD_{r,\alpha}^{-1}). \tag{27}$$

With $\alpha = 2$ the random variable $D_{r,\alpha}^{-1}$ obviously turns into $G_{r,r}$ so that, as in this case, we deal with the negative binomially distributed sample size considered in [4].

Corollary 7. *Let $\alpha \in (0,2]$ where $r > \frac{1}{\alpha}$. Let the random variable N_n be defined as (27) and be independent of the sequence $X_1, X_2, \ldots$ for each $n \in \mathbb{N}$. Then, the distribution of the sample quantiles constructed from samples with random sizes N_n converges to the generalized Student law $F_{r,\alpha}(x)$; that is,*

$$\mathsf{P}\Big(\frac{p(\xi_q)}{\sqrt{q(1-q)}} \cdot \sqrt{n}\big(X_{([qN_n]+1)} - \xi_q\big) < x\Big) \Longrightarrow F_{r,\alpha}(x).$$

Proof. It is easy to verify that the random variables N_n defined as (27) satisfy Condition (26) so that the desired result follows from Proposition 12. □

It should be noted that in Proposition 12 and Corollary 6, a non-random normalization and centering was used for the statistics constructed from samples with random sizes. This was performed because a reasonable approximation to the distribution of the basic statistics can be constructed only if both centering and normalizing values are non-random. Otherwise (that is, if normalization is random depending on the random sample size), the approximate asymptotic distribution function becomes random itself. For example, random normalization makes the problem of the evaluation of significance levels from the asymptotic distribution of the test statistic senseless.

3. Generalized Lomax Distribution

3.1. Definition and Basic Properties of the Generalized Lomax Distribution

The distribution of the random variable

$$|T_{r,\alpha}| \stackrel{d}{=} |Q_\alpha| \circ G_{r,r}^{-1/\alpha}$$

will be called a generalized Lomax distribution. When $\alpha = 1$, this distribution is known as Lomax distribution. In general, with an arbitrary $\alpha \in (0,2]$, the distribution of $|T_{r,\alpha}|$ can just as well be called folded generalized Student or one-sided generalized Student distribution. However, in what follows, we will keep to the term generalized Lomax distribution.

From (8), it is easy to see that the probability density $f^*_{r,\alpha}(x)$ of the generalized Lomax distribution has the form

$$f^*_{r,\alpha}(x) = \frac{\alpha}{r^{1/\alpha}\mathrm{B}(r, \frac{1}{\alpha})}\Big(1 + \frac{x^\alpha}{r}\Big)^{-(r+1/\alpha)}, \quad x \geq 0.$$

Recall that here, $\alpha \in (0,2]$ and $r > 0$ so that $\alpha r > 1$.

The expression for the moments of the generalized Lomax distribution is given by Proposition 2.

Proposition 13. *For $\alpha \in (0,1]$ and $r > \frac{1}{\alpha}$, the generalized Lomax distribution is mixed exponential.*

Proof. Since $|Q_1| \stackrel{d}{=} W_1$, from Proposition 10, it directly follows that

$$|T_{r,\alpha}| \stackrel{d}{=} \big(U_{1,\alpha} \circ G_{r,r}^{1/\alpha}\big)^{-1} \circ W_1. \tag{28}$$

□

Corollary 8. *For $\alpha \in (0,1]$ and $r > \frac{1}{\alpha}$, the generalized Lomax distribution is infinitely divisible.*

Proof. The statement follows from Proposition 13 and the result of [41], according to which it is sufficient that F is mixed exponential in order for a distribution function $F(x)$ such that $F(0) = 0$ to be infinitely divisible. □

Proposition 14. *For $\alpha \in (0,2]$ and $r > \frac{1}{\alpha}$, the scale mixtures of generalized Lomax distributions are identifiable; that is, if V_1 and V_2 are two nonnegative random variables, then the equality $|T_{r,\alpha}| \circ V_1 \stackrel{d}{=} |T_{r,\alpha}| \circ V_2$ implies $V_1 \stackrel{d}{=} V_2$.*

Proof. The proof is similar to that of Proposition 6. □

The generalized Lomax distribution can be just as well defined in terms of only (generalized) gamma distributions or only exponential power distributions, as is demonstrated in the following statement implied by Relationship (5).

Proposition 15. *For $\alpha \in (0,2]$ and $r > \frac{1}{\alpha}$, the following relationships hold:*

$$|T_{r,\alpha}| \stackrel{d}{=} \big(r|Q_\alpha| \circ |Q_{1/r}|^{-1/r}\big)^{1/\alpha} \stackrel{d}{=} \big(rG_{1/\alpha,1} \circ |Q_{1/r}|^{-1/r}\big)^{1/\alpha} \stackrel{d}{=}$$

$$\stackrel{d}{=} \big(G_{1/\alpha,r} \circ |Q_{1/r}|^{-1/r}\big)^{1/\alpha} \stackrel{d}{=} \big(G_{1/\alpha,r} \circ G_{r,1}^{-1}\big)^{1/\alpha}. \tag{29}$$

3.2. Generalized Lomax Distribution as a Scale Mixture of Folded Normal Distributions

From Proposition 7, we obviously obtain the following statement.

Corollary 9. *For any $\alpha \in (0,2]$ and any $r > \frac{1}{\alpha}$, the generalized Lomax distribution is a scale mixture of folded normal distributions:*

$$|T_{r,\alpha}| \stackrel{d}{=} \sqrt{D_{r,\alpha}} \circ |X|, \tag{30}$$

where

$$D_{r,\alpha} \stackrel{\text{def}}{=} \tfrac{1}{2}\big(U_{2,\alpha/2} \circ G_{r,r}^{2/\alpha}\big)^{-1} \stackrel{d}{=} \tfrac{1}{2}\big(U_{2,\alpha/2} \circ \overline{G}_{r,\alpha/2,r}\big)^{-1},$$

so that

$$\mathsf{P}(|T_{r,\alpha}| < x) = 2\int_0^\infty \Phi\Big(\frac{x}{\sqrt{y}}\Big)d\mathsf{P}(D_{r,\alpha} < y) - 1. \tag{31}$$

Moreover, if $\alpha \in (0,1]$, then $D_{r,\alpha} \stackrel{d}{=} 2W_1 \circ \big(U_{1,\alpha} \circ G_{r,r}^{1/\alpha}\big)^{-2}$.

3.3. Convergence of the Distributions of Maximum and Minimum Random Sums to the Generalized Lomax Distribution

In this section, it will be demonstrated that the generalized Lomax distribution can be the limit law for maximum sums of a random number of independent random variables (maximum random sums), minimum random sums, and absolute values of random sums.

In addition to the notation $S_n = X_1 + \ldots + X_n$ introduced in Section 2.3, for $n \in \mathbb{N}$, denote $\overline{S}_n = \max_{1\le i\le n} S_i$, where $\underline{S}_n = \min_{1\le i\le n} S_i$. The random variables $X_1, X_2, \ldots$ will be assumed to satisfy the Lindeberg condition (22). It is well-known that under these assumptions, not only does $\mathsf{P}(S_n < B_n x) \Longrightarrow \Phi(x)$ (see Section 2.3), but also $\mathsf{P}(\overline{S}_n < B_n x) \Longrightarrow 2\Phi(x) - 1$, $x \ge 0$, and $\mathsf{P}(\underline{S}_n < B_n x) \Longrightarrow 2\Phi(x)$, $x \le 0$.

Let, as usual, $N_1, N_2, \ldots$ be a sequence of nonnegative random variables such that for each $n \in \mathbb{N}$ the random variables $N_n, X_1, X_2, \ldots$ are independent. For $n \in \mathbb{N}$, let $S_{N_n} = X_1 + \ldots + X_{N_n}$, $\overline{S}_{N_n} = \max_{1\le i\le N_n} S_i$, and $\underline{S}_{N_n} = \min_{1\le i\le N_n} S_i$ (for definiteness, assume that $S_0 = \overline{S}_0 = \underline{S}_0 = 0$). Let $\{d_n\}_{n\ge1}$ be an arbitrary infinitely increasing sequence of positive numbers. Here, the convergence is meant as $n \to \infty$.

Lemma 9 ([44]). *Assume that the random variables $X_1, X_2, \ldots$ and $N_1, N_2, \ldots$ satisfy the conditions specified above. In particular, let the Lindeberg Condition (22) hold and let $N_n \to \infty$ in probability. Then, the distributions of normalized random sums weakly converge to some distribution; that is, there exists a random variable Y such that $d_n^{-1}S_{N_n} \Longrightarrow Y$ if and only if there exists a nonnegative random variable U such that $Y \stackrel{d}{=} \sqrt{U} \circ X$ and if any of the following conditions holds:*

(i) $d_n^{-1}|S_{N_n}| \Longrightarrow |Y|$;
(ii) *There exists a random variable* $\overline{Y}$ *such that* $d_n^{-1}\overline{S}_{N_n} \Longrightarrow \overline{Y}$;
(iii) *There exists a random variable* $\underline{Y}$ *such that* $d_n^{-1}\underline{S}_{N_n} \Longrightarrow \underline{Y}$;
(iv) *There exists a nonnegative random variable* U *such that* $d_n^{-2}B_{N_n}^2 \Longrightarrow U$.

Moreover,

$$\mathsf{P}(\underline{Y} < x) = 2\mathsf{E}\Phi(xU^{-1/2}),\ x \le 0;\ \ \mathsf{P}(\overline{Y} < x) = \mathsf{P}(|Y| < x) = 2\mathsf{E}\Phi(xU^{-1/2}) - 1,\ x \ge 0.$$

Lemma 9 and Corollary 8 imply the following statement.

Proposition 16. *Let* $\alpha \in (0,2]$. *Assume that the random variables* $X_1, X_2, \dots$ *and* $N_1, N_2, \dots$ *satisfy the conditions specified above. In particular, let the Lindeberg Condition (22) hold. Moreover, let* $N_n \to \infty$ *in probability. Then the following five statements are equivalent:*

$$d_n^{-1}S_{N_n} \Longrightarrow T_{r,\alpha};\ d_n^{-1}\overline{S}_{N_n} \Longrightarrow |T_{r,\alpha}|;\ d_n^{-1}\underline{S}_{N_n} \Longrightarrow -|T_{r,\alpha}|;$$

$$d_n^{-1}|S_{N_n}| \Longrightarrow |T_{r,\alpha}|;\ d_n^{-2}B_{N_n}^2 \Longrightarrow D_{r,\alpha}.$$

3.4. Generalized Lomax Distribution as a Mixed Weibull Distribution (with $1 \le \alpha \le 2$) and as a Mixed Fréchet Distribution (with $0 < \alpha \le 1$)

In addition to the auxiliary information presented in the Introduction, in this section, we will need some more definitions and auxiliary results.

In the paper [53], it was shown that any gamma distribution with a shape parameter no greater than one is mixed exponential. Namely, the density $g(x; r, \mu)$ of a gamma distribution with $0 < r < 1$ can be represented as

$$g(x; r, \mu) = \int_0^\infty ze^{-zx}p(z; r, \mu)dz,$$

where

$$p(z; r, \mu) = \frac{\mu^r}{\Gamma(1-r)\Gamma(r)} \cdot \frac{\mathbb{I}_{[\mu,\infty)}(z)}{(z-\mu)^r z}. \tag{32}$$

Moreover, a gamma distribution with a shape parameter $r > 1$ cannot be represented as a mixed exponential distribution.

In [54], it was proved that if $r \in (0,1)$, $\mu > 0$, and $G_{r,1}$ and $G_{1-r,1}$ are independent gamma-distributed random variables, then the density $p(z; r, \mu)$ defined by (32) corresponds to the random variable

$$Z_{r,\mu} = \frac{\mu(G_{r,1} + G_{1-r,1})}{G_{r,1}} \stackrel{d}{=} \mu Z_{r,1} \stackrel{d}{=} \mu\left(1 + \tfrac{1-r}{r}R_{1-r,r}\right), \tag{33}$$

where $R_{1-r,r}$ is a random variable with the Snedecor–Fisher distribution defined by the probability density

$$f(x; 1-r, r) = \frac{(1-r)^{1-r}r^r}{\Gamma(1-r)\Gamma(r)} \cdot \frac{\mathbb{I}_{(0,\infty)}(x)}{x^r[r + (1-r)x]}. \tag{34}$$

In other words, if $r \in (0,1)$, then

$$G_{r,\mu} \stackrel{d}{=} Z_{r,\mu}^{-1} \circ W_1. \tag{35}$$

In [32], it was proved that if $\alpha \ge 1$, then the one-sided EP distribution is a scale mixture of Weibull distributions:

$$|Q_\alpha| \stackrel{d}{=} Z_{1/\alpha,1}^{-1/\alpha} \circ W_\alpha. \tag{36}$$

Recall that the random variable W_α^{-1} is said to have an *inverse Weibull* or *Fréchet* distribution:

$$\mathsf{P}(W_\alpha^{-1} < x) = \mathsf{P}(W_\alpha \geq \tfrac{1}{x}) = \exp\{x^{-\alpha}\}, \quad x \geq 0.$$

From (5) and Gleser's result (35), we obtain the following statement.

Proposition 17. *(i). If $1 < \alpha \leq 2$ and $\frac{1}{\alpha} < r < 1$, then the generalized Lomax distribution is a scale mixture of Fréchet distributions:*

$$|T_{r,\alpha}| \stackrel{d}{=} |Q_\alpha| \circ Z_{r,r}^{1/\alpha} \circ W_\alpha^{-1} \stackrel{d}{=} \big(G_{1/\alpha,r} \circ Z_{r,1}\big)^{1/\alpha} \circ W_\alpha^{-1}. \tag{37}$$

(ii). If $1 < \alpha \leq 2$ and $r > \frac{1}{\alpha}$, then the generalized Lomax distribution is a scale mixture of Weibull distributions:

$$|T_{r,\alpha}| \stackrel{d}{=} \big(Z_{1/\alpha,1} \circ G_{r,r}\big)^{-1/\alpha} \circ W_\alpha. \tag{38}$$

Proof. Relationship (37) follows from Proposition 15 and (35). Relationship (38) follows from Proposition 15, (36), and (2) with $\gamma = \alpha$. □

3.5. Some Limit Theorems for Extreme Order Statistics in Samples with Random Sizes

Proposition 17 states that the generalized Lomax distributions with $\alpha \geq 1$ can be represented as scale mixtures of the Weibull distribution or as scale mixtures of the Fréchet distribution. In other words, Relationship (38) can be expressed in the following form: for any $x \geq 0$,

$$\mathsf{P}(|T_{r,\alpha}| < x) = \int_0^\infty (1 - e^{-zx^\alpha})d\,\mathsf{P}(Z_{1/\alpha,1} \circ G_{r,r} < z), \tag{39}$$

whereas Relationship (37) can be rewritten as

$$\mathsf{P}(|T_{r,\alpha}| < x) = \int_0^\infty e^{-zx^{-\alpha}}d\,\mathsf{P}(Z_{r,1} \circ G_{1/\alpha,r} < z). \tag{40}$$

At the same time, in the case that $0 < \alpha \leq 1$, Relationship (28) can be written in the form

$$\mathsf{P}(|T_{r,\alpha}| < x) = \int_0^\infty (1 - e^{-zx})d\,\mathsf{P}(U_{1,\alpha} \circ G_{r,r}^{1/\alpha} < z). \tag{41}$$

As is well known, all the parent distributions in these mixtures can be limiting for extreme-order statistics.

From (39) and (40), it follows that the generalized Lomax distribution with $\alpha \geq 1$ can appear as a limit distribution in limit theorems for extreme-order statistics in samples with random sizes. To illustrate this, we will consider the limit setting dealing with the max-compound and min-compound doubly stochastic Poisson processes.

Recall that the definition of a doubly stochastic Poisson process (Cox process) was given in Section 2.3.

Now, let $N(t)$, where $t \geq 0$, be the a doubly stochastic Poisson process (Cox process) lead by the process $L(t)$. Let $T_1, T_2, \ldots$ be the jump points of the process $N(t)$. Consider a marked Cox point process $\{(T_i, X_i)\}_{i\geq 1}$, where $X_1, X_2, \ldots$ are independent identically distributed random variables independent of the process $N(t)$. Most studies dealing with the point process $\{(T_i, X_i)\}_{i\geq 1}$ deal with a traditional *compound Cox process* $S(t)$ defined for each $t \geq 0$ as the *sum* of all marks X_i of the points T_i of the marked Cox point process that do not exceed the time t. In $S(t)$, the compounding operation is *summation*. In many applied problems, of no less importance are the other functions of the marked Cox point process $\{(T_i, X_i)\}_{i\geq 1}$: the so-called max-compound Cox process or min-compound Cox process that differ from $S(t)$ in that the compounding operation of summation is replaced by the operation of taking the maximum or minimum of the marking random variables, respectively. The analytic and asymptotic properties of max-compound and min-compound Cox processes were considered in [55–57].

Let $N(t)$ be a Cox process. The process $M(t)$ defined as

$$M(t) = \begin{cases} -\infty, & \text{if } N(t) = 0, \\ \max\limits_{1 \le k \le N(t)} X_k, & \text{if } N(t) \ge 1, \end{cases}$$

where $t \ge 0$, is called a *max-compound Cox process*.

The process $m(t)$ defined as

$$m(t) = \begin{cases} +\infty, & \text{if } N(t) = 0, \\ \min\limits_{1 \le k \le N(t)} X_k, & \text{if } N(t) \ge 1, \end{cases}$$

where $t \ge 0$, is called a *min-compound Cox process*.

The common distribution function of the random variables X_j will be denoted $F(x)$. In what follows, we will use the conventional notation

$$\text{lext}(F) = \inf\{x : F(x) > 0\}, \quad \text{rext}(F) = \sup\{x : F(x) < 1\}.$$

Lemma 10. *Assume that there exists a positive infinitely increasing function $d(t)$ and a positive random variable L such that*

$$\frac{L(t)}{d(t)} \Longrightarrow L \tag{42}$$

as $t \to \infty$. Let us also assume that $\text{lext}(F) > -\infty$ and the distribution function $P_F(x) \equiv F(\text{lext}(F) - x^{-1})$ satisfies the condition that there exists a number $\gamma > 0$ such that for any $x > 0$

$$\lim_{y \to \infty} \frac{P_F(yx)}{P_F(y)} = x^{-\gamma}. \tag{43}$$

Then, there exist functions $a(t)$ and $b(t)$ such that

$$\mathsf{P}\Big(\frac{m(t) - a(t)}{b(t)} < x\Big) \Longrightarrow H(x)$$

as $t \to \infty$, where

$$H(x) = \begin{cases} \displaystyle\int_0^\infty (1 - e^{-zx^\gamma}) d\mathsf{P}(L < z), & x \ge 0, \\ 0, & x < 0. \end{cases}$$

Moreover, the functions $a(t)$ and $b(t)$ can be defined as

$$a(t) = \text{lext}(F), \quad b(t) = \sup\Big\{x : F(x) \le \frac{1}{d(t)}\Big\} - \text{lext}(F). \tag{44}$$

Proof. This lemma can be proved in the same way as Theorem 2 in [55] dealing with max-compound Cox processes using the fact that

$$\min\{X_1, \ldots, X_{N(t)}\} = -\max\{-X_1, \ldots, -X_{N(t)}\}.$$

□

Proposition 18. *Let $0 < \alpha \le 1$, $r > \frac{1}{\alpha}$. Assume that there exists a positive infinitely increasing function $d(t)$ such that condition (42) holds with*

$$L \stackrel{d}{=} U_{1,\alpha} \circ G_{r,r}^{1/\alpha}.$$

Let us also assume that $\mathrm{lext}(F) > -\infty$ *and the distribution function* $P_F(x) \equiv F\big(\mathrm{lext}(F) - x^{-1}\big)$ *satisfies Condition* (43) *with* $\gamma = 1$. *Then, there exist functions* $a(t)$ *and* $b(t)$ *such that*

$$\frac{m(t) - a(t)}{b(t)} \Longrightarrow |T_{r,\alpha}| \tag{45}$$

as $t \to \infty$. *Moreover, the functions* $a(t)$ *and* $b(t)$ *can be defined by* (44).

Proof. This statement directly follows from Lemma 10 with the account of (41). □

Proposition 19. *Let* $1 \le \alpha \le 2$, *where* $r > \frac{1}{\alpha}$. *Assume that there exists a positive infinitely increasing function* $d(t)$ *such that Condition* (42) *holds with*

$$L \stackrel{d}{=} Z_{1/\alpha,1} \circ G_{r,r}.$$

Let us also assume that $\mathrm{lext}(F) > -\infty$ *and the distribution function* $P_F(x) \equiv F\big(\mathrm{lext}(F) - x^{-1}\big)$ *satisfies Condition* (43) *with* $\gamma = \alpha$. *Then, there exist functions* $a(t)$ *and* $b(t)$ *such that*

$$\frac{m(t) - a(t)}{b(t)} \Longrightarrow |T_{r,\alpha}| \tag{46}$$

as $t \to \infty$. *Moreover, the functions* $a(t)$ *and* $b(t)$ *can be defined by* (44).

Proof. This statement directly follows from Lemma 10 with the account of (39). □

Lemma 11. *Assume that there exist a positive infinitely increasing function* $d(t)$ *and a nonnegative random variable* L *such that Condition* (42) *holds. Let us also assume that* $\mathrm{rext}(F) = \infty$ *and there exists a positive number* γ *such that*

$$\lim_{y \to \infty} \frac{1 - F(yx)}{1 - F(y)} = x^{-\gamma} \tag{47}$$

for any $x > 0$. *Then, there exist a positive function* $b(t)$ *and a distribution function* $H_1(x)$ *such that*

$$\mathsf{P}\Big(\frac{M(t)}{b(t)} < x\Big) \Longrightarrow H_1(x)$$

as $t \to \infty$. *Moreover,*

$$H_1(x) = \begin{cases} 0, & x < 0, \\ \displaystyle\int_0^\infty e^{-zx^{-\gamma}} d\mathsf{P}(L < z), & x \ge 0, \end{cases}$$

and the function $b(t)$ *can be defined as*

$$b(t) = \inf\Big\{x : \, 1 - F(x) \le \frac{1}{d(t)}\Big\}. \tag{48}$$

Proposition 20. *Let* $1 \le \alpha \le 2$, $r > \frac{1}{\alpha}$. *Assume that there exists a positive infinitely increasing function* $d(t)$ *such that Condition* (42) *holds with*

$$L \stackrel{d}{=} Z_{r,1} \circ G_{1/\alpha,r}.$$

Let us also assume that $\mathrm{rext}(F) = \infty$ *and Condition* (47) *holds with* $\gamma = \alpha$. *Then, there exists a positive function* $b(t)$ *such that*

$$\frac{M(t)}{b(t)} \Longrightarrow |T_{r,\alpha}| \tag{49}$$

as $t \to \infty$. *Moreover, the function* $b(t)$ *can be defined by* (48).

Proof. This statement directly follows from Lemma 10 with the account of (40). □

It is very simple to give examples of processes satisfying the conditions described in Propositions 18 and 19. Let $L(t) \equiv Ut$ and $d(t) \equiv t$, where $t \geq 0$, where U is a positive random variable. Then, choosing an appropriately distributed U, we can provide the validity of the corresponding condition for the convergence of $L(t)/d(t)$. Moreover, the parameter t may not have the meaning of physical time. For example, it may be some location parameter of $L(t)$, so that the statements of this section concern the case of the large mean intensity of the Cox process.

3.6. Convergence of the Distributions of Mixed Geometric Random Sums to the Generalized Lomax Distribution And Extensions of the Rényi Theorem

In the preceding section, we made sure that the generalized Lomax distribution can be limiting for extreme-order statistics in samples of random sizes. Here, it will be demonstrated that this distribution can also be used as an asymptotic approximation for the distributions of sums of independent random variables.

According to Proposition 13, if $\alpha \in (0,1]$ and $r > \frac{1}{\alpha}$, then the generalized Lomax distribution is mixed exponential. According to Corollary 7, it is infinitely divisible and hence, by the Lévy–Khintchin theorem, can be limiting for sums of independent random variables in the double array limit scheme under the condition of the uniform negligibility of summands.

However, the classical summation scheme is far from the only summation model within which the generalized Lomax distribution can be an asymptotic distribution. To be sure of this, consider two limit settings dealing with mixed geometric and mixed Poisson random sums. In both of these settings, we will deal with versions of the law of large numbers for random sums where, unlike the classical situation, the limit may be random [45].

First, consider mixed geometric random sums.

Let $p \in (0,1)$ and let V_p be a random variable having a geometric distribution with the parameter p: $\mathsf{P}(V_p = k) = p(1-p)^{k-1}, k = 1, 2, \ldots$. This means that

$$\mathsf{P}(V_p > m) = \sum_{k=m+1}^{\infty} p(1-p)^{k-1} = (1-p)^m$$

for any $m \in \mathbb{N}$. Let $(\pi_n)_{n \geq 1}$ be a sequence of positive random variables taking values in the interval $(0,1)$, and, moreover, for each $n \geq 1$ and all $p \in (0,1)$, the random variables π_n and V_p are independent.

For each $n \in \mathbb{N}$, let $N_n = V_{\pi_n}$. Hence,

$$\mathsf{P}(N_n > m) = \int_0^1 (1-z)^m \, d\mathsf{P}(\pi_n < z) \tag{50}$$

for any $m \in \mathbb{N}$. The distribution of the random variable N_n will be called *π_n-mixed geometric* (for more details, see [58]).

Let $X_1, X_2, \ldots$ be a sequence of independent identically distributed random variables such that the expectation $\mathsf{E}X_1$ exists. Assume that $\mathsf{E}X_1 \equiv a \neq 0$. According to the Kolmogorov strong law of large numbers, this condition implies that

$$\frac{1}{na} \sum_{j=1}^{n} X_j \longrightarrow 1 \tag{51}$$

almost surely as $n \to \infty$.

For $n \in \mathbb{N}$, let $S_n = X_1 + \cdots + X_n$. Let N_n be a random variable with a π_n-mixed geometric distribution (50). Assume that for each $n \in \mathbb{N}$, the random variable N_n is independent of the sequence $X_1, X_2, \ldots$. Our nearest aim is to study the asymptotic behavior of the random sum S_{N_n} as $n \to \infty$.

Lemma 12 ([58]). *Assume that the random variables $X_1, X_2, \ldots$ satisfy Condition (51). Let for each $n \in \mathbb{N}$ the random variable N_n have a π_n-mixed geometric distribution (50) and be independent of the sequence $X_1, X_2, \ldots$. Assume that there exists a positive random variable N such that*

$$n\pi_n \Longrightarrow N$$

as $n \to \infty$. Then

$$\frac{S_{N_n}}{n} \Longrightarrow aN^{-1} \circ W_1 \quad (n \to \infty).$$

Proposition 21. *Let $\alpha \in (0,1]$ and $r > \frac{1}{\alpha}$. Assume that the random variables $X_1, X_2, \ldots$ satisfy Condition (51). Let for each $n \in \mathbb{N}$ the random variable N_n have a π_n-mixed geometric distribution (50) and be independent of the sequence $X_1, X_2, \ldots$. Assume that*

$$n\pi_n \Longrightarrow U_{1,\alpha} \circ G_{r,r}^{1/\alpha} \tag{52}$$

as $n \to \infty$. Then,

$$\lim_{n\to\infty} \sup_{x\geq 0} \big|\mathsf{P}(S_{N_n} < na \cdot x) - \mathsf{P}(|T_{r,\alpha}| < x)\big| = 0.$$

Proof. By Lemma 12 with $N \stackrel{d}{=} U_{1,\alpha} \circ G_{r,r}^{1/\alpha}$ and (28), Condition (52) implies

$$\frac{S_{N_n}}{na} \Longrightarrow \big(U_{1,\alpha} \circ G_{r,r}^{1/\alpha}\big)^{-1} \circ W_1 \stackrel{d}{=} |T_{r,\alpha}|. \tag{53}$$

Now it remains for us to refer to the Dini theorem, according to which, since the distribution function of the limit random variable is continuous, convergence in distribution (53) implies the uniform convergence of the distribution functions. □

Proposition 21 is an example of extension of the famous Rényi theorem on the asymptotic behavior of the distributions of geometric sums (or rarefied renewal processes) [59] to the case of mixed geometric sums. In turn, the Rényi theorem can be regarded as an example of the law of large numbers for geometric random sums.

Now, we turn to mixed Poisson random sums. For each $n \in \mathbb{N}$, define the random variable N_n as $N_n = \Pi(L_n)$, where $\Pi(t)$, with $t \geq 0$, is the Poisson process with unit intensity and L_n is a positive random variable independent of the process $\Pi(t)$. The distribution of N_n is a mixed Poisson distribution, as follows:

$$\mathsf{P}(N_n = k) = \frac{1}{k!}\int_0^\infty e^{-u}u^k d\,\mathsf{P}(L_n < u), \quad k = 0, 1, 2, \ldots \tag{54}$$

Proposition 22. *Let $\alpha \in (0,2]$ and let $r > \frac{1}{\alpha}$. Assume that the random variables $X_1, X_2, \ldots$ satisfy Condition (51). Let for each $n \in \mathbb{N}$ the random variable N_n have a mixed Poisson distribution (54). Then,*

$$\lim_{n\to\infty} \sup_{x} \big|\mathsf{P}(S_{N_n} < na \cdot x) - \mathsf{P}(|T_{r,\alpha}| < x)\big| = 0$$

if and only if

$$\frac{L_n}{n} \Longrightarrow D_{r,\alpha} \stackrel{d}{=} \tfrac{1}{2}\big(U_{2,\alpha/2} \circ \overline{G}_{r,\alpha/2,r}\big)^{-1}.$$

Proof. This statement is the direct consequence of Theorem 1 in [60] and the Dini theorem mentioned above. □

Funding: This research was funded by the Russian Science Foundation, grant 22-11-00212.

Data Availability Statement: Data is contained within the article

Acknowledgments: The author thanks the anonymous reviewers for their helpful remarks and thanks Alexander Zeifman for his help in the preparation of the manuscript.

Conflicts of Interest: The author declares no conflict of interest.

References

1. Student (Gosset, W.S.). The probable error of a mean. *Biometrica* **1908**, *6*, 1–25. [CrossRef]
2. Fisher, R.A. Applications of 'Student's' distribution. *Metron* **1925**, *5*, 90–104.
3. Li, R.; Nadarajah, S. A review of Student's t distribution and its generalizations. *Empir. Econ.* **2020**, *58*, 1461–1490. [CrossRef]
4. Bening, V.; Korolev, V. On an application of the Student distribution in the theory of probability and mathematical statistics. *Theort Probab. Appl.* **2005**, *49*, 377–391. [CrossRef]
5. Koepf, W.; Masjed-Jamei, M. A generalization of Student's t-distribution from the viewpoint of special functions. *Integral Transform. Spec. Funct.* **2006**, *17*, 863–875. [CrossRef]
6. Reyes, J.; Rojas, M.A.; Arrué, J. A new generalization of the Student's t distribution with applications in quantile regression. *Symmetry* **2021**, *13*, 2444. [CrossRef]
7. McDonald, J.B.; Newey, W.K. Partially adaptive estimation of regression models via the generalized tdistribution. *Econom. Theory* **1988**, *4*, 428–457. [CrossRef]
8. Butler, R.J.; McDonald, J.B.; Nelson, R.D.; White, S.B. Robust and partially adaptive estimation of regression models. *Rev. Econom. Statist.* **1990**, *72*, 321–327. [CrossRef]
9. Hansen, J.V.; McDonald, J.B.; Turley, R.S. Partially adaptive robust estimation of regression models and applications. *Eur. J. Oper. Res.* **2006**, *170*, 132–143. [CrossRef]
10. Theodossiou, P. Financial data and the skewed generalized *t* distribution. *Manag. Sci.* **1998**, *44*, 1650–1661. [CrossRef]
11. Harvey, A.; Lange, R.-J. Volatility Modeling with a Generalized t-distribution. *J. Time Ser. Anal.* **2017**, *38*, 175–190. [CrossRef]
12. Zhu, D.; Galbraith, J.W. A generalized asymmetric Student-t distribution with application to financial econometrics. *J. Econom.* **2010**, *157*, 297–305. [CrossRef]
13. Zhu, D.; Galbraith, J.W. Modeling and forecasting expected shortfall with the generalized asymmetric Student-t and asymmetric exponential power distributions. *J. Financ.* **2011**, *18*, 765–778. [CrossRef]
14. Arslan, O. Family of multivariate generalized t distributions. *J. Multivar. Anal.* **2004**, *89*, 329–337. [CrossRef]
15. Samorodnitsky, G.; Taqqu, M. *Stable Non-Gaussian Random Processes: Stochastic Models with Infinite Variance*; Chapman and Hall/Routledge: London, UK, 1994. [CrossRef]
16. Korolev, V.Y.; Chertok, A.V.; Korchagin, A.Y.; Kossova, E.V. A note on functional limit theorems for compound Cox processes. *J. Math. Sci.* **2016**, *218*, 182–194. [CrossRef]
17. Lomax, K.S. Business failures; Another example of the analysis of failure data. *J. Am. Stat. Assoc.* **1954**, *49*, 847–852. [CrossRef]
18. Bryson, M.C. Heavy-tailed distributions: Properties and tests. *Technometrics* **1974**, *16*, 61–68. [CrossRef]
19. Atkinson, A.B.; Harrison, A.J. *Distribution of Total Wealth in Britain*; Cambridge University Press: Cambridge, UK, 1978.
20. Hassan, A.S.; Al-Ghamdi, A.S. Optimum step-stress accelerated life testing for Lomax distribution. *J. Appl. Sci. Res.* **2009**, *5*, 2153–2164.
21. Alzaghal, A.; Hamed, D. New families of generalized Lomax distributions: Properties and applications. *Int. J. Stat. Probab.* **2019**, *8*, 51–68. [CrossRef]
22. Shams, T.M. The Kumaraswamy-generalized Lomax distribution. *Middle-East J. Sci. Res.* **2013**, *17*, 641–646. [CrossRef]
23. Al-Marzouki, S. A new generalization of power Lomax distribution. *Int. J. Math. Appl.* **2018**, *7*, 59–68.
24. Oguntunde, P.E.; Khaleel, M.A.; Ahmed, M.T.; Adejumo, A.O.; Odetunmibi, O.A. A new generalization of the Lomax distribution with increasing, decreasing, and constant failure rate. *Hindawi Model. Simul. Eng.* **2017**, *2017*, 6043169. [CrossRef]
25. Alghamdi, A. Study of Generalized Lomax Distribution and Change Point Problem. Ph.D. Thesis, Graduate College of Bowling Green State University, Bowling Green, OH, USA, 2018.
26. Naser, S.J. The generalized transmuted Lomax distribution. *AIP Conf. Proc.* **2022**, *2394*, 070017. [CrossRef]
27. Zolotarev, V.M. *One-Dimensional Stable Distributions*; American Mathematical Society: Providence, RI, USA, 1986.
28. Upadhye, N.S.; Barman, K. A unified approach to Stein's method for stable distributions. *Probab. Surv.* **2022**, *19*, 533–589. [CrossRef]
29. Schneider, W.R. Stable distributions: Fox function representation and generalization. In *Stochastic Processes in Classical and Quantum Systems*; Albeverio, S., Casati, G., Merlini, D., Eds.; Springer: Berlin/Heidelberg, Germany, 1986; pp. 497–511.
30. Uchaikin, V.V.; Zolotarev, V.M. *Chance and Stability. Stable Distributions and their Applications*; VSP: Utrecht, The Netherlands, 1999.
31. Subbotin, M.T. On the law of frequency of error. *Mat. Sb.* **1923**, *31*, 296–301.
32. Korolev, V. Some properties of univariate and multivariate exponential power distributions and related topics. *Mathematics* **2020**, *8*, 1918. [CrossRef]
33. Zhu, D.; Zinde-Walsh, V. Properties and estimation of asymmetric exponential power distribution. *J. Econom.* **2009**, *148*, 86–99. [CrossRef]
34. West, M. On scale mixtures of normal distributions. *Biometrika* **1987**, *74*, 646–648. [CrossRef]

35. Gnedenko, B.V.; Kolmogorov, A.N. *Limit Distributions for Sums of Independent Random Variables*; Addison-Wesley: Cambridge, MA, USA, 1954.
36. Slutsky, E. Über stochastische Asymptoten und Grenzwerte. *Metron* **1925**, *5*, 3–89.
37. Cramér, H. *Mathematical Methods of Statistics*; Princeton University Press: Princeton, NJ, USA, 1946.
38. Gradshtein, I.S.; Ryzhik, I.M. *Tables of Integrals, Series and Products*, 7th ed.; Academic Press: Amsterdam, The Netherlands, 2007.
39. Teicher, H. Identifiability of mixtures. *Ann. Math. Stat.* **1961**, *32*, 244–248. [CrossRef]
40. Antonov, S.N.; Koksharov, S.N. On the asymptotic behavior of tails of scale mixtures of normal distributions. *J. Math. Sci.* **2017**, *220*, 660–671. [CrossRef]
41. Goldie, C.M. A class of infinitely divisible distributions. *Math. Proc. Camb. Philos. Soc.* **1967**, *63*, 1141–1143. [CrossRef]
42. Feller, W. *An Introduction to Probability Theory and Its Applications*; Wiley: New York, NY, USA; London, UK; Sydney, Australia, 1966; Volume 2.
43. Grosswald, E. The Student t-distribution of any degree of freedom is infinitely divisible. *Z. Wahrscheinlichkeitstheorie Verw. Gebiete* **1976**, *36*, 103–109. [CrossRef]
44. Korolev, V.Y. Convergence of random sequences with independent random indexes. I. *Theory Probab. Appl.* **1994**, *39*, 313–333. [CrossRef]
45. Gnedenko, B.V.; Korolev, V.Y. *Random Summation: Limit Theorems and Applications*; CRC Press: Boca Raton, FL, USA, 1996.
46. Teugels, J.L. A note on Poisson-subordination. *Ann. Math. Stat.* **1972**, *43*, 676–680. Available online: http://www.jstor.org/stable/2240010 (accessed on 19 June 2023). [CrossRef]
47. Sengar, A.S.; Upadhye, N.S. Subordinated compound Poisson processes of order *k*. *Mod. Stoch. Theory Appl.* **2020**, *7*, 395–413. [CrossRef]
48. Kumar, A.; Nane, E.; Vellaisamy, P. Time-changed Poisson processes. *Stat. Probab. Lett.* **2011**, *81*, 1899–1910. [CrossRef]
49. Korolev, V.Y. Asymptotic properties of sample quantiles constructed from samples with random sizes. *Theory Probab. Appl.* **2000**, *44*, 394–399. [CrossRef]
50. Bening, V.; Korolev, V. *Generalized Poisson Models and Their Applications in Insurance and Finance*; Walter de Gruyter: Berlin, Germany, 2012.
51. Korolev, V.Y. Convergence of random sequences with independent random indexes. II. *Theory Probab. Appl.* **1995**, *40*, 770–772. [CrossRef]
52. Mosteller, F. On some useful "inefficient" statistics. *Ann. Math. Stat.* **1946**, *17*, 377–408. [CrossRef]
53. Gleser, L.J. The gamma distribution as a mixture of exponential distributions. *Am. Stat.* **1989**, *43*, 115–117. [CrossRef]
54. Korolev, V.Y. Analogs of Gleser's theorem for negative binomial and generalized gamma distributions and some their applications. *Inform. Appl.* **2017**, *11*, 2–17. [CrossRef]
55. Korolev, V.Y.; Sokolov, I.A.; Gorshenin, A.K. Max-Compound Cox Processes. I. *J. Math. Sci.* **2019**, *237*, 789–803. [CrossRef]
56. Korolev, V.Y.; Sokolov, I.A.; Gorshenin, A.K. Max-Compound Cox Processes. II. *J. Math. Sci.* **2020**, *246*, 488–502. [CrossRef]
57. Korolev, V.Y.; Sokolov, I.A.; Gorshenin, A.K. Max-Compound Cox Processes. III. *J. Math. Sci.* **2022**, *267*, 273–288. [CrossRef]
58. Korolev, V.Y. Limit distributions for doubly stochastically rarefied renewal processes and their properties. *Theory Probab. Appl.* **2017**, *61*, 649–664. [CrossRef]
59. Kalashnikov, V.V. *Geometric Sums: Bounds for Rare Events with Applications*; Kluwer Academic Publishers: Dordrecht, The Netherlands, 1997.
60. Korolev, V.Y. On convergence of distributions of compound Cox processes to stable laws. *Theory Probab. Appl.* **1999**, *43*, 644–650. [CrossRef]

mathematics

Article

Equivalent Conditions of Complete p-th Moment Convergence for Weighted Sum of ND Random Variables under Sublinear Expectation Space

Peiyu Sun [1,2], Dehui Wang [3] and Xili Tan [2,*]

[1] School of Mathematics, Jilin University, Changchun 130012, China
[2] School of Mathematics and Statistics, Beihua University, Jilin 132013, China
[3] School of Mathematics and Statistics, Liaoning University, Shenyang 110031, China
* Correspondence: txl@beihua.edu.cn

Abstract: We investigate the complete convergence for weighted sums of sequences of negative dependence (ND) random variables and p-th moment convergence for weighted sums of sequences of ND random variables under sublinear expectation space. Using moment inequality and truncation methods, we prove the equivalent conditions of complete convergence for weighted sums of sequences of ND random variables and p-th moment convergence for weighted sums of sequences of ND random variables under sublinear expectation space.

Keywords: complete convergence; ND random variables; sublinear expectation space

MSC: 60F10; 60F05

Citation: Sun, P.; Wang, D.; Tan, X. Equivalent Conditions of Complete p-th Moment Convergence for Weighted Sum of ND Random Variables under Sublinear Expectation Space. *Mathematics* **2023**, *11*, 3494. https://doi.org/10.3390/math11163494

Academic Editors: Irina Shevtsova and Victor Korolev

Received: 24 July 2023
Revised: 9 August 2023
Accepted: 11 August 2023
Published: 13 August 2023

1. Introduction

The nonadditive probabilities theory and nonadditive expectations theory are useful tools for researching measures of risk, uncertainties in statistics, non-linear stochastic calculus and superhedging in finance, cf. Peng [1,2], Denis [3], Gilboa [4], Marinacci [5]. This paper considers the general sublinear expectations which were introduced by Peng [6–8] in a general space by relaxing the linear property of the classical expectation to the subadditivity and positive homogeneity (cf. Definition 1 below). The sublinear expectation conception provided a very flexible framework to model the problems which are not additive. Inspired by the work of Peng, researchers have tried to study lots of limit theorems under linear expectation space to extend the corresponding results in probability and statistics. Zhang [9–11] studied the exponential inequalities, Rosenthal's inequalities, Hölder's inequalities and Donsker's invariance principle under sublinear expectation space. Chen [12–14] studied the strong laws of large numbers, the weak laws of large numbers, and the large deviation for ND random variables under sublinear expectations, respectively. Wu [15] obtained precise asymptotics for complete integral convergence under sublinear expectation space. For more research about limit theorems of sublinear expectation space, the reader could refer to the articles of Hu and Peng [15], Li and Li [16], Liu [17], Ding [18], Wu [19], Guo and Zhang [20,21], Dong and Tan [22].

Recently, Guo and Shan [23] studied equivalent conditions of complete q-th moment convergence for sums of sequences of negatively orthant dependent (NOD) variables under the classical space. Xu and Cheng [24,25] obtained equivalent conditions of complete convergence for sums of independence identical distribution (i.i.d.) random variables sequences and p-th moment convergence for sums of i.i.d. random variables sequences under sublinear expectation space. ND sequences have wide applications in penetration theory, multivariable statistics, etc. Therefore, it is necessary to generalize the properties of independent sequences to ND sequences. Hence, it is meaningful to extend the results of

Xu and Cheng [24,25] to ND random variables under sublinear expectation space. In this paper, we try to prove the equivalent conditions of complete convergence random variables and p-th moment convergence for weighted sums of sequences of ND random variables under sublinear expectation space.

2. Preliminaries

We use the framework of Peng [8]. Suppose that $(\Omega, \mathcal{F})$ is a given measurable space, $\mathcal{H}$ is a linear space of real functions defined on Ω such that $I_A \in \mathcal{H}$, where $A \in \mathcal{F}$, I_A denotes the indicator function of A, and if $(X_1, X_2, \dots, X_n) \in \mathcal{H}$, then $\varphi(X_1, X_2, \dots, X_n) \in \mathcal{H}$ for each $\varphi \in C_{l,Lip}(\mathbb{R}^n)$, where $C_{l,Lip}(\mathbb{R}^n)$ is the linear space of local Lipschitz continuous functions φ satisfying

$$|\varphi(x) - \varphi(y)| \le C(1 + |x|^m + |y|^m)|x - y|, \ \ \forall x, y \in \mathbb{R}^n,$$

for some $C > 0$, $m \in \mathbb{N}$ depending on φ. We also denote $C_{b,Lip}(\mathbb{R}^n)$ as the linear space of bounded Lipschitz continuous functions, for some $C > 0$, φ satisfying

$$|\varphi(x) - \varphi(y)| \le C|x - y|, \ \ \forall x, y \in \mathbb{R}^n.$$

Definition 1. *A sublinear expectation $\mathbb{E}$ on $\mathcal{H}$ is a function $\mathbb{E} : \mathcal{H} \to \overline{\mathbb{R}}$ satisfying the following properties: for all $X, Y \in \mathcal{H}$, we have*

(1) *Monotonicity: if $X \ge Y$ then $\mathbb{E}[X] \ge \mathbb{E}[Y]$;*
(2) *Constant preserving: $\mathbb{E}[c] = c$;*
(3) *Sub-additivity: $\mathbb{E}[X+Y] \le \mathbb{E}[X] + \mathbb{E}[Y]$ whenever $\mathbb{E}[X] + \mathbb{E}[Y]$ is not of the form $+\infty - \infty$ or $-\infty + \infty$;*
(4) *Positive homogeneity: $\mathbb{E}[\lambda X] = \lambda \mathbb{E}[X], \lambda \ge 0$.*
Here, $\overline{\mathbb{R}} = [-\infty, \infty]$. The triple $(\Omega, \mathcal{H}, \mathbb{E})$ is called a sublinear expectation space. Give a sublinear expectation $\mathbb{E}$, let us denote the conjugate expectation $\mathcal{E}$ of $\mathbb{E}$ by

$$\mathcal{E}[X] := -\mathbb{E}[-X], \quad \forall X \in \mathcal{H}.$$

A set function $V : \mathcal{F} \mapsto [0, 1]$ is called a capacity if

(1) $V(\emptyset) = 0, V(\Omega) = 1;$
(2) $V(A) \le V(B), A \subset B, A, B \in \mathcal{F}.$

In this paper, given a sublinear expectation space $(\Omega, \mathcal{H}, \mathbb{E})$, we set the capacity $\mathbb{V}(A) := \mathbb{E}[I_A]$ for $A \in \mathcal{F}$. We set the Choquet expectations $\mathcal{C}_{\mathbb{V}}$ by

$$\mathcal{C}_{\mathbb{V}} := \int_{-\infty}^{0} (\mathbb{V}(X \ge x) - 1) + \int_{0}^{\infty} \mathbb{V}(X \ge x) dx.$$

Definition 2. *Let X_1 be a n-dimensional random vector defined in sublinear expectation space $(\Omega_1, \mathcal{H}_1, \mathbb{E}_1)$ and X_2 be a n-dimensional random vector defined in sublinear expectation space $(\Omega_2, \mathcal{H}_2, \mathbb{E}_2)$. They are called 'identically distributed', denoted by $X_1 \overset{d}{=} X_2$, if*

$$\mathbb{E}_1[\varphi(X_1)] = \mathbb{E}_2[\varphi(X_2)], \quad \forall \varphi \in C_{b,Lip}(\mathbb{R}_n).$$

Definition 3. *In a sublinear expectation space $(\Omega, \mathcal{H}, \mathbb{E})$, a random vector $Y = (Y_1, \dots, Y_n), Y_i \in \mathcal{H}$ is said to be independent to another random vector $X = (X_1, \dots, X_m)$, $X_i \in \mathcal{H}$ under $\mathbb{E}$ if*

$$\mathbb{E}[\varphi(X, Y)] = \mathbb{E}[\mathbb{E}[\varphi(x, Y)]|_{x=X}], \quad \forall \varphi \in C_{b,Lip}(\mathbb{R}_m \times \mathbb{R}_n).$$

Random variables $\{X_n, n \ge 1\}$ are said to be independent, if X_{i+1} is independent to $(X_1, \dots, X_i)$ for each $i \ge 1$.

From the definition of independence, it is easily seen that, if Y is independent to X and $X, Y \in \mathcal{L}$, $\mathcal{L} = \{X \in \mathcal{H} : \mathbb{E}[|X|] < \infty\}$. $X \geq 0, \mathbb{E}[Y] \geq 0$, then

$$\mathbb{E}[XY] = \mathbb{E}[X]\mathbb{E}[Y].$$

Further, if Y is independent to X and $X, Y \in \mathcal{L}$ and $X \geq 0, Y \geq 0$, then

$$\mathcal{E}[XY] = \mathcal{E}[X]\mathcal{E}[Y].$$

Definition 4. *A sequence of random variables $\{X_n, n \geq 1\}$ is said to be i.i.d., if $X_i \stackrel{d}{=} X_1$ and X_{i+1} is independent to $(X_1, \ldots, X_i)$ for each $i \geq 1$.*

Definition 5. *(i) In a sublinear expectation space $(\Omega, \mathcal{H}, \mathbb{E})$, a random vector $Y = (Y_1, \ldots, Y_n)$, $Y_i \in \mathcal{H}$ is said to be ND to another random vector $X = (X_1, \ldots, X_m)$, $X_i \in \mathcal{H}$ under $\mathbb{E}$ if for each pair of test functions $\varphi_1 \in C_{l,Lip}(\mathbb{R}_m)$ and $\varphi_2 \in C_{l,Lip}(\mathbb{R}_n)$, we have $\mathbb{E}[\varphi_1(X)\varphi_2(Y)] \leq \mathbb{E}[\varphi_1(X)]\mathbb{E}[\varphi_2(Y)]$ whenever $\varphi_1(X) \geq 0$, $\mathbb{E}[\varphi_2(Y)] \geq 0$, $\mathbb{E}[\varphi_1(X)\varphi_2(Y)] < \infty$, $\mathbb{E}[\varphi_1(X)] < \infty$, $\mathbb{E}[\varphi_2(Y)] < \infty$, and either φ_1 and φ_2 are coordinate-wise non-increasing.*
(ii) Let $\{X_n, n \geq 1\}$ be a sequence of random variables in the sublinear expectations. $X_1, X_2, \ldots$ are said to be ND if X_{i+1} is ND to $(X_1, \ldots, X_i)$ for each $i \geq 1$.

From the definition of independence and ND, if Y is independent to X, then Y is ND to X. Furthermore, let $\{X_n, n \geq 1\}$ be a sequence of independent random variables and $f_1(x), f_2(x), \ldots \in C_{l,Lip(\mathbb{R})}$, then $\{f_n(X_n), n \geq 1\}$ is also a sequence of independent random variables; let $\{X_n, n \geq 1\}$ be a sequence of ND random variables, $f_1(x), f_2(x), \ldots \in C_{l,Lip(\mathbb{R})}$ are non-decreasing (non-increasing) functions, then $\{f_n(X_n), n \geq 1\}$ is also a sequence of ND.

In the sequel we suppose that $\mathbb{E}$ is sub-additive. Let C denote a positive constant which may differ from place to place. $a_n \ll b_n$ denote that there exists a constant $C > 0$ such that $a_n \leq C b_n$ for n large enough, $a_n \approx b_n$ means that $a_n \ll b_n$ and $b_n \ll a_n$, $\log x$ means $\ln(\max\{e, x\})$. $I(A)$ or I_A represents the indicator function of A.

We present several necessary lemmas to prove our main results.

Lemma 1 ([9])**.** *Let $p, q > 1$ be two real numbers satisfying $\frac{1}{p} + \frac{1}{q} = 1$. Then, for two random variables X, Y in $(\Omega, \mathcal{H}, \mathbb{E})$ we have $\mathbb{E}[|XY|] \leq (\mathbb{E}[|X|^p])^{\frac{1}{p}} (\mathbb{E}[|X|^q])^{\frac{1}{q}}$.*

Lemma 2 ([9])**.** *If $\mathbb{E}$ is countably subadditive and $C_{\mathbb{V}}(|X|) < \infty$, then*

$$\mathbb{E}[|X|] \leq C_{\mathbb{V}}(|X|).$$

Lemma 3 ([9])**.** *Suppose that X_k is ND to $(X_{k+1}, \ldots, X_n)$ for each $k = 1, \ldots, n-1$, or X_{k+1} is ND to $(X_1, \ldots, X_k)$ for each $k = 1, \ldots, n-1$. Then, for $p \geq 2$,*

$$\mathbb{E}\left[\max_{k \leq n} |S_k|^p\right] \leq C_p \left\{ \sum_{k=1}^{n} \mathbb{E}[|X_k|^p] + \left(\sum_{k=1}^{n} \mathbb{E}\left[|X_k|^2\right] \right)^{p/2} + \left(\sum_{k=1}^{n} ((\mathcal{E}[X_k])^- + (\mathbb{E}[X_k])^+) \right)^p \right\},$$

where $S_k = \sum_{i=1}^{k} X_k$, C_p is a positive constant depending only on p.

Lemma 4 ([24]). *Let Y be a random variable under sublinear expectation space $(\Omega, \mathcal{H}, \mathbb{E})$. Then, for any $\alpha > 0$, $\gamma > 0$, and $\beta > -1$*

$$(i) \quad \int_1^\infty u^\beta \mathcal{C}_{\mathbb{V}}(|Y|^\alpha I(|Y| > u^\gamma))du \le C\mathcal{C}_{\mathbb{V}}(|Y|^{(\beta+1)/\gamma+\alpha}),$$

$$(ii) \quad \int_1^\infty u^\beta \log(u)\mathcal{C}_{\mathbb{V}}(|Y|^\alpha I(|Y| > u^\gamma))du \le C\mathcal{C}_{\mathbb{V}}(|Y|^{(\beta+1)/\gamma+\alpha})\log(1+|Y|).$$

Lemma 5. *Let $\{X_n, n \ge 1\}$ be a sequence of ND random variables under sublinear expectation space $(\Omega, \mathcal{H}, \mathbb{E})$. Then, the condition that for all $x > 0$,*

$$\lim_{n\to\infty} \mathbb{V}\left(\max_{1\le j\le n} |X_j| > x\right) = 0, \tag{1}$$

implies that there exist constants C such that for all $x > 0$, and n large enough,

$$\left[1 - \mathbb{V}\left(\max_{1\le j\le n} |X_j| > x\right)\right]^2 \sum_{j=1}^n \mathbb{V}(|X_j| > x) \le C\mathbb{V}\left(\max_{1\le j\le n} |X_j| > x\right). \tag{2}$$

Proof. Write $\alpha_n = \mathbb{V}\left(\max_{1\le j\le n} |X_j| > x\right)$. Without the loss of generality, we may assume that $\alpha_n > 0$. Since $\{I(X_k > x) - \mathbb{E}I(X_k > x),\ k \ge 1\}$ and $\{I(X_k < -x) - \mathbb{E}I(X_k < -x),\ k \ge 1\}$ are sequences of ND under sublinear expectation space, denote $A_k = (X_k > x), B_k = (X_k < -x), D_k = (|X_k| > x)$, combining C_r inequality and Lemma 3 results in

$$\begin{aligned}
&\mathbb{E}\left[\sum_{k=1}^n (I(A_k) - \mathbb{E}I(A_k))\right]^2 \\
\le& C\sum_{k=1}^n \mathbb{E}\left[(I(A_k) - \mathbb{E}I(A_k))^2\right] + C\left(\sum_{k=1}^n ((\mathcal{E}[I(A_k) - \mathbb{E}I(A_k)])^- + (\mathbb{E}[I(A_k) - \mathbb{E}I(A_k)])^+\right)^2 \\
\le& C\sum_{k=1}^n \mathbb{E}\left[(I(A_k) - \mathbb{V}(A_k))^2\right] + C\left(\sum_{k=1}^n 2\mathbb{E}[|I(A_k) - \mathbb{E}I(A_k)|]\right)^2 \\
\le& C\sum_{k=1}^n \mathbb{E}\left[I(A_k) - (\mathbb{V}(A_k))^2\right] + C\left(\sum_{k=1}^n \mathbb{E}[I(A_k) - \mathbb{V}(A_k)]\right)^2 \\
\le& C\sum_{k=1}^n \mathbb{V}(A_k) + C\left(\sum_{k=1}^n \mathbb{V}(A_k)\right)^2.
\end{aligned}$$

In the same way, we could obtain

$$\mathbb{E}\left[\sum_{k=1}^n (I(B_k) - \mathbb{E}I(B_k))\right]^2 \le C\sum_{k=1}^n \mathbb{V}(B_k) + C\left(\sum_{k=1}^n \mathbb{V}(B_k)\right)^2.$$

It follows that

$$\begin{aligned}
&\mathbb{E}\left[\sum_{k=1}^n (I(D_k) - \mathbb{E}I((D_k))\right]^2 \\
\le& \mathbb{E}\left[\sum_{k=1}^n ((I(A_k) - \mathbb{E}I(A_k)) + (I(B_k) - \mathbb{E}I(B_k))\right]^2
\end{aligned}$$

$$
\begin{aligned}
&\leq 2\mathbb{E}\left[\sum_{k=1}^{n}(I(A_k)-\mathbb{E}I(A_k))\right]^2+2\mathbb{E}\left[\sum_{k=1}^{n}(I(B_k)-\mathbb{E}I(B_k))\right]^2\\
&\leq C\sum_{k=1}^{n}\mathbb{V}(A_k)+C\left(\sum_{k=1}^{n}\mathbb{V}(A_k)\right)^2+C\sum_{k=1}^{n}\mathbb{V}(B_k)+C\left(\sum_{k=1}^{n}\mathbb{V}(B_k)\right)^2\\
&\leq C\sum_{k=1}^{n}\mathbb{V}(D_k)+C\left(\sum_{k=1}^{n}\mathbb{V}(D_k)\right)^2.
\end{aligned}
$$

Similar to the proof of Lemma 2.5 in Xu [24], by positive homogeneity of sublinear expectation space, Lemma 1 and the subadditivity of expectations, we conclude that

$$
\begin{aligned}
&\sum_{k=1}^{n}\mathbb{V}(D_k)=\sum_{k=1}^{n}\mathbb{E}[I(D_k)]=\sum_{k=1}^{n-2}\mathbb{E}[I(D_k)]+\mathbb{E}[I(D_{n-1})+\mathbb{E}[I(D_n)]]\\
&=\sum_{k=1}^{n-2}\mathbb{E}[I(D_k)]+\mathbb{E}[I(D_{n-1})+I(D_n)]=\ldots=\mathbb{E}\left[I(D_1)+\mathbb{E}\left[\sum_{k=2}^{n}I(D_k)\right]\right]\\
&=\mathbb{E}\left[\sum_{k=1}^{n}I(D_k)\right]=\mathbb{E}\left[\sum_{k=1}^{n}I(D_k\bigcup_{j=1}^{n}D_j)\right]=\mathbb{E}\left[\sum_{k=1}^{n}I(D_k)I(\bigcup_{j=1}^{n}D_j)\right]\\
&\leq\mathbb{E}\left[\sum_{k=1}^{n}(I(D_k)-\mathbb{E}I(D_k))I\left(\bigcup_{j=1}^{n}D_j\right)\right]+\sum_{k=1}^{n}\mathbb{V}(D_k)\mathbb{V}\left(\bigcup_{j=1}^{n}D_j\right)\\
&\leq\left(\mathbb{E}\left[\sum_{k=1}^{n}(I(D_k)-\mathbb{E}I(D_k))\right]^2\mathbb{E}\left[I\left(\bigcup_{j=1}^{n}D_j\right)\right]\right)^{\frac{1}{2}}+\alpha_n\sum_{k=1}^{n}\mathbb{V}(D_k)\\
&\leq\left(C\alpha_n\left(\sum_{k=1}^{n}\mathbb{V}(D_k)+\left(\sum_{k=1}^{n}\mathbb{V}(D_k)\right)^2\right)\right)^{\frac{1}{2}}+\alpha_n\sum_{k=1}^{n}\mathbb{V}(D_k)\\
&\leq C\alpha_n^{\frac{1}{2}}\sum_{k=1}^{n}\mathbb{V}(D_k)+\frac{1}{2}\left(\frac{C\alpha_n}{1-\alpha_n}+(1-\alpha_n)\sum_{k=1}^{n}\mathbb{V}(D_k)\right)+\alpha_n\sum_{j=1}^{n}\mathbb{V}(D_k).
\end{aligned}
$$

which combined with (1) results in (2) immediately. Therefore the proof is finished. □

Lemma 6 ([25]). *Assume that Y is a random variable under sublinear expectation space $(\Omega,\mathcal{H},\mathbb{E})$. Then, for $p>0,\ q>0,\ r>0$, the following is equivalent:*

(i)

$$
\begin{cases}
C_{\mathbb{V}}(|Y|^p)<\infty, & \text{for } p>r/q,\\
C_{\mathbb{V}}(|Y|^{r/q}\log|Y|)<\infty, & \text{for } p=r/q,\\
C_{\mathbb{V}}(|Y|^{r/q})<\infty, & \text{for } p<r/q.
\end{cases}
$$

(ii)

$$
\int_1^{\infty}dy\int_1^{\infty}y^{r-1}\mathbb{V}(|Y|>x^{1/p}y^q)dx<\infty.
$$

Lemma 7 ([25]). *Assume that Y is a random variable under sublinear expectation space $(\Omega,\mathcal{H},\mathbb{E})$. Then, for $p>0,\ q>0,\ r>0$, the following is equivalent:*

(i)

$$
\begin{cases}
C_{\mathbb{V}}(|Y|^p)<\infty, & \text{for } p>r/q,\\
C_{\mathbb{V}}(|Y|^{r/q}\log^2|Y|)<\infty, & \text{for } p=r/q,\\
C_{\mathbb{V}}(|Y|^{r/q}\log|Y|)<\infty, & \text{for } p<r/q.
\end{cases}
$$

(ii)

$$
\int_1^{\infty}dy\int_1^{\infty}y^{r-1}\mathbb{V}(|Y|>x^{1/p}y^q)dx<\infty.
$$

3. Main Results

Our main results are as follows.

Theorem 1. *Assume that $\{X_n, n \geq 1\}$ is a ND random variables sequence under sublinear expectation space $(\Omega, \mathcal{H}, \mathbb{E})$, which is identically distributed as X. Suppose that $r > 1$, $q > \frac{1}{2}$, $\beta + q > 0$, moreover, for $\frac{1}{2} < q \leq 1$,*

$$\mathbb{E}(X) = -\mathbb{E}(-X) = 0.$$

Furthermore, let $\{a_{ni} \approx (i/n)^{\beta}(1/n)^{q},\ 1 \leq i \leq n,\ n \geq 1\}$ be a triangular array of real numbers. Then, the following is equivalent:
(i)

$$\begin{cases} C_{\mathbb{V}}(|X|^{r/q}) < \infty, & \text{for } \beta > -q/r, \\ C_{\mathbb{V}}(|X|^{(r-1)/(q+\beta)}) < \infty, & \text{for } -q < \beta < -q/r, \\ C_{\mathbb{V}}(|X|^{r/q}\log(1+|X|)) < \infty, & \text{for } \beta = -q/r. \end{cases} \tag{3}$$

(ii)

$$\sum_{n=1}^{\infty} n^{r-2}\mathbb{V}\left(\max_{1\leq k\leq n}\left|\sum_{i=1}^{k} a_{ni}X_i\right| > \epsilon\right) < \infty,\ \forall \epsilon > 0 \tag{4}$$

Theorem 2. *Assume that $\{X_n, n \geq 1\}$ is a ND random variables sequenceunder sublinear expectation space $(\Omega, \mathcal{H}, \mathbb{E})$, which is identically distributed as X. Suppose that $r > 1$, $q > \frac{1}{2}$, $\beta > -q/r$, moreover, for $\frac{1}{2} < q \leq 1$,*

$$\mathbb{E}(X) = -\mathbb{E}(-X) = 0.$$

Furthermore, let $\{a_{ni} \approx (i/n)^{\beta}(1/n)^{q},\ 1 \leq i \leq n,\ n \geq 1\}$ be a triangular array of real numbers. Then the following is equivalent:
(i)

$$\begin{cases} C_{\mathbb{V}}(|X|^{p}) < \infty, & \text{for } p > r/q, \\ C_{\mathbb{V}}(|X|^{r/q}) < \infty, & \text{for } p < r/q, \\ C_{\mathbb{V}}(|X|^{r/q}\log|X|) < \infty, & \text{for } p = r/q. \end{cases} \tag{5}$$

(ii)

$$\sum_{n=1}^{\infty} n^{r-2} C_{\mathbb{V}}\left(\left(\max_{1\leq k\leq n}\left|\sum_{i=1}^{k} a_{ni}X_i\right|^{p} - \epsilon\right)^{+}\right) < \infty,\ \forall \epsilon > 0 \tag{6}$$

Theorem 3. *Assume that $\{X_n, n \geq 1\}$ is a ND random variables sequence under sublinear expectation space $(\Omega, \mathcal{H}, \mathbb{E})$, which is identically distributed as X. Suppose that $r > 1$, $q > \frac{1}{2}$, $\beta = -q/r < 0$, moreover, for $\frac{1}{2} < q \leq 1$,*

$$\mathbb{E}(X) = -\mathbb{E}(-X) = 0.$$

Furthermore, let $\{a_{ni} \approx (i/n)^{\beta}(1/n)^{q},\ 1 \leq i \leq n,\ n \geq 1\}$ be a triangular array of real numbers. Then, (6) equivalent to

$$\begin{cases} C_{\mathbb{V}}(|X|^{p}) < \infty, & \text{for } p > r/q, \\ C_{\mathbb{V}}(|X|^{r/q}\log|X|) < \infty, & \text{for } p < r/q, \\ C_{\mathbb{V}}(|X|^{r/q}\log^{2}|X|) < \infty, & \text{for } p = r/q. \end{cases} \tag{7}$$

Theorem 4. *Assume that* $\{X_n, n \geq 1\}$ *is a ND random variables sequence under sublinear expectation space* $(\Omega, \mathcal{H}, \mathbb{E})$*, which is identically distributed as X. Suppose that* $r > 1$, $q > \frac{1}{2}$, $-q < \beta < -q/r < 0$*, moreover, for* $\frac{1}{2} < q \leq 1$,

$$\mathbb{E}(X) = -\mathbb{E}(-X) = 0.$$

Furthermore, let $\{a_{ni} \approx (i/n)^{\beta}(1/n)^{q},\ 1 \leq i \leq n,\ n \geq 1\}$ *be a triangular array of real numbers. Then (6) equivalent to*

$$\begin{cases} C_{\mathbb{V}}(|X|^{p}) < \infty, & \text{for } p > (r-1)/(q+\beta), \\ C_{\mathbb{V}}(|X|^{(r-1)/(q+\beta)}) < \infty, & \text{for } p < (r-1)/(q+\beta), \\ C_{\mathbb{V}}(|X|^{(r-1)/(q+\beta)} \log|X|) < \infty, & \text{for } p = (r-1)/(q+\beta). \end{cases} \tag{8}$$

4. Proof of the Main Results

4.1. Proof of Theorem 1

We first prove (3) $\Rightarrow$ (4). Choose $\delta > 0$, small enough, and a sufficiently large integer K. For all $1 \leq i \leq n,\ n \geq 1$, we write

$$\begin{aligned} X_{ni}^{(1)} &= -n^{-\tau} I(a_{ni}X_i < -n^{-\tau}) + a_{ni}X_i I(|a_{ni}X_i| \leq n^{-\tau}) + n^{-\tau} I(a_{ni}X_i > n^{-\tau}), \\ X_{ni}^{(2)} &= (a_{ni}X_i - n^{-\tau}) I(n^{-\tau} < a_{ni}X_i < \frac{\epsilon}{K}), \\ X_{ni}^{(3)} &= (a_{ni}X_i + n^{-\tau}) I(\frac{\epsilon}{K} < a_{ni}X_i < -n^{-\tau}), \\ X_{ni}^{(4)} &= (a_{ni}X_i + n^{-\tau}) I(a_{ni}X_i \leq -\frac{\epsilon}{K}) + (a_{ni}X_i - n^{-\tau}) I(a_{ni}X_i \geq \frac{\epsilon}{K}). \end{aligned} \tag{9}$$

Obviously, $\sum_{i=1}^{k} a_{ni}X_i = \sum_{i=1}^{k} X_{ni}^{(1)} + \sum_{i=1}^{k} X_{ni}^{(2)} + \sum_{i=1}^{k} X_{ni}^{(3)} + \sum_{i=1}^{k} X_{ni}^{(4)}$. Notice that

$$\left(\max_{1 \leq k \leq n} \left| \sum_{i=1}^{k} a_{ni}X_i \right| \geq 4\epsilon \right) \subseteq \bigcup_{j=1}^{4} \left(\max_{1 \leq k \leq n} \left| \sum_{i=1}^{k} X_{ni}^{(j)} \right| \geq \epsilon \right). \tag{10}$$

Thus, in order to establish (4), it suffices to prove that

$$I_j := \sum_{n=1}^{\infty} n^{r-2} \mathbb{V}\left(\max_{1 \leq k \leq n} \left| \sum_{i=1}^{k} X_{ni}^{(j)} \right| \geq \epsilon \right) < \infty,\ j = 1, 2, 3, 4. \tag{11}$$

In order to estimate I_1, we verify that

$$\max_{1 \leq k \leq n} \left| \sum_{i=1}^{k} \mathbb{E}X_{ni}^{(1)} \right| \to 0 \text{ as } n \to \infty.$$

By Lemma 2 and (3), we could obtain $\mathbb{E}|X|^{1/q} < \infty$, $\mathbb{E}|X|^{r/q} < \infty$. When $q > 1$, notice that $|X_{ni}^{(1)}| \leq n^{-\tau}$ and $|X_{ni}^{(1)}| \leq |a_{ni}X_i|$, it follows that

$$\begin{aligned} \max_{1 \leq k \leq n} \left| \sum_{i=1}^{k} \mathbb{E}X_{ni}^{(1)} \right| &\leq \sum_{i=1}^{k} \mathbb{E}\left| X_{ni}^{(1)} \right| \\ &\leq n^{-\tau(1-1/q)} \sum_{i-1}^{k} \mathbb{E}|a_{ni}X_i|^{1/q} \\ &\ll n^{-\tau(1-1/q)} \sum_{i=1}^{k} n^{-(\beta+q)/q} i^{\beta/q} \\ &\approx n^{-\tau(1-1/q)} \to 0 \text{ as } n \to \infty. \end{aligned}$$

When $\frac{1}{2} < q \le 1$, note that $\mathbb{E}(X) = -\mathbb{E}(-X) = 0$, by choosing τ small enough such that$-\tau(1 - r/q) + 1 - r < 0$, we obtain

$$\begin{aligned}
\max_{1\le k\le n}\left|\sum_{i=1}^{k}\mathbb{E}X_{ni}^{(1)}\right| &\le 2\sum_{i=1}^{n}\mathbb{E}|a_{ni}X_i|I(|a_{ni}X_i| > n^{-\tau}) \\
&\le 2n^{-\tau(1-r/q)}\sum_{i=1}^{n}\mathbb{E}|a_{ni}X_i|^{r/q} \\
&\ll n^{-\tau(1-r/q)}\sum_{i=1}^{n}|a_{ni}|^{r/q} \\
&\ll n^{-\tau(1-r/q)}\left(\sum_{i=1}^{n}n^{-r(\beta+q)/q}i^{r\beta/q}\right)
\end{aligned}$$

$$\approx \begin{cases} n^{\tau-r(-\tau+\beta+q)/q}, & -q < \beta < -q/r, \\ n^{-\tau(1-r/q)+1-r}\log n, & \beta = -q/r, \\ n^{-\tau(1-r/q)+1-r}, & \beta > -q/r, \end{cases} \quad \to 0 \text{ as } n \to \infty.$$

Hence, to prove $I_1 < \infty$, it suffices to prove that

$$I_1^* := \sum_{n=1}^{\infty} n^{r-2}\mathbb{V}\left(\max_{1\le k\le n}\left|\sum_{i=1}^{k}\left(X_{ni}^{(1)} - \mathbb{E}X_{ni}^{(1)}\right)\right| \ge \epsilon\right) < \infty.$$

From the property of ND random variables under sublinear expectation space, we could obtain $X_{ni}^{(1)}$ is also a sequence of ND random variables under sublinear expectation space. By Markov's inequality and Cr's inequality under sublinear expectation, Lemma 3, it can be shown that for a suitably large M,

$$\begin{aligned}
&\mathbb{V}\left(\max_{1\le k\le n}\left|\sum_{i=1}^{k}\left(X_{ni}^{(1)} - \mathbb{E}X_{ni}^{(1)}\right)\right| \ge \epsilon\right) \\
&\ll \sum_{i=1}^{n}\mathbb{E}\left[|X_{ni}^{(1)}|^M\right] + \left(\sum_{i=1}^{n}\mathbb{E}\left[|X_{ni}^{(1)}|^2\right]\right)^{M/2} + \left(\sum_{i=1}^{n}\left((\mathcal{E}[X_{ni}^{(1)}])^- + (\mathbb{E}[X_{ni}^{(1)}])^+\right)\right)^M
\end{aligned}$$

Taking M sufficiently large such that $-2 - \tau M + (\tau - \beta)r/q < -1, -1 - \tau M + \tau r/q < -1$, we have

$$\begin{aligned}
&\sum_{n=1}^{\infty} n^{r-2}\sum_{i=1}^{n}\mathbb{E}\left[|X_{ni}^{(1)}|^M\right] \\
&\ll \sum_{n=1}^{\infty} n^{r-2}\sum_{i=1}^{n}n^{-\tau(M-r/q)}\mathbb{E}\left[|a_{ni}X_i|^{r/q}\right] \\
&\approx \begin{cases} \sum_{n=1}^{\infty} n^{-2-\tau M+(\tau-\beta)r/q}, & -q < \beta < -q/r, \\ \sum_{n=1}^{\infty} n^{-1-\tau M+\tau r/q}\log n, & \beta = -q/r, \\ \sum_{n=1}^{\infty} n^{-1-\tau M+\tau r/q}, & \beta > -q/r, \end{cases} \\
&<\infty.
\end{aligned}$$

When $r/q \geq 2$, (3) implies $\mathbb{E}X^2 < \infty$. Noting that $\beta + q > 0$, $q > 1/2$, we can choose a sufficiently large M such that $r - 2 - M(q + \beta) < -1$, $r - 2 - qM + M/2 < -1$, then

$$\begin{aligned}
&\sum_{n=1}^{\infty} n^{r-2}\left(\sum_{i=1}^{n} \mathbb{E}\left[|X_{ni}^{(1)}|^2\right]\right)^{M/2} \\
\ll &\sum_{n=1}^{\infty} n^{r-2}\left(\sum_{i=1}^{n} a_{ni}^2\right)^{M/2} \\
\approx &\begin{cases} \sum_{n=1}^{\infty} n^{r-2-M(q+\beta)}, & -q < \beta < -1/2, \\ \sum_{n=1}^{\infty} n^{r-2-qM+M/2}(\log n)^{M/2}, & \beta = -1/2, \\ \sum_{n=1}^{\infty} n^{r-2-qM+M/2}, & \beta > -1/2, \end{cases} \\
< &\infty.
\end{aligned}$$

When $r/q < 2$, we could choose a sufficiently large M such that $r - 2 - (r + r\beta/q + (2 - r/q)\tau)M/2 < -1$, $r - 2 - (r - 1 + (2 - r/q)\tau)M/2 < -1$, then

$$\begin{aligned}
&\sum_{n=1}^{\infty} n^{r-2}\left(\sum_{i=1}^{n} \mathbb{E}\left[|X_{ni}^{(1)}|^2\right]\right)^{M/2} \\
\ll &\sum_{n=1}^{\infty} n^{r-2} n^{-\tau M(2-r/q)/2}\left(\sum_{i=1}^{n} a_{ni}^{r/q}\right)^{M/2} \\
\approx &\begin{cases} \sum_{n=1}^{\infty} n^{r-2-(r+r\beta/q+(2-r/q)\tau)M/2}, & -q < \beta < -q/r, \\ \sum_{n=1}^{\infty} n^{r-2-(r-1+(2-r/q)\tau)M/2}(\log n)^{M/2}, & \beta = -q/r, \\ \sum_{n=1}^{\infty} n^{r-2-(r-1+(2-r/q)\tau)M/2}, & \beta > -q/r, \end{cases} \\
< &\infty.
\end{aligned}$$

From $\beta + q > 0$, $q > 1/2$, $|X_{ni}^{(1)}| \leq n^{-\tau}$ and $|X_{ni}^{(1)}| \leq |a_{ni}X_i|$, choosing a sufficiently large M such that $r - 2 - (\tau + r - (\tau - \beta)r/q)M < -1$, $r - 2 - (r - 1 - \tau - \tau r/q)M < -1$, we obtain

$$\begin{aligned}
&\sum_{n=1}^{\infty} n^{r-2}\left(\sum_{i=1}^{n}\left((\mathcal{E}[X_{ni}^{(1)}])^- + (\mathbb{E}[X_{ni}^{(1)}])^+\right)\right)^{M} \\
\leq &\sum_{n=1}^{\infty} n^{r-2}\left(\sum_{i=1}^{n}\left(\mathbb{E}[|X_{ni}^{(1)}|] + \mathbb{E}[|X_{ni}^{(1)}|]\right)\right)^{M} \\
\leq &C\sum_{n=1}^{\infty} n^{r-2}\left(\sum_{i=1}^{n}\left(\mathbb{E}[n^{-\tau(1-r/q)}|a_{ni}X_i|^{r/q}]\right)\right)^{M} \\
\approx &\begin{cases} \sum_{n=1}^{\infty} n^{r-2-(r-1-\tau-\tau r/q)M}, & -q < \beta < -q/r, \\ \sum_{n=1}^{\infty} n^{r-2-(\tau+r-(\tau-\beta)r/q)M}(\log n)^{M}, & \beta = -q/r, \\ \sum_{n=1}^{\infty} n^{r-2-(\tau+r-(\tau-\beta)r/q)M}, & \beta > -q/r, \end{cases} \\
< &\infty.
\end{aligned}$$

By the definition $X_{ni}^{(2)}$, we have $0 < X_{ni}^{(2)} < \frac{\epsilon}{K}$. It follows that

$$\begin{aligned}
&\mathbb{V}\left(\max_{1\le k\le n}\left|\sum_{i=1}^{k} X_{ni}^{(2)}\right| \geq \epsilon\right) \\
=&\mathbb{V}\left(\sum_{i=1}^{n} X_{ni}^{(2)} \geq \epsilon\right) \\
\leq&\mathbb{V}(\text{there are at least } K \text{ indices } i \in [1,n], \text{ such that } a_{ni}X_i > n^{-\tau}) \\
\leq& \sum_{1\le i_1<i_2<\ldots<i_K\le n} \mathbb{V}(|a_{ni_1}X_{i_1}| > n^{-\tau}, \ldots, |a_{ni_K}X_{i_K}| > n^{-\tau}) \\
\leq&\left(\sum_{i=1}^{n} \mathbb{E}[I(|a_{ni_1}X| > n^{-\tau}, \ldots, I(|a_{ni_K}X| > n^{-\tau})]\right) \\
\leq&\left(\sum_{i=1}^{n} \mathbb{E}[I(|a_{ni}X| > n^{-\tau})]\right)^K \\
\leq&\left(\sum_{i=1}^{n} \mathbb{V}(|a_{ni}X| > n^{-\tau})\right)^K.
\end{aligned}$$

Hence, by Markov's inequality under sublinear expectation, it follows that

$$\begin{aligned}
I_2 &\leq \sum_{n=1}^{\infty} n^{r-2}\left(\sum_{i=1}^{n} \mathbb{V}(|a_{ni}X| > n^{-\tau})\right)^K \\
&\leq C\sum_{n=1}^{\infty} n^{r-2}\left(\sum_{i=1}^{n} n^{r\tau/p}|a_{ni}|^{r/p}\mathbb{E}|X|^{r/p}\right)^K \\
&\approx \begin{cases} \sum_{n=1}^{\infty} n^{r-2-Kr(q+\beta-\tau/q)}, & -q < \beta < -q/r, \\ \sum_{n=1}^{\infty} n^{r-2-K(r-1-r\tau/q)} \log^K n, & \beta = -q/r, \\ \sum_{n=1}^{\infty} n^{r-2-K(r-1-r\tau/q)}, & \beta > -q/r. \end{cases}
\end{aligned}$$

Notice that $r > 1, q+\beta > 0$, we could choose $\tau > 0$, small enough, and a sufficiently large integer K such that $r-2-Kr(q+\beta-\tau/q) < -1$ and $r-2-K(r-1-r\tau/q) < -1$. Hence, by Lemma 2, we obtain $I_2 < \infty$. Similarly, we could obtain $I_3 < \infty$.

By the definition of $X_{ni}^{(4)}$, we have

$$\left(\max_{1\le j\le n}\left|\sum_{i=1}^{j} X_{ni}^{(4)}\right| \geq \epsilon\right) \subseteq \left(\max_{1\le i\le n}|a_{ni}X_i| \geq \frac{\epsilon}{K}\right).$$

Since $\{a_{ni} \approx (i/n)^{\beta}(1/n)^{q}\}$, by Lemma 4, we see that

$$
\begin{aligned}
I_4 &\le \sum_{n=1}^{\infty} n^{r-2}\mathbb{V}\Big(|a_{ni}X_i| \ge \frac{\epsilon}{K}\Big)\\
&\le \sum_{n=1}^{\infty} n^{r-2}\mathbb{V}\Big(|X| \ge \frac{\epsilon}{K}n^{q+\beta}i^{-\beta}\Big)\\
&\approx \int_1^{\infty} x^{r-2}\int_1^{x}\mathbb{V}\Big(|X| > \frac{\epsilon}{CK}x^{q+\beta}y^{-\beta}\Big)dydx \text{ (Letting } u = x^{q+\beta}, v = y)\\
&= \frac{1}{q+\beta}\int_1^{\infty} du\int_1^{u^{1/q}} u^{(r-1)/(q+\beta)-1}v^{\beta(r-1)/(q+\beta)}\mathbb{V}\Big(|X| \ge \frac{\epsilon}{CK}u\Big)dv\\
&\approx \begin{cases} C\int_1^{\infty} u^{(r-1)/(q+\beta)-1}\mathbb{V}(|X| \ge \frac{\epsilon}{CK}u)du \ll \mathcal{C}_{\mathbb{V}}(|X|^{(r-1)/(q+\beta)}), & -q<\beta<-q/r;\\ C\int_1^{\infty} u^{r/q-1}\ln(u)\mathbb{V}(|X| \ge \frac{\epsilon}{CK}u)du \ll \mathcal{C}_{\mathbb{V}}(|X|^{r/q}\log(1+|X|)), & \beta=-q/r;\\ C\int_1^{\infty} u^{r/q-1}\mathbb{V}(|X| \ge \frac{\epsilon}{CK}u)du \ll \mathcal{C}_{\mathbb{V}}(|X|^{r/q}), & \beta>-q/r. \end{cases}
\end{aligned}
$$

Then by (3), we conclude $I_4 < \infty$. Now we prove (4) $\Rightarrow$ (3). Since

$$\max_{1\le k\le n}|a_{nk}X_k| \le 2\max_{1\le k\le n}\Big|\sum_{i=1}^{k}a_{ni}X_i\Big|,$$

applying (4), we have

$$\mathbb{V}\Big(\max_{1\le k\le n}|a_{nk}X_k| \ge \epsilon\Big) \to 0, \quad n\to\infty.$$

By Lemma 5, it follows that, for all $\epsilon > 0$

$$\sum_{i=1}^{n}\mathbb{V}(|a_{ni}X_i| \ge \epsilon) \ll \mathbb{V}\Big(\max_{1\le k\le n}|a_{nk}X_k| \ge \epsilon\Big). \tag{12}$$

Now, combining (12) with (4) gives

$$\sum_{n=1}^{\infty} n^{r-2}\sum_{i=1}^{n}\mathbb{V}(|a_{ni}X_i| \ge \epsilon) < \infty. \tag{13}$$

By the process of proof of $I_4 < \infty$, we see that (13) is equivalent to (3). The proof of Theorem 1 is finished.

4.2. Proof of Theorem 2

We first prove that (5) $\Rightarrow$ (6). Notice that

$$
\begin{aligned}
&\sum_{n=1}^{\infty} n^{r-2}\mathcal{C}_{\mathbb{V}}\left(\left(\max_{1\le k\le n}\Big|\sum_{i=1}^{k}a_{ni}X_i\Big|^p-\epsilon\right)^+\right)\\
&=\sum_{n=1}^{\infty} n^{r-2}\int_0^{\infty}\mathbb{V}\left(\max_{1\le k\le n}\Big|\sum_{i=1}^{k}a_{ni}X_i\Big|^p \ge \epsilon+x\right)dx\\
&=\sum_{n=1}^{\infty} n^{r-2}\int_{\epsilon}^{1}\mathbb{V}\left(\max_{1\le k\le n}\Big|\sum_{i=1}^{k}a_{ni}X_i\Big|^p \ge x\right)dx+\sum_{n=1}^{\infty} n^{r-2}\int_1^{\infty}\mathbb{V}\left(\max_{1\le k\le n}\Big|\sum_{i=1}^{k}a_{ni}X_i\Big|^p \ge x\right)dx\\
&=\sum_{n=1}^{\infty} n^{r-2}\int_{\epsilon}^{1}\mathbb{V}\left(\max_{1\le k\le n}\Big|\sum_{i=1}^{k}a_{ni}X_i\Big| \ge x^{1/p}\right)dx+\sum_{n=1}^{\infty} n^{r-2}\int_1^{\infty}\mathbb{V}\left(\max_{1\le k\le n}\Big|\sum_{i=1}^{k}a_{ni}X_i\Big| \ge x^{1/p}\right)dx\\
&:=I+II
\end{aligned}
$$

From Theorem 1, we see that $I < \infty$. We next establish $II < \infty$. Choose $0 < \alpha < 1/p$, $\delta > 0$, sufficiently small, and a large enough integer K. For every $1 \le i \le n$, $n \ge 1$, we note the fact that n is sufficiently large to guarantee $x^\alpha n^{-\tau} < \frac{x^{1/p}}{4K}$. Without the loss of restrictions, we could write

$$
\begin{aligned}
Y_{ni}^{(1)} &= -x^\alpha n^{-\delta} I(a_{ni}X_i < -x^\alpha n^{-\tau}) + a_{ni}X_i I(|a_{ni}X_i| \le x^\alpha n^{-\tau}) + x^\alpha n^{-\delta} I(a_{ni}X_i > x^\alpha n^{-\tau});\\
Y_{ni}^{(2)} &= (a_{ni}X_i - x^\alpha n^{-\tau}) I\left(x^\alpha n^{-\tau} < a_{ni}X_i < \frac{x^{1/p}}{4K}\right);\\
Y_{ni}^{(3)} &= (a_{ni}X_i + x^\alpha n^{-\tau}) I\left(-\frac{x^{1/p}}{4K} < a_{ni}X_i < -x^\alpha n^{-\tau}\right);\\
Y_{ni}^{(4)} &= (a_{ni}X_i + x^\alpha n^{-\tau}) I\left(a_{ni}X_i \le -\frac{x^{1/p}}{4K}\right) + (a_{ni}X_i - x^\alpha n^{-\tau}) I\left(a_{ni}X_i \ge \frac{x^{1/p}}{4K}\right).
\end{aligned}
$$

It is obvious that $\sum_{i=1}^k a_{ni}Y_i = \sum_{i=1}^k Y_{ni}^{(1)} + \sum_{i=1}^k Y_{ni}^{(2)} + \sum_{i=1}^k Y_{ni}^{(3)} + \sum_{i=1}^k Y_{ni}^{(4)}$. Notice that

$$\left(\max_{1\le l\le n}\left|\sum_{i=1}^l a_{ni}Y_i\right| \ge x^{1/p}\right) \subseteq \bigcup_{j=1}^4 \left(\max_{1\le l\le n}\left|\sum_{i=1}^l Y_{ni}^{(j)}\right| \ge x^{1/p}/4\right).$$

Thus, in order to establish (6), we only need to prove that

$$J_j := \sum_{n=1}^\infty n^{r-2}\int_1^\infty \mathbb{V}\left(\max_{1\le l\le n}\left|\sum_{i=1}^l Y_{ni}^{(j)}\right| \ge x^{1/p}/4\right)dx < \infty,\ j = 1,2,3,4.$$

In order to estimate J_1, we verify that

$$\sup_{x\ge 1}\frac{1}{x^{1/p}}\max_{1\le l\le n}\left|\sum_{i=1}^l \mathbb{E}Y_{ni}^{(1)}\right| \to 0 \text{ as } n\to\infty.$$

Lemmas 1 and 2, and (5) imply that

$$\mathbb{E}|X|^{1/q} < \infty,\quad \mathbb{E}|X|^{r/q} < \infty.$$

When $q > 1$, since $|Y_{ni}^{(1)}| \le x^\alpha n^{-\tau}$ and $|Y_{ni}^{(1)}| \le |a_{ni}X_i|$, by Lemma 2, it follows that

$$
\begin{aligned}
&\max_{1\le k\le n}\left|\sum_{i=1}^k \mathbb{E}Y_{ni}^{(1)}\right|\\
\le&\sum_{i=1}^n \mathbb{E}\left|Y_{ni}^{(1)}\right|\\
\le&(x^\alpha n^{-\tau})^{1-1/q}\sum_{i=1}^n \mathbb{E}|a_{ni}X_i|^{1/q}\\
\ll& x^{\alpha(1-1/q)}n^{-\tau(1-1/q)}\sum_{i=1}^n |a_{ni}|^{1/q}\\
\le& x^{\alpha(1-1/q)}n^{-\tau(1-1/q)}n^{(r-1)/r}\left(\sum_{i=1}^n |a_{ni}|^{r/q}\right)^{1/r}\\
\approx& x^{\alpha(1-1/q)}n^{-\tau(1-1/q)}.
\end{aligned}
\tag{14}
$$

Since $q > 1, 0 < \alpha < 1$, we could know $(1-1/q)\alpha < \alpha < 1/p$. Then by (14), for $x \ge 1$, we obtain

$$\sup_{x\ge 1}\frac{1}{x^{1/p}}\max_{1\le l\le n}\left|\sum_{i=1}^l \mathbb{E}Y_{ni}^{(1)}\right| \ll n^{-\tau(1-1/q)} \to 0 \text{ as } n\to\infty.$$

When $1/2 < q \le 1$, noticing that $\mathbb{E}(X) = -\mathbb{E}(-X) = 0$, taking a sufficiently small τ such that $-\tau(1 - r/q) + 1 - r < 0$, we obtain

$$\begin{aligned}
&\max_{1\le l\le n}\left|\sum_{i=1}^{l}\mathbb{E}Y_{ni}^{(1)}\right| \\
\le& 2\sum_{i=1}^{n}\mathbb{E}|a_{ni}X_i|I\big(|a_{ni}X_i| > x^{\alpha}n^{-\tau}\big) \\
\le& 2x^{\alpha(1-r/q)}n^{-\tau(1-r/q)}\sum_{i=1}^{n}\mathbb{E}|a_{ni}X_i|^{r/q} \\
\le& 2x^{\alpha(1-r/q)}n^{-\tau(1-r/q)}\sum_{i=1}^{n}\mathbb{E}|a_{ni}|^{r/q} \\
\approx& x^{\alpha(1-r/q)}n^{-\tau(1-r/q)+1-r}.
\end{aligned}$$

Observing that $1 - r/q < 0$, we have

$$\sup_{x\ge 1}\frac{1}{x^{1/p}}\max_{1\le k\le n}\left|\sum_{i=1}^{k}\mathbb{E}Y_{ni}^{(1)}\right| \ll n^{-\tau(1-r/q)+1-r} \to 0 \text{ as } n \to \infty.$$

Then, to prove $J_1 < \infty$, we only need to show

$$J_1^* := \sum_{n=1}^{\infty} n^{r-2}\int_1^{\infty}\mathbb{V}\left(\max_{1\le k\le n}\left|\sum_{i=1}^{k}\left(Y_{ni}^{(1)} - \mathbb{E}Y_{ni}^{(1)}\right)\right| \ge \frac{x^{1/p}}{8}\right)dx < \infty.$$

It is obvious that $Y_{ni}^{(1)}$ is a sequence of negatively dependent random variables under sublinear expectation space. It follows from Markov's inequality and Cr's inequality under sublinear expectation, Lemma 3, that for a sufficiently large M,

$$\begin{aligned}
&\mathbb{V}\left(\max_{1\le k\le n}\left|\sum_{i=1}^{k}\left(Y_{ni}^{(1)} - \mathbb{E}Y_{ni}^{(1)}\right)\right| \ge \frac{x^{1/p}}{8}\right) \\
\ll& x^{-M/p}n^{M/2-1}(\log n)^M\sum_{i=1}^{n}\mathbb{E}[|Y_{ni}^{(1)}|]^M.
\end{aligned}$$

Taking a suitably large M such that $-(1/p - \alpha)M - r\alpha/q < -1$, $-2 - \tau(M - r/q) + M/2 < -1$, we have

$$\begin{aligned}
&\sum_{n=1}^{\infty} n^{r-2+M/2-1}(\log n)^M\sum_{i=1}^{n}\int_1^{\infty}x^{-M/p}E[|Y_{ni}^{(1)}|]^M dx \\
\ll& \sum_{n=1}^{\infty} n^{r-2+M/2-1}n^{-\tau(M-r/q)}(\log n)^M\sum_{i=1}^{n}|a_{ni}|^{r/q}\int_1^{\infty}x^{-M(1/p-\alpha)-r\alpha/q}dx \\
\ll& \sum_{n=1}^{\infty} n^{-2-\tau(M-r/q)+M/2}\log n^M < \infty.
\end{aligned}$$

Consequently, we obtain $J_1^* < \infty$. Similar to the proof of (9), we could obtain

$$\mathbb{V}\left(\max_{1\le k\le n}\left|\sum_{i=1}^{k}Y_{ni}^{(2)}\right| \ge x^{1/p}/4\right) \le \left(\sum_{i=1}^{n}\mathbb{V}(|u_{ni}X| > x^{\alpha}n^{\ \ \tau})\right)^K.$$

From $\beta > -q/r$, and $a_{ni} \approx (i/n)^{\beta}(1/n)^q$, we obtain

$$\sum_{i=1}^{n}a_{ni}^{r/q} \approx \sum_{i=1}^{n}n^{-r(q+\beta)/q}i^{\beta r/q} \approx n^{1-r}$$

By Maokov's inequality under sublinear expectations, we conclude that

$$\begin{aligned}
J_2 &\leq \sum_{n=1}^{\infty} n^{r-2} \int_1^{\infty} \left(\sum_{i=1}^{n} \mathbb{V}(|a_{ni}X| > \mu x^{\alpha} n^{-\tau}) \right)^K dx \\
&\leq C \sum_{n=1}^{\infty} n^{r-2} \int_1^{\infty} \left(\sum_{i=1}^{n} x^{-r\alpha/q} n^{r\tau/q} \mathbb{E}|X|^{r/q} \right)^K dx \\
&\approx \sum_{n=1}^{\infty} n^{r-2-K(r-1-r\tau/q)} \int_1^{\infty} x^{-rK\alpha/q} dx.
\end{aligned}$$

Since $\alpha > 0, r > 1$, we could take a sufficiently small τ and sufficiently large K such that $-rK\alpha/q < -1$ and $-2+r-K(r-1-r\tau/q) < -1$. It follows that $J_2 < \infty$. Similarly, we can obtain $J_3 < \infty$. It is obvious that $\beta > -q/r$ implies $\beta(r-1)/(q+\beta) > -1$. Then,

$$\int_1^{s^{1/q}} t^{\beta(r-1)/(q+\beta)} dt \approx s^{\frac{1}{q} + \frac{\beta(r+1)}{q(q+\beta)}}. \tag{15}$$

It follows that

$$\begin{aligned}
J_4 &\leq \sum_{n=1}^{\infty} n^{r-2} \sum_{i=1}^{n} \int_1^{\infty} \mathbb{V}\left(|a_{ni}X_i| > \frac{x^{1/p}}{4K} \right) dx \\
&\approx \sum_{n=1}^{\infty} n^{r-2} \sum_{i=1}^{n} \int_1^{\infty} \mathbb{V}\left(|X| > \frac{x^{1/p}}{4CK} n^{q+\beta} i^{-\beta} \right) dx \\
&\approx \int_1^{\infty} dx \int_1^{\infty} v^{r-2} dv \int_1^{v} \mathbb{V}\left(|X| > \frac{x^{1/p}}{4CK} v^{q+\beta} u^{-\beta} \right) du \\
&\approx \int_1^{\infty} dx \int_1^{\infty} ds \int_1^{s^{1/q}} s^{(r-1)/(q+\beta)-1} y^{\beta(r-1)/(q+\beta)} \mathbb{V}\left(|X| > \frac{x^{1/p}}{4CK} s \right) dy \\
&\approx \int_1^{\infty} dx \int_1^{\infty} s^{r/q-1} \mathbb{V}\left(|X| > \frac{x^{1/p}}{4CK} s \right) ds.
\end{aligned}$$

Hence, from Lemma 6 and (5), we obtain $J_4 < \infty$. Now we prove (6) $\Rightarrow$ (5). By Markov's inequality under sublinear expectations, (6), and Lemma 2, we have

$$\begin{aligned}
&\sum_{n=1}^{\infty} n^{r-2} \mathbb{V}\left(\max_{1 \leq k \leq n} \left| \sum_{i=1}^{k} a_{ni} X_i \right| \geq \epsilon \right) \\
&= \sum_{n=1}^{\infty} n^{r-2} \mathbb{E}\left[I\left(\max_{1 \leq k \leq n} \left| \sum_{i=1}^{k} a_{ni} X_i \right| \geq \epsilon \right) \right] \\
&\leq \sum_{n=1}^{\infty} n^{r-2} \mathbb{E}\left[\left(\left(\max_{1 \leq k \leq n} \left| \sum_{i=1}^{k} a_{ni} X_i \right|^p - (\epsilon/2)^p \right)^+ / (\epsilon/2)^p \right) I\left(\max_{1 \leq k \leq n} \left| \sum_{i=1}^{k} a_{ni} X_i \right| \geq \epsilon \right) \right] \\
&\leq \sum_{n=1}^{\infty} n^{r-2} \mathbb{E}\left[\left(\left(\max_{1 \leq k \leq n} \left| \sum_{i=1}^{k} a_{ni} X_i \right|^p - (\epsilon/2)^p \right)^+ / (\epsilon/2)^p \right) \right] \\
&\leq \sum_{n=1}^{\infty} n^{r-2} \mathbb{E}\left[\left(\max_{1 \leq k \leq n} \left| \sum_{i=1}^{k} a_{ni} X_i \right|^p - (\epsilon/2)^p \right)^+ \right] / (\epsilon/2)^p < \infty.
\end{aligned}$$

similar proofs of (3.17) are available in Guo [23], we have

$$\mathbb{V}\left(\max_{1 \leq k \leq n} |a_{nk} X_k| > \epsilon \right) \to 0, \quad n \to \infty.$$

By Lemma 5, it follows that, for all $\epsilon > 0$

$$\sum_{i=1}^{n} \mathbb{V}(|a_{ni}X_i| > \epsilon) \ll \mathbb{V}\left(\max_{1 \le k \le n} |a_{nk}X_k| > \epsilon \right). \tag{16}$$

Now, combining (16) with (4) gives

$$\sum_{n=1}^{\infty} n^{r-2} \int_{\epsilon}^{\infty} \sum_{i=1}^{n} \mathbb{V}\left(|a_{ni}X_i| > x^{1/p} \right) < \infty. \tag{17}$$

By the process of proof of $I_4 < \infty$, we see that (17) is equivalent to (3). The proof of Theorem 2 is finished.

4.3. *Proof of Theorem 3*

From the supposition of Theorem 3, for $\beta = -q/r$, one can obtain

$$\sum_{i=1}^{n} a_{ni}^{r/q} \approx \sum_{i=1}^{n} n^{-r(q+\beta)/q} \log n, \tag{18}$$

and

$$\int_{1}^{s^{1/q}} t^{\beta(r-1)/(q+\beta)} dt = \int_{1}^{s^{1/q}} t^{-1} dt \approx \log s, \tag{19}$$

By the same argument as the proof of Theorem 2, with Lemma 7 in place of Lemma 6, together with (18) and (19), we could prove Theorem 3. Therefore, the proof is omitted.

4.4. *Proof of Theorem 4*

From the supposition of Theorem 4, for $\beta < -q/r$, one can obtain

$$\sum_{i=1}^{n} a_{ni}^{r/q} \approx \sum_{i=1}^{n} n^{-r(q+\beta)/q} i^{\beta r/q} \approx n^{-r(q+\beta)/q}, \tag{20}$$

and

$$\int_{1}^{s^{1/q}} t^{\beta(r-1)/(q+\beta)} dt \approx C. \tag{21}$$

By the same argument as the proof of Theorem 2, with (21) in place of (15), we could prove Theorem 4. Therefore, the proof is omitted.

5. Conclusions

In this paper, using the moment inequality for ND random variables sequences under sublinear expectation space and the truncation method, the authors establish the equivalent conditions of complete convergence for sums of ND random variables sequences and p-th moment convergence for sums of ND random variables sequences. The results extend the corresponding results from the classical probability space to the sublinear expectation space, as well as extending i.i.d random variables to ND random variables. In the future, we will try to establish the corresponding results for other dependent sequences under sublinear expectation space.

Author Contributions: P.S., D.W. and X.T. contributed equally to the development of this paper. All authors have read and agreed to the published version of the manuscript.

Funding: Department of Science and Technology of Jilin Province (Grant No. YDZJ202101ZYTS156), Natural Science Foundation of Jilin Province (Grant No. YDZJ202301ZYTS373).

Data Availability Statement: No new data were created or analyzed in this study.

Conflicts of Interest: The authors declare no conflict of interest.

References

1. Peng, S.G. Backward SDE and related G-Expectation. *Pitman Res. Notes Math. Ser.* **1997**, *364*, 141–159.
2. Peng, S.G. Monotonic limit theorem of BSDE and nonlinear decomposition theorem of Doob-Meyer type. *Probab. Theory Relat. Fields* **1999**, *113*, 473–499. [CrossRef]
3. Denis, L.; Martini, C. A theoretical framework for the pricing of contingent claims in the presence of model uncertainty. *Ann. Appl. Probab.* **2006**, *16*, 827–852. [CrossRef]
4. Gilboa, I. Expected utility with purely subjective non-additive probabilities. *J. Math. Econ.* **1987**, *16*, 65–88. [CrossRef]
5. Marinacci, M. Limit laws for non-additive probabilities and their frequentist interpretation. *J. Econ. Theory* **1999**, *84*, 145–195. [CrossRef]
6. Peng, S.G. G-Gxpectation, G-Brownian motion and related stochastic calculus of Ito's type. *Stoch. Anal. Appl.* **2006**, *2*, 541–567.
7. Peng, S.G. Multi-dimensional G-Brownian motion and related stochastic calculus under G-expectation. *Stoch. Proc. Appl.* **2008**, *118*, 2223–2253. [CrossRef]
8. Peng, S.G. *Nonlinear Expectations and Stochastic Calculus under Uncertainty*, 1st ed.; Springer: Berlin/Heidelberg, Germany, 2010.
9. Zhang, L.X. Exponential inequalities under the sub-linear expectations with applications to laws of the iterated logarithm. *Sci. China Math.* **2016**, *59*, 2503–2526. [CrossRef]
10. Zhang, L.X. Rosenthal's inequalities for independent and negatively dependent random variables under sub-linear expectations with applications. *Sci. China Math.* **2016**, *59*, 751–768. [CrossRef]
11. Zhang, L.X. Donsker's invariance principle under the sub-linear expectation with an application to chung's law of the iterated logarithm. *Commun. Math. Stat.* **2015**, *3*, 187–214. [CrossRef]
12. Zhang, M.; Chen, Z.J. Strong laws of large numbers for sub-linear expectations. *Sci. China Math.* **2016**, *59*, 945–954.
13. Chen, Z.J.; Liu, Q.; Zong, G. Weak laws of large numbers for sublinear expectation. *Math. Control Relat. Fields* **2018**, *8*, 637–651. [CrossRef]
14. Chen, Z.J.; Feng, X.F. Large deviation for negatively dependent random variables under sublinear expectation. *Comm. Stat. Theory Methods* **2016**, *45*, 400–412. [CrossRef]
15. Wu, Q.Y. Precise Asymptotics for Complete Integral Convergence under Sublinear Expectations. *Math. Probl. Eng.* **2020**, *13*, 3145935. [CrossRef]
16. Li, M.; Shi, Y.F. A general central limit theorem under sublinear expectations. *Sci. China Math.* **2010**, *53*, 1989–1994. [CrossRef]
17. Liu, W.; Zhang, Y. Large deviation principle for linear processes generated by real stationary sequences under the sub-linear expectation. *Comm. Stat. Theory Methods* **2023**, *52*, 5727–5741. [CrossRef]
18. Ding, X. A general form for precise asymptotics for complete convergence under sublinear expectation. *AIMS Math.* **2022**, *7*, 1664–1677. [CrossRef]
19. Wu, Y.; Wang, X.J. General results on precise asymptotics under sub-linear expectations. *J. Math. Anal. Appl.* **2022**, 511, 126090. [CrossRef]
20. Guo, S.; Zhang, Y. Central limit theolrem for linear processes generated by m-dependent random variables under the sub-linear expectation. *Comm. Stat. Theory Methods* **2023**, *52*, 6407–6419. [CrossRef]
21. Guo, S.; Zhang, Y. Moderate deviation principle for m-dependent random variables under the sublinear expectation. *AIMS Math.* **2022**, *7*, 5943–5956. [CrossRef]
22. Dong, H.; Tan, X.L.; Yong, Z. Complete convergence and complete integration convergence for weighted sums of arrays of rowwise m-END under sub-linear expectations space. *AIMS Math.* **2023**, *8*, 6705–6724. [CrossRef]
23. Guo, M.L.; Shan, S. Equivalent conditions of complete qth monent convergence for weighted sums of sequences of negatively orthant dependent raodom variables. *Chin. J. Appl. Probab. Stat.* **2020**, *36*, 381–392.
24. Xu, M.Z.; Cheng, K. Convergence of sums of i.i.d. random variables under sublinear expectations. *J. Inequal. Appl.* **2021**, *2021*, 157. [CrossRef]
25. Xu, M.Z.; Cheng, K. Equivalent conditions of complete p-th moment convergence for weighted sums of i.i.d. random variables under sublinear expectations. *arXiv* **2021**, arXiv:2109.08464.

mathematics
MDPI

Article

A Rényi-Type Limit Theorem on Random Sums and the Accuracy of Likelihood-Based Classification of Random Sequences with Application to Genomics

Leonid Hanin [1,*] and Lyudmila Pavlova [2]

[1] Department of Mathematics and Statistics, Idaho State University, 921 S. 8th Avenue, Stop 8085, Pocatello, ID 83209-8085, USA
[2] School of Applied Mathematics and Computational Physics, Peter the Great St. Petersburg Polytechnic University, Polytechnicheskaya ul. 29, 195251 St. Petersburg, Russia; lyu0510@gmail.com
* Correspondence: hanin@isu.edu

Abstract: We study classification of random sequences of characters selected from a given alphabet into two classes characterized by distinct character selection probabilities and length distributions. The classification is based on the sign of the log-likelihood score (LLS) consisting of a random sum and a random term depending on the length distributions for the two classes. For long sequences selected from a large alphabet, computing misclassification error rates is not feasible either theoretically or computationally. To mitigate this problem, we computed limiting distributions for two versions of the normalized LLS applicable to long sequences whose class-specific length follows a translated negative binomial distribution (TNBD). The two limiting distributions turned out to be plain or transformed Erlang distributions. This allowed us to establish the asymptotic accuracy of the likelihood-based classification of random sequences with TNBD length distributions. Our limit theorem generalizes a classic theorem on geometric random sums due to Rényi and is closely related to the published results of V. Korolev and coworkers on negative binomial random sums. As an illustration, we applied our limit theorem to the classification of DNA sequences contained in the genome of the bacterium *Bacillus subtilis* into two classes: protein-coding genes and standard noncoding open reading frames. We found that TNBDs provide an excellent fit to the length distributions for both classes and that the limiting distributions capture essential features of the normalized empirical LLS fairly well.

Keywords: Rényi theorem; sequence classification; classification accuracy; random sum; translated negative binomial distribution; Kullback–Leibler distance; Erlang distribution; protein-coding gene; open reading frame

MSC: 60F05; 92D20

Citation: Hanin, L.; Pavlova, L. A Rényi-Type Limit Theorem on Random Sums and the Accuracy of Likelihood-Based Classification of Random Sequences with Application to Genomics. *Mathematics* **2023**, *11*, 4254. https://doi.org/10.3390/math11204254

Academic Editors: Irina Shevtsova and Victor Korolev

Received: 21 August 2023
Revised: 6 October 2023
Accepted: 8 October 2023
Published: 11 October 2023

1. Introduction

This study concerns classification of sequences of characters selected randomly and independently of each other from a given alphabet of $M \geq 2$ characters. The length, N, of any such sequence is assumed to be a random variable (rv) independent of the sequence content. Suppose that there are two models of sequence assembly: one where characters are selected from the alphabet with positive probabilities $p(1), p(2), \ldots, p(M)$ and the sequence length has a certain distribution P (model A), and another where characters are selected with positive probabilities $q(1), q(2), \ldots, q(M)$ and the length has a distribution Q (model B). The two vectors of character selection probabilities (or equivalently, probability measures on $\{1, 2, \ldots, M\}$) are assumed to be distinct and will be denoted by $\mathcal{P}$ and $\mathcal{Q}$. Then, the model-generating probabilities are $P_A = \mathcal{P} \times P$ and $P_B = \mathcal{Q} \times Q$.

The sequence classification problem consists of deciding, for a given sequence of characters $C = (C_1, C_2, \ldots, C_n)$, which model generated this sequence. To simplify our notation, in what follows we will adopt the following convention: if C_k is the n_k-th character of the alphabet, then we will write $p(C_k) = p(n_k)$ and likewise $q(C_k) = q(n_k)$, $1 \leq k \leq n$. A natural approach to solving the classification problem is to compare the likelihoods of a sequence C associated with models A and B:

$$L_A(C) = P(n)\Pi_{k=1}^{n} p(C_k) \quad \text{and} \quad L_B(C) = Q(n)\Pi_{k=1}^{n} q(C_k). \tag{1}$$

Specifically, if $L_A(C) > L_B(C)$, then we decide that sequence C is generated by model A, while in the case where $L_B(C) > L_A(C)$, the sequence C is attributed to model B (in the unlikely case where $L_A(C) = L_B(C)$, the sequence C is not assigned to any model). Equivalently, denoting by $\mathcal{L}(C)$ the log-likelihood

$$\mathcal{L}(C) = \log \frac{L_A(C)}{L_B(C)}, \tag{2}$$

we classify sequence C as being generated by model A if $\mathcal{L}(C) > 0$ and by model B if $\mathcal{L}(C) < 0$.

Formulas (1) and (2) suggest that the log-likelihood ratio for a randomly and independently generated sequence $(C_1, C_2, \ldots, C_N)$ of random length N is a rv

$$X = \log \frac{P(N)}{Q(N)} + \sum_{n=1}^{N} \log \frac{p(C_n)}{q(C_n)} = f(N) + U, \tag{3}$$

where $f(N) = \log[P(N)/Q(N)]$ and

$$U = \sum_{n=1}^{N} X_n \tag{4}$$

is a random sum generated by independent and identically distributed (iid) rvs

$$X_n = \log \frac{p(C_n)}{q(C_n)}.$$

The expected value of rvs X_n for sequences generated by models $\mathcal{P}$ and $\mathcal{Q}$ is given by

$$\mu_{\mathcal{P}} = \sum_{m=1}^{M} p(m) \log \frac{p(m)}{q(m)} \quad \text{and} \quad \mu_{\mathcal{Q}} = \sum_{m=1}^{M} q(m) \log \frac{p(m)}{q(m)}. \tag{5}$$

It follows from Jensen's inequality [1] that $\mu_{\mathcal{Q}} < 0$, hence also $\mu_{\mathcal{P}} > 0$. Note that $\mu_{\mathcal{P}}$ represents the Kullback–Leibler distance [2] between distributions $\mathcal{P}$ and $\mathcal{Q}$: $\mu_{\mathcal{P}} = d_{KL}(\mathcal{P}, \mathcal{Q})$ and similarly $\mu_{\mathcal{Q}} = -d_{KL}(\mathcal{Q}, \mathcal{P})$. We denote by $\sigma_{\mathcal{P}}^2$ and $\sigma_{\mathcal{Q}}^2$ the corresponding variances.

An alternative way of looking at rv U arises from the following observation. For $1 \leq m \leq M$, denote by ν_m the number of occurrences of the m-th letter of the alphabet in a random sequence of length N. Then, $\nu_1 + \nu_2 + \ldots + \nu_M = N$ and

$$U = \sum_{m=1}^{M} \nu_m \log \frac{p(m)}{q(m)}. \tag{6}$$

Suppose the sequence is generated by model A. Note that, conditional on $N = n$, the random vector $(\nu_1, \nu_2, \ldots, \nu_M)$ follows the multinomial distribution $Mult(n; p(1), p(2), \ldots p(M))$. In particular, the distribution of rv ν_m is binomial $B(n, p(m))$, $1 \leq m \leq M$. Then, from Formulas (4)–(6), we obtain the following expression for the expected value of rv U under model A:

$$\mathbb{E}_A U = \sum_{n=1}^{\infty} P(N = n) \sum_{m=1}^{M} np(m) \log \frac{p(m)}{q(m)} = \mu_{\mathcal{P}} \mathbb{E}_{\mathcal{P}} N. \tag{7}$$

Similarly, under model B we have $\mathbb{E}_B U = \mu_Q \mathbb{E}_Q N$. Thus, rv U is closely related to the multinomial process with M outcomes and a random number of replications. The above formulas for the expectation of rv U under models A and B can also be obtained directly by applying Wald's identity [3] to the random sum (4).

Computation of various measures of classification accuracy including important misclassification error rates $P_A(X \leq 0)$ and $P_B(X \geq 0)$ requires the knowledge of the distribution of the log-likelihood score X under models A and B. However, in applications with a large alphabet size, computing these distributions for long sequences, let alone sequences of variable length, in closed form is a daunting task. This motivates studying approximations to the model-specific distributions of rv X arising for very long sequences. In this article, such approximations will be derived from the asymptotic distributions of two normalized versions of rv X,

$$Y = \frac{X}{\mathbb{E}X} \quad \text{and} \quad Z = \frac{X - \mathbb{E}X}{\sigma(X)}, \tag{8}$$

where, as usual, $\mathbb{E}X$ is the expected value of rv X and $\sigma(X)$ is its standard deviation under a given model of sequence assembly. The two asymptotic distributions are identified in Theorem 1 (see below). This theorem implies (see Section 4) that the two misclassification error rates for very long sequences are negligible, i.e., that the likelihood-based classification rule is asymptotically accurate (Theorem 2).

As an illustration of our results, we consider in Section 5 the classification of sequences of triplets of nucleotides contained in the deoxyribonucleic acid (DNA) of a given organism as protein-coding genes or noncoding open reading frames (ORFs). This classification problem is central in computational gene finding for newly sequenced or incompletely annotated genomes [4–6]. One of the most powerful tools used for this purpose is Hidden Markov models, see, e.g., [5–8]. In this setting, triplets of nucleotides (or individual nucleotides) generated by the *same* hidden state are emitted independently and have a random length, i.e., they meet our model assumptions.

In many cases of practical interest, sequences of characters must be sufficiently long. In the case of protein-coding genes, this is due to the fact that, in order to perform various biological functions, e.g., to serve as enzymes, proteins must have certain structural features that can only arise if they contain sufficiently many amino acids. Let $\ell \geq 1$ be the minimum allowed length, then $N \geq \ell$ with probability 1.

The limiting distribution of rvs Y and Z will be obtained in the case where the sequence length in models A and B follows respective translated negative binomial distributions (TNBDs) $NB(a,p) + \alpha$ and $NB(b,q) + \beta$, where $0 < p,\ q < 1$ and a, b, α, β are integers such that $a, b \geq 1$ and $\alpha, \beta \geq 0$. Recall that there are two closely related kinds of negative binomial distributions $NB(r,p)$. The first is the distribution of the "waiting time" to r-th "success" in a sequence of Bernoulli trials with the success probability p *including* the first r successes, while the second is the distribution of the number of "failures" preceding the r-th success. The latter distribution has a natural extension, sometimes called the Pólia distribution, for any real number $r > 0$ [9]. For compelling biological reasons associated with the structure of genes and elucidated in Section 5, see also [10], we will be modeling the length of DNA segments using negative binomial distributions $NB(r,p)$ of the *first kind* with integer $r \geq 1$. Thus,

$$P(N = n) = \binom{n - \alpha - 1}{a - 1} p^a (1-p)^{n-\alpha-a}, \quad n \geq a + \alpha, \tag{9a}$$

and similarly

$$Q(N = n) = \binom{n - \beta - 1}{b - 1} q^b (1-q)^{n-\beta-b}, \quad n \geq b + \beta. \tag{9b}$$

In what follows, the minimum sequence length under the two models will be assumed the same:

$$\ell = a + \alpha = b + \beta. \tag{10}$$

Parameters a, b, α, β of TNBDs, related to each other through Formula (10), will be assumed to be fixed. Therefore, limiting distributions of rvs Y and Z for very long sequences under models A and B will be computed under the conditions $p \to 0$ and $q \to 0$.

Our main goal in Sections 2 and 3 is to prove the following limit theorem. To formulate it, recall that the Erlang distribution $E(a, \lambda)$ is a gamma distribution $G(a, \lambda)$ with an integer shape parameter a. Also, if S is a probability distribution on $\mathbb{R}$ and $\tau \in \mathbb{R}$, then $S + \tau$ denotes the translated distribution and $-S$ stands for the distribution S reflected about the origin.

Theorem 1. *Suppose the sequence length distributions under models A and B are $P = NB(a, p) + \alpha$ and $Q = NB(b, q) + \beta$, respectively, with $a + \alpha = b + \beta = \ell$.*

(i) If $p,\ q \to 0$ in such a way that $p \log q \to 0$, then under model A, rvs Y and Z converge in distribution to $E(a, a)$ and $E(a, \sqrt{a}) - \sqrt{a}$, respectively;
(ii) If $p,\ q \to 0$ in such a way that $q \log p \to 0$, then under model B, rvs Y and Z converge in distribution to $E(b, b)$ and $\sqrt{b} - E(b, \sqrt{b})$, respectively.

In the case where rv X is just the random sum U, see Formula (4), the limit theorem for plain (untranslated) negative binomial distributions was known previously. Specifically, for $a = 1$, the fact that the limiting distribution of rv Y is $Exp(1)$ represents a classic theorem due to Rényi [11], see also [12]. A generalization of Rényi's theorem to negative binomial distributions $NB(r, p)$ of the second kind with arbitrary $r > 0$ was obtained by Korolev and Zeifman [13] based on an estimate of the Zolotarev distance [14] between the distributions of the normalized random sum U and $E(r, r)$; for a review of relevant results and methodology, see the article by Korolev [9] and references therein. Although it is probably possible to prove Theorem 1 by reduction to the known limit theorems for the normalized random sum U, we here prefer, for greater insight and the reader's convenience, to give a direct, self-contained, and fairly elementary proof of Theorem 1. In particular, the proof clearly demonstrates that conditions $p \log q \to 0$ and $q \log p \to 0$ in Theorem 1 make the term $f(N)$ in (3) negligible in the limit. The meaning of these conditions is that the expected length of random sequences generated by one model cannot tend to infinity exponentially faster than for sequences generated by the other model.

The article is organized as follows. In Section 2, we study the asymptotic behavior of the expected value and variance of rv X for long sequences generated by models A or B under the conditions of Theorem 1. Section 3 delivers the proof of Theorem 1. In Section 4, we show that, under the conditions of Theorem 1, the likelihood-based classification of random sequences is asymptotically accurate. In Section 5, we delve into genomics and describe in detail the problem of classification of DNA sequences as protein-coding genes or noncoding ORFs using the genome of bacterium *Bacillus subtilis* as an example. In the same section, we estimate the sequence length distributions from data and make a visual comparison of the empirical and theoretical distributions of rvs Y and Z. Finally, in Section 6, we discuss our findings from mathematical and bioinformatics perspectives.

2. Asymptotic Behavior of the Expectation and Variance of the Log-Likelihood Score

Our goal in this section is to establish the following result:

Proposition 1. *Let character selection probabilities under models A and B be governed by the respective probability distributions $\mathcal{P}$ and $\mathcal{Q}$ with expected values $\mu_{\mathcal{P}}$ and $\mu_{\mathcal{Q}}$. Also, let the respective sequence length distributions under models A and B be $P = NB(a, p) + \alpha$ and $Q = NB(b, q) + \beta$ with $a + \alpha = b + \beta = \ell$. Suppose that $p,\ q \to 0$. Then, for the expected value and variance of the log-likelihood score X under models A and B, we have the following asymptotic relations:*

(i) *If* $p\log q \to 0$, *then* $p\,\mathbb{E}_A X \to a\mu_{\mathcal{P}}$ *and* $p^2 Var_A X \to a\mu_{\mathcal{P}}^2$;
(ii) *If* $q\log p \to 0$, *then* $q\,\mathbb{E}_B X \to b\mu_{\mathcal{Q}}$ *and* $q^2 Var_B X \to b\mu_{\mathcal{Q}}^2$.

The following two lemmas will be instrumental in proving Proposition 1.

Lemma 1. *Let* $\ell \in \mathbb{Z}_+$ *and* $\{P_p(k) : k \geq \ell\}$, $0 < p < 1$, *be a family of probability distributions on* $\{\ell, \ell+1, \ell+2, \dots\}$. *Suppose there is a constant* $C > 0$ *independent of* p *such that* $p\,\mathbb{E}P_p \leq C$ *for all* p. *Then, for any sequence* $\{c(j)\}_{j=0}^{\infty}$ *such that*

$$\frac{c(j)}{j} \to 0 \quad as \quad j \to \infty, \tag{11}$$

we have

$$p\sum_{j=0}^{\infty} c(j)P_p(j+\ell) \to 0 \quad as \quad p \to 0. \tag{12}$$

Proof. We may assume without loss of generality that $c(j) \geq 0$ for all $j \geq 0$. Fix $\varepsilon > 0$. In view of (11), there exists $K \geq 0$, which we will also fix, such that $c(j) \leq j\varepsilon$ for all $j > K$. Let $M_K = \max\{c(j) : 0 \leq j \leq K\}$. Then,

$$p\sum_{j=0}^{\infty} c(j)P_p(j+\ell) = p\sum_{j=0}^{K} c(j)P_p(j+\ell) + p\sum_{j=K+1}^{\infty} c(j)P_p(j+\ell)$$

$$\leq pM_K\sum_{j=0}^{K} P_p(j+\ell) + \varepsilon p\sum_{j=K+1}^{\infty} jP_p(j+\ell)$$

$$\leq pM_K + \varepsilon p\sum_{j=K+1}^{\infty}(j+\ell)P_p(j+\ell) \leq pM_K + \varepsilon p\,\mathbb{E}P_p \leq pM_K + C\varepsilon.$$

Clearly, $pM_K \leq \varepsilon$ for all sufficiently small p. Therefore, for such p, we have

$$p\sum_{j=0}^{\infty} c(j)P_p(j+\ell) \leq (C+1)\varepsilon.$$

□

The second lemma concerns the asymptotic behavior of the Kullback–Leibler distance $d_{KL}(P,Q)$ between two TNBDs.

Lemma 2. *Let* $\ell \in \mathbb{Z}_+$, $P = NB(a,p) + \alpha$ *and* $Q = NB(b,q) + \beta$ *with* $a + \alpha = b + \beta = \ell$. *Suppose that* p, $q \to 0$ *in such a way that* $p\log q \to 0$. *Then,* $p\, d_{KL}(P,Q) \to 0$.

Proof. We have

$$d_{KL}(P,Q) = \sum_{n=\ell}^{\infty} P(n)\log\frac{P(n)}{Q(n)} = \sum_{j=0}^{\infty} P(j+\ell)\log\frac{P(j+\ell)}{Q(j+\ell)}. \tag{13}$$

In view of Formulas (9),

$$\frac{P(j+\ell)}{Q(j+\ell)} = \frac{\binom{j+a-1}{a-1}p^a(1-p)^j}{\binom{j+b-1}{b-1}q^b(1-q)^j}$$

independently of ℓ, so that

$$\log \frac{P(j+\ell)}{Q(j+\ell)} = a \log p - b \log q + j \log \frac{1-p}{1-q} + c(j), \tag{14}$$

where the sequence

$$c(j) = \log \frac{\binom{j+a-1}{a-1}}{\binom{j+b-1}{b-1}}, \quad j \geq 0, \tag{15}$$

clearly has property (11). From (13) and (14), we conclude that

$$d_{KL}(P,Q) = a \log p - b \log q + \log \frac{1-p}{1-q} \sum_{j=0}^{\infty} jP(j+\ell) + \sum_{j=0}^{\infty} c(j)P(j+\ell).$$

Recall that the expected value of the distribution $NB(r,p)$ is r/p. Together with (10), this implies

$$\sum_{j=0}^{\infty} jP(j+\ell) = \sum_{j=0}^{\infty} (j+\ell)P(j+\ell) - \ell = \frac{a}{p} + \alpha - \ell = a\left(\frac{1}{p} - 1\right). \tag{16}$$

Therefore,

$$d_{KL}(P,Q) = a \log p - b \log q + a\left(\frac{1}{p} - 1\right) \log \frac{1-p}{1-q} + \sum_{j=0}^{\infty} c(j)P(j+\ell). \tag{17}$$

We now apply Lemma 1 to the family of TNBDs $P_p = NB(a,p) + \alpha,\ 0 < p < 1$, and the sequence $\{c(j)\}_{j=0}^{\infty}$ given by (15). Note that the assumption of Lemma 1 regarding distributions P_p is met because $p\,\mathbb{E}P_p = a + \alpha p \leq a + \alpha = \ell$ for all p. Therefore, using (12), we infer from (17) that if

$$p,\ q \to 0 \quad \text{in such a way that} \quad p \log q \to 0, \tag{18}$$

then $p\, d_{KL}(P,Q) \to 0$, which completes the proof of Lemma 2. □

Remark 1. *A similar proof would show that if $p,\ q \to 0$ in such a way that $q \log p \to 0$, then $q\, d_{KL}(Q,P) \to 0$.*

Proof. We now proceed to proving part (i) of Proposition 1 assuming that conditions (18) are met. Recall that the expected value $\mu_{\mathcal{P}}$ and variance $\sigma_{\mathcal{P}}^2$ of the TNBD (9a) are given by $\mu_{\mathcal{P}} = a/p + \alpha$ and $\sigma_{\mathcal{P}}^2 = a(1-p)/p^2$. In view of (3) and (7), we find that

$$\mathbb{E}_A X = d_{KL}(P,Q) + \mu_{\mathcal{P}}\left(\frac{a}{p} + \alpha\right). \tag{19}$$

Then, according to Lemma 2, we have $p\, \mathbb{E}_A X \to a\mu_{\mathcal{P}}$.

We turn to the asymptotic behavior of the variance of the log-likelihood score X under model A. As a reminder, $X = f(N) + U$, where $f(N) = \log[P(N)/Q(N)]$ and $U = X_1 + X_2 + \ldots + X_N$ is a random sum, see (4). Then, for sequences generated by model A, we have

$$Var_A(X) = Var_{\mathcal{P}}[f(N)] + Var_{\mathcal{P}}(U) + 2Cov_A[f(N),U]. \tag{20}$$

We begin with the term $Var_{\mathcal{P}}[f(N)]$:

$$Var_{\mathcal{P}}[f(N)] = \mathbb{E}_{\mathcal{P}} f^2(N) - [\mathbb{E}_{\mathcal{P}} f(N)]^2 \leq \mathbb{E}_{\mathcal{P}} f^2(N). \tag{21}$$

Using the inequality $(x+y+z)^2 \le 3(x^2+y^2+z^2)$, we find on account of (14) that

$$\mathbb{E}_P f^2(N) = \sum_{j=0}^{\infty} P(j+\ell) \log^2 \frac{P(j+\ell)}{Q(j+\ell)} \le 3\,(a\log p - b\log q)^2$$

$$+3\log^2 \frac{1-p}{1-q} \sum_{j=0}^{\infty} j^2 P(j+\ell) + 3\sum_{j=0}^{\infty} c^2(j) P(j+\ell). \tag{22}$$

For the first term after the inequality sign in (22), we have, under the conditions in (18), $p^2(a\log p - b\log q)^2 \to 0$. Regarding the second term, we first estimate the second moment,

$$M_2(P) = \sum_{j=0}^{\infty} (j+\ell)^2 P(j+\ell),$$

of the TNBD $P = NB(a,p) + \alpha$ as follows:

$$M_2(P) = \frac{a(1-p)}{p^2} + \left(\frac{a}{p} + \alpha\right)^2 \le \frac{a + (a+\alpha)^2}{p^2} = \frac{a+\ell^2}{p^2}.$$

Therefore,

$$p^2 \log^2 \frac{1-p}{1-q} \sum_{j=0}^{\infty} j^2 P(j+\ell) \le p^2 \log^2 \frac{1-p}{1-q} \sum_{j=0}^{\infty} (j+\ell)^2 P(j+\ell)$$

$$\le (a+\ell^2) \log^2 \frac{1-p}{1-q} \to 0 \quad \text{as} \quad p,\, q \to 0.$$

Next, since $c^2(j)/j \to 0$ as $j \to \infty$, we conclude from Lemma 1 that

$$p \sum_{j=0}^{\infty} c^2(j) P(j+\ell) \to 0.$$

Combining the above limit relations for the three terms in Formula (22), we obtain $p^2 \mathbb{E}_P f^2(N) \to 0$, which, in view of (21), implies

$$p^2 Var_P[f(N)] \to 0. \tag{23}$$

We now focus on the second term in (20). According to the formula for the variance of a random sum [3],

$$Var_{\mathcal{P}}(U) = \sigma_{\mathcal{P}}^2\, \mathbb{E}_P N + \mu_{\mathcal{P}}^2\, Var_P(N) = \left(\frac{a}{p} + \alpha\right)\sigma_{\mathcal{P}}^2 + \frac{a(1-p)}{p^2}\mu_{\mathcal{P}}^2,$$

then

$$p^2 Var_{\mathcal{P}}(U) \to a\mu_{\mathcal{P}}^2 \quad \text{as} \quad p \to 0. \tag{24}$$

Finally, for the third term in (20), we obtain by the Cauchy–Schwarz inequality

$$p^2 \mid Cov_A[f(N), U] \mid \le \sqrt{p^2 Var_P[f(N)]}\sqrt{p^2 Var_{\mathcal{P}}(U)}.$$

It follows from (23) and (24) that $p^2 Cov_A[f(N), U] \to 0$.

In summary, Formula (20) and the limit relations for its terms yield $p^2 Var_A X \to a\mu_{\mathcal{P}}^2$.

To prove part (ii) of Proposition 1, notice that, in the case of model B, Formula (19) takes on the form

$$\mathbb{E}_B X = \mu_Q\left(\frac{b}{q} + \beta\right) - d_{KL}(Q, P),$$

which implies that if $p,\ q \to 0$ and $q \log p \to 0$, then $q\,\mathbb{E}_B X \to b\mu_{\mathcal{Q}}$. The proof of the limit relation for the variance of rv X under model B is identical to that for model A. □

Remark 2. *Asymptotic formulas for the expected value of rv X in Proposition 1 hold for any sequence of iid rvs (X_n) with finite expectation and, similarly, asymptotic formulas for the variance of rv X are valid for any such sequence of rvs with a finite second moment.*

3. Proof of Theorem 1

Because models A and B can be treated similarly, we only prove Theorem 1 for model A. As a preliminary, we compute the characteristic function (ch. f.) of rvs X and $Y = X/\mathbb{E}_A X$. To compute the ch. f. of rv X, denote by $\varphi_{\mathcal{P}}$ the ch. f. of rvs X_n for sequences generated by model A. Conditioning on rv N and using its independence of rvs $X_1, X_2, \ldots$, we find that

$$\Phi_X(s) = \mathbb{E}_A e^{isX} = \mathbb{E}_A e^{is[f(N)+U]} = \sum_{n=\ell}^{\infty} P(n) e^{is\log[P(n)/Q(n)]}\ \mathbb{E}_{\mathcal{P}} e^{is(X_1+X_2+\ldots+X_n)}$$

$$= \sum_{n=\ell}^{\infty} P(n) e^{is\log[P(n)/Q(n)]} \varphi_{\mathcal{P}}^n(s). \tag{25}$$

Also, for the ch. f. of rv Y, we have

$$\Phi_Y(t) = \mathbb{E}_A e^{itY} = \Phi_X(t/\mathbb{E}_A X). \tag{26}$$

The following result shows that the presence of the exponential factor $e^{is\log[P(n)/Q(n)]}$ in (25) does not affect the asymptotic behavior of $\Phi_X(t/\mathbb{E}_A X)$.

Lemma 3. *Under the conditions in (18),*

$$\Phi_X(t/\mathbb{E}_A X) - \sum_{n=\ell}^{\infty} P(n)\varphi_{\mathcal{P}}^n(t/\mathbb{E}_A X) \to 0\,, \quad t \in \mathbb{R}.$$

Proof. Recall that $|\ \varphi_{\mathcal{P}}(s)\ | \le 1$ for all $s \in \mathbb{R}$. Using the inequality $|\ e^{ix} - 1\ | \le |\ x\ |,\ x \in \mathbb{R}$, we obtain in view of (25)

$$|\ \Phi_X(s) - \sum_{n=\ell}^{\infty} P(n)\varphi_{\mathcal{P}}^n(s)\ | = |\ \sum_{n=\ell}^{\infty} P(n)\varphi_{\mathcal{P}}^n(s)\left(e^{is\log[P(n)/Q(n)]} - 1\right)\ |$$

$$\le \sum_{n=\ell}^{\infty} P(n)\ |\ e^{is\log[P(n)/Q(n)]} - 1\ | \le |\ s\ | \sum_{n=\ell}^{\infty} P(n)\ |\ \log\frac{P(n)}{Q(n)}\ |\,.$$

We set here $s = t/\mathbb{E}_A X$ and invoke (14) and (16) to find that

$$|\ \Phi_X(t/\mathbb{E}_A X) - \sum_{n=\ell}^{\infty} P(n)\varphi_{\mathcal{P}}^n(t/\mathbb{E}_A X)\ |$$

$$\le \frac{|\ t\ |}{p\,\mathbb{E}_A X}\left[ap\ |\ \log p\ | + bp\ |\ \log q\ | + a(1-p)\ |\ \log\frac{1-p}{1-q}\ | + S_p\right], \tag{27}$$

where

$$S_p = p\sum_{j=0}^{\infty} |\ c(j)\ |\ P(j+\ell)$$

and sequence $\{c(j)\}$ is defined by (15). By Lemma 1, we have $S_p \to 0$ as $p \to 0$. Also, in view of Proposition 1,under the conditions in (18),

$$p\,\mathbb{E}_A X \to a\mu_{\mathcal{P}} > 0. \tag{28}$$

The conclusion of Lemma 3 now follows immediately from (27). □

Next, we prove Theorem 1 starting with the limiting distribution of rv Y. To identify the latter, we have to find the limit of the ch. f. of rv Y given by (26). According to Lemma 3, we only have to compute the limit of the function

$$\Omega(s) = \sum_{n=\ell}^{\infty} P(n)\varphi_{\mathcal{P}}^{n}(s) = \Psi_P[\varphi_{\mathcal{P}}(s)]$$

evaluated at $s = t/\mathbb{E}_A X$, where

$$\Psi_P(z) = \sum_{n=\ell}^{\infty} P(n)z^n = z^{\alpha}\left[\frac{pz}{1-(1-p)z}\right]^a, \quad |z| < \frac{1}{1-p},$$

is the probability generating function of the TNBD $P = N(a,p) + \alpha$.

Since the distribution of rvs X_n under model $\mathcal{P}$ has a finite first moment, we can use the first-order Taylor expansion of its ch. f.:

$$\varphi_{\mathcal{P}}(s) = 1 + \varphi_{\mathcal{P}}'(0)s + s\rho(s) = 1 + i\mu_{\mathcal{P}}s + s\rho(s),$$

where $\rho(s) \to 0$ as $s \to 0$. Then,

$$\begin{aligned}\Omega(s) &= [\varphi_{\mathcal{P}}(s)]^{\alpha}\left[\frac{p\varphi_{\mathcal{P}}(s)}{1-(1-p)\varphi_{\mathcal{P}}(s)}\right]^a \\ &= [1 + i\mu_{\mathcal{P}}s + s\rho(s)]^{\alpha}\left[\frac{p(1 + i\mu_{\mathcal{P}}s + s\rho(s))}{1-(1-p)(1 + i\mu_{\mathcal{P}}s + s\rho(s))}\right]^a \\ &= [1 + i\mu_{\mathcal{P}}s + s\rho(s)]^{\alpha}\left[\frac{1 + i\mu_{\mathcal{P}}s + s\rho(s)}{1-(1-p)(i\mu_{\mathcal{P}} + \rho(s))s/p}\right]^a.\end{aligned}$$

Setting here $s = t/\mathbb{E}_A X$, we find, due to (28), that under the conditions in (18), s/p has a finite limit $t/(a\mu_{\mathcal{P}})$, which implies that $s \to 0$. Therefore, we conclude from (29) that

$$\Omega(t/\mathbb{E}_A X) \to \left(1 - \frac{it}{a}\right)^{-a}.$$

Thus, by Lemma 3, we also have

$$\Phi_Y(t) \to \left(1 - \frac{it}{a}\right)^{-a}. \tag{29}$$

This limiting function represents the ch. f. of the Erlang distribution $E(a,a)$.

To find the limiting distribution of rv Z under model A, notice that in view of (8)

$$Z = k(X)(Y-1), \tag{30}$$

where $k(X) = \mathbb{E}_A X/\sigma_A(X)$. By Proposition 1, under the conditions in (18)

$$k(X) \to a\mu_{\mathcal{P}}/(\sqrt{a}\mu_{\mathcal{P}}) = \sqrt{a}. \tag{31}$$

Therefore, from (30)–(32),

$$\Phi_Z(t) = e^{-ik(X)t}\Phi_Y[k(X)t] \to e^{-i\sqrt{a}\,t}\left(1 - \frac{it}{\sqrt{a}}\right)^{-a}.$$

Thus, the limiting distribution of rv Z under model A is the Erlang distribution $E(a,\sqrt{a})$ translated by $\sqrt{a}$ to the left, or symbolically $E(a,\sqrt{a}) - \sqrt{a}$.

The limiting ch. f. for rv Y under model B can be computed along similar lines. In this case, one has to take into account that $\mu_Q < 0$, which brings about a change of the sign in the analogs of formulas (28) and (32). As a result, under conditions $p,\ q \to 0$ and $q \log p \to 0$,

$$\Phi_Y(t) \to \left(1 - \frac{it}{b}\right)^{-b} \quad \text{and} \quad \Phi_Z(t) \to e^{i\sqrt{b}\,t}\left(1 + \frac{it}{\sqrt{b}}\right)^{-b}.$$

Therefore, the limiting distributions of rvs Y and Z are, respectively, the Erlang distribution $E(b,b)$ and the reflected Erlang distribution $E(b,\sqrt{b})$, translated by $\sqrt{b}$ to the right, or symbolically $\sqrt{b} - E(b,\sqrt{b})$.

Remark 3. *Theorem 1 holds for any sequence (X_n) of iid rvs with a finite second moment that has a positive expected value under model A and a negative expected value under model B.*

Remark 4. *It follows from (8) that, under model A, the distribution of rv X can be approximated by either an Erlang distribution $E(a,\lambda)$ with $\lambda = a\mathbb{E}_A X$ or by a transformed Erlang distribution $E(a,\gamma) + \tau$ with $\gamma = \sqrt{a}\,\sigma_A(X)$ and $\tau = \mathbb{E}_A X - \sqrt{a}\,\sigma_A(X)$. A similar remark also holds for model B.*

4. The Accuracy of the Likelihood-Based Classification of Random Sequences

Among the many measures of classification accuracy, perhaps the most informative ones are misclassification error rates $P_A(X \le 0)$ and $P_B(X \ge 0)$. The first of them represents the probability that a sequence generated by model A is not assigned to this model by the classification decision rule, i.e., it is either assigned to model B or not assigned to any model. A similar interpretation holds for the other error rate. An important question is whether, for very long sequences, the classification produces the correct result with a probability approaching 1; equivalently, this means that both misclassification error rates approach 0. We will call such a classification *asymptotically accurate*. The following statement about the asymptotic accuracy of the likelihood-based classification of random sequences described in the Introduction follows from Theorem 1.

Theorem 2. *Suppose that character selection probabilities $\mathcal{P}$ and $\mathcal{Q}$ for models A and B are distinct and that the sequence length distributions under these models are $P = NB(a,p) + \alpha$ and $Q = NB(b,q) + \beta$, respectively, with $a + \alpha = b + \beta = \ell$. If $p,\ q \to 0$ in such a way that $p \log q \to 0$ and $q \log p \to 0$, then the likelihood-based classification of such random sequences is asymptotically accurate.*

Proof. It follows from (28) that if p, q and $p \log q$ are all sufficiently small, then $\mathbb{E}_A X > 0$. Therefore, in view of Theorem 1 and due to the fact that the limiting distribution $E(a,a)$ does not have an atom at 0, we obtain

$$P_A(X \le 0) = P_A\left(\frac{X}{\mathbb{E}_A X} \le 0\right) \to P_A(V \le 0) = 0,$$

where V is a rv with Erlang distribution $E(a,a)$. Similarly, if p, q and $q \log p$ are all sufficiently small, then $\mathbb{E}_B X < 0$. Using Theorem 1, we conclude that

$$P_B(X \ge 0) = P_B\left(\frac{X}{\mathbb{E}_B X} \le 0\right) \to P_B(W \le 0) = 0,$$

where W is a rv with Erlang distribution $E(b,b)$. □

Recall that the meaning of the assumptions of Theorem 2 related to parameters p and q is that the expected length of long sequences generated by either model cannot be exponentially larger than that for sequences generated by the other model.

5. An Application to Genomics: Classification of DNA Sequences as Protein-Coding or Noncoding

In this section, we apply Theorem 1 to the classification of DNA sequences of bacterium *Bacillus subtilis* strain 168 as protein-coding or noncoding. *Bacillus subtilis* is a model bacterial organism with a well-annotated genome [15], which was extracted from the open source National Center for Biotechnology Information (NCBI) database (https://www.ncbi.nlm.nih.gov/nuccore/AF012532.1) accessed on 10 October 2023.

The annotated list of *Bacillus subtilis* genes is found at https://www.ncbi.nlm.nih.gov/genome/browse/#!/proteins/665/300274%7CBacillus%20subtilis%20subsp.%20subtilis%20str.%20168/chromosome/, accessed on 21 August 2023.

5.1. Background

Recall that (a) genetic information stored in the DNA can be represented as a sequence of nucleotides, A, C, T, G (adenine, cytosine, guanine, and thymine, respectively); (b) a protein is a sequence of amino acids; (c) each amino acid is encoded by one or several (up to six) triplets of DNA nucleotides, called *codons*; (d) a protein-coding gene is a sequence of codons encoding a protein; (e) the first codon of a gene is a START codon (typically ATG, encoding the amino acid methionine) signaling the start of transcription; (f) every gene is followed by a STOP triplet (TAA, TAG, or TGA) that does not encode an amino acid and signals the termination of the transcription process; (g) each gene belongs to one of the two complementary strands of the DNA; (h) genes of many prokaryotic organisms including all bacteria do not contain noncoding DNA segments, called *introns*. Thus, bacterial genes are contiguous sequences of codons starting with a START codon, followed by one of the three STOP triplets and not containing other in-frame STOP triplets. DNA sequences with these properties are called *open reading frames* (ORFs). DNA of various organisms, including *Bacillus subtilis,* contain numerous ORFs other than protein-coding genes. For more information about DNA, codons, genes, ORFs, amino acids, and proteins, see [16].

In what follows, we compare the Erlang distributions identified in Theorem 1 with the empirical distributions of the normalized log-likelihood scores Y and Z under models A and B associated with two respective classes of DNA sequences extracted from the *Bacillus subtilis* genome: protein-coding genes and a certain natural class, defined below, of protein noncoding ORFs. Parameters of these models of DNA sequence assembly were estimated based on the known membership of *Bacillus subtilis* ORFs in the two classes. A similar comparison can be performed for any other well-annotated prokaryotic genome without introns.

5.2. Protein-Coding Genes and Noncoding Open Reading Frames: Data and Models

The genome of *Bacillus subtilis* was found to contain no repeated genes or those with in-frame internal STOP triplets. A peculiar feature of the *Bacillus subtilis* genome is that only about 77.5% of its 4237 protein-coding genes begin with the standard START codon ATG. The vast majority of the remaining protein-coding genes begin with alternative START codons: TTG (coding for amino acid leucine) or GTG (coding for valine), which occur in 13% and 9% of all protein-coding genes, respectively. Additionally, 15 *Bacillus subtilis* protein-coding genes have nonstandard START codons: CTG encoding leucine and ATT encoding isoleucine.

To identify all protein noncoding ORFs within the *Bacillus subtilis* genome, we deleted all the protein-coding genes from the genome and read the resulting contiguous segments of nucleotides in the $5' \to 3'$ direction on the strand to which they belong. If the number, n, of nucleotides in any such segment was divisible by three then the segment was read in its natural frame; if n was of the form $n = 3k + 1$, then the segment was read in two reading frames (i.e., starting with the first or second nucleotide), while in the case $n = 3k + 2$, it was read in three reading frames (i.e., starting with the first, second, or third nucleotide). From all these reads, sequences of triplets beginning with the main START codon ATG utilized by *Bacillus subtilis*, followed by one of the STOP triplets, and not containing other in-frame STOP triplets were selected. This resulted in 4571 ORFs beginning with the standard START codon ATG. We will call them *standard noncoding ORFs*.

Note that some of them may actually represent genes encoding various kinds of RNA.

The following idea, borrowed from [10], allows one to view protein-coding genes and standard noncoding ORFs as randomly and independently assembled sequences of triplets of the kind discussed in the Introduction. Recall that any DNA sequence from each of these two classes is followed by a STOP triplet. Proceeding from any such STOP triplet, we move backwards adding new nucleotide triplets other than STOP triplets randomly and independently of each other. The alphabet used for such sequence assembly thus contains $M = 4^3 - 3 = 61$ triplets. The character selection probabilities for protein-coding genes and standard noncoding ORFs can be defined on empirical grounds as the respective frequencies of the 61 triplets found in all 4237 protein-coding genes and all 4571 standard noncoding ORFs, see Table 1. Also note that, under our independent model of DNA sequence assembly, the empirical frequency of a triplet coincides with the maximum likelihood estimate of the class-specific selection probability for the corresponding character given the data [8,17]. Based on the frequencies reported in Table 1, we found that $\mu_{\mathcal{P}} = 0.0709$, $\sigma_{\mathcal{P}} = 0.3575$ and $\mu_{\mathcal{Q}} = -0.0791$, $\sigma_{\mathcal{Q}} = 0.4182$.

Table 1. Observed frequencies of 61 triplets or codons for the two classes of DNA sequences of the *Bacillus subtilis* genome: *A* (protein-coding genes) and *B* (standard noncoding ORFs). Triplets are ordered lexicographically.

Triplets	*A*	*B*	Triplets	*A*	*B*
AAA	0.0496	0.0391	CTT	0.0232	0.0207
AAC	0.0172	0.0158	GAA	0.0493	0.0256
AAG	0.0211	0.0221	GAC	0.0186	0.0121
AAT	0.0223	0.0233	GAG	0.0232	0.0137
ACA	0.0223	0.0185	GAT	0.0332	0.0206
ACC	0.0086	0.0105	GCA	0.0217	0.0168
ACG	0.0145	0.0124	GCC	0.0159	0.0149
ACT	0.0087	0.0102	GCG	0.0202	0.0139
AGA	0.0108	0.0146	GCT	0.0190	0.0178
AGC	0.0142	0.0185	GGA	0.0218	0.0142
AGG	0.0038	0.0113	GGC	0.0235	0.0142
AGT	0.0066	0.0092	GGG	0.0112	0.0091
ATA	0.0094	0.0197	GGT	0.0127	0.0096
ATC	0.0271	0.0228	GTA	0.0134	0.0112
ATG	0.0271	0.0413	GTC	0.0174	0.0131
ATT	0.0372	0.0263	GTG	0.0178	0.0118
CAA	0.0197	0.0179	GTT	0.0193	0.0163
CAC	0.0074	0.0094	TAC	0.0121	0.0104
CAG	0.0187	0.0171	TAT	0.0228	0.0185
CAT	0.0153	0.0172	TCA	0.0148	0.0219
CCA	0.0070	0.0111	TCC	0.0080	0.0149
CCC	0.0033	0.0096	TCG	0.0063	0.0119
CCG	0.0159	0.0161	TCT	0.0129	0.0174
CCT	0.0105	0.0133	TGC	0.0043	0.0143
CGA	0.0040	0.0096	TGG	0.0103	0.0113
CGC	0.0085	0.0111	TGT	0.0036	0.0130
CGG	0.0064	0.0126	TTA	0.0192	0.0177
CGT	0.0074	0.0097	TTC	0.0142	0.0248
CTA	0.0049	0.0065	TTG	0.0155	0.0211
CTC	0.0109	0.0130	TTT	0.0308	0.0382
CTG	0.0233	0.0193			

In what follows, models A and B are used for describing DNA sequences representing protein-coding genes and standard noncoding ORFs, respectively. To specify these models completely, we need to determine their length distributions. Because the first triplet of any ORF is a START codon, random sequences anchored by a given STOP triplet and assembled as described above form a cluster of nested ORFs, each determined by the number, r, of START codons preceding the STOP triplet, as illustrated in Figure 1. Empirically, we found that the number r displays substantial variation, see Figure 2, showing the histogram for the values of r for all protein-coding genes beginning with the standard START codon ATG found in the *Bacillus subtilis* genome. According to our model of DNA sequence assembly, the length of protein-coding genes and standard noncoding ORFs with a *fixed* number $r \geq 1$ of START triplets ATG would follow respective negative binomial distributions $NB(r, p)$ and $NB(r, q)$, where $p = 0.0271$ and $q = 0.0413$ are the empirical frequencies of the START codon ATG for the two respective classes of ORFs, see Table 1. Therefore, the length distribution for protein-coding genes or standard noncoding ORFs is a mixture of such negative binomial distributions over all observed values of r, whose relative weights can also be determined empirically (for protein-coding genes with the START codon ATG, the absolute weights are given in Figure 2). Additionally, to encode functional proteins, genes have to be sufficiently long. In fact, the shortest protein-coding gene in the *Bacillus subtilis* genome has 20 codons. By comparison, the shortest standard noncoding ORF identified in this genome is 25 triplets long.

To account for such complexity of the length distribution, we assumed it to be TNBD $NB(a, p) + \alpha$ for model A and $NB(b, q) + \beta$ for model B, where $a + \alpha = b + \beta = \ell = 20$ triplets, with adjustable parameters a, b, p, q, to be estimated from the data.

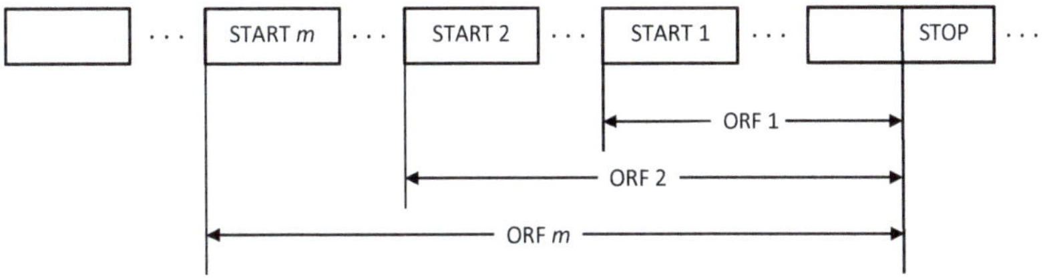

Figure 1. A nested cluster of ORFs anchored by a given STOP triplet. Empty boxes represent triplets of nucleotides other than START codons or STOP triplets. Reproduced with permission from [10].

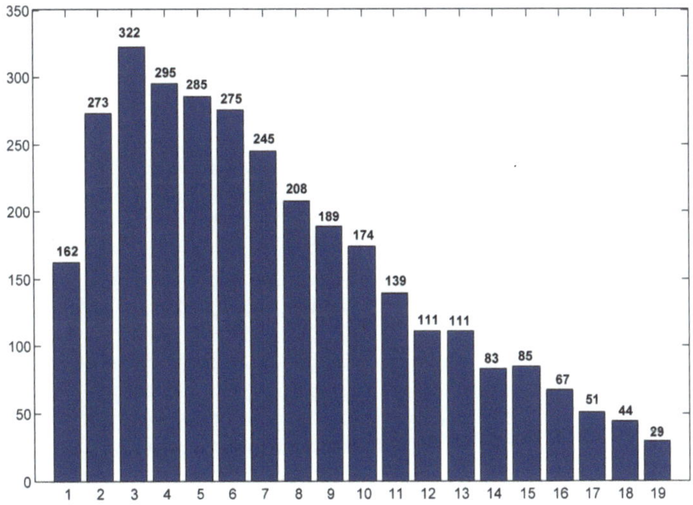

Figure 2. Histogram of the number of START codons ATG preceding a gene's STOP triplet for protein-coding *Bacillus subtilis* genes beginning with the START codon ATG.

5.3. Results

Parameters a, b, p, q of the two TNBDs were estimated by minimizing the total variation distance, d, between the assumed TNBDs and the empirical length distributions for protein-coding genes (model A) and standard noncoding ORFs (model B). The resulting optimal values were $a = 2,\ p = 0.0077$ for model A and $b = 1,\ q = 0.0467$ for model B, while the respective minimal total variation distances were found to be $d_A = 0.3945$ and $d_B = 0.4707$. Then, the translation parameters are $\alpha = \ell - a = 18$ codons for protein-coding genes and $\beta = \ell - b = 19$ triplets for standard noncoding ORFs. Thus, the best-fitting theoretical length distribution for standard noncoding ORFs is a translated geometric distribution $G(q) + \beta$. The relatively large magnitude of the minimum total variation distance is due to the fact that many lengths of protein-coding genes and standard noncoding ORFs carrying positive probabilities in the theoretical distributions are absent in the genome of *Bacillus subtilis*; yet another reason is the presence in this genome of a large number of anomalously long (in relative terms) sequences of both classes.

The profiles of the total variation distance as functions of parameters p and q for the optimal values $a = 2$ and $b = 1$ are shown in Figure 3. Notice that (i) if $p \to 0$ or $q \to 0$, then the corresponding theoretical length distributions "escape to infinity" so that $d \to 2$; (ii) if $p \to 1$, then $d \to 2[1 - P(20)]$, where $P(20) = 1/4237$ is the frequency of the minimum gene length of 20 codons; and (iii) by contrast, if $q \to 1$, then $d \to 2$ due to the fact that the shortest length of standard noncoding ORFs is 25 triplets rather than 20 triplets. The limiting behaviors (i)–(iii) are clearly seen in Figure 3. Finally, the estimated TNBDs and empirical length distributions approximated by suitable histograms are displayed in Figure 4A,B. We conclude from Figure 4 that TNBDs with the above-specified parameters provide an excellent visual fit to the empirical length distributions for the two classes of DNA sequences.

For the expected model-based lengths of protein-coding genes and standard noncoding ORFs, measured in triplets, we have

$$\mu_P = \frac{a}{p} + \alpha \simeq 278 \quad \text{and} \quad \mu_Q = \frac{b}{q} + \beta \simeq 40$$

while the corresponding standard deviations, also measured in triplets, are

$$\sigma_P = \frac{\sqrt{a(1-p)}}{p} \simeq 183 \quad \text{and} \quad \sigma_Q = \frac{\sqrt{b(1-q)}}{q} \simeq 21,$$

to be compared with their empirical counterparts $\bar{N}_A \simeq 290$, $\bar{N}_B \simeq 54$ and $s_A(N) \simeq 266$, $s_B(N) \simeq 91$. A few comments about the length distributions for the two classes of DNA sequences are in order:

(i) The genome of *Bacillus subtilis* contains a large number of very short standard noncoding ORFs. For example, the number of such ORFs with the length of 25 triplets (the shortest possible) is 273, while the number of those with the length ranging from 25 to 30 triplets is 1331 or 29%;

(ii) On average, protein-coding genes are much longer than standard noncoding ORFs. In fact, the ratio of their observed average lengths is about 5.4 and that of their model-based expected lengths is about 7.0;

(iii) The genome contains a significant number of very long protein-coding genes. The seven longest among them have lengths 3583, 3587, 3603, 4262, 4538, 5043, and 5488 codons, while the eighth longest gene is just 2561 codons long. This explains why the empirical standard deviation of gene length, $s_A(N) \simeq 266$ codons, is substantially larger than its theoretical counterpart, $\sigma_P \simeq 183$ codons. Without the seven longest genes, one would have $s_A(N) \simeq 208$ codons;

(iv) Although the number of anomalously long standard noncoding ORFs is disproportionately smaller than the number of very long protein-coding genes, their effect on the standard deviation of the length distribution is still considerable. For example, the longest standard noncoding ORF has 4428 triplets, while the length of the second longest ORF is 1190 triplets. Removing the longest ORF would reduce the standard deviation of ORF length from $s_B(N) \simeq 91$ to 64 triplets.

We also fitted TNBDs to the empirical length distribution for 3283 protein-coding genes beginning with the standard START codon ATG. This resulted in $a = 2$ (implying that $\alpha = 18$) and $p = 0.0078$, while the minimum total variation distance was 0.4313. Thus, the best-fitting TNBD is virtually indistinguishable from the same for the entire set of 4237 *Bacillus subtilis* protein-coding genes; however, surprisingly, the goodness of fit for the entire collection of genes is even better than for the seemingly more homogeneous subset of genes with the standard START codon ATG. That is why we used the entire set of protein-coding genes in our analysis.

Once models A and B are completely specified, one can evaluate the log-likelihood score X given by Formula (3) for each DNA sequence from either class. For the above-specified models of sequence length, the first term in (3) for any given sequence of length $N = n$ is

$$\log \frac{P(n)}{Q(n)} = \log \frac{p^2}{q} + \log(n-19) + (n-20)\log \frac{1-p}{1-q},$$

where $p = 0.0077$ and $q = 0.0467$. We then computed the class-specific normalized scores

$$Y_A = \frac{X}{\bar{X}_A}, \quad Y_B = \frac{X}{\bar{X}_B} \quad \text{and} \quad Z_A = \frac{X - \bar{X}_A}{s_A(X)}, \quad Z_B = \frac{X - \bar{X}_B}{s_B(X)},$$

where $\bar{X}_A \simeq 59.50$ and $\bar{X}_B \simeq -2.30$ are sample averages of the log-likelihood score X over all sequences in the two respective classes, while $s_A(X) \simeq 61.50$ and $s_B(X) \simeq 20.59$ are the corresponding sample standard deviations. Because the values of parameters p and q are small and have roughly the same order of magnitude, it would seem reasonable to compare empirical distributions of the samples Y_A, Y_B, Z_A, Z_B with the respective limiting distributions identified in Theorem 1, see Figures 5A,B and 6A,B, where empirical distributions are represented as histograms with appropriately chosen bins. We conclude from Figures 5 and 6 that the plain and transformed Erlang distributions found in Theorem 1 reproduce essential features of empirical distributions of the samples Y_A, Y_B, Z_A, Z_B such as range, shape, and mode fairly well.

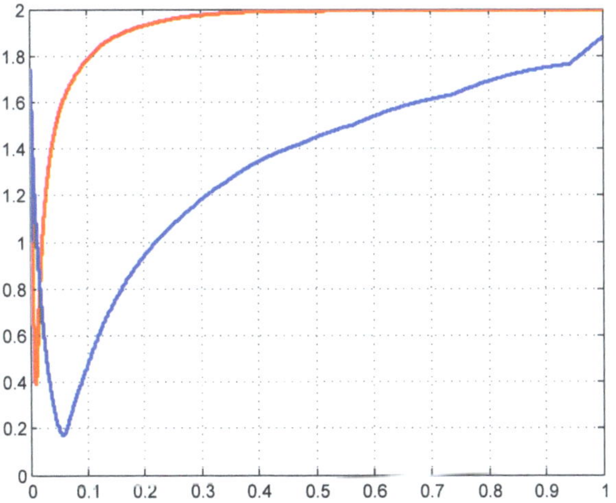

Figure 3. Red curve: plot of the total variation distance, d, between theoretical length distribution $NB(2, p) + 18$ for *Bacillus subtilis* protein-coding genes and its empirical counterpart as a function of parameter p. Blue curve: plot of the distance d between theoretical length distribution $G(q) + 19$ for *Bacillus subtilis* standard noncoding ORFs and its empirical counterpart as a function of parameter q.

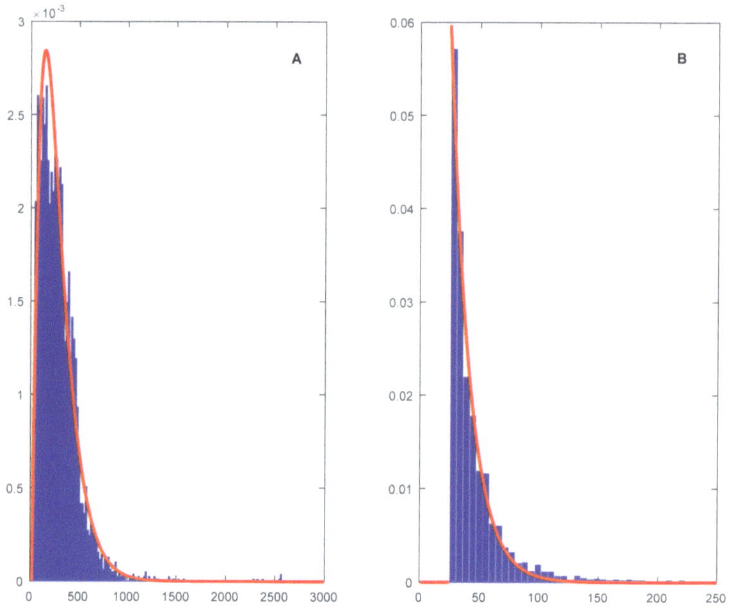

Figure 4. (**A**) Comparison of the empirical length distribution for all *Bacillus subtilis* protein-coding genes with the best-fitting TNBD $NB(2, p) + 18,\ p = 0.0077$. (**B**) Comparison of the empirical length distribution for *Bacillus subtilis* standard noncoding ORFs with the best-fitting translated geometric distribution $G(q) + 19,\ q = 0.0467$.

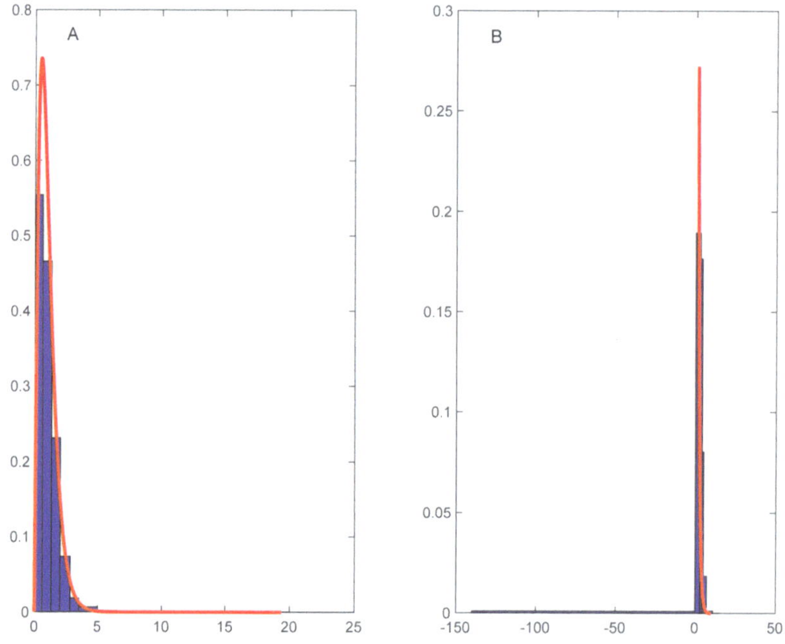

Figure 5. Comparison of the class-specific empirical distribution of the normalized log-likelihood score Y with its theoretical limiting counterpart identified in Theorem 1. (**A**) *Bacillus subtilis* protein-coding genes (class A); (**B**) *Bacillus subtilis* standard noncoding ORFs (class B).

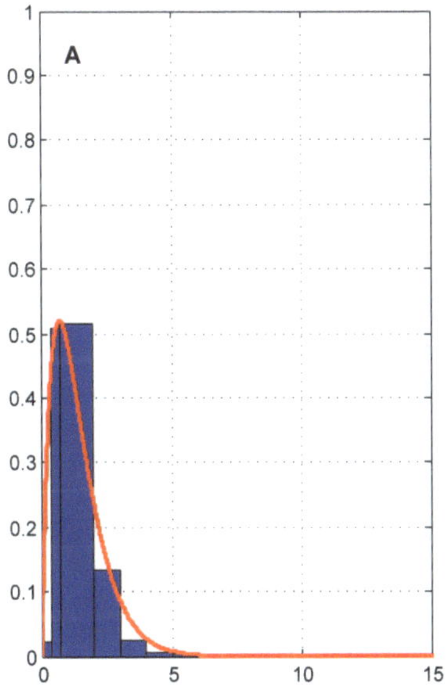

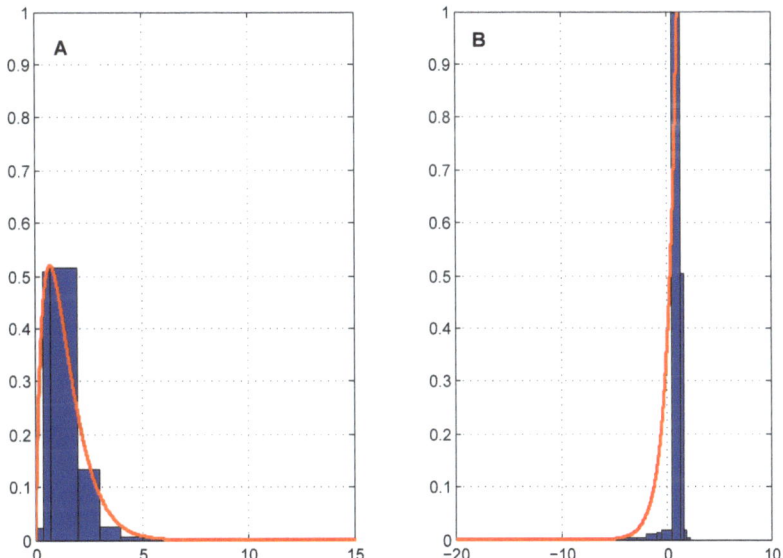

Figure 6. Comparison of the class-specific empirical distribution of the normalized log-likelihood score Z with its theoretical limiting counterpart identified in Theorem 1. (**A**) *Bacillus subtilis* protein-coding genes (class A); (**B**) *Bacillus subtilis* standard noncoding ORFs (class B).

6. Discussion

In this article, we derived a novel limit theorem for two natural normalizations, $Y = X/\mathbb{E}X$ and $Z = (X - \mathbb{E}X)/\sigma(X)$, of the log-likelihood score X, where the expectation and standard deviation are taken relative to either model A or B and it is assumed that the sequence length for these models follows respective TNBDs $NB(a,p) + \alpha$ and $NB(b,q) + \beta$. The limit theorem applies to long sequences ($p,q \to 0$) under the essential additional condition that the expected sequence length for either class is not exponentially larger than for the other class (more precisely, $p \log q \to 0$ and $q \log p \to 0$). The limiting distributions of rv Y under respective models A and B turned out to be Erlang distributions $E(a,a)$ and $E(b,b)$, while for rv Z, they came out as transformed Erlang distributions $E(a,\sqrt{a}) - \sqrt{a}$ and $\sqrt{b} - E(b,\sqrt{b})$, see Theorem 1. It is noteworthy that the limiting distributions depend on integer parameters a and b alone. Thus, the limiting behavior of the normalized log-likelihood score for long sequences represents, under the assumptions of Theorem 1, a fairly crude phenomenon.

Theorem 1 yields an important corollary: the asymptotic accuracy of the likelihood-based classification of random sequences, see Theorem 2.

To test the utility of our limit theorem, we applied it to the classification of open reading frames (ORFs), see Section 4, extracted from the genome of the bacterium *Bacillus subtilis* strain 168, as protein-coding genes (class A) and standard noncoding ORFs (class B). In this case, the alphabet consists of $M = 61$ triplets of DNA nucleotides other than STOP triplets. Since the genome of *Bacillus subtilis* is well annotated, class membership of all ORFs is known with certainty, which allowed us to empirically estimate character selection probabilities and length distributions for both classes of DNA sequences, see Table 1 and Figure 4. As was explained in Section 4, under the model of independent DNA sequence assembly, the length distributions for both classes are mixtures of negative binomial distributions, which we approximated, for each class of sequences, by a single TNBD. The best-fitting distributions from this family provided a surprisingly good fit to the empirical length distributions for both classes of DNA sequences, see Figure 4. This serves as an indirect validation of our model of DNA sequence assembly. This also corroborates earlier findings that the length of protein-coding genes in many organisms can be approximated by negative binomial distributions [6] or gamma distributions [18], which serve as a continuous analog of negative binomial distributions.

The aforementioned (transformed) Erlang distributions with $a = 2$ and $b = 1$ and their empirical counterparts (i.e., the distributions of the observed normalized log-likelihood scores Y and Z for the two classes of DNA sequences) are compared in Figures 5 and 6. They reveal that the theoretical limiting distributions provide a reasonable fit to the empirical distributions and capture some of their salient features such as range, shape, and mode. This is somewhat unexpected given that (a) the limiting distributions are one-parametric; (b) the model of random independent DNA sequence assembly is quite simplistic; (c) frequencies of the codons immediately following the START codon and immediately preceding the STOP triplet in protein-coding genes are distinct from those for internal codons [6]; and (d) our model disregards various additional features such as the presence in bacterial genomes of short regulatory nucleotide sequences at characteristic distances from the gene's START codon including ribosome binding sites (or Shine–Dalgarno sequences) and binding sites for transcription factors [5,6].

Our results can be applied to the classification of binary sequences ($M = 2$), DNA sequences viewed at the level of individual nucleotides ($M = 4$), and proteins represented as sequences of amino acids ($M = 20$). They may also potentially have applications in the areas of natural language processing and artificial intelligence.

The principal limitation of this work is the use of an independent (or zero-order Markov chain) model of sequence assembly. It was found long ago that DNA sequences are characterized by the presence of substantial short-range [7] and long-range [8] correlations between nucleotides and their triplets. As a result, efficient modern methods of computational gene finding employ higher-order, or even variable-order, Markov chain models and Hidden Markov models at the level of individual nucleotides [4–6]. For example, a gene finder called GeneMark [5] employs a 5th-order Markov chain model, while GLIMMER gene finder [4] combines k-th order Markov chain models for $0 \leq k \leq 8$. Although the accuracy of gene finding generally increases with k (the order of the Markov chain), the use of large values of k is prohibited by the large number, 4^{k+1}, of Markov transition probabilities that have to be estimated from a training set and the sparsity of $(k+1) -$ tuples of nucleotides used for estimation purposes. Thus, to make our limit theorem a better discriminator between protein-coding genes and noncoding ORFs in prokaryotic genomes, it should be extended to higher-order Markov chain models and Hidden Markov models of DNA sequence assembly, and to more general sequence length distributions including translated mixtures of negative binomial distributions.

On the mathematical side, our limit theorem would be more practical if augmented with a tight estimate of the Zolotarev metric [9,14] or another suitable distance [19] between the empirical distribution of the normalized log-likelihood score and its theoretical limiting counterpart.

Author Contributions: Methodology, L.H.; Formal analysis, L.H. and L.P.; Investigation, L.H. and L.P.; Writing—original draft, L.H.; Writing—review and editing, L.H. and L.P. All authors have read and agreed to the published version of the manuscript.

Funding: This research received no external funding.

Institutional Review Board Statement: Not applicable.

Informed Consent Statement: Not applicable.

Data Availability Statement: Not applicable.

Acknowledgments: We are grateful to Yegor Marin for his help with the extraction and processing of bioinformatics data on *Bacillus subtilis*. We also acknowledge the helpful comments and suggestions by three anonymous reviewers.

Conflicts of Interest: The authors declare no conflict of interest.

References

1. Hardy, G.H.; Littlewood, J.E.; Polya, G. *Inequalities*, 2nd ed.; Cambridge University Press: Cambridge, UK, 1952.
2. Kullback, S.; Leibler, R.A. On information and sufficiency. *Ann. Math. Stat.* **1951**, *22*, 79–86. [CrossRef]
3. Ross, S.M. *Introduction to Probability Models*, 6th ed.; Academic Press: San Diego, CA, USA, 1997.
4. Salzberg, S.L.; Delcher, A.L.; Kasif, S.; White, O. Microbial gene identification using interpolated Markov models. *Nucleic Acids Res.* **1998**, *26*, 544–548. [CrossRef] [PubMed]
5. Besemer, J.; Lomsadze, A.; Borodovsky, M. GeneMarkS: A self-training method for prediction of gene starts in microbial genomes. Implications for finding sequence motifs in regulatory regions. *Nucleic Acids Res.* **2001**, *29*, 2607–2618. [CrossRef]
6. Larsen, T.S.; Krogh, A. EasyGene—A prokaryotic gene finder that ranks ORFs by statistical significance. *BMC Bioinform.* **2003**, *4*, 21. [CrossRef] [PubMed]
7. Almagor, H. A Markov analysis of DNA sequences. *J. Theor. Biol.* **1983**, *104*, 633–645. [CrossRef] [PubMed]
8. Li, W. The study of correlation structures of DNA sequences: A critical review. *Comput. Chem.* **1997**, *21*, 257–271. [CrossRef] [PubMed]
9. Korolev, V. Bounds for the rate of convergence in the generalized Rényi theorem. *Mathematics* **2022**, *10*, 4252. [CrossRef]
10. Hanin, L. A tour of discrete probability guided by a problem in genomics. *Coll. Math. J.* **2020**, *51*, 284–294. [CrossRef]
11. Rényi, A. A characterization of Poisson processes. *Magy. Tud. Akad. Mat. Kut. Int. Kzl.* **1957**, *1*, 519–527.
12. Gnedenko, B.V. Limit theorems for sums of a random number of positive independent random variables. In Proceedings of the 6th Berkeley Symposium on Mathematical Statistics and Probability, Berkeley, CA, USA, 21 June–18 July 1970 ; pp. 537–549.
13. Korolev, V.Y.; Zeifman, A.I. Bounds for convergence rate in laws of large numbers for mixed Poisson random sums. *Stat. Probab. Lett.* **2021**, *168*, 108918. [CrossRef]
14. Zolotarev, V.M. Properties of and relations among certain types of metrics. *J. Sov. Math.* **1981**, *17*, 2218–2232. [CrossRef]
15. Kunst, F.J.; Ogasawara, N.; Moszer, I.; Albertini, A.M.; Alloni, G.; Azevedo, V.; Bertero, M.G.; Bessières, P.; Bolotin, A.; Borchert, S.; et al. The complete genome sequence of the gram-positive bacterium bacillus subtilis. *Nature* **1997**, *390*, 249–256. [CrossRef] [PubMed]
16. Watson, J.D.; Baker, T.A.; Bell, S.P.; Gann, A.; Levine, M.; Losick, R. *Molecular Biology of the Gene*, 6th ed.; Pearson Education: Cold Spring Harbor, NY, USA, 2008.
17. Ekisheva, S.; Borodovsky, M. Probabilistic models for biological sequences: Selection and Maximum Likelihood estimation. *Int. J. Bioinform. Res. Appl.* **2006**, *2*, 305–324. [CrossRef] [PubMed]
18. Tiessen, A.; Pérez-Rodríguez, P.; Delaya-Oredondo, L.J. Mathematical modeling and comparison of protein size distribution in different plant, animal, fungal and microbial species reveals a negative correlation between protein size and protein number, thus providing insight into the evolution of proteomes. *BMC Res. Notes* **2012**, *5*, 85. [CrossRef] [PubMed]
19. Rachev, S.T.; Klebanov, L.; Stoyanov, S.V.; Fabozzi, F. *The Methods of Distances in the Theory of Probability and Statistics*; Springer: New York, NY, USA, 2013.

mathematics

MDPI

Article

Estimates of the Convergence Rate in the Generalized Rényi Theorem with a Structural Digamma Distribution Using Zeta Metrics

Alexey Kudryavtsev [1,2,*] and Oleg Shestakov [1,2,3,*]

1 Faculty of Computational Mathematics and Cybernetics, M. V. Lomonosov Moscow State University, Moscow 119991, Russia
2 Moscow Center for Fundamental and Applied Mathematics, Moscow 119991, Russia
3 Federal Research Center "Computer Science and Control" of the Russian Academy of Sciences, Moscow 119333, Russia
* Correspondence: aakudryavtsev@cs.msu.ru (A.K.); oshestakov@cs.msu.ru (O.S.)

Abstract: This paper considers a generalization of the Rényi theorem to the case of a structural distribution with a scale parameter. In terms of the zeta metric, some estimates of the convergence rate in the generalized Rényi theorem are obtained when the structural mixed Poisson distribution of the summation index is a scale mixture of the generalized gamma distribution. Estimates of the convergence rate for the structural digamma distribution are given as a special case. The paper extends the results previously obtained for the generalized gamma distribution.

Keywords: generalized Rényi theorem; estimates of the convergence rate; generalized gamma distribution; digamma distribution; zeta metrics

MSC: 60F05

Citation: Kudryavtsev, A.; Shestakov, O. Estimates of the Convergence Rate in the Generalized Rényi Theorem with a Structural Digamma Distribution Using Zeta Metrics. *Mathematics* **2023**, *11*, 4477. https://doi.org/10.3390/math11214477

Academic Editor: Jin-Ting Zhang

Received: 20 September 2023
Revised: 20 October 2023
Accepted: 27 October 2023
Published: 29 October 2023

1. Introduction

Beta and gamma classes of distributions traditionally play an important role in modeling real processes with the use of probability theory techniques. The properties of infinite divisibility and stability inherent to some types of generalized gamma and beta distributions make it possible to use them as adequate asymptotic approximations in various popular limit theorems.

In 1925, the Italian researcher L. Amoroso, who studied the problems of dynamic equilibrium, considered the distribution [1], a special form of which is usually called the generalized gamma distribution $GG(\nu, p, \delta)$ with the density

$$g_{\nu,p,\delta}(x) = \frac{|\nu| x^{\nu p-1} e^{-(x/\delta)^{\nu}}}{\delta^{\nu p}\Gamma(p)}, \quad \nu \neq 0, \quad p > 0, \quad \delta > 0, \quad x > 0. \tag{1}$$

This distribution, along with its special cases, has found wide application in the study of many applied problems.

A natural generalization of distributions from the gamma class is the digamma distribution proposed in [2,3].

Definition 1. *A random variable $\rho_\delta \equiv \rho_{r,\nu,p,q,\delta}$ has a digamma distribution $DiG(r, \nu, p, q, \delta)$ with the characteristic index $r \in \mathbb{R}$ and the parameters of shape $\nu \neq 0$, concentration $p, q > 0$ and scale $\delta > 0$, if its Mellin transform is*

$$\mathcal{M}_{\rho_\delta}(z) = \frac{\delta^z \Gamma(p + z/\nu)\Gamma(q - rz/\nu)}{\Gamma(p)\Gamma(q)}, \quad p + \frac{\mathrm{Re}(z)}{\nu} > 0, \quad q - \frac{r\mathrm{Re}(z)}{\nu} > 0. \tag{2}$$

In addition to the generalized gamma distribution (1), the special cases of digamma distribution (2) also include [2,3] the generalized beta distribution of the second kind (McDonald distribution) [4] used primarily in econometrics and regression analysis, as well as the gamma-exponential distribution [5,6], proposed as a link between the gamma and beta classes.

The possibility of representing the digamma distribution as a scale mixture of generalized gamma laws

$$\rho_\delta \stackrel{d}{=} \delta \left(\frac{\lambda}{\mu^r} \right)^{1/\nu}, \tag{3}$$

where independent random variables λ and μ have gamma distributions $GG(1,p,1)$ and $GG(1,q,1)$, respectively, makes it possible to use the digamma distribution in the analysis of balance models [7,8], particulary for studying the asymptotic properties of the integral balance index [9].

One of the first and most important limit theorems related to the gamma family is the Rényi theorem [10] about the convergence of random sums with a geometric summation index to the standard exponential distribution. The classical Rényi theorem has a number of generalizations. In particular, it can be shown [9] that (2) can arise as a limiting distribution in the case when a mixed Poisson index is used instead of a geometric one.

The main accompanying task in the study of the asymptotic behavior of random sums is to estimate the rate of convergence to the limit law [11–15]. In particular, in Refs. [16–18], the estimation of the convergence rate in the Rényi theorem and some of its generalizations was carried out using the zeta metric, which was proposed in 1976 by V.M. Zolotarev [19]. The introduction of the zeta metric was motivated by the following considerations. Since in the presence of convergence there is always a question about its rate, it is necessary to have some metric that can be used to evaluate the accuracy of the approximation. When considering a weak convergence, it would also be desirable to have some "natural" metric. However, the class of continuous bounded functions present in the definition of weak convergence is too wide for presenting some convenient metric. For this reason, Zolotarev proposed to narrow the consideration to the class of Lipschitz differentiable bounded functions.

The paper proves a generalization of the Rényi theorem to the case of structural distributions that have a scale parameter. The results extend the approaches of [16–18], proposed for generalized gamma distributions, and are devoted to estimating the convergence rate in the generalized Rényi theorem with structural mixed generalized gamma distributions. In particular, some results for the structural digamma distribution are given.

2. Representations for Generalized Gamma and Negative Binomial Distributions

By $N_{p,0}$, we denote a random variable with the geometric distribution supported on non-negative integers:

$$\mathsf{P}(N_{p,0} = n) = p(1-p)^n, \ n = 0, 1, \ldots, \ p \in (0,1).$$

Let $S_{p,0}$ be the corresponding geometric random sum

$$S_{p,0} = \sum_{j=1}^{N_{p,0}} X_j.$$

Denote

$$S_n = \sum_{i=1}^{n} X_i, \ S_0 = 0.$$

By $G_{\nu,p,\delta}$, we denote a random variable having a generalized gamma distribution $GG(\nu,p,\delta)$ with the density (1). In what follows, a special form of (1) will be of particular interest, namely, the exponential distribution $GG(1,1,\delta)$.

Let $N_1(t)$ be the standard Poisson process. Let $N_1(t)$ and $G_{\nu,p,\delta}$ be independent for all t. We say that the random variable $N_{\nu,p,\delta} \equiv N_1(G_{\nu,p,\delta})$ has a generalized negative binomial distribution $GNB(\nu, p, \delta)$ [16]. Note that $N_{\nu,p,\delta t} \stackrel{d}{=} N_1(G_{\nu,p,\delta} t)$.

In Ref. [16], the following statement was proved.

Lemma 1. *If $\nu \in (0,1)$ and $p \in (0,1]$, then the generalized negative binomial distribution is the $Y_{\nu,p,\delta}$-mixed geometric distribution:*

$$\mathsf{P}(N_{\nu,p,\delta} = k) = \int_0^1 y(1-y)^k \, d\mathsf{P}(Y_{\nu,p,\delta} < y), \; k = 0,1,\ldots,$$

where the random variable $Y_{\nu,p,\delta}$ has the density

$$h_{\nu,p,\delta}(y) = \frac{\delta^2}{\Gamma(1-p)\Gamma(p)} \cdot \frac{1}{(1-y)^2} \int_1^\infty \frac{f_{\nu,1}(\delta^\nu y(1-y)^{-1} x^{-1/\nu}) \, dx}{(x-1)^p x^{1+2/\nu}}, \; 0 < y < 1, \tag{4}$$

where $f_{\nu,1}(x)$, $0 < \nu < 1$, is the density of a one-sided strictly stable law supported on the positive half-line, with a characteristic function

$$\phi_{\nu,1}(t) = \exp\left\{-|t|^\nu \exp\left\{-\frac{1}{2} i\pi\nu \mathrm{sgn} t\right\}\right\}.$$

In Ref. [17], the following statement for continuous analogues of generalized negative binomial and geometric distributions is proved.

Lemma 2. *If $\nu \in (0,1)$ and $p \in (0,1]$, then the generalized gamma distribution is a mixed exponential distribution:*

$$g_{\nu,p,\delta}(z) = \int_0^1 \frac{y}{1-y} e^{-\frac{y}{1-y} z} \cdot h_{\nu,p,\delta}(y) \, dy, \; z > 0,$$

where the density $h_{\nu,p,\delta}(y)$ is defined in (4).

3. Generalization of the Rényi Theorem for Distributions with a Scale Parameter

This section presents a generalization of the classical Rényi theorem [10] for structural distributions with a scale parameter [20]. The following theorem weakens the convergence requirements compared to the generalized Rényi theorem proved in Ref. [9].

Definition 2. *A random variable Λ has a distribution $D(\ldots, \delta)$ with the scale parameter $\delta > 0$, if $\hat{\Lambda} \stackrel{d}{=} \Lambda/\delta$ has a distribution $D(\ldots, 1)$, independent of δ.*

Note that all continuous distributions listed above have a scale parameter.

Let $\Lambda \sim D(\ldots, \delta)$ be a non-negative random variable with the scale parameter δ. Consider the standard Poisson process $N_1(t)$ and a sequence of identically distributed random variables $X_1, X_2, \ldots$ with a finite mathematical expectation $\mathsf{E}X_1 = a \neq 0$. Assume that $N_1(t), \Lambda, X_1, X_2, \ldots$ are independent for any $t \geq 0$.

Theorem 1. *Let $\hat{\Lambda} \stackrel{d}{=} \Lambda/\delta$. Then,*

$$\frac{S_{N_1(\Lambda t)}}{a\delta t} \Longrightarrow \hat{\Lambda}, \; \delta t \to \infty. \tag{5}$$

Proof of Theorem 1. Note that

$$\lim_{\delta t \to \infty} \mathsf{E} \exp\left\{is\left(\frac{N_1(\Lambda t)}{\delta t} - \frac{\Lambda}{\delta}\right)\right\} = 1.$$

Hence,

$$\frac{N_1(\Lambda t)}{\delta t} - \frac{\Lambda}{\delta} \xrightarrow{\mathsf{P}} 0, \quad \delta t \to \infty.$$

Since the distribution of $\hat{\Lambda}$ does not depend on δ, according to the Slutsky theorem [21], we conclude that

$$\frac{N_1(\Lambda t)}{\delta t} \Longrightarrow \hat{\Lambda}, \quad \delta t \to \infty.$$

The relation (5) follows from the transfer theorem for random sums, e.g., Theorem 2.2.1 from Ref. [22]. The theorem is proved. □

Remark 1. *Theorem 1 does not require that the parameters δ and t simultaneously tend to infinity.*

4. Estimation of the Rate of Convergence in the Classical Rényi Theorem Using the Zeta Metric

The Rényi theorem is a classical limit theorem. In the study of asymptotic approximations, the rate of convergence to the limit law is of particular interest. One of the approaches to analyzing the convergence rate is based on the use of an ideal metric.

Consider the ζ-metric proposed by V.M. Zolotarev. To demonstrate the importance of this metric, recall that the sequence of random variables Y_n weakly converges to the random variable Y if

$$\Delta_n = \mathsf{E}(f(Y_n) - f(Y)) \longrightarrow 0$$

as $n \to \infty$ for all $f \in \mathcal{F}$, where $\mathcal{F}$ is the set of all bounded and continuous functions. However, it is inconvenient to use the values of Δ_n to construct the convergence rate boundaries, since $\mathcal{F}$ is too large. V.M. Zolotarev proposed a definition of the so-called ideal ζ-metric, which narrows the class $\mathcal{F}$ to a subclass of Lipschitz differentiable bounded functions.

Let us introduce a formal definition of this metric. Let s be a positive number. Then, $s = m + \varepsilon$, where m is a non-negative integer and $\varepsilon \in (0,1]$. Let $\mathcal{F}_s$ be the set of all m times differentiable real-valued bounded functions f for which

$$\left| f^{(m)}(x) - f^{(m)}(y) \right| \le |x - y|^{\varepsilon}.$$

The ζ-metric $\zeta_s(X,Y) \equiv \zeta_s(F_X, F_Y)$ [19] is defined as

$$\zeta_s(X,Y) \equiv \zeta_{\mathcal{F}_s}(X,Y) = \sup_{f \in \mathcal{F}_s} |\mathsf{E}(f(X) - f(Y))|;$$

see also Refs. [23,24].

Note that the ζ-metric has the following property [24]:

$$\zeta_s(cX, cY) = c^s \zeta_s(X,Y), \quad c > 0. \tag{6}$$

According to the classical Rényi theorem, a geometric random sum, normalized by its mathematical expectation, weakly converges to the standard exponential distribution:

$$\frac{pS_{p,0}}{a(1-p)} \Longrightarrow G_{1,1,1}. \tag{7}$$

In the Refs. [18,25], the following estimates of the convergence rate in (7) were obtained in terms of ζ-metrics.

Lemma 3. *Suppose that $p \in (0,1)$. Let $X_1, X_2, \ldots$ be a sequence of identically distributed random variables independent of $N_{p,0}$ with $\mathsf{E}X_1 = a \neq 0$ and $\mathsf{E}X_1^2 < \infty$. Then,*

$$\zeta_1\left(\frac{p\sum_{i=1}^{N_{p,0}} X_i}{a(1-p)}, G_{1,1,1}\right) \leq \frac{p}{1-p}\cdot\frac{\mathsf{E}X_1^2}{a^2}.$$

Lemma 4. *Suppose that* $p \in (0,1)$. *Let* $X_1, X_2, \ldots$ *be a sequence of identically distributed random variables independent of* $N_{p,0}$ *with* $\mathsf{E}X_1 = a \neq 0$ *and* $\mathsf{E}X_1^2 < \infty$. *Then, for* $1 \leq s \leq 2$

$$\zeta_s\left(\frac{p\sum_{i=1}^{N_{p,0}} X_i}{a(1-p)}, G_{1,1,1}\right) \leq \frac{1}{s}\left[\frac{p}{1-p}\cdot\frac{\mathsf{E}X_1^2}{a^2}\right]^{s/2},$$

in particular,

$$\zeta_2\left(\frac{p\sum_{i=1}^{N_{p,0}} X_i}{a(1-p)}, G_{1,1,1}\right) \leq \frac{p}{2(1-p)}\cdot\frac{\mathsf{E}X_1^2}{a^2}.$$

5. Convergence Rate Estimates in the Generalized Rényi Theorem with a Structural Generalized Gamma Distribution

The statements of this section are the generalization of the results proved in Refs. [16,18] for the structural gamma distribution.

Lemma 5. *Suppose that* $\nu \in (0,1]$ *and* $p \in (0,1)$. *Let* $X_1, X_2, \ldots$ *be a sequence of identically distributed random variables with* $\mathsf{E}X_1 = a \neq 0$ *and* $N_1(t), G_{\nu,p,\delta}, X_1, X_2, \ldots$ *be independent for all* $t \geq 0$. *Then,*

$$\zeta_s\left(\frac{\sum_{i=1}^{N_1(G_{\nu,p,\delta t})} X_i}{a\delta t}, G_{\nu,p,1}\right) \leq \frac{1}{(\delta t)^s}\int_0^1 \frac{(1-y)^s}{y^s}\zeta_s\left(\frac{yS_{y,0}}{(1-y)a}, G_{1,1,1}\right)\cdot h_{\nu,p,\delta t}(y)\,dy$$

where the density $h_{\nu,p,\delta t}(y)$ *is defined in (4).*

Proof of Lemma 5. According to the property (6) of ζ-metrics

$$\zeta_s\left(\frac{\sum_{i=1}^{N_1(G_{\nu,p,\delta t})} X_i}{a\delta t}, G_{\nu,p,1}\right) = \frac{1}{(a\delta t)^s}\zeta_s\left(\sum_{i=1}^{N_1(G_{\nu,p,\delta t})} X_i, aG_{\nu,p,\delta t}\right).$$

Using Lemma 1, we get

$$\mathsf{P}\left(\sum_{i=1}^{N_1(G_{\nu,p,\delta t})} X_i < x\right) = \sum_{n=0}^{\infty}\int_0^1 y(1-y)^n h(y;\nu,p,\delta t)\,dy\mathsf{P}(S_n < x)$$

$$= \int_0^1 \sum_{n=0}^{\infty} y(1-y)^n \mathsf{P}(S_n < x) h(y;\nu,p,\delta t)\,dy = \int_0^1 \mathsf{P}(S_{y,0} < x) h(y;\nu,p,\delta t)\,dy.$$

Therefore, for any continuous bounded function f

$$\mathsf{E}f\left(\sum_{i=1}^{N_1(G_{\nu,p,\delta t})} X_i\right) = \int_0^1 \mathsf{E}f(S_{y,0})h(y;\nu,p,\delta t)\,dy.$$

Similarly, using Lemma 2,

$$\mathsf{E}f(aG_{\nu,p,\delta t}) = \int_0^\infty f(az)g_{\nu,p,\delta t}(z)\,dz = \int_0^1 \mathsf{E}f\left(aG_{1,1,\frac{1-y}{y}}\right)\cdot h_{\nu,p,\delta t}(y)\,dy.$$

Hence,

$$\zeta_s\left(\sum_{i=1}^{N_1(G_{\nu,p,\delta t})} X_i, aG_{\nu,p,\delta t}\right) = \sup_{f\in\mathcal{F}_s}\left|\mathsf{E}f\left(\sum_{i=1}^{N_1(G_{\nu,p,\delta t})} X_i\right) - \mathsf{E}f(aG_{\nu,p,\delta t})\right|$$

$$= \sup_{f\in\mathcal{F}_s}\left|\int_0^1 \mathsf{E}f(S_{y,0})h_{\nu,p,\delta t}(y)\,dy - \int_0^1 \mathsf{E}f\left(aG_{1,1,\frac{1-y}{y}}\right)\cdot h_{\nu,p,\delta t}(y)\,dy\right|$$

$$\leq \int_0^1 \zeta_s\left(S_{y,0}, aG_{1,1,\frac{1-y}{y}}\right)\cdot h_{\nu,p,\delta t}(y)\,dy$$

Thus,

$$\zeta_s\left(\frac{\sum_{i=1}^{N_1(G_{\nu,p,\delta t})} X_i}{a\delta t}, G_{\nu,p,1}\right) \leq \frac{1}{(a\delta t)^s}\int_0^1 \zeta_s\left(S_{y,0}, aG_{1,1,\frac{1-y}{y}}\right)\cdot h_{\nu,p,\delta t}(y)\,dy$$

$$= \frac{1}{(\delta t)^s}\int_0^1 \frac{(1-y)^s}{y^s}\zeta_s\left(\frac{yS_{y,0}}{(1-y)a}, G_{1,1,1}\right)\cdot h_{\nu,p,\delta t}(y)\,dy.$$

The lemma is proved. □

The following statement is a generalization of Lemmas 3 and 4 to the case of a structural generalized gamma distribution.

Lemma 6. *Suppose that $\nu \in (0,1]$ and $p \in (0,1)$. Let $X_1, X_2, \ldots$ be a sequence of identically distributed random variables with $\mathsf{E}X_1 = a \neq 0$, $\mathsf{E}X_1^2 < \infty$ and $N_1(t), G_{\nu,p,\delta}, X_1, X_2, \ldots$ be independent for all $t \geq 0$. Then,*

$$\zeta_1\left(\frac{\sum_{i=1}^{N_1(G_{\nu,p,\delta t})} X_i}{a\delta t}, G_{\nu,p,1}\right) \leq \frac{\mathsf{E}X_1^2}{a^2\delta t};$$

for $1 \leq s \leq 2$

$$\zeta_s\left(\frac{\sum_{i=1}^{N_1(G_{\nu,p,\delta t})} X_i}{a\delta t}, G_{\nu,p,1}\right) \leq \frac{1}{(\delta t)^{s/2}}\cdot\frac{\Gamma(p+s/(2\nu))}{s\Gamma(p)\Gamma(1+s/2)}\cdot\left[\frac{\mathsf{E}X_1^2}{a^2}\right]^{s/2},$$

in particular,

$$\zeta_2\left(\frac{\sum_{i=1}^{N_1(G_{\nu,p,\delta t})} X_i}{a\delta t}, G_{\nu,p,1}\right) \leq \frac{1}{\delta t}\cdot\frac{\Gamma(p+1/\nu)}{\Gamma(p)}\cdot\frac{\mathsf{E}X_1^2}{2a^2}.$$

Proof of Lemma 6. From Lemma 3 we get

$$\zeta_1\left(\frac{yS_{y,0}}{(1-y)a}, G_{1,1,1}\right) \leq \frac{y}{1-y}\cdot\frac{\mathsf{E}X_1^2}{a^2}.$$

Hence,

$$\zeta_1\left(\frac{\sum_{i=1}^{N_1(G_{\nu,p,\delta t})} X_i}{a\delta t}, G_{\nu,p,1}\right) \leq \frac{1}{\delta t}\int_0^1 \frac{1-y}{y}\zeta_1\left(\frac{yS_{y,0}}{(1-y)a}, G_{1,1,1}\right)\cdot h_{\nu,p,\delta t}(y)\,dy \leq \frac{\mathsf{E}X_1^2}{a^2\delta t}.$$

Let $1 \leq s \leq 2$. Then, by Lemma 4

$$\zeta_s\left(\frac{\sum_{i=1}^{N_1(G_{\nu,p,\delta t})} X_i}{a\delta t}, G_{\nu,p,1}\right) \leq \frac{1}{(\delta t)^s}\int_0^1 \frac{(1-y)^s}{y^s}\zeta_s\left(\frac{yS_{y,0}}{(1-y)a}, G_{1,1,1}\right)\cdot h_{\nu,p,\delta t}(y)\,dy$$

$$\leq \frac{1}{(\delta t)^s}\int_0^1 \frac{(1-y)^s}{y^s}\frac{1}{s}\left[\frac{y}{1-y}\cdot\frac{\mathsf{E}X_1^2}{a^2}\right]^{s/2}\cdot h_{\nu,p,\delta t}(y)\,dy$$

$$= \frac{1}{(\delta t)^s}\cdot\frac{1}{s}\cdot\left[\frac{\mathsf{E}X_1^2}{a^2}\right]^{s/2}\mathsf{E}\frac{(1-Y_{\nu,p,\delta t})^{s/2}}{Y_{\nu,p,\delta t}^{s/2}}.$$

Since by Lemma 2

$$G_{\nu,p,\delta}\stackrel{d}{=}\frac{1-Y_{\nu,p,\delta}}{Y_{\nu,p,\delta}}\cdot G_{1,1,1},$$

where $Y_{\nu,p,\delta}$ and $G_{1,1,1}$ can be considered independent, we obtain

$$\mathsf{E}(G_{\nu,p,\delta})^{s/2} = \mathsf{E}G_{1,1,1}^{s/2}\mathsf{E}\left(\frac{1-Y_{\nu,p,\delta t}}{Y_{\nu,p,\delta t}}\right)^{s/2}.$$

Thus,

$$\zeta_s\left(\frac{\sum_{i=1}^{N_1(G_{\nu,p,\delta t})} X_i}{a\delta t}, G_{\nu,p,1}\right) \leq \frac{1}{(\delta t)^s}\cdot\frac{1}{s}\cdot\left[\frac{\mathsf{E}X_1^2}{a^2}\right]^{s/2}\frac{\mathsf{E}(G_{\nu,p,\delta})^{s/2}}{\mathsf{E}G_{1,1,1}^{s/2}}$$

$$= \frac{1}{(\delta t)^{s/2}}\cdot\frac{\Gamma(p+s/(2\nu))}{s\Gamma(p)\Gamma(1+s/2)}\cdot\left[\frac{\mathsf{E}X_1^2}{a^2}\right]^{s/2}.$$

The lemma is proved. □

6. Convergence Rate Estimates in a Generalized Rényi Theorem with a Structural Mixed Generalized Gamma Distribution

This section provides an estimate of the convergence rate in the generalized Rényi theorem with a structural distribution that is a scale mixture of the generalized gamma distribution.

Let Q be a non-negative random variable.

Theorem 2. *Suppose that $\nu \in (0,1]$ and $p \in (0,1)$. Let $X_1, X_2, \ldots$ be a sequence of identically distributed random variables with $\mathsf{E}X_1 = a \neq 0$ and $Q, N_1(t), G_{\nu,p,\delta}, X_1, X_2, \ldots$ be independent for all $t \geq 0$. Assume that there is an estimate*

$$\zeta_s\left(\frac{\sum_{i=1}^{N_1(G_{\nu,p,\delta t})} X_i}{a\delta t}, G_{\nu,p,1}\right) \leq \Delta_s(\delta t).$$

Then,

$$\zeta_s\left(\frac{\sum_{i=1}^{N_1(Q\cdot G_{\nu,p,\delta t})} X_i}{a\delta t}, Q\cdot G_{\nu,p,1}\right) \leq \int_0^\infty y^s \Delta_s(y\delta t)\,dF_Q(y).$$

Proof of Theorem 2. Averaging over the distribution of Q, we obtain

$$\zeta_s\left(\frac{\sum_{i=1}^{N_1(Q\cdot G_{\nu,p,\delta}t)}X_i}{a\delta t}, Q\cdot G_{\nu,p,1}\right)=\int_0^\infty \zeta_s\left(\frac{\sum_{i=1}^{N_1(G_{\nu,p,\delta}yt)}X_i}{a\delta t}, yG_{\nu,p,1}\right)dF_Q(y)$$

$$\leq \int_0^\infty y^s\Delta_s(y\delta t)\,dF_Q(y).$$

The theorem is proved. □

Lemma 6 and Theorem 2 imply the validity of the following statements.

Corollary 1. *Suppose that $\nu \in (0,1]$ and $p \in (0,1)$. Let $X_1, X_2, \ldots$ be a sequence of identically distributed random variables with $\mathsf{E}X_1 = a \neq 0$, $\mathsf{E}X_1^2 < \infty$, and $Q, N_1(t), G_{\nu,p,\delta}, X_1, X_2, \ldots$ be independent for all $t \geq 0$. Then,*

$$\zeta_1\left(\frac{\sum_{i=1}^{N_1(G_{\nu,p,\delta}t)}X_i}{a\delta t}, G_{\nu,p,1}\right)\leq \frac{\mathsf{E}X_1^2}{a^2\delta t},$$

and hence,

$$\zeta_1\left(\frac{\sum_{i=1}^{N_1(Q\cdot G_{\nu,p,\delta}t)}X_i}{a\delta t}, Q\cdot G_{\nu,p,1}\right)\leq \frac{\mathsf{E}X_1^2}{a^2\delta t}.$$

Corollary 2. *Suppose that $\nu \in (0,1]$ and $p \in (0,1)$. Let $X_1, X_2, \ldots$ be a sequence of identically distributed random variables with $\mathsf{E}X_1 = a \neq 0$, $\mathsf{E}X_1^2 < \infty$, and $Q, N_1(t), G_{\nu,p,\delta}, X_1, X_2, \ldots$ be independent for all $t \geq 0$. Then by Lemma 4 and Theorem 3 for $1 \leq s \leq 2$*

$$\zeta_s\left(\frac{\sum_{i=1}^{N_1(G_{\nu,p,\delta}t)}X_i}{a\delta t}, G_{\nu,p,1}\right)\leq \frac{1}{(\delta t)^{s/2}}\cdot\frac{\Gamma(p+s/(2\nu))}{s\Gamma(p)\Gamma(1+s/2)}\cdot\left[\frac{\mathsf{E}X_1^2}{a^2}\right]^{s/2},$$

and hence,

$$\zeta_s\left(\frac{\sum_{i=1}^{N_1(Q\cdot G_{\nu,p,\delta}t)}X_i}{a\delta t}, Q\cdot G_{\nu,p,1}\right)\leq \frac{\mathsf{E}Q^{s/2}}{(\delta t)^{s/2}}\cdot\frac{\Gamma(p+s/(2\nu))}{s\Gamma(p)\Gamma(1+s/2)}\cdot\left[\frac{\mathsf{E}X_1^2}{a^2}\right]^{s/2}.$$

In particular,

$$\zeta_2\left(\frac{\sum_{i=1}^{N_1(Q\cdot G_{\nu,p,\delta}t)}X_i}{a\delta t}, Q\cdot G_{\nu,p,1}\right)\leq \frac{\mathsf{E}Q}{\delta t}\cdot\frac{\Gamma(p+1/\nu)}{\Gamma(p)}\cdot\frac{\mathsf{E}X_1^2}{2a^2}.$$

As a special case of a scale mixture of the generalized gamma distribution, consider the digamma distribution: $\rho_\delta \sim DiG(r,\nu,p,q,\delta)$.

Since the representation (3) in the form of a scale mixture of generalized gamma distributions is valid for the digamma distribution, the following statements hold.

Corollary 3. *Suppose that $\nu \in (0,1]$, $p \in (0,1)$ or $-\nu/r \in (0,1]$, $q \in (0,1)$. Let $X_1, X_2, \ldots$ be a sequence of identically distributed random variables with $\mathsf{E}X_1 = a \neq 0$, $\mathsf{E}X_1^2 < \infty$, and $N_1(t), \rho_\delta, X_1, X_2, \ldots$ be independent for all $t \geq 0$. Then,*

$$\zeta_1\left(\frac{\sum_{i=1}^{N_1(\rho_\delta t)}X_i}{a\delta t}, \rho_1\right)\leq \frac{\mathsf{E}X_1^2}{a^2\delta t}.$$

Corollary 4. *Suppose that $\nu \in (0,1]$, $p \in (0,1)$ or $-\nu/r \in (0,1]$, $q \in (0,1)$. Let $X_1, X_2, \ldots$ be a sequence of identically distributed random variables with $\mathsf{E}X_1 = a \neq 0$, $\mathsf{E}X_1^2 < \infty$, and $N_1(t), \rho_\delta, X_1, X_2, \ldots$ be independent for all $t \geq 0$. Then, for $1 \leq s \leq 2$*

$$\zeta_s\left(\frac{\sum_{i=1}^{N_1(\rho_\delta t)} X_i}{a\delta t}, \rho_1\right) \leq \frac{1}{(\delta t)^{s/2}} \cdot \frac{\Gamma(q - rs/(2\nu))}{\Gamma(q)} \cdot \frac{\Gamma(p + s/(2\nu))}{s\Gamma(p)\Gamma(1+s/2)} \cdot \left[\frac{\mathsf{E}X_1^2}{a^2}\right]^{s/2}.$$

In particular,

$$\zeta_2\left(\frac{\sum_{i=1}^{N_1(\rho_\delta t)} X_i}{a\delta t}, \rho_1\right) \leq \frac{1}{\delta t} \cdot \frac{\Gamma(q - r/\nu)}{\Gamma(q)} \cdot \frac{\Gamma(p + 1/\nu)}{\Gamma(p)} \cdot \frac{\mathsf{E}X_1^2}{2a^2} = \frac{\mathsf{E}\rho_1}{\delta t} \cdot \frac{\mathsf{E}X_1^2}{2a^2}.$$

7. Conclusions

In this paper, a generalization of the Rényi theorem is obtained for a class of structural distributions with a scale parameter, which includes a generalized gamma distribution and a generalized beta distribution of the second kind. For the case when the distribution of the summation index is a scale mixture of the generalized gamma distribution, the estimates of the convergence rate in the generalized Rényi theorem are obtained, expressed in terms of zeta metrics. In particular, such estimates are obtained for the structural digamma distribution that arises in the study of Bayesian balance models. The paper extends the results previously obtained only for the generalized gamma distribution.

Author Contributions: Conceptualization, A.K. and O.S.; methodology, A.K. and O.S.; formal analysis, A.K. and O.S.; investigation, A.K. and O.S.; writing—original draft preparation, A.K. and O.S.; writing—review and editing, A.K. and O.S.; supervision, A.K. and O.S.; funding acquisition, O.S. All authors have read and agreed to the published version of the manuscript.

Funding: This research was supported by the Ministry of Science and Higher Education of the Russian Federation, project No. 075-15-2020-799.

Data Availability Statement: Data sharing not applicable.

Conflicts of Interest: The authors declare no conflict of interest.

References

1. Amoroso, L. Ricerche intorno alla curva dei redditi. *Ann. Mat. Pura Appl.* **1925**, *21*, 123–159. [CrossRef]
2. Kudryavtsev, A.A.; Nedolivko, Y.N.; Shestakov, O.V. Main Probabilistic Characteristics of the Digamma Distribution and the Method of Estimating Its Parameters. *Moscow Univ. Comput. Math. Cybern.* **2022**, *46*, 79–86. [CrossRef]
3. Kudryavtsev, A.A.; Shestakov, O.V. Limit distributions for the estimates of the digamma distribution parameters constructed from a random size sample. *Mathematics* **2023**, *11*, 1778. [CrossRef]
4. McDonald, J.B. Some Generalized Functions for the Size Distribution of Income. *Econometrica* **1984**, *52*, 647–665. [CrossRef]
5. Kudryavtsev, A.A. On the representation of gamma-exponential and generalized negative binomial distributions. *Inform. Appl.* **2019**, *13*, 78–82. (In Russian)
6. Kudryavtsev, A.A.; Shestakov, O.V. The estimators of the bent, shape and scale parameters of the gamma-exponential distribution and their asymptotic normality. *Mathematics* **2022**, *10*, 619. [CrossRef]
7. Kudryavtsev, A.A. Bayesian balance models. *Inform. Appl.* **2018**, *12*, 18–27. (In Russian)
8. Kudryavtsev, A.A.; Shestakov, O.V. Asymptotically normal estimators for the parameters of the gamma-exponential distribution. *Mathematics* **2021**, *9*, 273. [CrossRef]
9. Kudryavtsev, A.A.; Shestakov, O.V. Digamma Distribution as a Limit for the Integral Balance Index. *Moscow Univ. Comput. Math. Cybern.* **2022**, *46*, 133–139. [CrossRef]
10. Kalashnikov, V.V. *Geometric Sums: Bounds for Rare Events with Applications;* Kluwer Academic Publishers: Dordrecht, The Netherlands, 2013.
11. Pekoz, E.A.; Rollin, A. New rates for exponential approximation and the theorems of Renyi and Yaglom. *Ann. Probab.* **2011**, *39*, 587–608. [CrossRef]
12. Hung, T.L. On the rate of convergence in limit theorems for geometric sums. *Southeast Asian J. Sci.* **2013**, *2*, 117–130.

13. Hung, T.L.; Kein, P.T. On the rates of convergence in weak limit theorems for normalized geometric sums. *Bull. Korean Math. Soc.* **2020**, *57*, 1115–1126.
14. Slepov, N.A. Convergence rate of random geometric sum distributions to the Laplace law. *Theory Probab. Appl.* **2021**, *66*, 121–141. [CrossRef]
15. Bulinski, A.; Slepov, N. Sharp Estimates for Proximity of Geometric and Related Sums Distributions to Limit Laws. *Mathematics* **2022**, *10*, 4747. [CrossRef]
16. Korolev, V.Y; Zeifman, A.I. Generalized negative binomial distributions as mixed geometric laws and related limit theorems. *Lith. Math. J.* **2019**, *59*, 366–388. [CrossRef]
17. Shevtsova, I.; Tselishchev, M. On the Accuracy of the Generalized Gamma Approximation to Generalized Negative Binomial Random Sums. *Mathematics* **2021**, *9*, 1571. [CrossRef]
18. Korolev, V. Bounds for the Rate of Convergence in the Generalized Renyi Theorem. *Mathematics* **2022**, *10*, 4252. [CrossRef]
19. Zolotarev, V.M. Approximation of distributions of sums of independent random variables with values in infinite-dimensional spaces. *Theory Probab. Appl.* **1976**, *21*, 721–737. [CrossRef]
20. Chen, W.; Xie, M.; Wu, M. Parametric estimation for the scale parameter for scale distributions using moving extremes ranked set sampling. *Stat. Probab. Lett.* **2013**, *83*, 2060–2066. [CrossRef]
21. Serfling, R.J. *Approximation Theorems of Mathematical Statistics*; John Wiley & Sons, Inc.: New York, NY, USA, 2002.
22. Gnedenko, B.V.; Korolev, V.Y. *Random Summation: Limit Theorems and Applications*; CRC Press: Boca Raton, FL, USA, 1996.
23. Zolotarev, V.M. Ideal metrics in the problem of approximating distributions of sums of independent random variables. *Theory Probab. Appl.* **1977**, *22*, 433–449. [CrossRef]
24. Zolotarev, V.M. *Modern Theory of Summation of Random Variables*; VSP: Utrecht, The Netherlands, 1997.
25. Shevtsova, I.; Tselishchev, M. A generalized equilibrium transform with application to error bounds in the Renyi theorem with no support constraints. *Mathematics* **2020**, *8*, 577. [CrossRef]

Article

Limit Distributions of Products of Independent and Identically Distributed Random 2 × 2 Stochastic Matrices: A Treatment with the Reciprocal of the Golden Ratio

Santanu Chakraborty

School of Mathematical and Statistical Sciences, University of Texas Rio Grande Valley, 1201 West University Drive, Edinburg, TX 78539-2999, USA; santanu.chakraborty@utrgv.edu

Abstract: Consider a sequence $(X_n)_{n \geq 1}$ of i.i.d. 2×2 stochastic matrices with each X_n distributed as μ. This μ is described as follows. Let $(C_n, D_n)^T$ denote the first column of X_n and for a given real r with $0 < r < 1$, let $r^{-1}C_n$ and $r^{-1}D_n$ each be Bernoulli distributions with parameters p_1 and p_2, respectively, and $0 < p_1, p_2 < 1$. Clearly, the weak limit of the sequence μ^n, namely λ, is known to exist, whose support is contained in the set of all 2×2 rank one stochastic matrices. In a previous paper, we considered $0 < r \leq \frac{1}{2}$ and obtained λ explicitly. We showed that λ is supported countably on many points, each with positive λ-mass. Of course, the case $0 < r \leq \frac{1}{2}$ is tractable, but the case $r > \frac{1}{2}$ is very challenging. Considering the extreme nontriviality of this case, we stick to a very special such r, namely, $r = \frac{\sqrt{5}-1}{2}$ (the reciprocal of the golden ratio), briefly mention the challenges in this nontrivial case, and completely identify λ for a very special situation.

Keywords: random walk; stochastic matrices; limiting measure; golden ratio

MSC: 60B15

1. Introduction

As the title of the paper suggests, the reader can understand that this paper deals with a situation where one considers products of independent and identically distributed random 2×2 stochastic matrices and their limiting behavior. In other words, here we are considering a probability measure μ on a collection of 2×2 stochastic matrices and studying the limiting behavior of the convolution sequence μ^n. To a reader new to this area, the author would like to refer the reader to the book by Hognas and Mukherjea [1]. This book starts from the very basic concepts, such as the definition of a semigroup, topological semigroups, semigroups of matrices, etc., in chapter 1 and then moves forward to more complex concepts, such as probability measures of semigroups, convolution products of probabilities and convergence, random walks on semigroups, random walks on semigroups of nonnegative matrices (and in particular stochastic matrices), etc. The current author collaborated on a few papers in this area [2–6].

For complete understanding of this article, we will go over a few details about convergence of convolution products of probability measures on semigroups of matrices. If $\mathbb{B}$ denotes the collection of Borel subsets of a set S, then $P(S)$ can be the set of all regular probability measures μ on $\mathbb{B}$. Then, denoting the collection of continuous functions on S as $C(S)$, for $\mu, \nu \in P(S)$, and $f \in C(S)$, one defines the following iterated integral:

$$I(f) = \int \int f(xy) \mu(dx) \nu(dy)$$

By the Riesz representation theorem, there exists a unique regular probability measure λ such that for any function $f \in C(S)$ with compact support, we have

Citation: Chakraborty, S. Limit Distributions of Products of Independent and Identically Distributed Random 2 × 2 Stochastic Matrices: A Treatment with the Reciprocal of the Golden Ratio. *Mathematics* **2023**, *11*, 4993. https://doi.org/10.3390/math11244993

Academic Editors: Irina Shevtsova and Victor Korolev

Received: 27 September 2023
Revised: 4 December 2023
Accepted: 6 December 2023
Published: 18 December 2023

Copyright: © 2023 by the author. Licensee MDPI, Basel, Switzerland. This article is an open access article distributed under the terms and conditions of the Creative Commons Attribution (CC BY) license (https://creativecommons.org/licenses/by/4.0/).

$$I(f) = \int f d\lambda$$

Then, λ is called the convolution of the probability measures μ and ν. There is a proposition in [1] that shows that for $\mu, \nu \in P(S)$, and $B \in \mathbb{B}$,

$$\mu * \nu(B) = \int \mu(Bx^{-1})\nu(dx) = \int \nu(x^{-1}B)\mu(dx)$$

Having defined the convolution product of regular probability measures on semigroups, one can consider a sequence of regular probability measures $\mu_1, \mu_2, \mu_3, \ldots$, construct a sequence of convolution products of these regular probability measures $\mu_1, \mu_1 \star \mu_2, \mu_1 \star \mu_2 \star \mu_3, \ldots$, and talk about conditions when such convolution sequences will converge. Then, one can specialize to the independent identically distributed situation where for each i, we have, $\mu_i = \mu$ for $i = 1, 2, 3, \ldots$. Then, the convolution sequence looks like μ^n for $n = 1, 2, 3, \ldots$. In all these situations, [1] assumes that S is a locally compact, second countable Hausdorff topological semigroup.

Then, if someone further specializes to the situation when S is a semigroup of non-negative matrices or say, stochatic matrices of a fixed order d, then one considers the usual matrix topology. There have been quite a few papers that study the conditions when the convolution sequence μ^n converges. Mukherjea [7] first gave conditions when such a sequence converges for i.i.d. 2×2 stochastic matrices. Then, subsequently such conditions for higher order stochastic matrices were obtained [5,6]. But none of these papers performed detailed study on the nature of the corresponding limiting measures. But motivated by a paper by Chamayou and Letac [8], we have investigated the nature of the limiting measure λ for a very special μ on 2×2 i.i.d. stochastic matrices.

Before proceeding further, let us denote the probability measure on stochastic matrices of a fixed order d by μ and its support by $S(\mu)$. So, $S(\mu)$ is a subcollection of stochastic matrices of a fixed order d. Thus, for any convolution product μ^n, we will denote its support by $S(\mu^n)$ and the support of the limiting measure λ (if it exists) by $S(\lambda)$.

If we denote the closure of an arbirary set E by $\overline{E}$, then

$$S(\mu^n) = \overline{\{A_1 A_2 \cdots A_n \mid \text{for each } i,\ A_i \in S(\mu),\ 1 \le i \le n\}}$$

where n is a positive integer and

$$\mathcal{S} = \overline{\cup_{n=1}^{\infty} S(\mu^n)}$$

Also, denote $\mathbb{P}$ to be the set of $d \times d$ strictly positive stochastic matrices in $\mathcal{S}$.

Chamayou and Letac [8] proved that if $(X_n)_{n \ge 1}$ is a sequence of $d \times d$ i.i.d. stochastic matrices such that $P(\min_{i,j}(X_1)_{ij} = 0) < 1$, then $Y = \lim_{n \to \infty} X_n X_{n-1} \cdots X_1$ exists almost surely and $P(Y \text{ has rank } 1) = 1$; furthermore, if for any Borel B of $d \times d$ stochastic matrices (with usual R^{d^2}-topology), we denote $\mu(B) = P(X_1 \in B)$ and $\lambda(B) = P(Y \in B)$, and then λ is the unique solution of the convolution equation $\lambda \star \mu = \lambda$.

Then, in [2], we noted that this wonderful result of Chamayou and Letac also holds under the (slightly weaker) condition that $\mu^m(\mathbb{P}) > 0$ for some positive integer m (as opposed to just 1, instead of m, taken in [8]) where μ^m is the distribution of the product $X_m \cdots X_1$ and $\mathbb{P}$ is the set of $d \times d$ strictly positive stochastic matrices. The reason is as follows: the Chamayou and Letac result shows that under the weaker condition, the subsequence $Y_{nm} = X_{nm} X_{nm-1} \cdots X_1$ converges almost surely to some $d \times d$ rank one stochastic matrix, Y_0, and consequently, any subsequence $X_{n_k} X_{n_k - 1} \cdots X_1$ with $n_k > s_k m$ (for some s_k) will also converge almost surely to a $d \times d$ stochastc matrix $VY_0 (= Y_0$, as Y_0 has rank one), where V is a limit point of the product subsequence $X_{n_k} X_{n_k - 1} \cdots X_{s_k m + 1}$. This establishes our observation.

Next we mention below some situations when $S(\lambda)$ consists of all rank one matrices:

Situation 1: If $(X_i)_{i\geq 1}$, as before, is i.i.d. $d \times d$ stochastic matrices such that for some positive integer $m \geq 1$,

$$\mu^m(\mathbb{P}) > 0 \tag{1}$$

then the sequence μ^n, where $\mu(B) = P(X_1 \in B)$ for Borel sets B of $d \times d$ stochastic matrices, converges weakly to a probability measure λ and $S(\lambda)$ consists of all rank one stochastic matrices in $\mathcal{S}$ such that $\lambda(\mathbb{P}) > 0$.

Situation 2: When λ is the weak limit of $(\mu^n)_{n\geq 1}$ and $\mathcal{S}$ contains a rank one matrix, then the support of λ, $S(\lambda)$ consists of all rank one stochastic matrices in $\mathcal{S}$. This is an algebraic fact for the support of an idempotent probability measure (note that $\lambda = \lambda \star \lambda$; see [1]).

In the same paper, Chamayou and Letac (see also [9]) tried to identify λ in the case when the rows of X_1 above are independent, and for $1 \leq i \leq d$, the i-th row of X_1 has Dirichlet distribution with positive parameters $\alpha_{i1}, \alpha_{i2}, \ldots, \alpha_{id}$, and they were successful in the case when $\sum_{j=1}^{d} \alpha_{ij} = \sum_{j=1}^{d} \alpha_{ji}$, $1 \leq i \leq d$. Indeed, there are only very few (other than those given in [8–10]) examples in the literature even for 2×2 stochastic matrices when the limit distribution λ has been identified completely in the above context. Our paper [2] is an example.

In [2], we considered 2×2 i.i.d. stochastic matrices $(X_n)_{n\geq 1}$ with $X_n = \begin{pmatrix} C_n & 1-C_n \\ D_n & 1-D_n \end{pmatrix}$, each X_n is distributed as μ and $r^{-1}C_n$ and $r^{-1}D_n$ are each Bernoulli distributions (with possibly different parameters p_1 and p_2, $0 < p_1, p_2 < 1$) for a real r satisfying $0 < r \leq 1$. Our goal was to identify λ, the distribution of $\lim_{n\to\infty} X_n X_{n-1} \cdots X_1$. Clearly, there are exactly four matrices in the support of μ, each with positive mass. It is well known that that μ^n converges weakly to a limiting measure λ and the support of λ consists of rank one matrices. In particular, if r equals 1, the support of λ has exactly two matrices, namely, $\begin{pmatrix} 0 & 1 \\ 0 & 1 \end{pmatrix}$ and $\begin{pmatrix} 1 & 0 \\ 1 & 0 \end{pmatrix}$. In [2], a complete solution is given to the problem for $0 < r \leq \frac{1}{2}$ and also for $r = 1$.

The situation $\frac{1}{2} < r < 1$ is much more challenging. Before explaining where the challenge lies, let us make the following convention:

From now on, we will often denote the matrix $\begin{pmatrix} x & 1-x \\ x & 1-x \end{pmatrix}$ by simply x when there is no fear of confusion. Thus, for the limiting measure λ, $\lambda(x)$ will mean $\lambda\begin{pmatrix} x & 1-x \\ x & 1-x \end{pmatrix}$ and if we write that the support of λ, $S(\lambda)$ is contained in $[0, 1]$, then this means the following:

$$S(\lambda) \subset \left\{ \begin{pmatrix} x & 1-x \\ x & 1-x \end{pmatrix} : 0 \leq x \leq 1 \right\}$$

Now, we are going to explain why the case $\frac{1}{2} < r < 1$ is more challenging. Although we find it quite easy to observe that $\lambda(0)$ and $\lambda(r)$ have the same expressions as in the previous case, it is indeed hard to exhibit a point in $(0, r)$ with positive λ-mass.

However, there is a special situation when things are more tractable, namely, $r = \frac{\sqrt{5}-1}{2}$ (the reciprocal of the golden ratio). We denote this special r as r_g. Notice that r_g satisfies the equation $r_g^2 + r_g - 1 = 0$. Using this equation extensively, we completely solve for λ in this particular situation. It can be seen that although this is just one case, the proof is highly nontrivial. According to the author, the reason why r_g works for us is because of the fact that $\lambda(1 - r_g)$ could be found out easily and so this technique of proof worked.

It may be mentioned here that there have been numerous studies in the literature involving the golden ratio. One very recent study invloving golden ratio is in the context of machine learning [11].

As in the case of $0 < r \leq \frac{1}{2}$, here also λ is discrete with masses at countably many points. Our main theorem appears in Section 4.

One gets a feeling that for any other r satisfying $\frac{1}{2} < r < 1$, finding the value of $\lambda(1-r)$ itself will be a challenge, making it quite nontrivial. Thus, for a general $\frac{1}{2} < r < 1$, a different technique of proof might be needed to obtain a complete solution.

In the next section (Section 2), we describe our set up, state the results proved in [2] for $0 < r \leq \frac{1}{2}$, and briefly discuss the more challenging situation $\frac{1}{2} < r < 1$. In Section 3, we focus on $r = r_g = \frac{\sqrt{5}-1}{2}$ (reciprocal of the golden ratio) and prove two important propostions. We prove our main theorem and a series of lemmas leading to it in Section 4. We have some concluding remarks and comments in Section 5.

2. Preliminaries

In our case, we are considering the case of a probability measure μ on 2×2 stochastic matrices. $S(\mu)$ denotes its support, which is a subcollection of 2×2 stochastic matrices. $S(\mu^n)$ denotes the support of μ^n where μ^n is the convolution sequence. As pointed out in [7], μ^n converges if and only if $S(\mu)$ is not a singleton:

$$S(\mu) \neq \left\{ \begin{pmatrix} 0 & 1 \\ 1 & 0 \end{pmatrix} \right\}$$

And in case there is a strictly positive matrix in $S(\mu)$, then the support $S(\lambda)$ of the limiting measure λ consists of rank one matrices. Our special case satisfies that condition:

We consider 2×2 i.i.d. stochastic matrices $(X_n)_{n \geq 1}$ with $X_n = \begin{pmatrix} C_n & 1-C_n \\ D_n & 1-D_n \end{pmatrix}$, such that each X_n is distributed as μ. Also, assume that for a given r with $0 < r \leq 1$, both $r^{-1}C_n$ and $r^{-1}D_n$ are Bernoulli distributions with parameters p_1 and p_2 respectively .

Then, the support of μ has exactly four matrices as $S(\mu)$ is given by:

$$S(\mu) = \left\{ \begin{pmatrix} 0 & 1 \\ 0 & 1 \end{pmatrix}, \begin{pmatrix} 0 & 1 \\ r & 1-r \end{pmatrix}, \begin{pmatrix} r & 1-r \\ 0 & 1 \end{pmatrix}, \begin{pmatrix} r & 1-r \\ r & 1-r \end{pmatrix} \right\}$$

Let the μ-masses at these points be denoted by $p_{00}, p_{01}, p_{10}, p_{11}$ respectively so that $p_{00} + p_{01} = 1 - p_1, p_{00} + p_{10} = 1 - p_2, p_{10} + p_{11} = p_1$ and $p_{01} + p_{11} = p_2$.

Let λ be the distribution of $\lim_{n \to \infty} X_n X_{n-1} \cdots X_1$.

In case r equals 1, one can easily observe that λ is a Bernoulli distribution with parameters entirely dependent on the probability mass function of μ, namely,

$$\lambda(0) = \frac{p_{00} + p_{01}}{1 - p_{10} + p_{01}}$$

This follows by solving for $\lambda(0)$ and $\lambda(1)$ in the convolution equation $\lambda \star \mu = \lambda$.

For $0 < r < 1$, the support of μ^n, $S(\mu^n)$ and consequently $\mathcal{S}$ is contained in the set

$$\left\{ \begin{pmatrix} x & 1-x \\ y & 1-y \end{pmatrix} : 0 \leq x \leq r, 0 \leq y \leq r \right\}$$

This can be proved using induction on n. One assumes up to some positive integer l and proves for $l+1$ by noticing that when one multiplies a matrix in $S(\mu^l)$ by a matrix in $S(\mu)$, the entiries in the product matrix satisfies the condition that each entry in the first column is between 0 and r because each entry in the first column of the matrices from $S(\mu^l)$ and $S(\mu)$ is so.

Also, since the relation $\lambda \star \mu = \lambda$ holds, the support of λ, namely, $S(\lambda)$ consists of all rank one matrices in $\mathcal{S}$. As a result, $S(\lambda) \subset \{x : 0 \leq x \leq r\}$, where x stands for $\begin{pmatrix} x & 1-x \\ x & 1-x \end{pmatrix}$. Moreover, exploiting the identity $\lambda \star \mu = \lambda$, we have

$$\lambda(0) = \frac{p_{00}}{1 - p_{10}}, \quad \lambda(r) = p_{11} + \lambda(0)p_{01} = \frac{p_{11}(1 - p_{10}) + p_{00}p_{01}}{1 - p_{10}}$$

and for other points x with $0 < x < r$ with positive λ-masses, we have

$$\lambda(x) = \lambda(r^{-1}x)p_{10} + \lambda(1 - r^{-1}x)p_{01} \tag{2}$$

Next, we state the results proved in [2] for $0 < r \leq \frac{1}{2}$:

2.1. Case: $0 < r \leq \frac{1}{2}$

First of all, we introduce some notations. For each $i \geq 1$, define

$$A_i = \left\{ \sum_{j=1}^{k} (-1)^{j-1} r^{i_j} : 1 \leq i_1 < i_2 < i_3 < \cdots < i_k = i,\, k \leq i \right\}, \quad A = \cup_{i=1}^{\infty} A_i$$

We have two propositions for taking care of the cases $0 < r < \frac{1}{2}$ and $r = \frac{1}{2}$:

Proposition 1. *For $0 < r < \frac{1}{2}$, we have the following:*

(i) For every positive integer $i \geq 1$, $|A_i| = 2^{i-1}$ and each point in A_i has positive λ-mass. These are the only points of degree i in the support of λ with positive λ-mass.

(ii) Each such point has λ-measure equal to $\lambda(r)p_{10}^{i-1-k}p_{01}^{k}$. For every $i > 1$, $\lambda(A_i) = \lambda(r)[p_{10} + p_{01}]^{i-1}$.

(i) $\lambda(0) + \sum_{i=1}^{\infty} \lambda(A_i) = \lambda(0) + \lambda(r) \cdot \left[\sum_{i=1}^{\infty} (p_{10} + p_{01})^{i-1}\right] = 1$.

Proposition 2. *For $r = \frac{1}{2}$, we have the following:*

(i) The only points that have positive λ-masses are the dyadic rationals in $[0, \frac{1}{2}]$. Thus, for every i, there are exactly 2^{i-2} dyadic rationals of the form $\frac{k}{2^i}$ with $k \leq 2^{i-1}$ and k odd with positive λ-mass. A_i consists of exactly these points. Also, $|A_i| = 2^{i-2}$.

(ii) A typical point in A_i has λ-measure equal to $\lambda\left(\frac{1}{2}\right)(p_{10} + p_{01})p_{10}^{i-1-k}p_{01}^{k-1}$ for some positive integer k. For every $i > 1$, $\lambda(A_i) = \lambda\left(\frac{1}{2}\right)[p_{10} + p_{01}]^{i-1}$.

(iii) The sum of the λ-masses of all dyadic rationals in $\left[0, \frac{1}{2}\right]$ along with the λ-mass at zero equals 1. Equivalently, $\lambda(0) + \sum_{i=1}^{\infty} \lambda(A_i) = \lambda(0) + \lambda\left(\frac{1}{2}\right) \cdot \left[\sum_{i=1}^{\infty} (p_{10} + p_{01})^{i-1}\right] = 1$

The case $\frac{1}{2} < r < 1$ turns out to be quite nontrivial. We briefly introduce that case below:

2.2. Case: $\frac{1}{2} < r < 1$

The case $\frac{1}{2} < r < 1$ is distinctly different from the case $r < \frac{1}{2}$ because now we have $1 - r < r$. Since for each r, λ has masses at 0 and r, it is not absolutely continuous for any r. Now, suppose we continue with the same notation of A introduced in the case $0 < r \leq \frac{1}{2}$. Thus, $A = \cup_{i=1}^{\infty} A_i$ where, for every positive integer i,

$$A_i = \left\{ \sum_{j=1}^{k} (-1)^{j-1} r^{i_j} : 1 \leq i_1 < i_2 < i_3 < \cdots < i_k = i,\, k \leq i \right\}$$

It then easily follows that each of these points in A also has positive mass even in the case $\frac{1}{2} < r < 1$. However, it is indeed a challenge to calculate λ-masses at these points.

Also, since $1 - r \in (0, r)$, it is natural to have points of the form $1 + \sum_{j=1}^{k} (-1)^j r^{i_j}$, $1 \leq i_1 < i_2 < i_3 < \cdots < i_k = i$, $k \leq i$ for any positive integer i in the interval $(0, r)$ (to see this, notice that $r^{i_1} > \sum_{j=2}^{k} (-1)^j r^{i_j}$). Accordingly, define $A^* = \cup_{i=1}^{\infty} A_i^*$, where

$$A_i^* = \left\{ 1 + \sum_{j=1}^{k} (-1)^j r^{i_j} : 1 \leq i_1 < i_2 < i_3 < \cdots < i_k = i,\, k \leq i \right\}$$

Recall that, for $0 < r \leq \frac{1}{2}$, each point in A has positive λ-mass and each point in A^* is outside $(0, r)$ and has zero λ-mass.

For $\frac{1}{2} < r < 1$, of course, each polynomial in A is in $(0, r)$. But, although some polynomials in A^* are numerically less than r, it is not easy to see which of these points have positive λ-masses. Clearly, some polynomials in A_i^* are outside $(0, r)$ and have zero λ-measure if i is large enough. For example, for a fixed r, it is possible to get a positive integer $m > 1$ such that $1 - r^m \geq r > 1 - r^{m-1}$. Next, consider $i_1 = l$ with $l \geq m$ for a polynomial $1 + \sum_1^k (-1)^j r^{i_j}$ in A_i^* with $1 \leq i_1 < i_2 < i_3 < \cdots < i_k = i, k \leq i$. Then, this polynomial is greater than or equal to $1 - r^m + \sum_2^k (-1)^j r^{i_j}$, which is obviously greater than r and has λ-measure zero. But, it is a possibility that some points in A^* could have positive λ-masses too.

Recall the very special r, $r = r_g$, the reciprocal of the golden ratio. We know r_g satisfies the equation $r_g^2 + r_g - 1 = 0$ and $1 - r_g$ actually equals r_g^2, whose λ-measure can be found out easily. The next two sections deal with this special case.

3. $r = r_g$: Main Results

In this section and also in the next section, we deal with $r = r_g = \frac{\sqrt{5}-1}{2}$ unless stated otherwise. This is a very special case of $\frac{1}{2} < r < 1$. Note that r_g is the reciprocal of the golden ratio and is the positive solution of the equation $r^2 + r - 1 = 0$. To avoid dealing with too many radical signs and complicating matters, we will continue to use r_g in these two sections for this particluar choice of r.

Remark 1. *A polynomial* $1 + \sum_1^k (-1)^j r_g^{i_j}$ *in* A_i^* *with* $1 \leq i_1 < i_2 < i_3 < \cdots < i_k = i, k \leq i$ *and* $i_1 \geq 2$ *has zero* λ*-measure.*

This is because, $1 - r_g^2 = r_g$ implies that such a polynomial is greater than r_g in magnitude. However, for $i_1 = 1$, such a polynomial may have positive λ-measure as well.

In order to notice this, first observe that, $\lambda(1 - r_g) > 0$. This is because, using (2), we have

$$\lambda(1 - r_g) = \lambda(r_g^2) = \lambda(r_g)p_{10} + \lambda(1 - r_g)p_{01}$$

implying that $\lambda(1 - r_g) = \frac{p_{10}}{1-p_{01}}\lambda(r_g)$ where $\lambda(r_g)$ is already known.

Next, consider a nontrivial example, say, the polynomial $1 - r_g + r_g^2 - r_g^3$. Using (2) repeatedly and Remark 2, we find that its λ- measure equals

$$\lambda(r_g^2)p_{10}^2 p_{01} + \lambda(1 - r_g^2)p_{10}p_{01}^2 = \lambda(1 - r_g)p_{10}^2 p_{01} + \lambda(r_g)p_{10}p_{01}^2$$

implying that the polynomial under consideration has non-zero λ-measure. Since we know $\lambda(r_g)$ and $\lambda(1 - r_g)$, it is possible to find out $\lambda(1 - r_g + r_g^2 - r_g^3)$ explicitly.

But, this is only a particular example. Can we make a general observation? Yes. Look at the following result.

Proposition 3. *Any polynomial in* A^* *either has* λ*-measure* 0 *or can be written as a polynomial in* A.

Proof. To fix ideas, we assume that our polynomial in A^* is $1 + \sum_{j=1}^k (-1)^j r_g^{i_j}$ with $1 \leq i_1 < i_2 < i_3 < \cdots < i_k = i$ and $k \leq i$. Because of Remark 3.0, we can assume that $i_1 = 1$. Then, we consider the following cases:

Case 1: $i_j = j$ for $j = 2, 3, \ldots, k$.

Then, the given polynomial equals $1 - r_g + r_g^2 - \cdots + (-1)^k r_g^k$

Subcase 1: k is even, say, $k = 2m$. Then, the above polynomial equals $1 - r_g + r_g^2 - \cdots + r_g^{2m}$. Notice that $r_g^j - r_g^{j+1} = r_g^{j+1} - r_g^{j+3}$ for $j = 0, 1, 2, \ldots$. Thus, the given polynomial equals $r_g - r_g^3 + r_g^3 - r_g^5 + \cdots + r_g^{2m-1} - r_g^{2m+1} + r_g^{2m}$ which equals $r_g - r_g^{2m+1} + r_g^{2m} > r_g$. So, it has λ-measure 0.

Subcase 2: k is odd, $k = 2m+1$. Then, the above polynomial equals $1 - r_g + r_g^2 - \cdots + r_g^{2m} - r_g^{2m+1}$. Once again recall that $r_g^j - r_g^{j+1} = r_g^{j+1} - r_g^{j+3}$ for $j = 0,1,2,\ldots$. So, the given polynoimal equals $r_g - r_g^3 + r_g^3 - r_g^5 + \cdots + r_g^{2m-1} - r_g^{2m+1} + r_g^{2m+1} - r_g^{2m+3} = r_g - r_g^{2m+3}$. And it is a polynomial in A.

Case 2: There exists an l such that $i_l > l$ and $i_j = j$ for $j < l$. Then, the given polynomial equals $1 - r_g + r_g^2 - \cdots + (-1)^{l-1} r_g^{l-1} + \sum_{j=l}^{k} (-1)^j r_g^{i_j}$.

Subcase 1: l is even, say, $l = 2m$. Then, the polynomial equals $1 - r_g + r_g^2 - \cdots - r_g^{2m-1} + \sum_{j=2m}^{k} (-1)^j r_g^{i_j}$. Again, we use $r_g^j - r_g^{j+1} = r_g^{j+1} - r_g^{j+3}$ for $j = 0,1,2,\ldots$ so that the given polynomial equals $r_g - r_g^3 + r_g^3 - r_g^5 + \cdots + r_g^{2m-1} - r_g^{2m+1} + \sum_{j=2m}^{k} (-1)^j r_g^{i_j}$. If $i_{2m} = 2m+1$, then this polynomial equals $r_g - r_g^3 + r_g^3 - r_g^5 + \cdots + r_g^{2m-1} - r_g^{2m+1} + r_g^{2m+1} + \sum_{j=2m+1}^{k} (-1)^j r_g^{i_j}$, which equals $r_g + \sum_{j=2m+1}^{k} (-1)^j r_g^{i_j}$. This is, of course, a polynomial in A . On the other hand, if $i_{2m} > 2m+1$, then the above polynomial equals $r_g - r_g^{2m+1} + \sum_{j=2m}^{k} (-1)^j r_g^{i_j}$. Once again, it is a polynomial in A.

Subcase 2: l is odd, say, $l = 2m+1$. Then, the given polynomial equals $1 - r_g + r_g^2 - \cdots - r_g^{2m-1} + r_g^{2m} + \sum_{j=2m+1}^{k} (-1)^j r_g^{i_j}$. Applying once again $r_g^j - r_g^{j+1} = r_g^{j+1} - r_g^{j+3}$ for $j = 0,1,2,\ldots$, this polynomial equals $r_g - r_g^3 + r_g^3 - r_g^5 + \cdots + r_g^{2m-1} - r_g^{2m+1} + r_g^{2m} + \sum_{j=2m+1}^{k} (-1)^j r_g^{i_j}$. This simplifies to $r_g - r_g^{2m+1} + r_g^{2m} + \sum_{j=2m+1}^{k} (-1)^j r_g^{i_j} = r_g + r_g^{2m+2} + \sum_{j=2m+1}^{k} (-1)^j r_g^{i_j}$. If $i_{2m+1} = 2m+2$, then the above equals $r_g + \sum_{j=2m+2}^{k} (-1)^j r_g^{i_j} > r_g$. So, it has λ-measure zero. If $i_{2m+1} > 2m+2$, then the given polynomial equals $r_g + r_g^{2m+2} + \sum_{j=2m+1}^{k} (-1)^j r_g^{i_j}$ which is same as $r_g + r_g^{2m+2} - r_g^{i_{2m+1}} + \sum_{j=2m+2}^{k} (-1)^j r_g^{i_j} > r_g$. So, it has λ-measure equal to zero. □

Remark 2. *Because of the above proposition, it is good enough to consider only polynomials in A. We will rather consider the same polynomials as in the case $0 < r < \frac{1}{2}$ and will try to work out their λ-measures.*

We have seen in Section 2 that the number of elements in A_n equals 2^{n-1}. But, because of the relationship $1 - r_g = r_g^2$ in the current situation, there will be redundancy and all polynomials are not distinct. So, we will see that we need to consider at most 2^{n-2} elements from A_n for each $n \geq 3$:

Proposition 4. *There are at most 2^{n-2} distinct elements in A_n for each $n \geq 3$.*

Proof. Once again, the identity $1 - r_g = r_g^2$ has a big role to play. For $n = 1,2,3$ or 4, it is trivial to observe. For general n, first notice that $r_g^n = r_g^{n-2} - r_g^{n-1}$, and so r_g^n can be considered to be in A_{n-1}. More generally, define

$$Q_n = \left\{r_g^n\right\} \cup \left\{ \sum_{j=1}^{k} (-1)^{j-1} r_g^{i_j} : 1 \leq i_1 < \cdots < i_{k-1} < i_k;\ i_{k-1} < n,\ i_k = n;\ k < n;\ n - i_{k-1} \geq 2 \right\}$$

and

$$R_n = \left\{ \sum_{j=1}^{k} (-1)^{j-1} r_g^{i_j} : 1 \leq i_1 < \cdots < i_{k-1} < i_k;\ i_{k-1} = n-1,\ i_k = n,\ k \leq n \right\}$$

Let $Q = \cup_{n=3}^{\infty} Q_n$ and $R = \cup_{n=3}^{\infty} R_n$. Then, observe that each polynomial in Q is numerically equal to a polynomial in R of less degree.

We see this as follows:

Consider an $n > 2$. Take a polynomial in Q_n. If it is r_g^n, we have already provided the argument, that is, $r_g^n = r_g^{n-2} - r_g^{n-1} \in R_{n-1}$. Otherwise, consider a typical element from Q_n, say, $r_g^{i_1} - r_g^{i_2} + \cdots + (-1)^{k-1} r_g^{i_{k-1}} + (-1)^k r_g^n$ with $1 \leq i_1 < i_2 < \cdots < n$ and for some $k < n$. If $n - i_{k-1} = 2$, then $r_g^{i_{k-1}} - r_g^n = r_g^{n-2} - r_g^n = r_g^{n-1} = r_g^{n-3} - r_g^{n-2}$. As a result, the given polynomial equals $r_g^{i_1} - r_g^{i_2} + \cdots + +(-1)^{k-1} r_g^{n-3} + (-1)^k r_g^{n-2}$. So, it is a polynomial in R of less degree $(n-2)$. On the other hand, if $n - i_{k-1} > 2$, then $r_g^{i_{k-1}} - r_g^n = r_g^{i_{k-1}} - r_g^{n-2} + r_g^{n-1}$. So, the given polynomial equals $r_g^{i_1} - r_g^{i_2} + \cdots + (-1)^{k-1} r_g^{i_{k-1}} + (-1)^k r_g^{n-2} + (-1)^{k+1} r_g^{n-1}$. Once again, this is a polynomial in R of less degree $(n-1)$.

It is clear that for each n, $A_n = Q_n \cup R_n$ and hence $A = Q \cup R$. So, because of this observation, the only polynomials in A that can be considered for λ-mass calculation are the ones in R. Also, it follows that for $n \geq 3$, R_n has at most 2^{n-2} distinct polynomials. Consequently, A_n also has at the most 2^{n-2} distinct elements and the proposition follows. □

Remark 3. *Thus, for each n, we have fewer polynomials of degree n compared to the situation* $0 < r < \frac{1}{2}$.

Now, it is time we prove our main theorem. We prove it in the next section.

4. $r = r_g$: Proof of the Main Theorem

Here is our main theorem:

Theorem 1. *Consider* $r = r_g = \frac{\sqrt{5}-1}{2}$. *Then*

$$\lambda(0) + \lambda(r_g) + \lambda(r_g^2) + \lambda(r_g - r_g^2) + \lambda(R) = 1$$

where $R = \cup_{n=3}^{\infty} R_n$ *with*

$$R_n = \left\{ \sum_{j=1}^{k} (-1)^{j-1} r_g^{i_j} : 1 \leq i_1 < i_2 < \cdots < i_{k-2} < i_{k-1} < i_k;\ i_{k-1} = n-1,\ i_k = n,\ k \leq n \right\}$$

First, notice that, using (2), it follows that $\lambda(r_g^2) = \frac{p_{10}}{1-p_{01}} \lambda(r_g)$ and $\lambda(r_g - r_g^2) = \left(\frac{p_{10}^2}{1-p_{01}} + p_{01} \right) \lambda(r_g)$. Thus, in order to prove the theorem, it is enough to prove:

$$\lambda(R) = \frac{p_{10} + p_{01}}{1 - p_{10} - p_{01}} \lambda(r_g - r_g^2) \tag{3}$$

because then,

$$\lambda(r_g - r_g^2) + \lambda(R) = \left(1 + \frac{p_{10} + p_{01}}{1 - p_{10} - p_{01}} \right) \lambda(r_g - r_g^2)$$

As a result,

$$\lambda(0) + \lambda(r_g) + \lambda(r_g^2) + \lambda(r_g - r_g^2) + \lambda(R) = \lambda(0) + \frac{1}{1 - p_{10} - p_{01}} \lambda(r_g)$$

But, recall from Section 3:

$$\lambda(0) = \frac{p_{00}}{1 - p_{10}}, \quad \lambda(r_g) = p_{11} + \lambda(0) p_{01} = \frac{p_{11}(1 - p_{10}) + p_{00} p_{01}}{1 - p_{10}}$$

This implies that

$$\lambda(0) + \frac{1}{1 - p_{10} - p_{01}} \lambda(r_g) = 1$$

This is the reason that it is good enough to prove (3). For this, we proceed as follows.

First of all, notice that $R_3 = \{r_g^2 - r_g^3, r_g - r_g^2 + r_g^3\}$, $R_4 = \{r_g^3 - r_g^4, r_g^2 - r_g^3 + r_g^4, r_g - r_g^3 + r_g^4, r_g - r_g^2 + r_g^3 - r_g^4\}$ etc. and in general

$$R_n = \{r_g^{n-1} - r_g^n, r_g^{n-2} - r_g^{n-1} + r_g^n, \ldots, r_g - r_g^{n-1} + r_g^n, \ldots, r_g - r_g^2 + \cdots + r_g^{n-1} - r_g^n\}$$

Next, we introduce some notations for any $0 < r < 1$.

Define $g : R \to R$ and $f_j : R \to R$ for every positive integer j as follows: $g(p) = rp$ and $f_j(p) = r^j - p$. Thus, $R_3 = \{f_2(r^3), f_1f_2(r^3)\}$, $R_4 = \{f_3(r^4), f_2f_3(r^4), f_1f_3(r^4), f_1f_2f_3(r^4)\}$ etc., and in general,

$$R_n = \{f_{n-1}(r^n), f_{n-2}f_{n-1}(r^n), \ldots, f_1f_{n-1}(r^n), \ldots, f_1f_2\cdots f_{n-1}(r^n)\}$$

We further define operators F_j for $j \geq 2$ on R as follows: $F_2 = \{f_2, f_1f_2\}$, $F_3 = \{f_3, f_2f_3, f_1f_3, f_1f_2f_3\}$ etc., and in general,

$$F_{n-1} = \{f_{n-1}, f_{n-2}f_{n-1}, \ldots, f_1f_{n-1}, \ldots, f_1f_2\cdots f_{n-1}\}$$

Thus, $R_j = F_{j-1}(r^j)$ for $j = 3, 4, \ldots$ and

$$F_{j-1}(p) = \{f_{j-1}(p), f_{j-2}f_{j-1}(p), \ldots, f_1f_{j-1}(p), \ldots, f_1f_2\cdots f_{j-1}(p)\}$$

In general, one would anticipate $|F_2(p)| = 2$, $|F_3(p)| = 4, \ldots, |F_{j-1}(p)| = 2^{j-2}$. But, for $r = r_g$, equality is replaced by $\leq$ for some ps.

Now, in order to prove (3), we will use a series of Lemmas 1–5. Lemma 1 identifies that connsecutive R_is have nonempty overlaps for $i \geq 3$, Lemma 2 evaluates the cardinality of the consecutive overlaps, Lemma 3 evaluates the cardinality of the consecutive differences, Lemma 4 calculates the λ- measures of these differences, and, finally, Lemma 5 puts them together to evaluate the λ-measure of R thereby proving (3). Thus, once Lemmas 1–5 are proved, (3) is proved and the proof of the theorem is complete.

Lemma 1. *Consecutive R_is (R_i and R_{i+1}) have nonempty intersections for $i \geq 3$. In fact, $R_4 \cap R_3 = \emptyset$ but $R_{j+1} \cap R_j \neq \emptyset$ for $j > 3$*

Proof. It is trivial to observe that $R_4 \cap R_3 = \phi$. Now, notice that $r_g^2 - r_g^4 + r_g^5, r_g - r_g^2 + r_g^4 - r_g^5 \in R_5 \cap R_4$ because $r_g^2 - r_g^4 + r_g^5 = r_g - r_g^2 + r_g^5 = r_g - r_g^2 + r_g^3 - r_g^4 \in R_4$ and automatically, $r_g - r_g^2 + r_g^4 - r_g^5 = r_g - (r_g - r_g^2 + r_g^3 - r_g^4) = r_g^2 - r_g^3 + r_g^4 \in R_4$. Thus, $R_5 \cap R_4 = F_2(r_g^4 - r_g^5)$ and $|R_5 \cap R_4| = 2$. In general, $R_{j+1} \cap R_j \supseteq F_{j-2}(r_g^j - r_g^{j+1}) \cup F_{j-4}(r_g^j - r_g^{j+1})$ for $j \geq 6$. In fact, we can show that for positive integers $k \geq 3$

$$R_{2k-1} \cap R_{2k-2} = F_{2k-4}(r_g^{2k-2} - r_g^{2k-1}) \cup F_{2k-6}(r_g^{2k-2} - r_g^{2k-1}) \cup \cdots \cup F_2(r_g^{2k-2} - r_g^{2k-1})$$

$$R_{2k} \cap R_{2k-1} = F_{2k-3}(r_g^{2k-1} - r_g^{2k}) \cup F_{2k-5}(r_g^{2k-1} - r_g^{2k}) \cup \cdots \cup F_3(r_g^{2k-1} - r_g^{2k})$$

So, Lemma 1 is proved. □

Lemma 2. *For $i \geq 4$, $|R_i \cap R_{i+1}|$s are evaluated upper bounds for $|R_{i+1} - R_i|$ are determined as follows:*

For $k \geq 3$, we have,

$$|R_{2k-1} \cap R_{2k-2}| = \frac{2}{3}(2^{2k-4} - 1), \quad |R_{2k} \cap R_{2k-1}| = \frac{4}{3}(2^{2k-4} - 1)$$

so that

$$|R_{2k-1}-R_{2k-2}| \leq \frac{2^{2k-2}+2}{3}, \quad |R_{2k}-R_{2k-1}| \leq \frac{2^{2k-1}+4}{3}$$

Proof. From Lemma 1, it follows that $|R_5 \cap R_4| = 2$ implying $|R_5 - R_4| \leq 2^3 - 2 = 6$, $|R_6 \cap R_5| = 4$ implying $|R_6 - R_5| \leq 2^4 - 4 = 12$.

In general, notice that for $k \geq 4$,

$$|F_{2k-2l}(r_g^{2k-2l+2} - r_g^{2k-2l+3})| = 2^{2k-2l-1}$$

and

$$|F_{2k-2l+1}(r_g^{2k-2l+3} - r_g^{2k-2l+4})| = 2^{2k-2l}$$

for $2 \leq l \leq k-1$. Also,

$$|R_{2k-1} \cap R_{2k-2}| = 2^{2k-5} + 2^{2k-7} + \cdots + 2 = \frac{2}{3}\left(2^{2k-4} - 1\right)$$

implying that $|R_{2k-1} - R_{2k-2}| \leq 2^{2k-3} - \frac{2}{3}\left(2^{2k-4} - 1\right) = \frac{2^{2k-2}+2}{3}$ and

$$|R_{2k} \cap R_{2k-1}| = 2^{2k-4} + 2^{2k-6} + \cdots + 2^2 = \frac{4}{3}\left(2^{2k-4} - 1\right)$$

implying that $|R_{2k} - R_{2k-1}| \leq 2^{2k-2} - \frac{4}{3}\left(2^{2k-4} - 1\right) = \frac{2^{2k-1}+4}{3}$.

Thus, Lemma 2 is proved. □

Lemma 3. *For $i \geq 4$, $|R_{i+1} - R_i|$s are evaluated exactly by getting rid of the redundancies:*

More explicitly, for $j \geq 6$, not all elements in R_j are distinct. In fact, for $k \geq 3$, R_{2k} has $2^{2k-4} - 2$ and R_{2k+1} has $2^{2k-3} - 2$ pairs of elements which are numerically equal so that

$$|R_{2k} - R_{2k-1}| = \frac{5 \cdot 2^{2k-4} + 10}{3}, \quad |R_{2k+1} - R_{2k}| = \frac{5 \cdot 2^{2k-3} + 8}{3}$$

Proof. From now on, we refer to duplicates as those pairs of polynomials or elements in R which have different algebraic expressions, but becaue of our choice of r, they are numerically equal. In order to exactly evaluate $|R_{i+1} - R_i|$ for $i \geq 4$, we need to identify such pairs.

Thus, $R_6 - R_5$ has two pairs of duplicates, namely, $r_g^2 - r_g^5 + r_g^6$ & $r_g - r_g^2 + r_g^4 - r_g^5 + r_g^6$; $r_g - r_g^2 + r_g^5 - r_g^6$ and $r_g^2 - r_g^4 + r_g^5 - r_g^6$ because

$$r_g - r_g^2 + r_g^4 - r_g^5 + r_g^6 = r_g^2 - r_g^4 + r_g^4 - r_g^5 + r_g^6 = r_g^2 - r_g^5 + r_g^6$$

$$r_g - r_g^2 + r_g^5 - r_g^6 = r_g^2 - r_g^4 + r_g^5 - r_g^6$$

In general, $R_{2k} - R_{2k-1}$ has $2 + 4 + \cdots + 2^{2k-5}$ pairs of duplicates implying that $|R_{2k} - R_{2k-1}| = \frac{2^{2k-1}+4}{3} - (2^{2k-4} - 2) = \frac{5 \cdot 2^{2k-4}+10}{3}$. Here, each pair in the union are disjoint sets.

Also, $R_{2k+1} - R_{2k}$ has $2 + 4 + \cdots + 2^{2k-5}$ pairs of duplicates implying that $|R_{2k+1} - R_{2k}| = \frac{2^{2k}+2}{3} - (2^{2k-3} - 2) = \frac{5 \cdot 2^{2k-3}+8}{3}$. Again, each pair in the union are disjoint sets.

Thus, Lemma 3 is proved. □

Lemma 4. *λ-measures of $R_{i+1} - R_i$ for $i \geq 3$ are calculated as:*

First of all, $\lambda(R_3) = \lambda(r_g - r_g^2)(p_{10} + p_{01})$ and for $k \geq 2$,

$$\lambda(R_{2k} - R_{2k-1}) = \lambda(R_{2k-1} - R_{2k-2})(p_{10} + p_{01}) + \lambda(r_g - r_g^2)p_{10}^{2k-3}p_{01}(p_{10} + p_{01})$$

which equals

$$\lambda(R_{2k}-R_{2k-1})=\lambda\left(r_g-r_g^2\right)(p_{10}+p_{01})^{2k-2}\left[1+\sum_{l=0}^{k-2}p_{10}^{2l+1}p_{01}\,(p_{10}+p_{01})^{-2l-1}-\sum_{l=1}^{k-3}p_{10}^{2l+1}p_{01}\,(p_{10}+p_{01})^{-2l-2}\right] \quad (4)$$

where for $k=2$, the last sum in the above equation is absent. Also, we have,

$$\lambda(R_{2k+1}-R_{2k})=\lambda(R_{2k}-R_{2k-1})(p_{10}+p_{01})-\lambda\left(r_g-r_g^2\right)p_{10}^{2k-3}p_{01}(p_{10}+p_{01})$$

which equals

$$\lambda(R_{2k+1}-R_{2k})=\lambda\left(r_g-r_g^2\right)(p_{10}+p_{01})^{2k-1}\left[1+\sum_{l=0}^{k-2}p_{10}^{2l+1}p_{01}\left[(p_{10}+p_{01})^{-2l-1}-(p_{10}+p_{01})^{-2l-2}\right]\right] \quad (5)$$

where for $k=2$, $R_{2k}-R_{2k-1}=R_4-R_3=R_4$ and $R_{2k-1}-R_{2k-2}=R_3-R_2=R_3$.

Proof. Recall that $R_3=F_2(r_g^3)=\{r_g^2-r_g^3,\ r_g-r_g^2+r_g^3\}$. Then, using (2) and Proposition 3, we have

$$\lambda(R_3)=\lambda(r_g^2-r_g^3)+\lambda(r_g-r_g^2+r_g^3)=\lambda(r_g-r_g^2)(p_{10}+p_{01})$$

Next, we have $R_4=F_3\left(r_g^4\right)=\{r_g^3-r_g^4,\ r_g^2-r_g^3+r_g^4,\ r_g-r_g^3+r_g^4,\ r_g-r_g^2+r_g^3-r_g^4\}$. We find λ-measures of these points by making use of (2) and Remark 2. Thus, we notice that

$$\lambda(1-r_g+r_g^2-r_g^3)=\lambda(r_g-r_g^3+r_g^4)=\lambda(r_g-r_g^2)p_{10}p_{01}$$

Putting all these together, $\lambda(R_4-R_3)$ equals

$$\lambda(r_g-r_g^2)(p_{10}+p_{01})^2+\lambda(1-r_g+r_g^2-r_g^3)(p_{10}+p_{01})=\lambda(r_g-r_g^2)(p_{10}+p_{01})^2+\lambda(r_g-r_g^2)\,p_{10}p_{01}(p_{10}+p_{01})$$

In other words,

$$\lambda(R_4-R_3)=\lambda(R_3)(p_{10}+p_{01})+\lambda(r_g-r_g^2)\,p_{10}p_{01}(p_{10}+p_{01}) \quad (6)$$

It is to be noted that $R_4\cap R_3=\emptyset$, and so $R_4-R_3=R_4$ which implies $\lambda(R_4-R_3)=\lambda(R_4)$.

Before proceeding further, we notice that $F_j\left(r_g^{j+1}\right)=g\left(F_{j-1}(r_g^j)\right)\cup f_1\circ g\left(F_{j-1}(r_g^j)\right)$ for $j\geq 4$ and $R_{j+1}-R_j$ equals $g(R_j-R_{j-1})\cup f_1\circ g(R_j-R_{j-1})$ for $j\geq 5$.

However, at the next stage, we have already noticed that $R_5\cap R_4\neq\emptyset$, and so $R_5-R_4\neq R_5$. In fact,

$$R_5=F_4\left(r_g^5\right)$$

and

$$R_5-R_4=F_4\left(r_g^5\right)-F_2\left(r_g^4-r_g^5\right)$$

Now, notice that

$$F_4\left(r_g^5\right)=g(R_4-R_3)\cup f_1\circ g(R_4-R_3)$$

So,

$$R_5-R_4=g(R_4-R_3)\cup f_1\circ g(R_4-R_3)-F_2\left(r_g^4-r_g^5\right)$$

This is the same as

$$\left[g(R_4-R_3)-g\left(r_g-r_g^3+r_g^4\right)\right]\cup\left[f_1\circ g(R_4-R_3)-f_1\circ g\left(r_g-r_g^3+r_g^4\right)\right]$$

Since $g(R_4 - R_3) - g\left(r_g - r_g^3 + r_g^4\right)$ and $f_1 \circ g(R_4 - R_3) - f_1 \circ g\left(r_g - r_g^3 + r_g^4\right)$ do not have overlaps, we deduce that

$$\lambda(R_5 - R_4) = \lambda(R_4 - R_3)(p_{10} + p_{01}) - \lambda\left(r_g - r_g^2\right) p_{10}p_{01}(p_{10} + p_{01}) \tag{7}$$

which equals

$$\lambda(R_5 - R_4) = \lambda\left(r_g - r_g^2\right)(p_{10} + p_{01})^3 + \lambda(r_g - r_g^2)\, p_{10}p_{01}(p_{10} + p_{01})^2 - \lambda(r_g - r_g^2)\, p_{10}p_{01}(p_{10} + p_{01}) \tag{8}$$

Thus, from Equations (6) and (8), we observe that Lemma 4 is proved for $k = 2$. For general k, one can use induction on k and carefully sort out the issues with the duplicates to complete the proof of the lemma. □

Lemma 5. *Finally, we calculate λ-measure of R:*

$$\lambda(R) = \sum_{j=3}^{\infty} \lambda(R_j - R_{j-1}) = \sum_{j=1}^{\infty} \lambda\left(r_g - r_g^2\right)(p_{10} + p_{01})^j = \lambda\left(r_g - r_g^2\right) \cdot \frac{p_{10} + p_{01}}{1 - p_{10} - p_{01}}$$

where we put $R_2 = \emptyset$.

Proof. Using (4) and (5) for $k \geq 2$, Lemma 5 follows trivially and the proof of the theorem is complete. □

5. Concluding Remarks

In the present context, it is interesting to recall an older problem, first introduced in [7]. It is as follows: consider the very simple situation of a μ that is supported on exactly two 2×2 stochastic matrices, namely, $\begin{pmatrix} a_1 & 1-a_1 \\ b_1 & 1-b_1 \end{pmatrix}$ and $\begin{pmatrix} a_2 & 1-a_2 \\ b_2 & 1-b_2 \end{pmatrix}$ with $a_i > b_i$ for $i = 1, 2$. Let the μ-masses at these two points be p and $1 - p$, respectively, where $0 < p < 1$. Let λ be the weak limit of the convolution sequence μ^n. What is the nature of λ? If we denote $a_1 - b_1 = s$ and $a_2 - b_2 = t$, then, in [12], some partial solution to this problem was mentioned. In the special case scenario when $s = t$ and $p = \frac{1}{2}$, it was observed in [13] that it is precisely the case of Bernoulli convolutions. In fact, the following proposition is stated in [13]:

Proposition 5. *Let μ be a probability measure giving equal mass to the matrices $\begin{pmatrix} a_1 & 1-a_1 \\ b_1 & 1-b_1 \end{pmatrix}$ and $\begin{pmatrix} a_2 & 1-a_2 \\ b_2 & 1-b_2 \end{pmatrix}$ with $a_i > b_i$ for $i = 1, 2$. Let, say, $a_1 - b_1 = a_2 - b_2 = t$. Then, the limiting measure λ of the convolution sequence μ^n is absolutely continuous (where the limt λ is identified as a probability on $[0, 1]$) iff the law of $\sum_{n=0}^{\infty} t^n \epsilon_n$ is absolutely continuous where ϵ_n's are i.i.d. $+1$ and -1 with equal probabilities.*

Although the century old problem of Bernoulli convolutions was finally solved in [14], there had been a lot of previous studies at various times in different directions in spite of it being apparently a simple problem with μ concentrated on two points only. Thus, it is quite possible that under our current set up of μ being concentrated on four matrices with $\frac{1}{2} < r < 1$, the problem may be at least as challenging as the Bernoulli convolution problem.

We bring in the context of Bernoulli convolutions here to make readers aware that for a nontrivial $\frac{1}{2} < r < 1$, one needs to explore a number of ideas to proceed towards a complete solution for our problem.

Funding: This research received no external funding.

Data Availability Statement: No new data were created or analyzed in this study. Data sharing is not applicable to this article.

Acknowledgments: I acknowledge my affiliation, the University of Texas Rio Grande Valley, for allowing me to use the university office, university library, and university computers for conducting my research.

Conflicts of Interest: The author declares no conflict of interest.

References

1. Hognas, G.; Mukherjea, A. *Probability Measures on Semigroups*, 2nd ed.; Springer: New York, NY, USA, 2011.
2. Chakraborty, S.; Mukherjea, A. Limit distributions of random walks on stochastic matrices. *Proc. Indian Acad. Sci. (Math Sci.)* **2014**, *124*, 603–612. [CrossRef]
3. Chakraborty, S. Cyclicity and weak convergence for convolution of measures on non-negative matrices. *Sankhya Indian J. Stat.* **2007**, *69*, 304–313.
4. Chakraborty, S.; Mukherjea, A. Completely simple semigroups of real $d \times d$ matrices and real random walks. *Contemp. Math.* **2010**, *516*, 99–108.
5. Chakraborty, S.; Rao, B.V. Convolution powers of probabilities on stochastic matrices of order 3. *Sankhya A* **1998**, *60*, 151–170.
6. Chakraborty, S.; Rao, B.V. Convolution powers of probabilities on stochastic matrices. *J. Theor. Probab.* **2001**, *14*, 599–603. [CrossRef]
7. Mukherjea, A. Limit Theorems: Stochastic matrices, ergodic markov chains and measures on semigroups. In *Probability Analysis and Related Topics*; Bharucha Reid, A.T., Ed.; Academic Press: New York, NY, USA, 1979; Volume 2, pp. 143–203.
8. Chamayou, J.F.; Letac, G. A transient random walk on stochastic matrices with Dirichlet distributions. *Ann. Prob.* **1994**, *22*, 424–430. [CrossRef]
9. Van Assche, W. Products of 2×2 stochastic matrices with random entries. *J. Appl. Prob.* **1986**, *23*, 1019–1024. [CrossRef]
10. Chassaing, P.; Letac, G.; Mora, M. *Brocot Sequences and Random Walks in SL(2,R)*; Springer: Berlin/Heidelberg, Germany, 1985; Volume 1034, pp. 37–50.
11. Jaeger, S. The Golden Ratio in Machine Learning. In Proceedings of the IEEE Applied Imagery Pattern Recognition Workshop (AIPR), Washington, DC, USA, 12–14 October 2021; pp. 1–7. [CrossRef]
12. Mukherjea, A.; Tserpes, N.A. *Measures on Topological Semigroups*; Lecture Notes in Mathematics; Springer: Berlin/Heidelberg, Germany, 1976; Volume 547.
13. Chakraborty, S.; Rao, B.V. Bernoulli Convolutions. In *Mathematical Models for Bioengineering and Probabilistic Systems*; Mishra, J.C., Ed.; Narosa Publishing House: New Delhi, India, 2005; pp. 380–404.
14. Solomyak, B. On the random series $\sum \pm\lambda^n$ (an Erdos problem). *Ann. Math.* **1995**, *142*, 611–625. [CrossRef]

mathematics

MDPI

Article

Poissonization Inequalities for Sums of Independent Random Variables in Banach Spaces with Applications to Empirical Processes

Igor Borisov

Sobolev Institute of Mathematics, 630090 Novosibirsk, Russia; sibam@math.nsc.ru

Abstract: Inequalities are obtained which connect the probability tails and moments of functions of the nth partial sums of independent random variables taking values in a separable Banach space and those for the accompanying infinitely divisible laws. Some applications to empirical processes are studied.

Keywords: sums of independent random variables; moment inequalities; accompanying infinitely divisible law; convex function; empirical process

MSC: 62G08

1. Introduction and the Main Results

Let $X_1, X_2, \ldots$ be independent random variables (r.v.s) taking values in a separable Banach space $(\mathcal{B}, \|\cdot\|)$ with respective distributions $P_1, P_2, \ldots$. In the i.i.d. case, we will denote by P the common distribution.

$Pois(\mu)$ denotes the compound Poisson distribution with Lévy measure μ:

$$Pois(\mu) := e^{-\mu(\mathcal{B})} \sum_{k=0}^{\infty} \frac{\mu^{*k}}{k!}, \tag{1}$$

where μ^{*k} is the k-fold convolution of a finite measure μ with itself; μ^{*0} is the Dirac measure with the atom at zero. $S_n := \Sigma_{i \le n} X_i$, where $S_0 = 0$ by definition. The compound Poisson distribution with Lévy measure $\mu \equiv \mu_n := \sum_{i \le n} P_i$ is called the accompanying infinitely divisible law for $\mathcal{L}(S_n)$ (see [1]); here and everywhere in the future, the symbol $\mathcal{L}(\zeta)$ denotes the distribution of a random variable (r.v.) ζ. We denote by τ_{μ_n} a r.v. having this distribution.

For every natural $m \le n$, let $\{X_{m,i}; i \ge 1\}$ be independent copies of the random variable X_m. We assume that all the sequences $\{X_i\}$, $\{X_{1,i}\}$, $\{X_{2,i}\}, \ldots$ are independent. Additionally, let $\pi(t), \pi_1(t), \ldots, \pi_n(t)$, $t \ge 0$ be independent Poisson random processes with unit intensity which do not depend on the sequences of r.vs above. From (1), it follows that

$$Pois(P) = \mathcal{L}\left(S_{\pi(1)}\right). \tag{2}$$

The characteristic functional of a $\mathcal{B}$-valued r.v. ζ is defined as follows:

$$\varphi_\zeta(l) := \mathbf{E}e^{il(\zeta)}, \quad l \in \mathcal{B}^*,$$

where $l(\cdot)$ is a bounded linear functional on $\mathcal{B}$, i.e., it is an element of the conjugate space $\mathcal{B}^*$. So, one obtains

$$\varphi_{\tau_P}(l) := \mathbf{E}e^{il(\tau_P)} = \exp\{\varphi_{X_1}(l) - 1)\}.$$

Citation: Borisov, I. Poissonization Inequalities for Sums of Independent Random Variables in Banach Spaces with Applications to Empirical Processes. *Mathematics* **2024**, *12*, 2803. https://doi.org/10.3390/math12182803

Academic Editors: Irina Shevtsova and Victor Korolev

Received: 27 July 2024
Revised: 2 September 2024
Accepted: 4 September 2024
Published: 10 September 2024

Next, the characteristic functional of the accompanying infinitely devisable law is calculated by the formula

$$\varphi_{\tau_{\mu_n}}(l) := \mathbf{E}e^{il(\tau_{\mu_n})} = \exp\left\{\sum_{i=1}^{n}\left(\varphi_{X_{1,i}}(l) - 1\right)\right\}. \tag{3}$$

In other words,

$$\mathcal{L}(\tau_{\mu_n}) = \mathcal{L}\left(\sum_{m=1}^{n} S_{m,\pi_m(1)}\right), \tag{4}$$

where the sums $S_{m,\pi_m(1)} := \sum_{i=1}^{\pi_m(1)} X_{m,i}$, $m = 1,\dots,n$ (with $\sum_{i=1}^{0} = 0$) are independent, and $\mathcal{L}\left(S_{m,\pi_m(1)}\right) = Pois(P_m)$ by virtue of (1). In the i.i.d. case, from (3), we obtain that Formula (4) can be rewritten as follows:

$$Pois(\mu_n) \equiv Pois(nP) = \mathcal{L}\left(S_{\pi(n)}\right). \tag{5}$$

The main goal of this paper is to obtain upper and lower moment inequalities for some measurable functions of S_n or of the collection $S_1,\dots,S_n$ via the analogous moments of the accompanying compound Poisson laws as well as to obtain upper bounds for the probability tail of these functionals. Results of this kind are related to Kolmogorov's problem of approximating sums of independent r.vs by various infinitely divisible laws, in particular, by the accompanying ones, as well as with an improvement of the classical probability inequalities for these sums.

In what follows, we consider functions of one or several (say, n) $\mathcal{B}$-valued arguments. In the latter case, we consider functions of the n-variate argument $\bar{z} := (z_1,\dots,z_n)$ from the new Banach space $\mathcal{B}^n := \mathcal{B}\times\cdots\times\mathcal{B}$ with the norm $\|\bar{z}\|_* := \left(\|z_1\|^2 + \ldots + \|z_n\|^2\right)^{1/2}$. So, for arbitrary Borel functions $f(z)$, $G(\bar{z})$ and $F(\bar{z})$, with $z\in\mathcal{B}$ and $\bar{z}\in\mathcal{B}^n$, introduce the following notation under appropriate moment conditions:

$$\phi(n) := \mathbf{E}f(S_n), \tag{6}$$

$$\Phi_F(\bar{k}_n) := \mathbf{E}F(S_{1,k_1},\dots,S_{n,k_n}), \tag{7}$$

$$g_n := \mathbf{E}G(S_1,\dots,S_n), \tag{8}$$

where $\bar{k}_n := (k_1,\dots,k_n)$, with $k_j \in Z_+$ (Z_+ is the set of all nonnegative integers). It is clear that the function $\phi(n)$ is a particular example of the function g_n. In turn, the latter function is a particular case of $\Phi_F(\bar{k}_n)$ if $k_1 = \ldots = k_n = 1$.

We say that a function $\psi : Z_+ \to R$ is convex (concave) if the difference $\Delta\psi(n) := \psi(n+1) - \psi(n)$ is a nondecreasing (nonincreasing, respectively) function in n.

The following two theorems, in particular, contain some results from [2] together with some new results.

Theorem 1. *The following assertions are valid*:

1. *For all $z\in\mathcal{B}$ and naturals m, let the functions $\phi_{m,z}(n) := \mathbf{E}f(S_{m,n}+z)$ be convex. Then,*

$$\mathbf{E}f(S_n) \le \mathbf{E}f(\tau_{\mu_n}) \tag{9}$$

provided that the expectation on the right-hand side of this inequality exists.

In the i.i.d. case, inequality (9) *holds if only the function $\phi(n)$ is convex.*

2. *Let the function* $\Phi_F(\bar{k}_n)$ *be convex with respect to each coordinate* $k_j \in Z_+$. *Then, for every vector* $\bar{k} \in Z_+^n$,

$$\Phi_F(\bar{k}_n) \leq \mathbf{E}F(\tau^{(1)}_{k_1P_1}, \ldots, \tau^{(n)}_{k_nP_n}) \tag{10}$$

if the expectation on the right-hand side of (10) *exists, where* $\{\tau^{(j)}_{k_jP_j}, j = 1, \ldots, n\}$ *are independent r.v-s with respective distributions* $\{Pois(k_jP_j), j = 1, \ldots, n\}$.

Remark 1. *If the functions* $\Phi_F(\bar{k}_n)$ *and* $\phi_{m,z}(n)$ *in Theorem 1 are concave, then, inequalities (9) and (10) are changed to the opposite. It follows from the well-known connection between convex and concave functions: concave =* $-$*convex.*

For a r.v. ζ with values in $\mathcal{B}$, $supp\,\zeta$ denotes the minimal closed subset of $\mathcal{B}$ such that $\zeta \in supp\,\zeta$ with probability 1. We need the notion of convexity in the direction determined by a subset of $\mathcal{B}$. We say that a measurable function f is convex in direction $\bigcup_{i\geq 1} suppX_i$ if for all $x \in \bigcup_{i\geq 1} supp\, S_i$ and all $z, h \in \bigcup_{i\geq 1} suppX_i$, this function satisfies the inequality

$$f(x+h) - f(x) \leq f(x+h+z) - f(x+z). \tag{11}$$

Notice that, in the one-dimensional case, convexity in direction R_+ (nonnegative summands) or Z_+ (integer-valued nonnegative summands) is the classical convexity. But in the multivariate case, the convexity of f does not imply the relation (11). As a counterexample, we consider the three-dimensional case and the convex function $f(x_1, x_2, x_3) = \max_{i\leq 3}|x_i|$. Put $x = (1,0,0)$, $h = (0,2,0)$ and z=(0,0,3). It is clear that inequality (11) for these parameters is false. However, this function satisfies the relation (11) in the direction determined by any one-dimensional subspace of $\mathbb{R}^3$.

Proposition 1. *In the i.i.d. case, let a measurable function* f *satisfy* (11). *Then, under the moment conditions above, inequality* (9) *holds.*

Example 1. *If* $X_i \geq 0$ *a.s., and* f *is an arbitrary convex function on* $[0,\infty)$, *then, inequalities (9) and (11) are valid.*

We now consider some particular cases of the scheme described in Proposition 1. Let $F_n^*(t)$ be the empirical distribution function based on a sample $\omega_1, \ldots, \omega_n$ from the $[0,1]$-uniform distribution. Then, the normalized empirical process $\nu_n(t) := nF_n^*(t)$ can be represented as the nth partial sum $\sum_{i=1}^{n} X_i$ of the indicator-type i.i.d. random processes $X_i := I_{\{s:\,s\leq t\}}(\omega_i)$ taking values in a Banach space, say, $L_2[0,1]$. It is well known that the accompanying compound Poisson r.v. $S_{\pi(n)}$ for this sum is a Poisson random process with intensity n, which coincides in distribution with the Poisson random process $\pi(nt)$, $t \in [0,1]$. Notice that the finite-dimensional distributions of the random process $\nu_n(\cdot)$ are multinomial. In particular, for each $t \in (0,1)$, the distribution $\mathcal{L}(\nu_n(t))$ is binomial with parameters (n,t).

As consequences of Proposition 1, we obtain the following two assertions.

Corollary 1. *Let* $f : Z_+ \to R$ *be a convex function. Then, for any* $t \in [0,1]$,

$$\mathbf{E}f(\nu_n(t)) \leq \mathbf{E}f(\pi(nt)), \tag{12}$$

whenever the right-hand side in (12) *is well-defined.*

Corollary 2. *Let G and f be nondecreasing convex functions on R. Then,*

$$\mathbf{E}G\left(\int_0^1 f(\nu_n(t))\lambda(dt)\right) \le \mathbf{E}G\left(\int_0^1 f(\pi(nt))\lambda(dt)\right)$$

if the right-hand side of this inequality is well defined, where $\lambda(\cdot)$ is an arbitrary finite measure on $[0,1]$.

One can slightly weaken the convexity property in Corollary 1 by studying power moments of the r.vs under consideration.

Proposition 2. *For every $t \in [0,1]$ and any naturals n and m, the following inequalities hold:*

$$\mathbf{E}(\nu_n(t)+x)^{2m-1} \le \mathbf{E}(\pi(nt)+x)^{2m-1}, \quad \forall x \ge -n, \tag{13}$$

and

$$|\mathbf{E}(\nu_n(t)+x)^{2m-1}| \le \mathbf{E}(\pi(nt)+x)^{2m-1}, \quad \forall x \ge -nt. \tag{14}$$

Remark 2. *It is worth noting that, from Corollary 2, one can easily obtain similar inequalities for all even moments and $x \in R$. Additionally, for all $x \ge 0$, inequalities (13) and (14) coincide and also follow from (12). So, the only nontrivial cases in (13) and (14) are $x \in [-n,0)$ and $x \in [-nt,0)$, respectively. We note that, for $x < -nt$, the right-hand sides in (13) and (14) may be negative (say, for $m = 1$).*

A direct consequence of Proposition 2 is as follows.

Corollary 3. *Let $f(x)$ be an entire function on $[0,\infty)$.*

1. *Assume that there is a point $x_0 \ge 0$ such that, for all $k \ge 2$, the values of k-th derivatives $f^{(k)}(x_0)$ at the point x_0 are nonnegative. Then, for every $t \in [0,1]$ and all $n \ge x_0$,*

$$\mathbf{E}f(\nu_n(t)) \le \mathbf{E}f(\pi(nt)) \tag{15}$$

provided that the expectation on the right-hand side of (15) is well defined.

2. *Assume that there is a point $x^* \ge 0$ such that*

$$f^*(x) := \sum_{k\ge 0} \frac{|f^{(k)}(x^*)|}{k!}(x-x^*)^k$$

is an entire function on $[0,\infty)$ as well. Then, for every $(0,1]$ and all $n \ge x^*/t$,

$$\mathbf{E}f(\nu_n(t)) \le \mathbf{E}f^*(\pi(nt)) \tag{16}$$

provided that the expectation on the right-hand side of (16) is well defined.

Example 2. *Let $f(x) := x^3 - 3rx^2$, $x \ge 0$, where $r > 0$. Put $x_0 = r$. Then, the conditions in item 1 of Corollary 3 are fulfilled, and inequality (15) is valid for all $n \ge r$. But the function $f(x)$ is convex only for $x \ge r$; otherwise, it is concave.*

Theorem 2. *Suppose that at least one of the following two conditions is fulfilled:*

1. *The function f is continuously differentiable in the Fréchet sense (i.e., $f'(x)[h]$ is continuous in x for each fixed h), and for each $x \in \bigcup_{i\ge 1} supp\, S_i$ and all $z, h \in \bigcup_{i\ge 1} supp\, X_i$,*

$$f'(x+th)[h] \le f'(x+z+th)[h] \quad \forall t \in [0,1]; \tag{17}$$

2. $\mathbf{E}X_k = 0$ *for all* k, f *is twice continuously differentiable in the Fréchet sense, and* $f''(x)[h,h]$ *is convex in* x *for each fixed* $h \in \bigcup_{i\geq 1} supp\, X_i$.

Then, the function $\phi(n)$ *is convex, i.e., inequality* (9) *is valid.*

Corollary 4. *If* $X_i \geq 0$ *a.s. and* $f : R_+ \to R$ *is a convex function, then, inequality* (11) *is valid. If* X_i *are random vectors in* R^k, $k \geq 2$, *or in the Hilbert space* l_2, *with nonnegative coordinates, then, the function* $f(x) := \|x\|^{2+\alpha}$, *where* $\|\cdot\|$ *is the corresponding Euclidean norm and* $\alpha \geq 0$, *satisfies inequalities* (11) *and* (17). *For the zero-mean Hilbert-space-valued r.vs* X_i, *the function* $f(x) := \|x\|^{\beta}$, *where* $\beta = 2, 4$ *or* $\beta \geq 6$, *satisfies condition 2 of Theorem 2. Therefore, in these cases, inequality* (9) *holds under the restriction* $\mathbf{E}|f(\tau_{\mu_n})| < \infty$.

Remark 3. *There exist functions* $f(x)$ *which do not satisfy the conditions of Theorem 2 but the corresponding function* $\phi(n)$ *is convex. For example, in the i.i.d. one-dimensional case, let us consider the function* $f(x) := x^5$ *and the centered summands* $\{X_i\}$. *It is clear that the conditions of Theorem 2 are not fulfilled. In this case, we have*

$$\phi(n) = \mathbf{E}(\sum_{i=1}^{n} X_i)^5 = n\mathbf{E}X_1^5 + 10n(n-1)\mathbf{E}X_1^3\mathbf{E}X_1^2,$$

i.e., it is a quadratic function with respect to the variable n. *Thus, if* $\mathbf{E}X_1^3 \geq 0$, *then, the function* $\phi(n)$ *is convex; otherwise, it is concave. In other words, in this case, we obtain upper and lower Poissonization inequalities in dependence on the sign of the moment* $\mathbf{E}X_1^3$.

The exactness of inequality (9) is characterized by the following two assertions.

Corollary 5. *For independent one-dimensional centered r.v.s* $\{X_i\}$, *consider the function* $f(x) := x^3$. *Since, for any fixed* $z \in R$, *the second derivative of the function* $F_z(x) = (z+x)^3$ *is convex and concave simultaneously, then, by item 2 of Theorem 2,*

$$\mathbf{E}S_n^3 = \mathbf{E}\tau_{\mu_n}^3. \tag{18}$$

Given a finite measure μ on $\mathcal{B}$ satisfying the condition $\mu(\{0\}) = 0$, we denote by $\phi_\mu(n)$ the function $\phi(n)$ in (6) defined in the i.i.d. case for the summand distribution $\mu(\cdot)/\mu(\mathcal{B})$.

Theorem 3 ([2]). *In the i.i.d. case, let the function* $\phi_\mu(k)$ *be convex. Then,*

$$\sup_{n,P} \mathbf{E}f(S_n) = \mathbf{E}f(\tau_\mu) \tag{19}$$

whenever the expectation on the right-hand side of (5) *is well defined, where* $\mathcal{L}(\tau_\mu) = Pois(\mu)$, *and the supremum is taken over all* n *and* P *such that* $nP(A \setminus \{0\}) = \mu(A)$ *for all Borel subsets* $A \subseteq \mathcal{B}$.

Remark 4. *Taking inequality (9) into account, we can easily reformulate Theorem 2 for the non-i.i.d. case. The idea of employing compound Poisson distributions for constructing upper bounds for the moments of the sums was first proposed by Prokhorov ([3,4]). In particular, relations (9) and (19) were obtained in [4] for the functions* $f(x) := x^{2m}$ *(m is an arbitrary natural) and* $f(x) := \mathrm{ch}(tx)$, $t \in R$, *in the case of one-dimensional symmetric* $\{X_i\}$. *Moreover, in the case of zero-mean one-dimensional summands, these relations for the functions* $f(x) := \exp(hx)$, $h \geq 0$, *can be easily deduced from [3] (see also [5]).*

A more general result in this direction was obtained by Utev [6]. Under condition 2 of Theorem 2, he proved extremal equality (19) for nonnegative functions $f(x)$ having an exponential majorant, using a technique by Kemperman [7]. In our opinion, the proof of item 2 of Theorem 2 (see Section 3) is much simpler than that in [6] and needs no additional restrictions on $f(x)$ and the sample space.

Relations like (9) and (19) can also be applied for obtaining sharp moments and the tail probability inequalities for sums of independent r.vs (for details, see [5–12]).

We now consider the centered empirical point process $\bar{\nu}_n(t) := \nu_n(t) - nt$, $t \in [0,1]$, that one can interpret as a sum of n i.i.d. centered r.vs $X_i := I_{\{s:\, s \le t\}}(\omega_i) - t$ taking values, say, in the Hilbert space $L_2([0,1], \lambda)$, where $\lambda(\cdot)$ is an arbitrary finite measure on $[0,1]$. The accompanying compound Poisson random process can be represented in the form $\pi_n^o(t) := \pi(nt) - t\pi(n)$, $t \in [0,1]$, which may be called as a "Poissonian bridge" with intensity n on the unit interval. By Corollary 5, we then obtain

$$\mathbf{E}\left(\int_0^1 (\bar{\nu}_n(t))^2 \lambda(dt)\right)^{\gamma} \le \mathbf{E}\left(\int_0^1 (\pi_n^o(t))^2 \lambda(dt)\right)^{\gamma}, \tag{20}$$

where $\gamma = 1, 2$ or $\gamma \ge 3$. If $\lambda(\cdot)$ is the Dirac measure with atom at a point t, then, a univariate analog of inequality (20) is as follows:

$$\mathbf{E}|\bar{\nu}_n(t)|^{\gamma} \le \mathbf{E}|\pi_n^o(t)|^{\gamma}, \tag{21}$$

with an arbitrary $\gamma \ge 3$ or $\gamma = 2$ and any $t \in [0,1]$. But compared to (20), we have here less restrictive conditions on γ due to item 2 of Theorem 2. It is clear that we can replace the power functions in (21) with any function f having a convex second derivative under appropriate moment conditions:

$$\mathbf{E}f(\bar{\nu}_n(t)) \le \mathbf{E}f(\pi_n^o(t)). \tag{22}$$

It is interesting to compare inequalities (21) and (22) with (12) and (13) taking Remark 2 into account and setting $x = -nt$ in (13). Put $\bar{\pi}(t) := \pi(t) - t$.

Proposition 3. *For every $t \in [0,1]$ and any even convex function f on R, the following two-sided inequality is valid:*

$$\max\{\mathbf{E}f(t\bar{\pi}(n(1-t))), \mathbf{E}f((1-t)\bar{\pi}(nt))\}$$

$$\le \mathbf{E}f(\pi_n^o(t)) \le \max\{\mathbf{E}f(\bar{\pi}(n(1-t))), \mathbf{E}f(\bar{\pi}(nt))\} \tag{23}$$

if only the Poissonian moments exist. Moreover, if $t \in [1/2, 1]$, then,

$$\mathbf{E}f(\pi_n^o(t)) \le \mathbf{E}f(\bar{\pi}(nt)). \tag{24}$$

Proposition 4. *For any $x \ge 0$, $t \in [0,1]$ and every natural number m,*

$$\mathbf{E}(\pi_n^o(t) + x)^m \le \mathbf{E}(\bar{\pi}(nt) + x)^m. \tag{25}$$

Thus, inequalities (21)–(25) improve the estimates (12)–(15).

We supplemented Corollary 2 and Theorem 2 with an example of an infinitely dimensional function space $\mathcal{B}$. Let $\mathcal{B} = C[0,1]$, with $||x|| := \sup_{0 \le t \le 1} |x(t)|$. Consider an integral-type functional of the form

$$f(x) := \int_0^1 g(x(t))\lambda(dt), \quad x \in C[0,1],$$

where $g(z)$ is a smooth function on R. In this case, the first two Fréchet derivatives of f are defined as follows:

$$f^{(1)}(x)[h] := \int_0^1 g'(x(t))h(t)\lambda(dt),$$

$$f^{(2)}(x)[h_1, h_2] := \int_0^1 g''(x(t))h_1(t)h_2(t)\lambda(dt), \quad h, h_1, h_2 \in C[0,1].$$

For example, if the continuous random processes $X_i = X_i(t), t \in [0,1]$, are nonnegative and the function g is convex (or the first derivative $g'(x)$ is nondecreasing in the positive direction), then, item 1 of Theorem 2 will be fulfilled. On the other hand, if $X_i(t)$ are centered random processes on $[0,1]$ and the second derivative $g''(z)$ is convex on R, then, item 2 of Theorem 2 will also be satisfied.

We can easily reformulate condition (11) and Theorem 2 for the functions $F(\bar{z})$ in (7) if for any $j = 1, \ldots, n$ and fixed $z_i \in \mathcal{B}$, we put

$$F_{\bar{z},j}(x) := F(z_1, \ldots z_{j-1}, x, z_{j+1}, \ldots, z_n) \tag{26}$$

and, under the conditions of Theorem 2, replace the function $f(x)$ with $F_{\bar{z},j}(x)$ for $\bar{z}$ from an appropriate subset.

Corollary 6. *For every fixed $j = 1, \ldots, n$, let the functions $F_{\bar{z},j}(x)$ satisfy (11) for all $x, h \in \bigcup_{i \geq 1} supp\, S_{j,i}$ and $z_k \in \bigcup_{i \geq 1} supp\, S_{k,i}$, $k \neq j$. Then, under the moment conditions above, inequality (10) holds.*

In (7), put

$$F(\bar{z}) := G(z_1, z_1 + z_2, \ldots, z_1 + \ldots + z_n). \tag{27}$$

Corollary 7. *Let the functions $F_{\bar{z},j}(x)$, defined in (26) by the function $F(\bar{z})$ in (27), satisfy the conditions of Theorem 2. Then,*

$$g_n \leq \mathbf{E}G(\tau_{P_1}^{(1)}, \tau_{P_1}^{(1)} + \tau_{P_2}^{(2)}, \ldots, \sum_{i=1}^{n} \tau_{P_i}^{(i)}), \tag{28}$$

where the independent r.v-s $\{\tau_{P_i}^{(i)}\}$ are defined in Theorem 1.

The above results deal with some type of convexity. However, one can obtain moment inequalities close to those mentioned above without any convexity conditions. The following result is valid for the r.vs $\{X_i\}$ such that $0 < \mathbf{Pr}(X_i = 0) < 1$ for all i.

Theorem 4. *In the i.i.d. case, for every nonnegative measurable function f, the following inequality holds:*

$$\mathbf{E}f(S_n) \leq \frac{1}{1-p}\mathbf{E}f(\tau_\mu), \tag{29}$$

where $p := \mathbf{Pr}(X_1 \neq 0)$.

Corollary 8. *For any measurable nonnegative function $F(\bar{z})$ in (7),*

$$\Phi_F(\bar{1}) \leq A_n \mathbf{E}F(\tau_{P_1}^{(1)}, \ldots, \tau_{P_n}^{(n)}), \tag{30}$$

with $A_n := \exp\{\sum_{i=1}^n p_i\}$, where $p_i := \mathbf{Pr}(X_i \neq 0)$. In particular, in the non-i.i.d. case, the factor $(1-p)^{-1}$ in (29) may be replaced with A_n.

For an arbitrary vector $\bar{k}_n \neq \bar{1}$,

$$\Phi_F(\bar{k}_n) \leq A_n^* \mathbf{E}F(\tau_{k_1 P_1}^{(1)}, \ldots, \tau_{k_n P_n}^{(n)}), \tag{31}$$

where $A_n^* := \prod_{i=1}^n (1-p_i)^{-1} < \exp\{\sum_{i=1}^n p_i(1-p_i)^{-1}\}$.

In Theorem 4 and Corollary 8, we do not require the existence of the expectations considering their values on the extended real line. It is clear that, in the non-i.i.d. case, inequalities (29) and (30) provide a sufficiently good upper bound under the so-called Poissonian setting when the summand distributions have large atoms at zero, i.e., the probabilities p_i are such that the constant A_n is not too large.

Notice that some particular cases of inequality (29) are contained in [1,13].

Remark 5. *In the case $n = 1$, there exists a slightly better upper bound than that in (29). In this case, the factor $(1-p)^{-1}$ on the right-hand side of (29) can be replaced with e^p. However, in the special case when $S_n = \sum_{i\le n} \nu_1^{(i)}(p_i)$, where $\{\nu_1^{(i)}(p_i)\}$ are independent Bernoulli r.vs with respective parameters $\{p_i\}$, there exists a better upper bound than that in (29). In this case, we can replace the factor A_n with $(1-\tilde{p})^{-2}$, where $\tilde{p} = \max\{p_i;\ i \le n\}$ (see [14,15]).*

Corollary 9. *Let g be a nonnegative function satisfying the condition $\mathbf{E}g(\pi(\lambda)) < \infty$ for some λ. Then, for every n and p satisfying the condition $np \le \lambda$, the following inequality holds:*

$$\mathbf{E}g(\nu_n(p)) \le \frac{e^{\lambda - np}}{1-p}\mathbf{E}g(\pi(\lambda)). \tag{32}$$

Moreover,

$$\lim_{n\to\infty,\, np\to\lambda-0} \mathbf{E}g(\nu_n(p)) = \mathbf{E}g(\pi(\lambda)). \tag{33}$$

Remark 6. *It is worth noting that, under the minimal moment condition above, we cannot replace the one-sided double limit in (33) with the classical double limit, and the condition $np \le \lambda$ in (32) cannot be omitted. Moreover, there exists a nonnegative function $g(k)$ (see Section 3) such that $\mathbf{E}g(\pi(\lambda)) < \infty$ and*

$$\lim \sup_{n\to\infty,\, np\to\lambda+0} \mathbf{E}g(\nu_n(p)) = \infty. \tag{34}$$

2. Applications to Empirical Point Processes

In this section, we formulate some consequences of the above theorems as well as some new similar results for empirical point processes indexed by subsets of a measurable space. These processes generalize the scheme of univariate empirical point processes $\nu_n(t)$ from the previous section. These results are a basis for the so-called Poissonization method for generalizing empirical point processes. Sometimes, it is more convenient to replace an empirical point process under study with the corresponding accompanying Poisson point process having a simpler structure for analysis (for example, independent "increments"). Some versions of this sufficiently popular and very effective method can be found in many papers. In particular, some probability inequalities connecting the distributions of empirical processes (in various settings) and those of the corresponding Poisson processes are contained in [13,16–18], etc.

Let $x_1, x_2, \ldots$ be i.i.d. r.vs taking values in an arbitrary measurable space $(\mathfrak{X}, \mathcal{A})$ and having a common distribution P. The empirical point process is introduced as

$$V_n(A) := \sum_{i=1}^{n} I_A(x_i), \quad A \in \mathcal{A}_c,$$

and the accompanying Poisson point process

$$\Pi_n(A) := \sum_{i=1}^{\pi(n)} I_A(x_i), \quad A \in \mathcal{A}_c,$$

where $\mathcal{A}_c \equiv \{A_i\}$ is a countable family of measurable sets, and a standard Poisson random process $\pi(\cdot)$ is independent of the collection $\{x_i\}$.

We will consider these processes as r.vs taking values in the separable Banach space $B_q(\mathcal{A}_c)$ of all functions $Y(\cdot)$ on $\mathcal{A}_c$ such that $\sum_{i\ge 1} |Y(A_i)|^q 2^{-i} < \infty$ for some $q \ge 1$, endowed with the norm

$$\|Y\|_q = \left(\sum_{i\ge 1} \frac{|Y(A_i)|^q}{2^i}\right)^{1/q}.$$

In the case $q = \infty$, we deal with the supnorm $\|Y\|_\infty := \sup_i |Y(A_i)|$. It is clear that the Banach space $B_q(\mathcal{A}_c)$ is isomorphic to the Banach space $L_q[\mathbb{N}, \lambda]$, where $\mathbb{N}$ is the set of natural numbers, and λ is a discrete probability measure on $\mathbb{N}$ with $\lambda(\{k\}) = 2^{-k}$. So, the point process $\Pi_n(\cdot)$ is the accompanying compound Poisson process for the point process $V_n(\cdot)$ in the Banach space $B_q(\mathcal{A}_c)$.

As a direct consequence of Proposition 1, the following assertion is valid.

Corollary 10. *Let $\Phi(\cdot)$ be a measurable functional on $B_1(\mathcal{A}_c)$, which is convex in the positive direction with respect to the standard pointwise partial order in function spaces. Then, under appropriate moment conditions, the following inequality holds:*

$$\mathbf{E}\Phi(V_n) \leq \mathbf{E}\Phi(\Pi_n). \tag{35}$$

As examples, one can consider functionals of the form

$$\Phi_{G,f}(Y) := G\left(\sum_{i\geq 1} f_i(Y(A_i))\right),$$

where G and $\{f_i\}$ are nondecreasing convex functions on $\mathbb{R}$ provided that $\sum_{i\geq 1} |f_i(x)| < \infty$ for all $x \in \mathbb{R}$. For such functionals, it is easy to verify the conditions of Corollary 10 (see the proof of Corollary 2).

By analogy with the univariate case, the centered empirical point process $V_n^o(A) := V_n(A) - nP(A)$ and the corresponding accompanying compound Poisson point process $\Pi_n^o(A) := \Pi_n(A) - nP(A)\Pi_n(\mathfrak{X})$ are introduced. For such processes, the second assertion of Theorem 2 can be reformulated as follows:

Corollary 11. *Let $\Phi(x)$ be a measurable functional on $B_1(\mathcal{A}_c)$ having a convex second Fréchet derivative. Then,*

$$\mathbf{E}\Phi(V_n^o) \leq \mathbf{E}\Phi(\Pi_n^o), \tag{36}$$

whenever the expectation on the right-hand side of this inequality exists.

As examples of such functionals, one can cite $\Phi_{G,f}(Y)$.

We now introduce the so-called *restricted empirical point processes*. Let $A_0 \in \mathcal{A}$ and $p := \mathbf{P}(x_1 \in A_0) \in (0,1)$. Consider the restrictions of the point processes $V_n(A)$ and $\Pi_n(A)$ on the set $\mathcal{A}_0 := \{A \in \mathcal{A}_c : A \subseteq A_0\}$, which is denoted by $V_n^*(A)$ and $\Pi_n^*(A)$, respectively. We call these processes *$\mathcal{A}_0$-restricted point processes*. In this case, $V_n^*(A) \equiv S_n = \sum_{i=1}^n X_i$, where $X_i := \{I_A(x_i);\ A \in \mathcal{A}_0\}$, $i = 1, \ldots, n$, are i.i.d. stochastic processes indexed by the elements from the family $\mathcal{A}_0$, with $p := \mathbf{P}(X_1 \neq 0) \in (0,1)$. We may consider $\{X_i\}$ as i.i.d. r.vs taking values in the Banach space $B_\infty(\mathcal{A}_c)$. As a direct consequence of Theorem 4, we then obtain

Corollary 12. *The following inequalities are valid:*

$$\mathcal{L}(V_n^*) \leq \frac{1}{1-p}\mathcal{L}(\Pi_n^*), \tag{37}$$

$$\mathbf{E}F(V_n^*) \leq \frac{1}{1-p}\mathbf{E}F(\Pi_n^*),$$

where $F(\cdot) \geq 0$ and the expectations take their values on the extended real line.

We now introduce a class of additive statistics of the empirical point processes. Let $\Delta_1, \Delta_2, \ldots$ be a finite or countable measurable partition of the sample space. We assume that $p_i := P(\Delta_i) > 0$ for all i and $p_1 \geq p_2 \geq p_3 \geq \ldots$. Denote $\nu_{in} := V_n(\Delta_i)$. We study a class of additive functionals of the form

$$\Phi_f(V_n) := \sum_{i\geq 1} f_{in}(\nu_{in}), \tag{38}$$

where $\{f_{in}\}$ is an array of functions on $\mathbb{Z}_+$, with $\sum_{i\geq 1} |f_{in}(0)| < \infty$.

Example 3. *We now give a few examples of additive statistics.*

(1) Given a finite partition $\{\Delta_i; i = 1, \ldots, m\}$, put $f_{in}(x) := \frac{(x-np_i)^2}{np_i}$, $i = 1, \ldots, m$. Then, we deal with a χ^2-statistic of the form

$$\Phi_{\chi^2}(V_n) = \sum_{i=1}^{m} \frac{(\nu_{in} - np_i)^2}{np_i}.$$

(2) The log-likelihood function can be represented as the following linear functional:

$$\Phi_l(V_n) := \sum_{i=1}^{N} \nu_{in} \log p_i.$$

(3) Fix a countable partition $\{\Delta_i; i \geq 1\}$. Let $f_{in}(x) \equiv f(x) := I_A(x)$. (For countable partitions, we assume that $0 \notin A$). Then, the functional

$$\Phi_I(V_n) = \sum_{i\geq 1} I_A(\nu_{in}) \tag{39}$$

is the number of cells Δ_i, each of them contains a number of the sample points X_i from the range defined by a subset A of naturals. It is the so-called infinite multinomial scheme of placing particles (balls) in cells (boxes) (for example, see [19–24]).

For additive functionals (38), one can also obtain Poissonization inequalities using the above mentioned inequalities for restricted empirical point processes. The next theorem is related to estimating the distribution tails of additive functionals (38) via the probability tails of the same functionals of the accompanying Poisson point process $\Pi_n(\cdot)$. The main property of the functionals $\Phi_f(\Pi_n)$ is that they have a structure of sums of independent r.vs.

Theorem 5. *Let $f_{i\tilde{n}}(\cdot) \geq 0$ for all i. Then, for any $x > 0$,*

$$\mathbf{P}(\Phi_f(V_n) \geq x) \leq 2C^* \mathbf{P}(\Phi_f(\Pi_n) \geq x/2), \tag{40}$$

where $C^* := \min_{k\geq 1} \max\Big\{ \big(\sum_{i\leq k} p_i\big)^{-1}, \big(\sum_{i>k} p_i\big)^{-1} \Big\}$. If, additionally,

$$\sup_x \sum_{i\leq m} f_{i\tilde{n}}(x) \leq C_{m,n}$$

for some natural number m, then,

$$\mathbf{P}(\Phi_f(V_n) \geq x) \leq \left(\sum_{i\leq m} p_i \right)^{-1} \mathbf{P}(\Phi_f(\Pi_n) \geq x - C_{m,n}). \tag{41}$$

Remark 7. *It is worth noting that, in (41), the constant $C_{m,n}$ may be interpreted as a level of truncation for the r.v. $\sum_{i\leq m} f_{i\tilde{n}}(\nu_{i_n})$. In this case, we should add the probability $\mathbf{P}\big(\sum_{i\leq m} f_{i\tilde{n}}(\nu_{i_n}) > C_{m,n}\big)$ to the right-hand side of inequality (41).*

Integrating both sides of inequality (40) in x on the positive half-line, we obtain

Corollary 13. *Under the conditions of Theorem 5, let F be a nondecreasing function defined on $\mathbb{R}_+$, continuous at zero and $F(0) = 0$. If $\mathbf{E}F(2\Phi_f(\overline{\Pi}_{\bar{n}})) < \infty$, then,*

$$\mathbf{E}F(\Phi_f(V_n)) \le 2C^*\mathbf{E}F(2\Phi_f(\Pi_n)). \tag{42}$$

As an example, consider the functional $\Phi_{I_B}(V_n)$ defined in (39). Then, as a consequence of (41) and Chernoff's upper bound (see [25]) for the probability tail of a sum of independent nonidentically distributed Bernoulli r.vs (the transition from finite sums to series in this case is obvious), we obtain the following result.

Corollary 14 ([24]). *Put $M_n(B) := \mathbf{E}\Phi_{I_B}(\Pi_{\bar{n}}) = \sum_{i\ge 1}\mathbf{P}(\pi_{in} \in B)$. Then, the following inequality holds for any $\varepsilon > (M_n(B))^{-1}$:*

$$\mathbf{P}\left(\left|\frac{\Phi_{I_B}(V_n)}{M_n(B)} - 1\right| > \varepsilon\right) \le 2p_1^{-1}e^{-\frac{\delta^2 M_n(B)}{2+\delta}}, \tag{43}$$

where $\delta := \varepsilon - \frac{1}{M_n(B)}$.

Remark 8. *We note that one can replace the Poissonian mean $M_n(B)$ in (43) with the mean $\mathbf{E}\Phi_{I_B}(\overline{V}_{\bar{n}})$, which differs from $M_n(B)$ by no more than 1 due to Barbour–Hall's estimate of the Poisson approximation to a binomial distribution (see [24,26]). Further, if the condition $M_n(B) \to \infty$ is met as $n \to \infty$, then, from (43), we obtain not only the law of large numbers (already formulated in Corollary 2) but at a certain growth rate of the sequence $M_n(B)$, the strong law of large numbers (SLLN). In particular, if $p_i = Ci^{-1-b}$, then, $M_n(B) \sim C(B)n^{\frac{1}{1+b}}$ for any subset of natural numbers B (see [24]). If in the case $m = 1$, we consider the infinite intervals $B \equiv B_k := \{i : i > k\}$ for any $k \in \mathbb{Z}_+$, then, the SLLN is valid only under the condition $p_i > 0$ for all i. This follows from estimate (43), monotonicity of the functions $I_{B_k}(x)$ and simple arguments in proving SLLN in [27] (see also [21]). Moreover, inequality (43) allows us to estimate the rate of convergence in SLLN. If $M_n(B) \to \infty$, this rate of convergence has the order $O(M_n^{-1/2}(B)\log^{1/2} n)$.*

3. Proofs

In this section, we prove some key assertions formulated in the previous two sections.

Proof of Proposition 1. In the i.i.d. case, the convexity of $\phi(k)$ directly follows from (11):

$$\phi(k+1) - \phi(k) \le \mathbf{E}(f(S_{k+1} + X_{k+2}) - f(S_k + X_{k+2})) = \phi(k+2) - \phi(k+1).$$

□

Proof of Corollary 2. Denote

$$F_{x,h,z} := \int_0^1 f(x(t) + h(t) + z(t))\lambda(dt),$$

where $x(t)$, $h(t)$ and $z(t)$ are nonnegative measurable bounded functions. Due to the convexity and monotonicity of f, one has

$$F_{x,0,0} \le F_{x,0,z}, \quad F_{x,h,0} - F_{x,0,0} \le F_{x,h,z} - F_{x,0,z}.$$

From these inequalities and convexity of G, we immediately obtain

$$G(F_{x,h,0}) - G(F_{x,0,0}) \le G(F_{x,h,z}) - G(F_{x,0,z}).$$

So, condition (11) is fulfilled. □

Proof of Proposition 2. First, we consider the case $n = 1$. In other words, we deal here with the Bernoulli r.v. $\nu_1(t)$ with parameter t.

Lemma 1. *For every natural m, the following inequalities hold:*

$$\mathbf{E}(\nu_1(t) + x)^{2m-1} \leq \mathbf{E}(\pi(t) + x)^{2m-1}, \quad \forall x \geq -1, \tag{44}$$

and

$$|\mathbf{E}(\nu_1(t) + x)^{2m-1}| \leq \mathbf{E}(\pi(t) + x)^{2m-1}, \quad \forall x \geq -t. \tag{45}$$

Proof. In order to prove (44), we first study the case $x = -1$.. We have

$$\mathbf{E}(\nu_1(t) - 1)^{2m-1} = t - 1,$$

$$\mathbf{E}(\pi(t) - 1)^{2m-1} = -e^{-t} + \sum_{k=2}^{\infty} \frac{(k-1)^{2m-1}}{k!} t^k e^{-t}$$

$$> -e^{-t} + \frac{1}{2} \sum_{k=2}^{\infty} \frac{(k-1)^{2m-3}}{(k-2)!} t^k e^{-t} = -e^{-t} + \frac{t^2}{2} \mathbf{E}(1 + \pi(t))^{2m-3}$$

$$> t - 1 - \frac{t^2}{2} + \frac{t^2}{2} \mathbf{E}(1 + \pi(t))^{2m-3} > t - 1, \tag{46}$$

where $m \geq 2$ (in the case $m = 1$, the assertion is trivial). We have proved inequalities of the form (44) for even moments and all $x \in \mathbb{R}$ (see Corollary 1). Therefore, inequality (44) remains true after derivation of both its sides with respect to x. So, inequality (44) follows from this fact and (46).

Taking inequality (44) into account, we conclude that, to prove (45), it suffices to deduce only the inequality

$$\mathbf{E}(t - \nu_1(t))^{2m-1} \leq \mathbf{E}(\pi(t) - t)^{2m-1}. \tag{47}$$

Denote $g_m(t) := \mathbf{E}(\pi(t) - t)^m$. We need the following recurrent relation for $g_m(t)$ (for details, see [16,28]):

$$g_m(t) = t \sum_{k=0}^{m-2} C_{m-1}^k g_k(t), \tag{48}$$

where $m \geq 2$, $g_0(t) \equiv 1$ and $g_1(t) \equiv 0$. From (48), we conclude that, for all naturals m, the functions $g_m(t)$ are nonnegative and nondecreasing on $[0, 1]$.

First, we assume that $t \leq 1/2$. Then, we have

$$\mathbf{E}(t - \nu_1(t))^{2m-1} = t(1-t)(t^{2m-2} - (1-t)^{2m-2}) \leq 0,$$

and (47) holds because of the nonnegativity of the functions $g_m(t)$.

In the case $t > 1/2$, we consider another Bernoulli r.v. $\tilde{\nu}_1(\tilde{t}) := 1 - \nu_1(t)$, with $\tilde{t} := 1 - t$. By (44), we then obtain

$$\mathbf{E}(t - \nu_1(t))^{2m-1} = \mathbf{E}(\tilde{\nu}_1(\tilde{t}) - \tilde{t})^{2m-1} \leq g_{2m-1}(\tilde{t}) \leq g_{2m-1}(t)$$

due to the monotonicity of the functions $g_m(t)$. The lemma is proven. □

Since $\nu_n(t)$ coincides in distribution with the sum of independent copies of the r.vs $\nu_{n-1}(t)$ and $\nu_1(t)$, the further proof of the theorem can be continued by induction on n (using (22) and the binomial formula). The proposition is proven. □

Proof of Corollary 3. Due to Fubini's theorem and the Taylor expansion of the function f at the point x_0, the existence of the moment $\mathbf{E}f(\pi(nt))$ implies the equality

$$\mathbf{E}f(\pi(nt)) = \sum_{k\geq 0} \frac{f^{(k)}(x_0)}{k!}\mathbf{E}(\pi(nt) - x_0)^k.$$

So, for all $n \geq x_0$, one can apply inequality (13) for every summand with $k \geq 2$ of the series on the right-hand side of the above identity that yields inequality (15). Here, we have taken into account the fact that

$$\mathbf{E}(\pi(nt) - x_0) = \mathbf{E}(\nu_n(t) - x_0),$$

i.e., the first two summands in the series representations of the expectations $\mathbf{E}f(\pi(nt))$ and $\mathbf{E}f(\nu_n(t))$ coincide.

Inequality (16) is proved similarly, using the estimate (14). □

Remark 9. *Inequality (53) is a part of a more general result in [15]. It is worth noting that this upper bound is an estimate for the so-called Radon–Nikodym derivative of a binomial distribution with respect to the accompanying Poisson law. This problem was studied by a number of authors ([14,29,30], and others). In particular, under some additional restriction on n and p, a slightly stronger estimate is contained in [29]. However, in general, the upper bound (53) cannot be essentially improved. Under some restrictions on n and p, a lower bound for the left-hand side of (53) has the form $(1 - cp)^{-1}$, where $c < 1$ is an absolute positive constant. For example, for $n = 1$, an unimprovable upper bound in (53) equals $e^p < (1 - p)^{-1}$. It is easy to check that $e^p > (1 - p/2)^{-1}$ for all $p \leq 1/2$.*

Proof of Corollary 8. Taking Remark 9 into account, we have a refinement of estimate (53) in the case $n = 1$, and as a consequence, we obtain

$$\mathbf{E}g(\nu_1(p)) \leq e^p g(\pi(p))$$

for any nonnegative function g. The further arguments of proving estimate (30) are quite similar to those in the proof of Theorem 1 below.

Estimate (31) is a direct consequence of estimate (53) and the arguments above. □

Proof of Corollary 9. Inequality (32) follows from Lemma 2 and the simple estimate

$$\sup_j \frac{\mathbf{P}(\pi(np) = j)}{\mathbf{P}(\pi(\lambda) = j)} = \sup_j \left(\frac{np}{\lambda}\right)^j e^{\lambda - np} \leq e^{\lambda - np}$$

if $np \leq \lambda$ only. Otherwise, there are no uniform upper bounds for the Radon–Nikodym derivative under consideration.

Relation (33) follows from the classical Poisson limit theorem and inequality (32), which provides fulfillment of the uniform integrability condition. The corollary is proven. □

To prove relation (34), we consider the function $g(k) := (1 \vee (k-2)!)\lambda^{-k}$. It is clear that $\mathbf{E}g(\pi(\lambda)) < \infty$. Otherwise, we have

$$\mathbf{E}g(\nu_n(p)) > \frac{1}{k_n(k_n - 1)} \prod_{j\leq k_n - 1}(1 - j/n)\left(\frac{np}{\lambda}\right)^{k_n}\left(1 - \frac{np}{n}\right)^{n-k_n},$$

where $n \geq 4$ and $k_n := [\sqrt{n}]$. Further, it easy to see that, as $n \to \infty$ and $np \to \lambda$,

$$\prod_{j\leq k_n-1}(1 - j/n) = \exp\left\{-\sum_{j\leq k_n-1} j/n + O(k_n^3/n^2)\right\} \sim \exp\{-k_n^2/2n\} \sim e^{-1/2}$$

and
$$\left(1-\frac{np}{n}\right)^{n-k_n} \sim e^{-\lambda}.$$

We now suppose that $np/\lambda = 1 + n^{-\alpha}$ for some $\alpha < 1/2$. Then,
$$\left(\frac{np}{\lambda}\right)^{k_n} \sim e^{k_n n^{-\alpha}} \to \infty,$$
which must be proved. □

Proof of Theorem 1. In the i.i.d. case, inequality (9) is a simple consequence of relation (5) and the classical Jensen inequality:
$$\mathbf{E}f(\tau_{\mu_n}) = \mathbf{E}\phi(\pi(n)) \geq \phi(n) = \mathbf{E}f(S_n).$$

In order to prove inequality (9) in the non-i.i.d. case, taking formula (4) into account, we put
$$\tau_{\mu_n} := \sum_{m=1}^{n} S_{m,\pi_m(1)}. \tag{49}$$

The further reasoning is quite analogous to the above. Put $z_1 := \sum_{m=2}^{n} S_{m,\pi_m(1)}$. Using the above arguments, we have
$$\mathbf{E}f(\tau_{\mu_n}) = \mathbf{E}\mathbf{E}_{z_1}\phi_{1,z_1}(\pi(1)) \geq \mathbf{E}\mathbf{E}_{z_1}\phi_{1,z_1}(1) = \mathbf{E}f(X_1 + z_1),$$
where the symbol $\mathbf{E}_{z_1}$ denotes the conditional expectation given z_1. Now, we put $z_2 := X_1 + \sum_{m=3}^{n} S_{m,\pi_m}$. Then, repeating the same calculation, we obtain the estimate
$$\mathbf{E}f(X_1 + z_1) = \mathbf{E}\mathbf{E}_{z_2}\phi_{2,z_2}(\pi_2) \geq \mathbf{E}\mathbf{E}_{z_2}\phi_{2,z_2}(1) = \mathbf{E}f(X_1 + X_2 + \sum_{m=3}^{n} S_{m,\pi_m}).$$

Continuing calculations in this way, we obtain inequality (9). Theorem 1 is proven. □

Proof of Theorem 2. The first assertion is trivial because, under condition 1, from Taylor's formula, we have
$$\begin{aligned} f(x+h) - f(x) &= \int_0^1 f'(x+th)[h]dt \leq \int_0^1 f'(x+z+th)[h]dt \\ &= f(x+z+h) - f(x+z) \end{aligned}$$
for every $x \in \mathcal{G}$ and $z, h \in \bigcup_{i\leq n} suppX_i$,, that is, inequality (11) is fulfilled.

To prove the second assertion, we only need to prove this in the i.i.d. case because, using the arguments in proving Theorem 1 above, we can reduce the problem to the i.i.d. case. It remains to observe that, under condition 2 and given z, the function $f(x+z)$ has a convex second derivative with respect to x. So, we prove the assertion in the i.i.d. case. Taking into account continuity in x of the function $f''(x)[h,h]$ for any fixed h and using Taylor's formula, we have
$$f(S_{k+1}) - f(S_k) = f'(S_k)[X_{k+1}] + \int_0^1 (1-t)f''(S_k + tX_{k+1})[X_{k+1}, X_{k+1}]dt. \tag{50}$$

First, we average both sides of (50) with respect to the distribution of X_{k+1} and use the fact that, for any centered (in Bochner sense) r.v. X and an arbitrary linear continuous functional $l(\cdot)$, the equality $\mathbf{E}l(X) = 0$ holds. Averaging both sides of this identity with respect to the other distributions, we then obtain the equality (with a probability interpretation of the remainder in (50))

$$\phi(k+1)-\phi(k)=\frac{1}{2}\mathbf{E}f''(S_k+\zeta X_{k+1})[X_{k+1},X_{k+1}]=\mathbf{E}f''(S_k+\zeta X_{k+2})[X_{k+2},X_{k+2}] \quad (51)$$

due to the i.i.d. condition of $\{X_k\}$, where ζ is a r.v. with the density $2(1-t)$ on the unit interval, which is defined on the main probability space and independent of the sequence $\{X_k\}$ (we may assume here that this space is reached enough). It is worth noting that, because of the integrability of the left-hand side of (50), the expectation on the right-hand side of (51) is well defined due to Fubini's theorem. In the i.i.d. case, by Jensen's inequality (for the conditional expectation $\mathbf{E}_{\zeta,X_{k+2}}$), we finally obtain from (51) the inequality we need:

$$\phi(k+1)-\phi(k)=\frac{1}{2}\mathbf{E}\mathbf{E}_{\zeta,X_{k+2}}f''(S_k+\zeta X_{k+2})[X_{k+2},X_{k+2}]$$

$$\leq\frac{1}{2}\mathbf{E}f''(S_{k+1}+\zeta X_{k+2})[X_{k+2},X_{k+2}]=\phi(k+2)-\phi(k+1).$$

The theorem is proven. □

Proof of Theorem 4. First, we prove two important lemmas which play a key role in proving the theorem. For the initial r.vs which are nondegenerate at zero, let $\{X_i^0\}$ be independent r.vs with respective distributions

$$\mathcal{L}(X_i^0):=\mathcal{L}(X_i|X_i\neq 0),$$

with $p:=\mathbf{Pr}(X_1\neq 0)\in(0,1)$. Denote $S_m^0:=\sum_{i\leq m}X_i^0$.

Lemma 2 ([2,31])**.** *In the i.i.d. case, under the above notation, the following relations hold:*

$$\mathcal{L}(S_n)=\mathcal{L}(S^0_{\nu_n(p)}),\quad Pois(n\mathcal{L}(X_1))=\mathcal{L}(S^0_{\pi(np)}), \quad (52)$$

where $\mathcal{L}(\nu_n(p))$ is the binomial distribution with parameters n and p; the pair $(\nu_n(p),\,\pi(np))$ does not depend on the sequence $\{X_i^0\}$.

The equalities in (52), which are very convenient in studying the accuracy of the Poisson approximation of the sums, are contained in various forms in many papers (see, for example, Refs. [29–35], and others). Actually, these relations also represent versions of the total probability formula and are easily proven.

Taking into account the representations in (52), we can reduce the problem to the simplest one-dimensional case when we estimate moments of a binomial distribution using, for example, convexity arguments as above. However, in this case, we can obtain sufficiently exact inequalities for the moments of arbitrary functions without convexity using the following lemma from [15] (see also [2]). For the convenience of the reader, we reproduce the proof of this assertion.

Lemma 3. *For each $p\in(0,1)$,*

$$\sup_{n,j}\frac{\mathcal{L}(\nu_n(p))(j)}{\mathcal{L}(\pi(np))(j)}\leq\frac{1}{1-p}. \quad (53)$$

Proof. For every nonnegative integer $j \le n$, we have

$$\frac{\mathbf{P}(\nu_n(p)=j)}{\mathbf{P}(\pi(np)=j)} = \frac{n(n-1)\cdots(n-j+1)}{n^j(1-p)^j}(1-p)^n e^{np}$$
$$= \exp\left\{n(p+\log(1-p)) - j\log(1-p) + \sum_{i=0}^{j-1}\log\left(1-\frac{i}{n}\right)\right\}$$
$$\le \exp\left\{-\log(1-p) + n(p+\log(1-p)) - (j-1)\log(1-p)\right.$$
$$\left. +n\int_0^{(j-1)/n}\log(1-x)dx\right\} \le \exp\left\{-\log(1-p) - nH_p\left(\frac{j-1}{n}\right)\right\},$$

where $H_p(x) = -p + x + (1-x)\log((1-x)/(1-p))$. The following properties of H_p are obvious:

$$H_p(1) = 1-p, \quad H_p(p) = 0, \quad \frac{d}{dx}H_p(p) = 0, \quad \frac{d^2}{dx^2}H_p(x) = 1/(1-x),$$

which implies $H_p(x) \ge 0$ for all $x \le 1$ due to the convexity of $H(x)$, i.e., inequality (13) is proven. □

Finally, as a consequence of Lemmas 1 and 2, we obtain the following moment inequality for any nonnegative function $g(\cdot)$:

$$\mathbf{E}g(\nu_n(p)) \le \frac{1}{1-p}g(\pi(np)),$$

and apply this inequality for the conditional expectation $\mathbf{E}_{\{X_i^0\}}f(S^0_{\nu_n(p)})$, given the sequence $\{X_i^0\}$. Theorem 4 is proven. □

Remark 10. *Inequality (53) is a part of a more general result in [15]. It is worth noting that this upper bound is an estimate for the so-called Radon–Nikodym derivative of a binomial distribution with respect to the accompanying Poisson law. This problem was studied by a number of authors ([14,29,30] and others). In particular, under some additional restriction on n and p, a slightly stronger estimate is contained in [29]. However, in general, the upper bound (53) cannot be essentially improved. Under some restrictions on n and p, a lower bound for the left-hand side of (53) has the form $(1-cp)^{-1}$, where $c < 1$ is an absolute positive constant. For example, for $n = 1$, an unimprovable upper bound in (53) equals $e^p < (1-p)^{-1}$. It is easy to confirm that $e^p > (1-p/2)^{-1}$ for all $p \le 1/2$.*

Proof of Corollary 8. Taking Remark 9 into account, we have a refinement of estimate (53) in the case $n = 1$, and as a consequence, we obtain

$$\mathbf{E}g(\nu_1(p)) \le e^p g(\pi(p))$$

for any nonnegative function g. The further arguments of proving estimate (30) are quite similar to those in the proof of Theorem 1, applying formulas (52) for $n = 1$ and the above inequality for the corresponding conditional expectations. Estimate (31) is a direct consequence of estimate (53) and the arguments above. □

Proof of Corollary 9. Inequality (32) follows from Lemma 2 and the simple estimate

$$\sup_j \frac{\mathbf{P}(\pi(np)=j)}{\mathbf{P}(\pi(\lambda)=j)} = \sup_j\left(\frac{np}{\lambda}\right)^j e^{\lambda-np} \le e^{\lambda-np}$$

if $np \leq \lambda$ only. Otherwise, there are no uniform upper bounds for the Radon–Nikodym derivative under consideration.

Relation (33) follows from the classical Poisson limit theorem and inequality (32), which provides fulfillment of the uniform integrability condition. The corollary is proven. □

To prove relation (34), we consider the function $g(k) := (1 \vee (k-2)!)\lambda^{-k}$. It is clear that $\mathbf{E}g(\pi(\lambda)) < \infty$. Otherwise, we have

$$\mathbf{E}g(\nu_n(p)) > \frac{1}{k_n(k_n-1)} \prod_{j \leq k_n - 1} (1 - j/n) \left(\frac{np}{\lambda}\right)^{k_n} \left(1 - \frac{np}{n}\right)^{n-k_n},$$

where $n \geq 4$ and $k_n := [\sqrt{n}]$. Further, it is easy to see that, as $n \to \infty$ and $np \to \lambda$,

$$\prod_{j \leq k_n - 1} (1 - j/n) = \exp\left\{ - \sum_{j \leq k_n - 1} j/n + O(k_n^3/n^2) \right\} \sim \exp\{-k_n^2/2n\} \sim e^{-1/2}$$

and

$$\left(1 - \frac{np}{n}\right)^{n-k_n} \sim e^{-\lambda}.$$

We now suppose that $np/\lambda = 1 + n^{-\alpha}$ for some $\alpha < 1/2$. Then,

$$\left(\frac{np}{\lambda}\right)^{k_n} \sim e^{k_n n^{-\alpha}} \to \infty,$$

which was to be proved. □

Proof of Theorem 5. For any natural k, we denote

$$\Phi_f^{(k)}(V_n) := \sum_{i \leq k} f_{in}(\nu_{in}).$$

It is clear that

$$\mathbf{P}\Big(\Phi_f(V_n) \geq x\Big) \leq \mathbf{P}\Big(\Phi_f^{(k)}(V_n) \geq \frac{x}{2}\Big) + \mathbf{P}\Big(\Phi_f(V_n) - \Phi_f^{(k)}(V_n) \geq \frac{x}{2}\Big). \tag{54}$$

In the notation of Theorem 1, let V_n^* be the restriction of the point process V_n to the set $A_0 := \bigcup_{i \leq k} \Delta_i$ with a hit probability $p := \sum_{i \leq k} p_i$. Under the sign of the first probability of the right-hand side of inequality (54), we replace the point process V_n with V_n^* and use inequality (37) for the distributions of the restrictions of the corresponding point processes under consideration.

The difference

$$\Phi_f(V_n) - \Phi_f^{(k)}(V_n) = \sum_{i > k} f_{in}(\nu_{in})$$

is an additive functional of the restriction of V_n to the set $\overline{A}_0 := \bigcup_{i > k} \Delta_i$ with hitting probability $p := \sum_{i > k} p_i$. For this functional, we also use estimate (37). As a result, taking into account the nonnegativity of all $f_{in}(\cdot)$, from (54) and Theorem 1, we easily obtain

$$\mathbf{P}\Big(\Phi_f(V_n) \geq x\Big) \leq \left(\sum_{i > k} p_i\right)^{-1} \mathbf{P}\Big(\Phi_f^{(k)}(\Pi_n) \geq \frac{x}{2}\Big)$$

$$+ \left(\sum_{i \leq k} p_i\right)^{-1} \mathbf{P}\Big(\Phi_f(\Pi_n) - \Phi_f^{(k)}(\Pi_n) \geq \frac{x}{2}\Big) \leq 2C^* \mathbf{P}\Big(\Phi_f(\Pi_n) \geq \frac{x}{2}\Big).$$

Inequality (41) is proved similarly:

$$\mathbf{P}\Big(\Phi_f(V_n) \geq x\Big) \leq \mathbf{P}\Bigg(\sum_{i>m} f_{in}(\nu_{in}) \geq x - C_{m,n}\Bigg) \leq \Bigg(\sum_{i\leq m} p_i\Bigg)^{-1} \mathbf{P}\Big(\Phi_f(\Pi_n) \geq x - C_{m,n}\Big).$$

The theorem is proven. □

Proof of Proposition 3. First, taking into account the fact that the increments of Poissonian processes are independent, we note that the r.v. $\pi_n^o(t) = \pi(nt) - t\pi(n)$ coincides in distribution with the r.v.

$$Y := (1-t)\bar{\pi}(nt) - t\bar{\pi}_1(n(1-t)). \tag{55}$$

Since the r.vs $\bar{\pi}(nt)$ and $\bar{\pi}_1(n(1-t))$ are independent and centered, the lower bound in (23) immediately follows from Jensen's inequality. The upper bound follows from the convexity and evenness of the function f.

Since the centered random process $\bar{\pi}(t)$ has independent increments, the expectation $\mathbf{E}f(\bar{\pi}(t))$ is a nondecreasing function in t in virtue of Jensen's inequality. So, for $t \in [1/2, 1]$, the right-hand side of (23) coincides with $\mathbf{E}f(\bar{\pi}(nt))$. □

Proof of Proposition 4. It is clear that it suffices to consider the case $x = 0$. Moreover, taking inequality (24) into account, we prove estimate (25) for every $t \in [0, 1/2]$ only. The characteristic function of Y has the form

$$\varphi_Y(s) := \exp\{g(s)\},$$

where $g(s) := nte^{i(1-t)s} + n(1-t)e^{-its} - n$. So, the mth moment of Y is calculated by the formula $\mathbf{E}Y^m = i^{-m}\varphi^{(m)}(0)$. We need the multiple differentiation formula of products:

$$(uv)^{(n)} = \sum_{k=0}^{n} C_n^k u^{(k)} v^{(n-k)},$$

with $\psi^{(0)} = \psi$. We then obtain

$$\varphi_Y^{(m)}(0) = (g'(s)\varphi_Y(s))_{s=0}^{(m-1)} = \sum_{k=0}^{m-1} C_{m-1}^k g^{(k+1)}(0)\varphi_Y^{(m-1-k)}(0). \tag{56}$$

A similar representation is valid for the characteristic function of $\bar{\pi}(nt)$:

$$\varphi_{\bar{\pi}(nt)}^{(m)}(0) = \sum_{k=0}^{m-1} C_{m-1}^k f^{(k+1)}(0)\varphi_{\bar{\pi}(nt)}^{(m-1-k)}(0), \tag{57}$$

where $f(s) := nt(e^{is} - 1) - isnt$ and $\varphi_{\bar{\pi}(nt)}(s) := e^{f(s)}$.

We now compare the coefficients in the sums in (56) and (57). One has

$$g^{(k)}(0) = i^k nt(1-t)[(1-t)^{k-1} + (-1)^k t^{k-1}],$$

$$f'(0) = 0, \;\; f^{(k)}(0) = i^k nt, \;\; \forall k \geq 2.$$

Moreover, for each $t \in [0, 1/2]$ and all naturals k,

$$0 \leq (1-t)[(1-t)^{k-1} + (-1)^k t^{k-1}] \leq 1.$$

In other words, for all naturals k,

$$0 \leq i^{-k} g^{(k)}(0) \leq i^{-k} f^{(k)}(0). \tag{58}$$

Since

$$i^{-m}\varphi_Y^{(m)}(0) = \sum_{k=0}^{m-1} C_{m-1}^k i^{-k-1} g^{(k+1)}(0) i^{k+1-m} \varphi_Y^{(m-1-k)}(0) \quad (59)$$

then, all the values $i^{-k}\varphi_Y^{(k)}(0)$ are nonnegative. Therefore, the inequalities

$$i^{-m}\varphi_Y^{(m)}(0) \leq i^{-m}\varphi_{\bar{\pi}(nt)}^{(m)}(0)$$

are easily proved by induction on m using the relations (56)–(59).

Thus, the proposition is proven. □

4. Conclusions

In the present paper, some inequalities were obtained for the distributions of sums of independent B-space-valued r.vs in terms of the accompanying infinitely divisible laws. As consequences of these results, similar inequalities were obtained for the distributions of empirical and accompanying Poisson point processes.

It is worth noting that the above arguments for additive statistics are also transferred to more general additive functionals of the U-statistic structure of empirical group frequencies:

$$U_{f,n}(V_n) := \sum_{1 \leq i_1 < \ldots < i_m} f_{n,i_1,\ldots,i_m}(\nu_{n,i_1}, \ldots, \nu_{n,i_m}),$$

where $\{f_{n,i_1,\ldots,i_m}(\cdot)\}$ is an array of finite functions defined on Z_+^m and satisfying only the restriction

$$\sum_{1 \leq i_1 < \ldots < i_m} |f_{n,i_1,\ldots,i_m}(0, \ldots, 0)| < \infty \quad \forall n,$$

with $\nu_{n,i} := V_n(\Delta_i)$ and finite or countable measurable partition $\{\Delta_i\}$ of $\mathcal{B}$. In this case, the problem is reduced to studying the distribution of the Poissonian version $U_{f,n}(\Pi_n)$ where one can use a martingale approach for estimating its moments and probability tail.

Funding: This study is supported by the Basic Research Program of the Siberian Branch of the Russian Academy of Sciences, project no. FWNF-2024-0001.

Data Availability Statement: No new data were created or analyzed in this study. Data sharing is not applicable for studies that did not create any new data.

Conflicts of Interest: The author declares no conflicts of interest.

References

1. Araujo, A.; Giné, E. *The Central Limit Theorem for Real and Banach Valued Random Variables*; Wiley: New York, NY, USA, 1980.
2. Borisov, I.S. Moment inequalities connected with accompanying Poisson laws in Abelian groups. *Intern. J. Math. Math. Sci.* **2003**, *44*, 2771–2786. [CrossRef]
3. Prokhorov, Y.V. An extremal problem in probability theory. *Theory Probab. Appl.* **1960**, *4*, 201–203. [CrossRef]
4. Prokhorov, Y.V. Extremal problems in limit theorems. In Proceedings of the 6th USSR Conference on Probability Theory and Mathematical Statistics, Vilnius, Lithuania, 5–14 September 1962; pp. 77–84. (In Russian)
5. Pinelis, I.F.; Utev, S.A. Exact exponential bounds for sums of independent random variables. *Theory Probab. Appl.* **1989**, *34*, 340–346. [CrossRef]
6. Utev, S.A. Inequalities for sums of weakly dependent random variables and rates of convergence in the invariance pronciple. *Mat. Tr.* **1985**, *5*, 56–75. (In Russian)
7. Kemperman, J.H.B. On a class of moments problems. In *Proceedings of the 6th Berkley Symposium on Mathematical Statistics and Probability, Berkley, CA, USA, 9–12 April 1971*; University California Press: Berkley, CA, USA, 1972; Volume 2.
8. Cox, D.C.; Kemperman, J.H.B. Sharp bounds on the absolute moments of a sum of two i.i.d. random variables. *Ann. Probab.* **1983**, *11*, 765–771. [CrossRef]
9. Pinelis, I.F.; Utev, S.A. Estimation of the moments of sums of independent random variables. *Theory Probab. Appl.* **1985**, *29*, 574–577. [CrossRef]
10. Utev, S.A. Extremal problems in moment inequalities. *Theory Probab. Appl.* **1984**, *29*, 411–412.
11. Ibragimov, R.; Sharakhmetov, S. On the exact constant for the Rosentahl inequality. *Theory Probab. Appl.* **1997**, *42*, 294–302. [CrossRef]

12. Ibragimov, R.; Sharakhmetov, S. The exact constant in the Rosentahl inequality for random variables with mean zero. *Theory Probab. Appl.* **2001**, *46*, 134–138. (In Russian)
13. Giné, E.M.; Mason, D.M.; Zaitsev, A.Y. The L_1-norm density estimator process. *Ann. Probab.* **2003**, *31*, 719–768. [CrossRef]
14. Barbour, A.D.; Chen, L.H.Y.; Choi, K.P. Poisson approximation for unbounded functions, I: Independent summands. *Stat. Sin.* **1995**, *5*, 749–766.
15. Borisov, I.S.; Ruzankin, P.S. Poisson approximation for expectation of unbounded functions of independent random variables. *Ann. Probab.* **2002**, *30*, 1657–1680. [CrossRef]
16. Borisov, I.S. Approximation of von Mises statistics with multidimensional kernels. *Siberian Math. J.* **1991**, *32*, 554–566. [CrossRef]
17. Deheuvels, P.; Mason, D.M. Functional laws of the iterated logarithm for increments of empirical and quantile processes. *Ann. Probab.* **1992**, *20*, 1248–1287. [CrossRef]
18. Einmahl, J.H.J. *Multivariate Empirical Processes*; CWI Tract 33; Centrum voor Wiskunde en Informatica: Amsterdam, The Netherlands, 1987.
19. Bahadur, R.R. On the number of distinct values in a large sample from an infinite discrete distribution. *Proceed. Nation. Inst. Sci. India* **1960**, *26A* (Suppl. II), 67–75.
20. Barbour, A.D.; Gnedin, A.V. Small counts in the infinite occupancy scheme. *Electr. J. Probab.* **2009**, *14*, 365–384. [CrossRef]
21. Karlin, S. Central limit theorems for certain infinite urn schemes. *J. Math. Mech.* **1967**, *17*, 373–401. [CrossRef]
22. Darling, D.A. Some limit theorems associated with multinomial trials. In Proceedings of the 5th Berkeley Symposium on Mathematical Statistics and Probability, Berkley, CA, USA, 21 June–18 July 1965; Volume 2(A), pp. 345–350.
23. Kolchin, V.F.; Sevastyanov, B.A.; Chistyakov, V.P. *Random Assignments*; Nauka: Moscow, Russia, 1976. (In Russian)
24. Borisov, I.S.; Jetpisbaev, M.J. Poissonization principle for additive functionals of empirical point processes. *Mathematics* **2022**, *10*, 4084. [CrossRef]
25. Hagerup, T.; Rüb, C. A guided tour of Chernoff bounds. *Inform. Process. Lett.* **1990**, *33*, 305–308. [CrossRef]
26. Barbour, A.D.; Hall, P. On the rate of Poisson convergence. *Math. Proc. Camb. Philos. Soc.* **1984**, *95*, 473–480. [CrossRef]
27. Loeve, M. *Probability Theory*; Russian Translation; Nauchnaya Literatura: Moscow, Russia, 1962.
28. Kendall, M.G. *The Advanced Theory of Statistics*; Griffin: London, UK, 1943; Volume 1.
29. Le Cam, L. An approximation theorem for the Poisson binomial distribution. *Pacific J. Math.* **1960**, *10*, 1181–1197. [CrossRef]
30. Chen, L.H.Y. An approximation theorem for convolutions of probability measures. *Ann. Probab.* **1975**, *3*, 992–999. [CrossRef]
31. Borisov, I.S. Poisson approximation of the partial sum process in Banach spaces. *Sib. Math. J.* **1996**, *37*, 627–634. [CrossRef]
32. Khintchine, A. *Asymptotishe Gesetze der Wahrscheinlichkeitsrechnung*; Springer: Berlin/Heidelberg, Germany, 1933.
33. Khintchine, A.Y. *Asymptotic Laws of Probability Theory*; Translation from German; United Scientific and Technical Publishing House of NKTP USSR: Moscow/Leningrad, Russia, 1936. (In Russian)
34. Le Cam, L. On the distribution of sums of independent random variables. In *Bernoulli, Bayes, Laplace (Anniversary Volume)*; Springer: Berlin/Heidelberg, Germany; New York, NY, USA, 1965; pp. 179–202.
35. Deheuvels, P.; Pfiefer, D. Poisson approximation of multinomial distributions and point processes. *J. Multivar. Anal.* **1988**, *25*, 65–89. [CrossRef]

MDPI AG
Grosspeteranlage 5
4052 Basel
Switzerland
Tel.: +41 61 683 77 34

Mathematics Editorial Office
E-mail: mathematics@mdpi.com
www.mdpi.com/journal/mathematics

www.ingramcontent.com/pod-product-compliance
Lightning Source LLC
LaVergne TN
LVHW072340090526
838202LV00019B/2448
9783725826957